Thoughtful Parenting

A MANUAL OF WISDOM FOR HOME & FAMILY

Edited by
R. PAUL STEVENS & ROBERT BANKS

InterVarsity Press
Downers Grove, Illinois

InterVarsity Press
P.O. Box 1400, Downers Grove, IL 60515-1426
World Wide Web: www.ivpress.com
E-mail: mail@ivpress.com

InterVarsity Press® is the book-publishing division of InterVarsity Christian Fellowship/USA®, a student movement active on campus at hundreds of universities, colleges and schools of nursing in the United States of America, and a member movement of the International Fellowship of Evangelical Students. For information about local and regional activities, write Public Relations Dept., InterVarsity Christian Fellowship/USA, 6400 Schroeder Rd., P.O. Box 7895, Madison, WI 53707-7895.

All Scripture quotations, unless otherwise indicated, are taken from the Holy Bible, New International Version®. NIV®. *Copyright ©1973, 1978, 1984 by International Bible Society. Used by permission of Zondervan Publishing House. All rights reserved.*

Some articles in this volume are reprinted from and some are revised from The Complete Book of Everyday Christianity, *edited by Robert Banks & R. Paul Stevens, ©1997 by Robert Banks & R. Paul Stevens, and published by InterVarsity Press. Used by permission.*

Cover photograph: Juan Silva/Image Bank

ISBN 0-8308-2245-3

Printed in the United States of America ∞

Library of Congress Cataloging-in-Publication Data

Thoughtful parenting: a manual of wisdom for home and family/edited by R. Paul Stevens & Robert Banks.
    p. cm.
Includes bibliographical references.
ISBN 0-8308-2245-3 (pbk.: alk. paper)
1. Parenting—Religious aspects—Christianity. 2. Family—Religious life. I. Stevens, R. Paul, 1937-II. Banks, Robert J.

BV4529 .T46 2001
248.8'45   2001024413

| 20 | 19 | 18 | 17 | 16 | 15 | 14 | 13 | 12 | 11 | 10 | 9 | 8 | 7 | 6 | 5 | 4 | 3 | 2 | 1 |
| 17 | 16 | 15 | 14 | 13 | 12 | 11 | 10 | 09 | 08 | 07 | 06 | 05 | 04 | 03 | 02 | 01 |

Contents

HOW TO USE THIS GUIDE
FOR ALL ITS WORTH

"Help! I'm a parent" is the heart cry of people trying to be family, friends, spouses and parents in a rapidly disintegrating society. While there is a spate of books telling us "how to do it successfully," this guide offers something different—a thoughtful reflection on "how come" as well as "how to." Relating rightly to the other sex, being married for good, and raising children and grandchildren in the "training and instruction of the Lord" (Eph 6:4) are tall orders. But as one after another article in this volume shows, there is a promise and blessing in family life. Both family and church (also a family experience for Christians) are meeting places with God. Many people think that finding God at home—sometimes called "domestic spirituality"—is a matter of bringing God into the home through family devotions and religious rituals, good as these may be. Indeed, there is an excellent article on family prayer. But the whole of family life itself is a spiritual discipline inviting us Godward. God made human beings to live in family because God—in Father, Son and Holy Spirit—dwells in family. Created human beings reflect that image on earth. So the most mundane as well as the most exalted family experiences—from reading a story to your children to planning a family vacation—as well as all the family transitions—from adolescence to empty nesting—are designed by God to be faith-evoking and life-affirming. Even family problems and domestic crises are opportunities as well as dangers.

So in this guide you will find general and introductory articles on parenting, marriage, family and sexuality (a good place to start). There are articles offering a biblical theology and spirituality of all kinds of family experiences: the Internet, play, breast-feeding, chores, tithing, clothing, meal preparation and the automobile—to mention only a few. Each article has a practical cast and contains both *how come* and *how to*. Specific problems such as abuse, conflict resolution, divorce, miscarriage, addiction and drugs are addressed. Ninety-three in all, these articles are written by a wide range of people from four continents: pastors, business people, counselors, physicians, homemakers, lawyers, professors and students. It is a people's book about ordinary domestic life.

The guide can be read from cover to cover over a period of time, as each article is bite-sized. But you may make the best use of the book by starting with your own questions and concerns. In the text of each article you will be directed to other articles by the presence of "*", and at the end of the article "See also" signals other entries you can consult on the subject you are exploring. "References and Resources" at the end of each subject indicates both the books quoted by the author and additional reading you can undertake. Cross-references between articles will help you find your way. For example, you might look up "Last Will" and find you are directed to "Will, Last," or consult "Cohabiting" and be directed to three articles that deal with this: "Dating," "Marriage" and "Sexuality."

Many of these articles were adapted from *The Complete Book of Everyday Christianity* (InterVarsity Press, 1997) edited by ourselves, but we have added several new ones to provide a more comprehensive guide to hearth and home, including character, discipline, shame and adoption. Enjoy this resource and grow in faith, hope and love through the contributions of a wide selection from the family of God.

R. PAUL STEVENS AND ROBERT BANKS

LIST OF ARTICLES

LIST OF
CONTRIBUTORS

Dr. Carol Anderson, physician: **Breast-Feeding; Conception; Miscarriage; New Reproductive Technology; Pregnancy**

Dr. David Augsburger, professor of pastoral counseling, Fuller Theological Seminary: **Love**

Dr. Judith K. Balswick, professor of marriage and family, Graduate School of Psychology, Fuller Theological Seminary: **Family Problems; Goals**

Dr. Jack Balswick, professor of marriage and family, Graduate School of Psychology, Fuller Theological Seminary: **Masculinity**

Julie Banks, author, homemaker: **Family History; Pets**

Dr. Robert Banks, theological educator, institute director: **Automobile; Chores; Conversation; Home; Mobility; Neighboring; Shopping; Telephone**

Dr. Roy Bell, emeritus professor of family ministries, Carey Theological College, Vancouver, B.C.: **Empty Nesting; Grandparenting**

Iain Benson, constitutional lawyer, lecturer, author, senior research fellow, Centre for Renewal in Public Policy, Ottawa, Ont.: **Character**

Rodney Clapp, editor, author: **Family; Mission**

Dr. John Court, director of Psychological Clinic, Fuller Theological Seminary: **Homosexuality**

Dr. Mark Davies, assistant professor of counseling and family studies, Carey Theological College, Vancouver, B.C.: **Abortion; Abuse; Health; Leisure; Stress**

Dr. John M. Dettoni, president, Chrysalis Ministries: **Adolescence**

Dr. John Drane, professor of practical theology, University of Aberdeen, Scotland: **Alternative Religions**

Paddy Ducklow, pastor, psychologist: **Communication, Family Systems, Marriage**

Maudine Fee, grandmother and teacher: **Prayer**

Dr. Michael Green, evangelist: **Baptism; Confirmation**

Angus M. Gunn, emeritus professor of education, University of British Columbia: **Schools, Public and Private**

Dr. Maxine Hancock, author, speaker, broadcaster, professor of interdisciplinary studies and spiritual theology, Regent College, Vancouver, B.C.: **Reading**

Dr. Archibald Hart, professor of psychology, Graduate School of Psychology, Fuller Theological Seminary: **Depression**

Dr. Simon Holt, lecturer, practical theology, Whitley College, University of Melbourne, Australia: **Eating; Home**

Dr. Edwin Hui, professor of medical ethics and spiritual theology, Regent College, Vancouver, B.C.: **Abortion; Contraception; Health**

Dr. Robert K. Johnston, professor of theology and culture, Fuller Theological Seminary: **Play**

Patricia Kerr, teacher, Buenos Aires Bible Institute, Argentina: **Hospitality**

Dr. Yea Sun E. Kim, associate professor of family counseling and Korean family studies, Fuller Theological Seminary: **Shame**

Dr. Cameron Lee, associate professor of family studies, Fuller Theological Seminary: **Discipline**

Paul W. Lermitte, registered financial planner: **Allowances**

Kathryn Lockhart, homemaker, humorist: **Clothing**

Sue Lyon, home educator

and potter: **Home Schooling**

Dr. Michael Maloney, physician: **Contraception**

Thomas H. McAlpine, director of urban evangelism, World Vision International: **Sleeping**

Theresa McKenna, single parents ministry coordinator: **Single Parenting**

Mike McLoughlin, director, Youth With A Mission, Marketplace Ministries, Kelowna, B.C. <www.scruples.org>: **Internet**

Hal Miller, software engineer: **Computer; Computer Games**

Robbie E. Monsma, retired lawyer and certified Christian concil-iator, Peacemaker Ministries: **Conflict Resolution**

David J. Montgomery, associate pastor, Knock Presbyterian Church, Belfast: **Forgiveness**

Dr. Barbara Mutch, assistant professor of ministry, Carey Theological College, Vancouver, B.C.: **Adoption**

Mike Nichols, pastor, counselor: **Character; Masturbation; Self-Esteem**

Susan Norman, homemaker: **Homemaking**

Valerie Pyke Parks, student: **Menstruation**

Dr. Elaine J. Ramshaw, associate professor of pastoral care, Luther Seminary: **Godparenting**

Dr. John Schneider, professor of theology, Calvin College: **Money**

Dr. Quentin J. Schultze, professor of communications, Calvin College: **Entertainment; Television; Videos**

Dr. Calvin Seerveld, professor of philosophical aesthetics, Institute of Christian Studies, Toronto: **Games**

Dr. Celeste N. Snowber, assistant professor of physical education and dance: **Femininity**

Gail Stevens, homemaker, chaplain: **Death**

Dr. R. Paul Stevens, David J. Brown Professor of Marketplace Theology and Leadership, Regent College, Vancouver, B.C.: **Blessing; Character; Credit Card; Dating; Death; Divorce; Family; Gift-Giving; Insurance; Listening; Parenting; Sabbath; Sexuality; Spiritual Formation; Tithing; Vacations; Values; Will, Last**

John R. Sutherland, director of public affairs, Christian Labour Association of Canada: **Debt**

Dr. John F. Van Wicklin, professor of psychology, Houghton College: **Drugs**

Mary Ruth Wilkinson, homemaker, hearthkeeper: **Fairy Tales; Meal Preparation**

Dan Williams, pastor, author: **Allowances**

Martha Zimmerman, author, homemaker: **Birthdays; Holidays—Christmas, Easter, Thanksgiving**

—ABORTION—

Abortion has been with us throughout the ages. While first accepted as a necessary measure or "therapy" in saving the life of the mother, it has also been accepted in many countries as a means of population control, "quality of life" control (in the case of deformed fetuses) and reproductive control. It is often a procedure used by teens and women in economic hardship who do not have the resources to care for a child, as well as for women who are victims of rape and incest. In modern Western culture the justification and acceptance of this practice has widened as women's rights and reproductive rights have come to the forefront. Often a woman's request for abortion is justification enough for the procedure.

Medical Considerations

Abortion is the termination of a pregnancy.* It can be classified as either *spontaneous* or *induced.* A spontaneous abortion is a miscarriage,* that is, the pregnancy ends usually due to various chromosomal or congenital defects, diseases or infections—of fetal or maternal origin. Unlike spontaneous abortion, an induced abortion is not a natural process of the body and involves a medical intervention. This intervention is of two types—therapeutic or elective—depending on the reason for the abortion. If the mother's life is in danger, as in the case of cardiovascular and hypertensive diseases, an abortion might be performed for therapeutic reasons. An elective or voluntary abortion, on the other hand, is requested for reasons other than maternal health and is the most commonly performed type of abortion in the West today. It is estimated that approximately 25 percent of all pregnancies in the world are terminated by elective abortion, making this the most common method of re-production limitation (see Contraception).

The method chosen for an abortion is commonly determined by factors like the duration of the pregnancy, the patient's health,* the experience of the physician and the physical facilities. The methods include (1) suction or surgical curettage; (2) induction of labor by means of intra- or extraovular injection of a hypertonic solution or other oxytocic agent; (3) extraovular placement of devices such as catheters, bougies or bags; (4) abdominal or vaginal hysterotomy and (5) menstrual* regulation. About 75 percent of induced abortions in the United States are performed by suction curettage for a pregnancy of twelve weeks' duration or less; these are usually performed in abortion outpatient clinics. There are, however, medical concerns about this spreading practice.

The two major medical reasons for limiting abortion today are fetal viability (which changes with technological capabilities) and medical consequences to the mother. Viability, the point at which a fetus can survive outside the mother's womb, now stands at twenty-four weeks, though some infants even younger have survived. Yet the consequences of an abortion procedure to the mother are debated and controversial. While most abortions, especially those done in the first trimester, are safe for women physically, the psychological consequences have gone undocumented. Some reports deny serious psychological effects of abortion, but most cite overwhelming statistics indicating dire long-term negative effects, including guilt, shame,* depression,* grief, anxiety, despair, low self-esteem,* distrust and hostility. Women with previous histories of psychiatric illnesses tend to be affected to a greater degree.

Pro-life Versus Pro-choice
The abortion debate is divided into two clearly opposing camps: the pro-life and the pro-choice, each entrenched in its respective uncompromising positions. The pro-life stance holds the view that the fetus is a developing human being with intrinsic values* and inviolable rights, as much a human being as the mother. So the sanctity of the fetal life in the womb, however developed, should have priority over the reproductive freedom of the woman. Abortion should be considered only when the life of the mother is in jeopardy. The basis of the pro-life position is largely grounded on divine authority and the belief that human life is a gift of God.

The pro-choice position does not see the fetus as possessing rights independent of the mother, who alone has the right to decide the fate of the fetus. This maternal right is in turn grounded in the principle of autonomy or self-determination. The pro-choice position also views access to abortion as necessary for women's complete social equality. Any restriction of the availability of abortion is interpreted as coercing women to carry pregnancies to term against their will.

Personhood
While it is seldom disputed that a fetus is human, there is hardly a consensus as to when the fetus becomes a human person. Personhood is still a crucial issue, since modern society accords a person certain moral rights, such as the right to life. General philosophical criteria for personhood include any one or all of the following: rationality, consciousness, self-consciousness, freedom to act on one's own reasons, capacity to communicate with others and to make moral judgments. Some hold that only when one or all of these qualities have been actualized should a human being be considered a person (actuality principle). Others feel that these qualities of personhood only emerge gradually in the course of fetal and early childhood development, so what counts in defining personhood is the potential that the human life possesses (potentiality principle). In this view, fetuses and infants are recognized as having different degrees of personhood and therefore are given different measures of right to life.

As support for the Christian doctrine of the image of God, Genesis 1:26-27 reads, "Then God said, 'Let us make man in our image, in our likeness, and let them rule.' . . . So God created man in his own image, in the image of God he created him; male and female he created them." Because God exists as three persons in communion, we also believe that human persons are created in his image to live in community. The most fundamental attribute of being in the image of God and human personhood, therefore, is relationality. God creates every single human person in order to relate to him or her. In response, every created human person seeks to relate to the Creator and other fellow creatures. Since each human being is created uniquely by God, every single human being is God's image bearer. This is the ground for personhood, uniqueness and the right to life. Life is sacred because God creates a particular life for a unique relationship between him as the Creator and us as his creatures. This relationship begins when a conceptus is formed as God permits a human sperm and ovum to unite in the creation of a new unique life. How that life unfolds and whether all the inherent potentialities are actualized or not do not take away the intrinsic value of that life as God's image bearer, a human person.

A Christian Response
Such a Christian understanding of personhood undergirds the proper attitude toward abortion. The sixth commandment in the Bible (not to kill; Ex 20:13) carries the positive mandate of stewardship of all lives as sacred to God. This means not that the value of life is absolute (Mt 24:9) but rather that no life is to be taken without an absolutely and unequivocally justifiable reason. As the Creator and Giver of life, it is God who ultimately has the sovereign right to take away life. So any attempt to terminate life, as in an abortion, must be done with the fullest sense of accountability before the sovereign God.

Family Concerns
One of the primary considerations the Supreme Court used in deciding that abortion was legal (Roe v. Wade) was the individual's right to privacy. This principle reflects the prevailing mood of society, where individual rights are considered more important than collective rights. The reality is that abortion does not affect only the mother. It also affects the fetus and typically has a significant effect on family life. Abortion is not merely a private decision that only affects one individual but typically has profound consequences for families.

Many Christians would prefer not to talk or even think about abortion. In attempting to explain it to our children, it is tempting to simply tell them that "it's wrong because God says it's wrong." But such an approach does little to empower our children to cope with the multifaceted non-Christian value system that they are exposed to on a daily basis. As they grow older, they will be challenged by many strong and compassionate arguments as to why abortion is a viable option. As part of discipling our children, Christian parents must be intentional in teaching them in word and in deed what they believe, why they believe it and how they live it out. Four critical areas should be addressed.

First, it is important to teach the sanctity of human life (Gen 1:27; Ps 139). All humans, regardless of race, class, IQ or physical ability, are created in the image of God. Scripture suggests that the very individuals who are most at risk to be aborted, those born into adverse circumstances, are the very ones that have a special place in God's heart. One of the most significant things parents can do in instilling this value of the sanctity of human life is to actively involve the entire family in some service to those less fortunate. There are very few things that will so deeply instill God's love for human beings than allowing our children to be involved in service to others.

Second, broaden the discussion about abortion to include sexuality.* Christians often believe that abortion is not something that they will ever have to deal with because their children are not having sex. This is simply not true. Research suggests that between 18 and 25 percent of Christians are engaging in

3

premarital sex leading to many unwanted pregnancies, which often end in abortion. Cameron found that 8 percent of all women who had obtained an abortion declared themselves to be "very devout" Christians, while another 15 percent identified themselves to be "moderately devout" (316-32). A godly perspective on sexuality, intimacy and love are critical components in helping young people act in a personally responsible way. Christians cannot truly understand all the factors surrounding the issue of abortion unless they understand God's perspective on sex and sexuality.

Third, teach them in an explicit manner what abortion involves. Typically when abortion is explained, it is done so in a simplistic manner that emphasizes the speed and painlessness of the procedure. Rarely discussed is what happens to the fetus during this procedure, as well as some of the negative effects that happen to women after the abortion. As mentioned above many postabortion women suffer from anxiety, depression, unresolved grief, and overwhelming guilt and shame. While the average parent may feel overwhelmed in taking on such an educational task (because they do not know much about it themselves), many Christian agencies, such as pregnancy crisis centers, have excellent educational materials and programs. This can be an opportunity for the whole family to become better informed.

Fourth, teach them to be agents of redemption and reconciliation. Typically the church is the last place a Christian or anyone else would turn to in dealing with the crisis that abortion evokes. Yet as Christians we are called to act redemptively. To be pro-life means we are for life for all people, including those who have had an abortion. In reaching out to help them find the forgiveness* and healing that Christ offers, we are not only ministering in a powerful way to the world we

live in but also to some of our own Christian brothers and sisters. We must attempt the delicate balancing act that our Lord taught us in dealing with the woman caught in adultery (Jn 8:1-11). He showed compassion toward the sinner without compromising the standards of God. Christians most act like Christ when they hold their values absolutely, yet from a stance of humility and service, rather than self-righteous moralizing, which often leads to harshness, rigidity and extremism. Our conviction about God's truth and values must be under girded with the ethic of love,* compassion and forgiveness.

The Church's Response

Resolving the dilemma of abortion takes more than ardently defending the sanctity of life in the unborn, for there is sacred life to embrace, though tragically unwanted, when abortion is opposed and denied. As a community that espouses Christian teachings and opposes abortion, the church and the families of the church must be prepared to parent any children, not just our own, as a shared obligation. This means taking concrete steps to receive unwanted children into our families as a gesture of taking seriously the sacred lives God has created and exercising stewardship.

Christians must, in addition to exercising the stewardship of life, honor our obligation of love. Love sees a woman seeking abortion as a neighbor in need of compassion. Regardless of whether abortion is given or denied, the pregnant mother, father and other members of the family will likely feel wounded. The Christian community must live out its spirit of *koinonia* by developing various forms of care and support during such a difficult time and by providing a context in which repentance, reconciliation, healing and nurturing may take place. Christian education in the form of counseling is also important, and participation with a Christlike humility and patience in organizations such as Pregnancy Crisis Center enables a Christian community to resolve and persevere with the abortion dilemma.

See also ADOPTION, CONCEPTION; MISCARRIAGE; PARENTING; SELF-ESTEEM; SEXUALITY.

References and Resources

T. Beauchamp and L. Walters, eds., *Contemporary Issues in Bioethics* (Belmont, Calif.: Wadsworth, 1989) 181-239; P. Cameron, "Abortion, Capital Punishment, and the Judeo-Christian Ethic," *Linacre Quarterly* 48, no. 4 (1981) 316-32; J. Davies and J. Jenkins, "Abortion—A Biblical Perspective," in *The Christian Educator's Handbook on Family Education*, ed. K. Gangel and J. Wilhoit (Grand Rapids: Baker, 1996), 269-84; S.

McFarland, "The Abortion Rotation," *Christianity Today* 39, no. 4 (1995) 25; F. Mathewes-Green, *Real Choices: Offering Practical, Life-Affirming Alternatives to Abortion* (Sisters, Ore.: Multnomah, 1994); M. L. Pernoll, ed., *Current Obstetric and Gynecologic Diagnosis and Treatment*, 7th ed. (Stamford, Conn.: Appleton & Lange, 1991); P. Ramsey, "Morality of Abortion," in *Life or Death: Ethics and Options* (Seattle: University of Washington Press, 1968) 60-93; D. C. Reardon, *Aborted Women, Silent No More* (Wheaton, Ill.: Crossway Books, 1987); N. Stotland, "Psychiatric Issue in Abortion, and the Implications of Recent Legal Choices for Psychiatric Practice," in *Psychiatric Aspects of Abortion*, ed. N. Stotland (Washington, D.C.: American Psychiatric Press, 1991) 1-16; J. R. W. Stott, "The Abortion Dilemma," in *Issues Facing Christians Today* (Old Tappan, N.J.: Revell, 1984) 2:187-214.

Edwin Hui and Mark Davies

—ABUSE—

Tragically, abuse in all its many forms most often happens within the home.* Estimates vary greatly, but the most common reports suggest that 25 percent of all married couples have engaged in physical abuse, at least 10 percent of all children have experienced severe forms of physical abuse by their parents within the past year, and 20 percent of all families will be forced to deal with some form of sexual abuse. It is little wonder that the American Medical Association has identified family abuse as the "silent epidemic" of the 1990s (Blue). The tragedy of family abuse is that it is perpetrated by those very individuals whom we believe we can trust and who are supposed to love us.

Dynamics of Abuse

Abuse is, in fact, very hard to define. For example, when does spanking become a form of physical abuse? There may be several suggestions as to how to determine this, but there is no one absolute standard that can be applied. Furthermore, all parents have overstepped the boundaries of verbal or physical punishment at one time or another. It is therefore more accurate to think of abuse in terms of being on a continuum rather

than being a true dichotomy. These realities make abuse very hard to measure accurately. While there are many sophisticated sociological and psychological measures of abuse, one important test of abuse is the fear test. Quite simply, the more fear there is in a family, the more likely that abuse at some level is occurring. The most important factors in understanding abuse and determining its effects include

□ The nature of the abuse. The more intense the abuse, the greater the damage done to the victim.

☐ The frequency and duration of abuse. The more frequent and prolonged the abuse is, the greater the damage.

☐ The relationship of the abused to the abuser. The closer the relationship is between the abused and the abuser, the more serious the consequences. Those who are in positions of power and trust (i.e., parents) and who use that position in order to abuse cause the greatest damage. This is why incest has even more serious psychological and spiritual consequences than rape by a stranger.

There are no simple answers as to why abuse occurs. Some psychologists believe that abuse is the result of psychopathology and point out that most abusers are narcissistic, immature, rigid, compulsive, anxious and lacking in empathy. Others suggest that abuse is the acting out of the inner pain of emptiness, depression,* guilt and fear that is felt within the family. Rather than dealing with these issues, families act out their pain by becoming abusive. A consistent finding is that the most accurate predictor of family abuse is whether or not individuals within the family were exposed to abuse growing up. The Bible teaches that the sins of the fathers are often passed on to the next generation (Ex 20:5). Children who grow up in abusive families learn that trauma, abuse or neglect are a way of life, and a significant proportion of abused children grow up to become abusers. Beyond the sociological and psychological explanations there is also a powerful spiritual reality underlying abuse. Satan inspires, supports and celebrates abuse. Jesus called Satan the father of lies (Jn 8:44) who carries out his work under a cloak of secrecy (Jn 3:19). Abuse in any form is dependent upon secrecy and lies for its continuance. Some of the greatest methods for

overcoming family cycles of abuse include prayer,* confession, forgiveness,* truth and the healing given by the Holy Spirit.

Abuse has to do with misuse of power, whether that power be emotional, physical or spiritual. It is significant that the vast majority of abuse still today is perpetrated against those who historically have had the least amount of power in our society—women and children. The relationship can be said to be abusive when power is used to hurt or coerce another. Being raised in an abusive home teaches children deeply held but sinful convictions about power and its use. Children learn that if you can not get your own way, then violence is permissible and that hitting people you love is acceptable (Strauss, Gelles, Steinmetz).

In contrast to a worldly concept of power, Christ taught us that greatness comes in serving others. Thus Christian parenting is not about lording power over our children. Christian parents should not try to get their children to do the things *we want* them to but get them to do the things *they need* to in order to grow, become autonomous and follow Christ. Authority is not about the right of anyone in power to do what he or she wants. Often abuse is justified as moral rightness—that it is acceptable to hit someone in order to enforce God's moral law. Biblical authority is always guided by the ethic of love* and service, and abuse promotes neither of these. Jesus was very clear about what would happen to those who harmed children (Mt 18:6), and his dealing with the woman caught in adultery is a corrective against the wrong use of power and morality.

Types of Abuse
The most common and widely accepted form of abuse is emotional abuse.

Emotional abuse. Most experts believe that at some level all parents have engaged in emotional abuse toward each other and toward their children. There is some evidence to suggest that emotional abuse can cause even greater fear than a physically abusive relationship because it happens so frequently. Emotional abuse includes humiliation, degradation, terrorization, isolation and exploitation. It is verbal aggression (O'Leary and Jouriles), and its main effect is to cause fear.

Emotional abuse is a serious form of abuse because words define and shape a child's identity and experience of the world. Hostile and demeaning belittling has an extremely negative effect on the individual. Another common form of emotional abuse is the "double bind." This is when a family member is placed in a no-win situation. An example of this is a drunken father demanding that his child bring him another beer. The child is caught in the terrible situation of supporting his father's drunkenness or risking verbal or physical abuse. Double binds, along with other forms of verbal abuse, lead to depression, anxiety, low self–esteem,* intense feelings of shame* and worthlessness, and even mental illness. Children who witness their parents engaging in emotional abuse with each other also suffer significant negative effects. Research has found that there is a strong link between verbal abuse and the potential for physical abuse.

Physical abuse. Physical abuse involves inflicting physical pain or injury on another or coercing another with physical force including violent acts. Family violence happens across all socioeconomic stratums and is strongly associated with social isolation, alcoholism, depression and poverty. There is a range from mild abuse (pushing, grabbing) to serious abuse (choking, beating). Victims of abuse tend to be less powerful than their abusers, are invested or dependent in the abusive relationship and are perceived by the abuser to be a source of stress (Larson, Goltz and Hobart). Common characteristics of abusive parents include low self-esteem, lack of self-confidence, social isolation, lack of empathy and a history of abuse in their own backgrounds. Results of physical abuse are fear, terror, low self-esteem, inability to trust, loneliness, depression, suicide and homicide. Abused children exhibit cognitive impairment, social skill deficits, depression, immaturity and delinquency, and they do poorly in school (Arias and Pape). The vast majority of physical abuse is perpetrated by husbands against their wives or by parents against their children. However, siblings often physically abuse each other, and sometimes children physically assault their parents. As well, elder abuse by children or grandchildren is gaining a significant amount of attention as a serious problem.

Sexual abuse. Though sexual abuse is very difficult to define, it is agreed that the most damaging form is incest— the ultimate form of betrayal. The child looks to his or her parent for support, care and love, yet is violated in a profoundly destructive way. In almost all cases it is the males who commit this crime. Females are at a much higher risk to be sexually abused than males, and the risk is increased if they are in a stepfamily. Sexual abuse of children has profoundly devastating consequences that often plague the victim over their entire life span. Victims suffer from depression, anxiety, posttraumatic stress disorder, dissociative identity disorder, anorexia and a host of other problems.

Spiritual abuse. Families are also damaged by spiritual abuse, which is most prevalent among highly religious families. At its most basic level, spiritual abuse occurs when the concept of God is taught in such a way that inspires fear and dependence among family members. This is achieved by parents portraying God to their children as an angry tyrant whom we can never please. God is portrayed as judgmental rather than merciful, angry rather than loving and condemning rather than forgiving. Salvation must be earned by being good enough. Families who pursue these lies are often rigid, authoritarian, distant and overcontrolling. The children often grow up with little emotional support and exhibit high amounts of fear, anxiety, guilt and depression. Rather than being set free by their faith, they are constricted and suffocated by legalism and guilt.

Dealing with Abuse

Breaking the cycle of abuse is very difficult. Walker has described abuse as cyclical in nature. The first stage is where there is increased tension and hostility within the family. Typically the victim tries to placate the abuser, but as the tension increases he or she becomes more fearful and pulls back. Next comes the uncontrollable discharge of aggression (verbal, physical or sexual) that is expressed, and tension is released. This is followed by the loving contrition phase where the abuser promises "never again." The abuser is kind and generous and works to restore the good relationship. The victim becomes trapped in the cycle, believing it won't happen again, but every time it is repeated, the victim's self-esteem is lowered, and he or she has fewer resources with which to flee from the abusive relationship.

Abused children are unable to believe that their parents are capable of such sinful behavior and thus introject their parents' sin into themselves. They end up believing that they are evil and deserve the actions of their parents. They believe that something is wrong with them. Even adults who have en-

dured ongoing abuse believe these lies. The result is that victims often accept responsibility for the abuse and work to maintain the relationship. Abuse has a pernicious effect of wearing down a person's self-esteem and warping his or her perception of reality. Both the abuser and abused begin to believe that the abuse itself is normal. Often victims do not leave because of the shame they feel. Many individuals can't leave due to dependency needs, and those who do often face a very difficult time, particularly adolescents.* Many victims are more intimidated by the thought of moving out of the abusive situation than they are by staying in it. As bad as it is, at least they know what to expect.

Usually the longer the abuse has existed, the more drastic the intervention is required to stop it. The most important intervention when abuse occurs is to protect the victims from further abuse. Often this means removing individuals physically from their families. Though the judicial system, social welfare system and health care has had a hard time dealing with this problem, some interventions such as shelters have been very positive. It has been found that laying charges against abusers has been more effective in stopping abusive behavior than mediation processes. Once abuse is stopped, then healing can begin to take place, both for the family as a whole and for each individual family member.

Family abuse has other issues underneath it. Not only does the pain of abuse have to be dealt with, but the family must face its other painful underlying issues. The process involved in helping families confront and recover from abuse includes: bringing secrets out into the open, dispelling lies and replacing them with truth, helping members gain insight with a focus on changing behavior, teaching family members to learn to talk about feelings, and helping them learn how to master coping skills.

Often well-meaning but ill-informed Christians counsel victims to remain in an abusive relationship. To be sure, God does not desire families to be split apart. The first step, however, in helping individuals or families is getting the abuse to stop. If the abuse does not stop, then family members must be protected from even more serious physical, emotional or sexual harm. Christians can play a significant role in helping families heal from abuse by refusing to support abusive behavior in any way, shape or form.

Helping to heal abusive families is usually work for professional counselors. However, pastors and churches play a critical role in the healing process. Simple acts of compassion, forgiveness* and acceptance often provide the spiritual base that abusive families need in order to heal. Often times those who have had a long history of abuse do not have any concept of how normal families work and being exposed to healthy family models is helpful. Churches must ensure that they are not a haven to shelter ongoing abuse by silence, cover up or inaction. One of the greatest ways to confront abuse is through prevention. Preaching, teaching and supporting healthy family values* both within the church and in the community can make a significant impact in helping grow healthy, godly families. The church and individual Christians can play a signifi-

cant role in healing and preventing the pain that comes from living in an abusive family situation.

See also CONFLICT RESOLUTION; DISCIPLINE; FAMILY PROBLEMS; FAMILY SYSTEMS; FORGIVENESS; SEXUALITY; SHAME.

References and Resources
I. Arias and K. Pape, "Physical Abuse," in L. L'Abate, ed., *Handbook of Developmental Family Psychology and Psychopathology* (New York: John Wiley, 1994) 284-308; B. Birns and S. Birns, "Violence Free Families," in S. Dreman, *The Family on the Threshold of the 21st Century* (Mahwah, N.J.: Lawrence Erlbaum, 1997) 129-46; K. Blue, "Abuse," in *The Complete Book of Everyday Christianity*, ed. R. Banks and R. P. Stevens, (Downers Grove, Ill.: InterVarsity Press, 1997) 4-8; K. Blue, *Healing Spiritual Abuse* (Downers Grove, Ill.: InterVarsity Press, 1993); J. Dobson, *Love Must be Tough* (Waco, Tex.: Word, 1983); J. Haugaard, "Sexual Abuse in Families, " in L. L'Abate, op. cit., 309-29; R. Kagan and S. Schlossberg, *Families in Perpetual Crisis* (New York: W. W. Norton, 1989); L. Larson, W. Goltz and C. Hobart, *Families in Canada* (Scarborough, Ont.: Prentice-Hall, 1994); K. O'Leary and E. Jouriles, "Psychological Abuse Between Adult Partners, " in L. L'Abate, op. cit., 330-49; W. Steele and M. Raider, *Working with Families in Crisis* (New York: Guilford Press, 1991); L. Steinberg, *Adolescence* (New York: McGraw-Hill, 1996); M. Strauss, R. Gelles and S. Steinmetz, *Behind Closed Doors: Violence in the American Family* (New York: Anchor Books, 1980); L. Walker, *The Battered Woman Syndrome* (New York: Springer, 1984).

Mark Davies

—ADOLESCENCE—

Adolescence is a special time of development in all areas of a young person's life. Development occurs as youth grow from less to more mature in all areas of their lives within their own social and cultural environment. Because of their development in several domains, adolescents sense new powers, abilities, interests and processes at work in them. Exploring these new avenues leads to new creations both internally and externally.

Internally, adolescents restructure and develop values* and ultimately a new understanding of the self, of "who I am." This occurs in the six domains of human development: physical—growing from a child's body to an adult body; cognitive—developing the ability to think abstractly (perform formal operations); social—learning to recognize and accept adult social and sex roles; affective—gaining control of one's emotions; moral—moving from making egocentric moral judgments and actions to those that are other-centered, then principle-driven and ultimately agape-based; spiritual—forming a personally owned, examined and internalized faith.

Externally, adolescents make many changes in their relationships with others. These changes take the forms of new processes by which adolescents relate to their entire world, new modes of behavior, new relationships and experiences, and new feelings and meanings about others and the external world.

These internal and external processes and relationships produce *intrapersonal* disruptions, changes, stresses and at times turmoil, as well as *interpersonal* conflicts between self and parents, relatives, friends, siblings, teachers and many other authority figures.

In short, adolescent development is the process within the total personhood from approximately age twelve through twenty-five by which various structural and development changes occur at identifiable stages along the way.

Adolescent development is manifested in various forms of behavior, some of which are socially acceptable. Other forms are questionable, and some are socially and personally destructive.

Culture and Adolescence

The world of adolescence in both Western and non-Western societies is composed of major dimensions or factors that are characteristics of any subculture. The astute youth worker or parent will want to keep in mind that youth subcultures go through dynamic changes. What might be in vogue today may be out tomorrow; something new will become all the rage

for anywhere from a few weeks to a few years or even longer. Only one thing is certain. Youth culture does not remain static; it is in a constant state of flux.

How can one address the needs of youth when the subculture is constantly changing? By studying youth culture and seeking to understand what is going on. All cultures have certain common factors, but particular subcultures exhibit them in unique ways.

Values and norms. These are the basis for decision-making and behavior. They are usually unique to youth and are often not understood by adults.

In-group language. Youths have their own words and language to communicate with each other that are unique to their own culture and time. This language is not shared by children or adults. In this way adolescents keep their secrets and keep out nonadolescents from their world.

Distinct channels of mass communication. MTV is their station. Rock music radio stations are also theirs. They have their own magazines, Internet pages and forums. This is how they communicate with each other and how the subculture is made more homogenous worldwide.

Unique styles and fads. Adolescents have distinct hair and clothing* styles, mannerisms and so on. These styles are usually fads that change, often within a year or two.

Sense of solidarity. Adolescents feel like they are in their own clan and are correct to a large degree. They are segregated into schools,* offered low-paying after-school jobs and generally kept separate from the adult world. They hang out together because they are pushed together by social institutions.

Status criteria. They have developed a way of measuring successful achievement, ownership and use of their subcultures' status symbols—language, fads, values, channels of communication and identification with their subculture. People who do not measure up are often shunned or treated badly because they do not conform to the criteria.

Influence and power of leaders. Adolescents are influenced by heroes and charismatic leaders, especially those disdained by adult cultures.

Subcultural institutions. Specialized institutions meet the needs that the main culture cannot, or does not, desire to meet; the entertainment*/recreational industry caters to teens by offering youth-oriented magazines and electronic malls.

Geography. This is where adolescents reside and where they go to learn, hang out, work, have fun, recreate, be entertained and play.* They have their own locations, be it a street corner, someone's house or a mall. Almost all American schools have particular sections on their campuses where various subgroups assemble.

Use of technology. Mechanical and electronic technology allows adolescents to escape (or leave) their immediate surroundings and go somewhere else. Teens escape by means of cars, bikes, skateboards, body/surfboards, radio and TV stations, movies, video games and concerts. Of increasing importance to adolescents are the Internet* and other electronic means of communicating.

Adolescents today are a subculture to themselves. What youth need is loving acceptance of them as real human beings, not some sort of otherworldly creatures that have to be tolerated until they "grow up." Adolescents are people *now*. They are people whom God loves, for whom Christ died and in whom the Holy Spirit may dwell. Christian teens are spiritually gifted people called into ministry just as are adults.

Jesus as an Adolescent

Jesus was a teenager! What is most amazing is that Jesus' adolescent behaviors in Luke 2:51-52 are similar to those that many teenagers evidence today—and with the same reactions from their parents as Jesus had from his. So the temple narrative provides parents with a great deal of encouragement that their own adolescents, whether they are twelve or twenty-two, are quite normal. Adolescents themselves can find comfort in this story if they recognize that the problems Jesus encountered are similar to their own and that he can be a model for how to handle similar ones today.

The narrative of Jesus in the temple illustrates all six of the previously stated major developmental domains or areas.

Physical development. Jesus was evidently a physically mature person, enough for him to take care of himself alone in the capital city of Jerusalem for at least three and perhaps up to five days.

Luke states, "Jesus grew in wisdom and stature " (2:52; see also v. 40). This, along with Hebrews 2 and 4, suggests that Jesus' physical body went through the same growth and development as any other adolescent. If this is so, then we can assume that he developed structurally and muscularly like any other teenager. He began to grow body hair and develop sexually just like any normal youth. His voice changed from a child's to that of an adult. He developed hand-eye coordination so that he could pound a nail in the carpenter shop in Nazareth without destroying either the wood or his fingers. He probably ate so much that his parents wondered if he had a bottomless pit for a stomach.

Cognitive development. According to Jewish custom Jesus would at this age begin to study the Law (Talmud) and to take on the responsibilities associated with the Law. His parents evidently felt he could be trusted to make informed judgments about what to do. They had to have allowed him much unsupervised time in Jerusalem. Jesus evidenced independence from his parents, seeking out his own interests and concerns. He knew enough about himself and what he was about to begin to enter into dialogue with the teachers in the temple.

Mary and Joseph did not seem to understand Jesus. First they thought he was with the pilgrims on the return trip; then they looked for him all through the city. Seemingly in exasperation and not without some sense of hopelessness, they finally went to the temple.

Why did Jesus go back to the temple? He was like any other cognitively growing adolescent. He had questions about life, about his experiences in the temple, about what he saw and heard as he went through Passover. One wonders what he might have been thinking if he recalled the words of Isaiah 53 and the suffering servant of other parts of Isaiah. His parents found him among the teachers in the temple, listening to them and asking questions. He was using his mind to inquire and learn. We can only speculate as to his questions. Whatever he asked and said, he amazed those around him with his understanding, insights and replies. The teachers and other adults present treated him as a person on a par with themselves. They did not dismiss him as a little child. They allowed him to interact with them. Adults are amazed when a younger person to-

day, like Jesus, listens carefully, asks thoughtful questions and offers responsible answers. So Jesus surprised those teachers in the temple.

In typical adolescent fashion he was developing a sense of self-identity and mission that would eventually lead him to Calvary. But in the temple, he knew that he was not just the son of Mary and Joseph. He, like adolescents today, had begun to distinguish self from others, to know what he was not and what he wanted to become, and to articulate that self-identity even though in only partial ways. His reply to Mary is instructive about his self-identity. He distinguished between Joseph and his heavenly Father and the need to be in his Father's house, and by implication, to be about his Father's instead of his father's business.

In one sense Jesus demonstrated what many adolescents want to demonstrate, namely, that they are growing up. They do not want to be considered children any longer. They are searching for new and exciting experiences to test their own sense of identity and development.

Social development. Jesus' parents evidently thought he was a "social" person, that he was somewhere with the crowd of friends and family on the return trip to Nazareth. They must have considered other occasions when Jesus would be gone for a long part of the day and had no great concern for his safety. Jesus, however, wasn't with his usual associates; he was holding his own with teachers and priests. Evidently he could talk and interact socially with many people in such a way that they did not think to consider his young age and his apparent lack of supervision.

Today's youth are similar to Jesus. They are increasingly socially adept in various situations. With the advent of the first totally TV* generations in history, adolescents around the world are ever more sophisticated in situations that would have discomforted their grandparents in the 1950s. Today's adolescents surprise many adults when given a chance to ask questions and state their thoughts or insights. The problem many adolescents face is not that they lack social skills but that adults will not carry on a serious conversation* with them. Often most of the communication from adults to youth is in the form of commands or prohibitions. The "Just Say No" campaign is a good example of well-meaning adults' failure to recognize the social and cognitive development of today's youth and the temptations surrounding them. Merely telling youth not to do something without giving them a chance to talk, share, inquire and question is a recipe for failure.

Affective development. Both Jesus' parents and Jesus himself showed affective, emotional development in the incident in Luke 2. His parents showed their astonishment and exasperation, if not even panic. Upon finding him in the temple, seemingly calmly interacting with the teachers, his mother let out a typical mother shout: "Son, why have you treated us like this? Your father and I have been anxiously searching for you." She was emotionally upset. Jesus had been missing for three or more days, depending on how one counts the days in the text. There had been no hint of where he could be. They were upset and rightly so. They did not understand why he had done what he had done.

This is a common plight of just about every parent in the world when it comes to adolescent sons and daughters. Parents continually ask the emotionally laden question "What have you done and why did you do it?" The often-asked question of parents is "What has become of our little boy/girl? You used to be so good. Now look at you. We do not understand what is happening to you."

Jesus, on the other hand, showed typical adolescent lack of thought about what consequences his actions might have for other people's feelings. He was looking for new experiences; he was caught up in the emotion of the event, finding great personal satisfaction by being in his Father's house. There is no suggestion that "the devil made him do it" or that he was driven to stay in the city by the Holy Spirit. It was his free choice, flowing from his decision to encounter more of the great delight that he found at the temple. Undoubtedly he was excited by the big city of Jerusalem compared to the small town of Nazareth. The activities of the Feast of the Passover with its sacrifice and meals stirred his heart, mind and soul to reflect on the lamb that was slain.

Moral development. Moral development focuses on the way a person decides what actions to take and which actions are considered good or bad. Children usually make moral judgments based on what is best for themselves. If they are punished, they know something is bad. If they like what they are doing and there is no punishment associated with it, then it must be good. In the temple story we see Jesus making a moral judgment that it was fine for him not to tell his parents where he was, to remain in Jerusalem without permission, and not to be accountable to any earthly person except himself. He was focused on his own needs, identity and desire to interact in the temple. He did not think about his parents and their needs. This should sound familiar to parents worldwide. Jesus evidenced typical moral judgments of a twelve year old. He may have been physically mature, precocious in intellectual or cognitive development and well adept at social relationships, but he was typical of early adolescence when it came to moral development.

When Mary rebuked him by her comment, Jesus responded with mild rebuke to her in the form of a question: "Why were you searching for me? . . . Didn't you know I had to be in my Father's house?" Regardless of Jesus' sinlessness, he responded typically of someone at his stage of moral development. Unfortunately, that response is often taken by authoritarian parents as being disrespectful, insolent and therefore offensive.

If we understand Jesus' developmental stage, we would not see it this way. Jesus' response to his mother's question should be taken as it is meant to be understood: a statement of a well-meaning young person who cannot understand why his parents were all upset by what appeared to him as innocent behavior. They should have known where to look for him. Why? Because Jesus knew what he was doing and where he was. He assumed, like most adolescents, that his parents would somehow know what he was thinking if he was thinking it. It takes a higher level of moral development for a young adolescent to be able to switch places with others to learn how they might understand a particular moral situation. Jesus was not mature enough at this point to do so and therefore responded in a typical way to his mother's excited question and statements.

Jesus demonstrated the way many adolescents make their moral choices. They view things only from their limited moral viewpoint; it takes time for normal adolescents to move from their immature egocentrism to a more mature stage.

Jesus, however, willingly submitted to his parents' authority. Though he had just alluded that Joseph was not his father, yet he went with his parents to Nazareth and was obedient to them. He recognized that they had authority over

him and that his role was to obey that rightful authority. Jesus' sinlessness comes to the fore at this point. Although all adolescents are tempted and often succumb to defying their parents' authority, Jesus, being tempted to do the same at the temple, did not. This is where Jesus' actions differ from those of adolescents: he did not consider his parents' lack of understanding of him, his actions and motives as sufficient grounds to disobey them. Parents would very much like to see Jesus' behavior copied by their own adolescent children.

Spiritual development. Jesus' faith development was evidenced in several ways in the narrative. He was in the temple with the teachers, obviously interested in the faith of his parents and nation. His cognitive and social development helped him to be comfortable asking questions, listening and processing the teachers' comments. He also was seemingly quite at home in his "Father's house." It seems by implication that he had spent a good amount of the days separated from his parents in the temple.

Like all adolescents, Jesus had a genuine interest in religious things, more so since he grew up in a society that enculturated the Jewish faith from infancy through adulthood. To be Jewish meant believing in the one true God of Abraham and the law of Moses. Today the vast majority of adolescents have a sense of religion and a high interest in spiritual matters. Few are truly atheists, especially younger adolescents. Not until young people arrive in university or college classes do they begin to "lose their faith" or to have serious doubts about what they have been taught.

Because Jesus was human, likely he had doubts about many things as he grew up. His faith development, however, continued and did not waver. Luke states, "And Jesus grew . . . in favor with God and men." His strong identification of himself with his Father's house indicated that his faith development was more mature than that of most adolescents his age. Yet while he was precocious in faith development, he was not totally off the normal faith development scale. He had questions to ask about his faith. Many youth have a strong identity with God and do not waver into unbelief even though they may have doubts from time to time. Many youth have a strong spiritual sense that continues to cause them to seek God and to keep on growing. It is not until the "cares of this life" in adulthood come upon them that they begin to lose some if not much of their enthusiasm for spiritual things. The message of Jesus' own life and the teachings of the Epistles suggest that while lack of continual spiritual development may not be too unusual, it is by no means the biblical norm. Jesus showed us that a young adolescent could be actively engaged in his own faith development and that such action is normal and welcomed.

Adolescence is a normal part of human development, as Jesus' example shows. Adults need to recognize the signs of normalcy in the lives of all the adolescents with whom they have contact. Adults should help adolescents along their developmental paths so they may continue as smoothly as possible in their growth and development into more and more mature adolescents and then adults.

See also FAMILY; PARENTING; STRESS.

References and Resources

D. P. Ausbel et al., *Theory and Problems of Adolescent Development* (New York: Green and Stratton, 1977); M. Brake, *The Sociology of Youth Culture and Youth Subcultures: Sex, Drugs and Rock 'n' Roll* (Boston: Kegan Paul, 1980); J. M. Dettoni, *Introduction to Youth Ministry* (Grand Rapids: Zondervan, 1993); D. Elkind, *All Grown Up and No Place to Go: Teenagers in Crisis* (Reading, Mass.: Addison-Welsey, 1984); T. Lickona, *Raising Good Children: Helping Your Child Through the Stages of Moral Development* (New York: Bantam, 1983); D. Offer, E. Ostrove et al., *The Teenage World* (New York: Plenum, 1988); S. Parks, *The Critical Years* (New York: Harper & Row, 1986); L. Parrott, *Helping the Struggling Adolescent* (Grand Rapids: Zondervan, 1993); Q. Schultz, R. M. Anker et al., *Dancing in the Dark: Youth Popular Culture and the Electronic Media* (Grand Rapids: Eerdmans, 1991); H. Sebold, *Adolescence: A Social Psychological Analysis* (Englewood Cliffs, N.J.: Prentice-Hall, 1984).

John M. Dettoni

—ADOPTION—

To adopt is to take a person into one's family legally and to rear as one's own child. Every year Americans adopt more than one hundred thousand children and Canadians about six thousand. Adoption directly affects another half-million or so people from the nuclear and extended families that adoptees join. With adoption affecting this many people, it forces us to replace the false notion of what comprises a "normal" family* with a more encompassing one: an adult or adults who provide a child, whether born or not born to them, with a loving, permanent family, a real family. Adoption is one way in which families are made.

Types of Adoptions

There are several different types of adoptions. *Agency adoptions* use organizations such as Family Services to coordinate the placement of a child with an adoptive family. Social workers conduct home studies of prospective families. If the agency worker decides that the home would benefit a child, the worker looks for a child to place in the home.* The social worker sends a referral to the court so the adoption may be finalized legally sometime after the child has been placed within the home. For prospective adoptive parents, placement of a child through an agency can require a long wait.

Independent adoptions are usually mediated by a third party such as a lawyer or doctor. This person seeks to connect an expectant mother with a potential family. In independent adoptions the home study is not usually as exhaustive, and the process is often quicker than going through an agency. Sometimes the adoptive parents agree to help pay for the mother's medical expenses during the pregnancy. Legal paperwork is still completed.

Open adoptions take a variety of forms. The continuum runs from semiopen (first-names-only, agency-mediated, minimal exposure, one-time-only meeting or exchange of letters and pictures at specified intervals) to wide-open involvement in each others' lives. The style of open adoption depends on the needs of the adoptee and the comfort level of the consenting adults. Open adoptions are being practiced with increasing frequency in recent years. Supporters of open adoptions believe that including birth parents in the ongoing lives of the adopted child enables adoptees to see that "the people who gave them life value them, even if they can't raise them. . . . Adoptees learn that choosing adoption was circumstance, rather than rejection or abandonment" (Webber, 82). Children are given direct access to the story surrounding their beginnings, birth parents may retain a link with their child, and adoptive families gain access to what may be critical information. At the same time, open adoptions are culturally unscripted and complex, and may make the adopting parents vulnerable to a birth parent's own possible need for parenting.*

International adoption refers to children who are born abroad and placed in a North American home for adoption. Many requirements of the governments of both countries must be met, and the cost of international adoptions is often considerable.

Black market adoptions occur when children are bought and sold outside the law. Mediators may not try to provide safety or follow-up for the child. Arrangements are made, money* is exchanged, and the location of the child becomes a mystery. Court documents are not filed to enable adoptees to be traced. Sometimes children are bought in developing countries and sold in North America, taking advantage of those who are most vulnerable and desperate.

Biblical Reflections
In the Old Testament childless Sarah urged Abraham to father a child by her concubine, knowing that this child would then be considered Sarah's by adoption (Gen 16:2). Pharaoh's daughter adopted Moses (Ex 2:10). God himself introduced the concept in the Davidic covenant by means of the "divine adoption formula": "I will be his father, and he will be my son" (2 Sam 7:14).

In the New Testament the theme of adoption is richly developed in the writings of Paul. In fact, adoption is defined as the purpose for which God sent Jesus. "But when the time had fully come, God sent his Son, born of a woman, born under law, to redeem those under law, that we might receive the full rights of sons" (Gal 4:4-5). This adoption is connected with the reception of the Spirit of the New Covenant. "Because you are sons, God sent the Spirit of his Son into our hearts, the Spirit who calls out, 'Abba, Father.' So you are no longer a slave, but a son; and since you are a son, God has made you also an heir" (vv. 6-7). The divine adoption formula expands to include daughters, in addition to sons (2 Cor 6:18). Even as Greek and Roman adoption granted adoptees the same status and privileges as natural-born heirs, divine adoption grants believers the privilege of addressing God as Abba Father, the same name Jesus uses.

In addition to the present privileges, there is also a future dimension to the theological meaning of adoption. Along with creation, believers long for their future redemption (Rom 8:23). This redemption is called adoption. When believers enter fully into the inheritance of their adoption, they will rule with the Son of God as sisters and brothers of the Son.

In contrast to the sole intent of the ancient Greeks and Romans to benefit the adoptive father, God's adoption concerns itself with the welfare of the adoptee. The family of God embraces both women and men, and adoption is not restricted to males. God extends adoption to those who were strangers and enemies to him. God's practice of adoption is a free and generous offer of kinship with Christ. He welcomes his adopted children into all the privileges of intimate address, as well as the promise of a future that includes communion with the Spirit of God. Father, Son and Holy Spirit are all part of this amazing gift of God, which he chooses to call adoption.

Practical Considerations

For those persons considering adoption, working through personal loss before adopting is important. Because adoption is usually a choice that follows infertility, complex emotions surrounding failure to conceive or carry a baby to term are inevitable. No parents, adoptive or otherwise, should expect their children to carry the burden for their emotional stability. Once those emotions and lost dreams have been dealt with, understand that families build ties more on love,* caring and nurturing than on bloodlines. A family formed by adoption is a real family facing all the joys and challenges of life together.

Once you have adopted, tell an adopted child the story of his/her adoption as early as possible. Give a simple, straightforward explanation and be prepared to repeat it as often as asked for. Telling the facts of a child's adoption is not a one-time event. It should be an integral part of the fabric of ongoing family communication.* Tell the truth, as far as you know it, and as far as the child is ready to receive it. Tell the story in a way that will not require later contradictions and be prepared to add to the child's understanding as the child matures.

Expect an adopted child to search at some point in his or her life for at least one birth parent. A child may not search, particularly if it is a boy, but be prepared, nonetheless. An adopted child's search does not signal parental rejection. Motivation is usually more to do with finding "missing pieces" than an attempt to find "replacement" parents. Believe in your child. Continue to tell your feelings to your child, trust your child, and strive to serve as a support in the discovery of their whole identity.

For adoptees considering a birth parent search, begin by pondering the following questions: Why do you want to contact a birth parent? What are your long-term hopes and expectations? What kind of a relationship would you like to have? How will you respond if your expectations are not met? What do you think will be the impact on your family? Try to anticipate what you might gain and lose through a search. Be prepared to learn that some birth parents cannot be found, do not want to be found or are deceased. Many provinces and states have adoption reunion registries staffed by trained persons sensitive to the complex dynamics of adoption searches and prepared to offer counsel in a variety of formats.

For those persons faced with the difficult decision of whether to raise an unexpected child or allow the baby to be placed for adoption, there are many questions to be considered. Do I understand what is involved in caring for a baby? Can I support a child financially? Will I commit myself to seek the well-being of this child through all the stages of infancy, childhood, adolescence and into adulthood? Am I willing to have my freedom affected to give this child all that it needs? Considering adoption is difficult, and major centers have a crisis pregnancy center with trained counselors prepared to help persons make thoughtful decisions. Planning the adoption of a child is the action of mature love. It is the product of love that chooses to place a child's well-being first. It takes a great deal of courage and maturity.

Adoption is one way of creating a family. It is also God's chosen way of making his family. Canadian actress and adoptive mother Sonja Smits identifies the radical theological nature of adoption in this way: "I have come to realize that making that choice to love and commit to a child you didn't bear comprises a threat to some people; perhaps because if one can love another's child as one's own, the next step is loving one's neighbour as oneself" (Webber, x). The mystery of adoption lies at the heart of the gospel.

See also ABORTION; FAMILY; NEW REPRODUCTIVE TECHNOLOGY; PARENTING; PREGNANCY; SINGLE PARENTING.

References and Resources
J. E. Greenberg and H. H. Carey, *Adopted* (New York: Franklin Watts, 1987); M. Komar, J. Kincaid, *Adopting for Good* (Downers Grove, Ill.: InterVarsity Press, 1997); *Communicating with the Adopted Child* (New York: Walker, 1992); J. M. Scott, *Adoption as Sons of God* (Tübingen: J. C. B. Mohr, 1992); M. Webber, *As if Kids Mattered: What's Wrong in the World of Child Protection and Adoption* (Toronto: Key Porter, 1998); M. Zimmerman, *Should I Keep My Baby?* (Minneapolis: Bethany House, 1997).

Barbara Horkoff Mutch

—ALLOWANCES—

Many people believe that the best way parents can give their children a financial education is to give them practical experience through an allowance. As you cannot learn to read without books, you cannot learn how to handle money* if you never touch it.

The Bible contains much about training up children in the way of the Lord (e.g., Deut 6:6-7; Eph 6:4), and personal finances are an important area in which to lay down a godly life pattern. There are many general references to handling money in the Scriptures, and many of these can be applied to the raising of godly and wise children. For example, insights such as "Whoever loves money never has money enough" (Eccles 5:10) and Jesus' comment on the sacrificial generosity of the widow's offering (Mk 12:41-44) are vital parts of a child's home "curriculum." The specific commandments against stealing and coveting that, according to Deuteronomy, are to be impressed upon children are certainly to the point. The passages in Proverbs about money are also applicable (e.g., Prov 1:19; 3:9; 13:11, 22; 15:16; 28:8). Certainly handling personal finances is one of the key ways in which a child needs to be trained. In our increasingly complicated and stressful economic world, as much practice with money as possible before adolescence* is particularly essential.

Two Kinds of Allowances

Some parents apply the word *allowance* only to regular money given to a child that is not tied to any chores* but just reflects the child's membership in the family.* Most families expect contributions by the child to the cleanliness of his or her body and bedroom, and usually some participation in household work, but the allowance is never seen as a direct reward for any duties. It is never removed as a punishment for "sins" of omission or commission in the area of personal responsibilities. With this approach, called the *true allowance*, additional funds can still be received by the child for assignments in the household that they take on voluntarily (e.g., grass cutting).

Other families downplay that type of allowance in favor of a pay-for-work approach. While these parents agree that personal hygiene, tidying one's closet and doing homework should be their own reward, they arrange (often in dialogue with the child) regular, age-appropriate duties that are real contributions to the household (e.g., dusting, laundry and gardening) to which all or most of the allowance is directly linked. This approach, called the *cooperative family economy*, emphasizes the Scriptures that teach against laziness (e.g., Prov 10:4; 2 Thess 3:11-12) and about the dignity of work.

For at least two reasons those taking this approach should not give up on some expression of the true allowance: (1) to avoid turning childhood into a job and caregivers into managers, and (2) to help regularize and control the inevitable gifts of money (for small treats) that flow from parent to child during a week.

Why not collect these "gifts" into a simple, true allowance and eliminate a lot of bother? On the other hand, for the biblical reasons already stated, true-allowance parents should also pay attention to the value of "money for work," recognizing that even young children can make a significant contribution to a family economy. In practice the two approaches often come together in child rearing, with a true allowance being emphasized in the earlier years and working directly for a share of the family income being stressed more with teenagers.

Guidelines

There are many specific systems used by parents to manage the distribution of family income. All parents can apply the following commonsense guidelines.

Progressive. Increase weekly money as the children get older, with consequently more responsibility for making purchases for themselves (e.g., teenagers purchasing clothes, personal grooming products and entertainment). One rule of thumb suggests a number of dollars each week equal to half the child's age, but each family needs to decide for itself what is realistic and reasonable.

Consistent. It is extremely important to give the allowance regularly, in full and at the same time each week (consider how adults would respond to an employer who operated any differently). Wisdom can be applied to the best timing (Sunday or Monday evening avoids the temptation of Saturday shopping* sprees), and extending advances should be kept to a minimum (having to save for a costlier purchase is usually a better discipline).

Independent. The benefit of an allowance includes freedom in spending. Though it is difficult to see children "wasting" money on sweets, there is no better way to learn to make decisions, plan ahead and determine value. Parental guidance is not thereby eliminated, but parents must be prepared to let their children grow through mistakes.

Positive. The temptation to use an allowance as a bribe or punishment should be avoided. Do not change the rules midstream and unilaterally and thus create a negative image around what should be a gift (true allowance) or compensation (cooperative family economy). Other strategies to change a child's behavior unrelated to the allowance should be used (e.g., removal of privileges for breaking curfew).

There will always be differences of opinion about how to handle allowances. The most important thing is to involve children as much as possible in setting up the system and the amounts in the context of an appreciation of the overall state of family finances, to embody the practice in wider teaching about God's will for money and stewardship, and to establish good attitudes and behaviors from the earliest age.

See also DISCIPLINE; GIFT-GIVING; GOALS; MONEY; TITHING; VALUES.

References and Resources
J. R. Peterson, *It Doesn't Grow on Trees* (Crozet, Va.: Betterway Publications, 1988); G. W. Weinstein, *Children and Money* (New York: Charterhouse, 1975).

Paul W. Lermitte and Dan Williams

—ALTERNATIVE RELIGIONS—

Alternative religions here mean those not part of a mainline religious tradition. It does not include world religions such as Islam or Buddhism but the various "designer spiritualities" so popular today, including especially those under the heading of New Age.

Parents do not have to look far to uncover such influences in the lives of their children. The story lines of many of the most popular TV* cartoon series are based on the search for the spiritual or extraterrestrial powers that will endow their heroes with extraordinary abilities. Talk shows frequently project the same worldview, as celebrities talk openly and without embarrassment of tuning in to spirit guides to help them make all sorts of life decisions. It is impossible to be a child today and not receive these messages as part of the cultural atmosphere. Not all children will accept this uncritically, but those who are struggling with other issues in the process of growing up will find much to attract them here.

Sources
This kind of eclectic spirituality is rooted in a disillusionment with modern Western culture, which is now widely perceived as having failed people. Though few would wish to discard the achievements of science and technology, it is obvious that they have not solved the world's problems, and the twentieth century has been one of the most brutal and dehumanizing periods in the whole of history. Instead of getting better, humankind seems to be getting worse, with rampant racism and genocide, as well as willful destruction of the planet. If we are to survive for long into the third millenni-

um, things will have to change. We will need a new paradigm with which to understand the world. But since Christianity has been the dominant faith of the old paradigm, there is a widespread assumption that Christian values* have contributed to the mess we are now in, and if they are part of the problem then by definition they will not be part of the solution. The alternatives now emerging are not new but are merely the latest manifestation of what Aldous Huxley once called "the perennial philosophy." Whenever materialist revelation has failed—whether secular or religious—Western culture has always reverted to an idealist, essentialist (and therefore timeless and universalist) way of understanding life. This is why today's spiritualities lay so much emphasis on non-Western sources and include Christianity only through aspects of the medieval mystical traditions or heterodox movements such as Gnosticism.

Issues for Christian Parents

The pluralistic spirituality of our day raises three issues of particular concern for Christians.

Personal power. Especially among children there is a growing feeling of powerlessness in our society. Things often seem to be in the control of forces we no longer know how to deal with—whether the unpredictable powers of nature unleashed by greenhouse gases and climate change or the marketing strength of multinational corporations that increasingly determine everything from the kind of food we eat to the news we hear. Awareness of this can leave people feeling disempowered and threatened, and in this context, anything that offers the possibility of gaining control is bound to be attractive. This is the perennial appeal of magic of all kinds, as well as movements such as Satanism, especially when they offer membership of an exclusive club thereby hiding the secret knowledge from the uninitiated.

Personal responsibility. When combined with belief in reincarnation, this search for personal power can be especially enticing. Reincarnation originated in the religious traditions of India, where it has a moral basis: in Hinduism, people's status in future lives is determined by the ways they behave in this one. But in today's alternative spiritualities this is regularly twisted by the incorporation of Western notions of individualism, so that the karma (baggage from the past) that people have today can be regarded as something they have individually chosen for themselves at some time in the past. This explains the popularity of therapies such as past-life recall and the emphasis on taking responsibility for our own actions, while being accountable to no one else. When taken to its logical conclusion, it presents serious ethical questions. For if we have all chosen to be who we now are, that means no one needs to have a social conscience. Those who are poor and marginalized must have chosen to be that way, just as the rich and famous have. Moreover—and New Age therapists do not hesitate to draw this conclusion—people afflicted with undeserved suffering must have brought it on themselves or chosen to go that way in order to achieve their own self-determined spiritual purposes.

It is little wonder that children brought up with that kind of worldview can end up not only being unbelievably self-centered but also having no moral framework within which to understand violence or suffering. If everyone chooses to do what they do, that makes cruelty, murder and rape morally neutral actions.

Truth. The New Age in particular sees itself as an inclusive worldview that can take elements from many cultures and transform them into a new way of being. By incorporating non-Western spiritualities, New Agers often claim they are making a valuable contribution to worldwide harmony. In reality, though, this can only come about by assuming that there is no such thing as truth and that all claims to truth are relative. Children can easily buy into this mix-and-match approach. That is how they buy their clothes* or choose their food—so why not do it with spirituality as well? What harm can it be doing, especially if it promotes international understanding?

Christian Responses
It is clearly both impossible and undesirable to insulate children from the wider culture around them. This is the world our children are growing up in, and they will need to deal with all this one day. It will be counterproductive merely to discredit and question what is going on. Children need to know that there are positive alternatives. In reality, there is a Christian understanding of all the issues that have been highlighted here.

Christians and personal power. In the Bible people are described as "made in God's image" (Gen 1:26). For many reasons, Christians have historically been more inclined to play that down, emphasizing sin and fallenness rather than power and blessing.* It is a simple fact that large numbers of those individuals with a low self-esteem* who seek power through alternative spiritualities have come from Christian homes,* where they have been so thoroughly imbued with a sense of worthlessness that they cannot see how being Christian is worthwhile.

Personal responsibility. Related to this, many people from Christian homes take with them an enormous burden of guilt, feeling responsible not only for their own shortcomings but for all the evil that is in the entire world.

The gospel is realistic about the human predicament—but at its heart is a message of forgiveness, telling us that life can be different not as we make selfish choices for ourselves but as we allow ourselves to be transformed to be like Jesus. Unfortunately, many Christians have adopted the individualistic lifestyles characteristic of our culture and live as if no one else mattered. This is a denial of the gospel, which is about taking up the cross and following Jesus. It is easy to ridicule many of today's spiritual seekers, but for a lot of them church would be just too bland and undemanding to have any appeal. They do genuinely want to be the best people they can possibly be and will do whatever it takes to accomplish that.

Truth. Christians should have something useful to say about ultimate values. Notions of absolute right and wrong, of truth and untruth, are key understandings that Christian parents ought to be passing on to their children. Many do, especially when "truth" is defined only in terms of theological correctness or doctrinal purity. But on morality and behavior, issues are often fudged. Children know their parents better than anyone else, and if the parents' behavior in the privacy of the home does not match what they say in church, no one should be surprised when children give up on faith as they grow older. If lifestyles do not have absolute integrity, children will be unable to tell the difference between what they see on the TV and what is supposed to be Christian. Similar comments could be made regarding the contemporary search for mystical experiences. For a generation nurtured on *The X-Files,* contact with the numinous and the spiritual can seem as natural as having a meal. There is certainly no shortage of examples of such encounters in the Bible, and yet Christians often react with embarrassed silence when asked about the supernatural foundations of their own faith, preferring to limit "truth" to matters that can be dealt with through cognitive and rational means.

Put simply, the best way to help children deal with the pluralistic beliefs and lifestyles they encounter in everyday life is for Christian families to live and believe differently, and for the gospel to be modeled as well as talked about in the home. As with other aspects of parenting,* there are no shortcuts to nurturing children to spiritual maturity.

See also COMPUTER GAMES; HOME SCHOOLING; PRAYER; READING; SCHOOLS, PUBLIC AND PRIVATE; TELEVISION; VALUES.

References and Resources
J. Drane, *What Is the New Age Still Saying to the Church?* (San Francisco: HarperSanFrancisco, 1999); J. Fowler, "Keeping Faith with God and our Children," in *Faithful Change: The Personal and Public Challenges of Postmodern Life* (Nashville: Abingdon, 1996); Z. Sardar, *Postmodernism and the Other: The New Imperialism of Western Culture* (Chicago: Pluto, 1998); C. Stonehouse, *Joining Children on the Spiritual Journey* (Grand Rapids: Baker, 1998); J. H. Westerhoff III, *Will Our Children Have Faith?* (New York: Seabury, 1976).

John Drane

ALTERNATIVE SCHOOLS. *See* HOME SCHOOLING.

—AUTOMOBILE—

Along with the clock, the automobile has had a profound effect on modern life. Most people are aware of its benefits, but increasing concern has been expressed about its social costs through road deaths, pollution and urban sprawl.

Unfortunately, little attention has been paid to its impact on individual attitudes and behavior, and upon the character and quality of family life, as well as upon the cost and shape of the houses in which we live. This is also true of its impact upon our attitude to time and place more generally and upon other significant relationships, as well as upon public transport and our contact with the poor and needy. In order to understand this we need to first step back into the era when the automobile began to exert its presence upon modern society.

Spread of the Automobile
The first gasoline-powered horseless carriage was sold in France in 1887 and in the United States in 1896. By 1910 almost half a million cars were on the road in America, and it soon became the leading automobile culture. The decisive factor in the democratization of the car was the introduction from 1908 onward of the Ford Model T. Other giant car manufacturers, such as General Motors, rapidly emerged. Within two decades over half the families in America owned cars. By the end of the thirties, public preference for the car was affecting the growth and quality of public transportation. At the end of World War II the car-propelled exodus to the suburbs received a massive impetus.

By the late seventies interstate highways were largely in place. Traffic density increased despite more roads, insurance* costs soared, and road deaths* continued to mount. In turn, the automobile played a key role in determining where suburbs, workplaces, malls, entertainment* centers and churches were located. People also based their decisions on where to reside and earn a living, as well as where to shop, play* and meet for worship on the basis of the automobile.

Advantages of the Automobile

In the early days the car was seen to have many advantages. It was cleaner than the horse, eliminating the problem of great quantities of manure and urine that were daily deposited on streets. Despite all the initial concerns about speed, automobiles were also considered safer. They were not only more reliable but more convenient than horses and horse-drawn public transportation. They opened up the benefits of the countryside to harried city dwellers. In particular, they offered greater flexibility and choice and were believed to keep the family together. Automobiles are still largely valued for the same reasons, even if there is now more realism attached to their ownership.

Significance of the Automobile

People have always valued the automobile apart from these practical advantages. The car often symbolizes status and wealth. It is, particularly for teenagers, a symbol of individual freedom and independence, and even for adults this is one of the reasons car pools are so difficult to begin. The car is a symbol of identity; for male members of the family in particular it is a sign of masculinity,* an expression of actual or fanciful self-image. It is a symbol of adulthood and citizenship, since it is in having a car rather than gaining the vote that a young person becomes a full participant in modern society. It is also a symbol of reward and punishment, for being grounded is the ultimate punishment for a teenager and having your car repossessed or driv-

er's license revoked is the ultimate deprivation for an adult.

The automobile is also an embodiment of priorities and dreams. The car ushers us into a private, climate-controlled, technological world that increases our withdrawal from the environment as well as from neighborliness and community. Children especially become conditioned to this from an early age. For teenagers and young adults it is also a place to play out fantasies about exercising power, confronting danger and overcoming fear.

Disadvantages of the Automobile

For several decades now some people have had second thoughts about the role of the car, however. The automobile seemed to be dividing the family more than uniting it, congesting cities as much as decentralizing them, generating regulations as well as increasing freedom and downgrading public transportation instead of complementing it.

Increasingly, psychologists and others have noticed the strange effect upon people of getting behind the wheel. Drivers tend to become one with their machine, an extension of it. How else do we explain the greater than usual competitiveness, rudeness and carelessness so many otherwise equable people exhibit on the road? During the last decades of the twentieth century the emergence of the Green movement has resulted in other protests about the effect of the car upon previously user-friendly space inside and outside the city. One of the key victims of the automobile is the experience of local neighborhood, which in turn diminishes the quality of family life. Since people drive to and from their homes, they do not see, greet or talk with each other much anymore.

Since they go greater distances to shop and relax, the corner store disappears, and the neighborhood park empties. Since streets become more unsafe, children lose spaces in which once they socialized and played. Since residents are somewhere else during the day, crime increases as houses become easy pickings for burglars. Even where people stay at home,* as traffic density on streets increases, the number and quality of relationships people have with others on the block dramatically decline.

The high social cost of the automobile has now begun to register, particularly on middle-class families. (1) The automobile is the largest cause of smog. In many places the average car puts into the air each year the equivalent of its weight in pollutants. (2) Automobiles kill and maim forty times as many people per miles traveled as do planes and buses, and eighty times as many as travel on trains. The number of people killed by the automobile worldwide per year is somewhere between 300,000 and 500,000. (3) Through the building of roads, parking lots, garages, median strips and gas stations, at least one-third of the land area in major cities is now given over to the car, thus making them less attractive places to raise families. (4) The car discriminates against the old, the infirm, the handicapped, the poor—all those who cannot afford to buy one or who are frightened to cross busy roads. Automobiles and roadside vans are increasing congestion in major national parks to urban proportions, both threatening their delicate ecological balance and making them less hospitable places.

Sanctification of the Automobile

For all these reasons we must seek to make the automobile more an instrument than an idol. Rather than our allowing it to captivate us, we need to bring our attitudes and use of it fully captive to Christ (2 Cor 10:5). Instead of conforming to its demands and possibilities, we need to be "transformed by the renew-

ing" of our attitudes toward it (Rom 12:2). We need to work out ways of expressing our family life, loving our neighbor and caring for the creation more in and through our cars.

What does this mean in practice? It involves more than going for additional family outings in the car, driving safely in a way that conserves energy or using our cars to get less mobile people to and from church. The basic starting point is to see ourselves not as the owners of our cars but as stewards of them. They are one of several ways of getting around that are granted us by God. As such, they are a gift from God for our own benefit and for the benefit of others.

From this perspective we may extract some practical guidelines: (1) Since we are able to walk, use bicycles (the most energy-efficient form of transportation) and take public transportation, both as families and individuals, using the car only when it is more appropriate to do so. Speed and convenience are not the only issues here. Other considerations are fitness, tension levels, enjoying company and opportunity to reflect or pray. (2) We should buy cars that will be more economical in use of gas and other basic materials, most appropriate for the number of people traveling and least damaging to the human and created environment. This should include considering ways that we could have less than one car per spouse or family member. (3) Given that cars absorb approximately a quarter of a person's or family's weekly or annual budget (it now costs more to travel by car overall than by taxi or airplane), we should purchase and use cars that will result in as little drain on our financial resources as possible. (4) Where feasible, we should combine journeys to different locations in the same or adjacent areas so that one longer trip takes the place of several shorter ones, and we should choose places to live, as well as to work, shop, relax and worship, that require the minimum of car use. (5) If the opportunity arises, consider replacing commuting with telecommuting by working some or most of the time at home. (6) Fast occasionally from the car, at least once a month but more if possible, breaking our dependence on it, giving the family more time together and supporting public transportation.

Putting the car in its proper place ultimately requires a combination of individual, group and also institutional responses to an incredibly complex but increasingly urgent area of modern life. Difficult though it may be, we must make the effort. In this respect we should "not be conformed to this world," as for the most part we are "but transformed through the renewing of [our] minds" (Rom 12:2 NRSV). If we were to follow through on this, then one day we might begin to see a reflection of the idyllic urban situation pictured in the book of Revelation. In the "holy" and "faithful" city, "once again old men

and women, so old that they use canes when they walk, will be sitting in the city squares. And the streets will again be full of boys and girls playing" (Zech 8:3-5 GNB).

See also MOBILITY; NEIGHBORING; VACATIONS.

References and Resources
T. Bendixson, *Instead of Cars* (London: Temple Smith, 1974); M. L. Berger, *The Devil Wagon in God's Country: The Automobile and Social Change in Rural America* (Hamden, Conn.: Archon, 1979); D. Engwicht, *Reclaiming Our Cities and Towns: Better Living with Less Traffic* (Philadelphia: New Society, 1993); J. J. Flink, *The Car Culture* (Boston: MIT Press, 1975); D. Lewis and L. Goldstein, eds., *The Automobile and American Culture* (Ann Arbor: University of Michigan Press, 1983); J. McInnes, *The New Pilgrims* (Sydney: Albatross, 1980); Organization for Economic and Cultural Development, *The Automobile and the Environment* (Boston: MIT Press, 1978); A. J. Walter, "Addicted to Mobility: The Morality of the Motor Car," *Third Way*, January 21, 1985, 21-23.

Robert Banks

—BAPTISM—

Baptism has a direct relationship to the theology and spirituality of daily life because (1) it takes an everyday experience—washing, bathing or cleaning—and elevates it to a special means of grace, thus giving us a lens through which we can see God's love for us; (2) it brings meaning by symbolizing and certifying that we are not alone but are truly members of the people of God; (3) as a special means of grace, baptism introduces us to the realm of the Spirit by which we are empowered to live extraordinary lives in ordinary situations. This article will consider the confusing testimony of the church on the matter, the examples of Jesus and John, a Christian understanding of baptism, the vexed question of its administration and, finally, the significance of baptism with the Holy Spirit.

One Baptism or Three?
There is one baptism (Eph 4:5), but you would never guess as much from the way Christians talk about it. For the Catholic,

it was his baptism as an infant that brought him into the church and made him a Christian. For the Baptist, her baptism was by immersion, administered after profession of faith. For the Pentecostal, baptism was in or by the Holy Spirit, normally accompanied by the gift of tongues: this Spirit baptism eclipses all else. All three are saying something important and stressing an important aspect of Christian baptism.

The Catholic tradition sees baptism as the way of gaining membership in the people of God. Just as you entered the old covenant people of Israel by circumcision, so you enter the new covenant people of God by baptism (Acts 2:40-41; Gal 3:27-29). This noble view, strong on God's act of incorporation, is weak on response. If we think of it as the only strand in Christian initiation, it degenerates into magic.

Churches in the Baptist tradition see baptism as a seal on the profession of faith (Acts 16:31-33). The church is the company of believers. This view is strong on response but very individualistic. It makes human commitment almost more significant than divine initiative. Moreover, it is very cerebral: it makes little room for those too young or too handicapped to make a decisive response.

Churches in the Pentecostal tradition see baptism very differently. The church is not so much a historical entity (which may well be apostate), not a company of believers (which may mean little more than intellectual assent). Reception of the life-giving Spirit of God is the authentic mark of the church. Baptism with the Holy Spirit is the only baptism worth having (Rom 8:9). Important though this emphasis undoubtedly is, it too is deficient. Cut off from historical continuity it can be, and often is, very divisive. Cut off from any serious emphasis on the content of the faith, it can easily go off the rails in doctrine or morals. There is such a thing as church history and Christian doctrine. The Spirit of God, the Word of God and the people of God need to walk hand in hand.

These different strands belong together. We find them all in Acts, where baptism is sometimes seen as the agency of salvation (Acts 2:38), sometimes as the seal of faith (16:31-33) and sometimes as the sovereign anointing of the Holy Spirit (10:44-48). The Catholics are right to see baptism as the objective mark of God's great rescue achieved on Calvary, to which we can make no contribution or addition. The Baptists are right to see in baptism a personal response, in repentance and faith, to the grace of God. The Pentecostals are right to see baptism as the way we are ushered into the world of the Spirit. Baptism is as deep and broad as the salvation of which it is the sacrament.

What Can We Learn from John's Baptism?

John's baptizing caused an immense stir. It was a mark of repentance. No pedigree, no good deeds, could bring a person into the coming kingdom: the only path lay through the baptismal waters of repentance. Moreover, John's baptism pointed ahead to the forgiveness* of sins and the gift of the Spirit that Jesus would bring. It was also a very public and humiliating act. Never before had Jews been baptized; baptism was one of the initiation ceremonies for Gentiles joining the people of God.

And finally, John's baptism was decisive. A person either went through the waters of God's judgment or else would have to face it in stark reality later on. In all these ways John's baptism, a landmark in Judaism, was an advertisement of the main feature: Christian baptism.

What Can We Learn from the Baptism of Jesus?

In his baptism Jesus identified with sinners, something that even John the Baptist found scandalous (Mt 3:14). It was an anticipation of Calvary, when his cross was to be his baptism—in blood (Lk 12:50). We cannot enter with Jesus into the unspeakable agonies of bearing the world's sin, but we can and should share in other aspects of his baptism.

The baptism of Jesus was an assurance of sonship (Mt 3:17). So it is with the Christian, adopted into the family* of God (Rom 8:15-16). The voice from heaven at Jesus' baptism, "You are my Son; in you I am well pleased," was a combination of two significant Old Testament texts (Ps 2:7; Is 42:1). Jesus, the Son of God, is also the Servant of God. Those servant songs in Isaiah, culminating in Isaiah 53, sketch the path of ministry and suffering. For the Christian, ministry and suffering are also inescapable: baptism points inexorably to that calling.

Christian baptism embraces us in the threefold baptism of Jesus—the baptism of repentance in the Jordan, the baptism of rescue on the cross and the baptism of power in the Holy Spirit. In our own baptism we see these same three realities. It calls us to repentance. It shows us where pardon is to be had. And it offers us the power of the Holy Spirit.

How Are We to Understand Christian Baptism?

In the light of these precedents of John and Jesus, how are we to understand Christian baptism? It is no optional extra: Jesus solemnly enjoined it upon us at the climax of his life on earth (Mt 28:18-20).

1. Christian baptism embodies God's challenge to repentance and faith. It cannot be conducted without some expression of both. Baptism says to us, *You are unclean. You need washing. I can do that for you. But you must change your ways.* It takes us to the heart of the gospel.

2. Christian baptism offers us the blessings of the new covenant. God approaches us in utterly unmerited grace. We respond in repentance and faith. And baptism signs over to us the blessings of the new covenant: forgiveness, adoption,* servanthood, the Holy Spirit, the new birth, justification and the promise of life after death.*

3. Christian baptism plunges us into the death and resurrection of Jesus. Baptism is the gateway to a complete revolution in morals and lifestyle, even though we shall never achieve perfection in this life. It embodies our aim to live out the life of Christ in our own daily circumstances.

4. Christian baptism initiates us into the worldwide church. It is the adoption certificate into the family of God. It is the mark of belonging, the badge of membership.

5. Christian baptism appoints us to work for the kingdom of God. Through our baptism, then, we are commissioned to engage in active ministry for Christ wherever we find ourselves—in our homes,* neighborhoods and workplaces.

6. Christian baptism does something! This New Testament emphasis is often overlooked by Protestants, many of whom prefer to think it symbolizes something. But the New Testament uses some strongly instrumental language about baptism. It is through baptism that we enter the "name" of the Trinity (Mt 28:19) and thus are saved (1 Pet 3:21), regenerated (Jn 3:5), united with Christ in his death and resurrection (Rom 6:3-8; Col 2:12), and incorporated into his body (1 Cor 12:13). To be sure, several of these references mention the Holy Spirit (the divine agency) or faith (the human agency), but there is an undeniably instrumental flavor about the language used by the biblical writers. This should not surprise us. Justification, regeneration, incorporation into Christ, baptism—these

are all different images of the way God makes us his own.

Baptism, then, is an efficacious sign of the new life. It is a palpable mark of belonging, like the wedding ring or the adoption certificate. Luther grasped this clearly. When he was tempted to doubt his own faith, he recalled the standing emblem of God's faithfulness marked upon him as an infant. He cried out in confidence, *Baptizatus sum,* "I have been baptized," realizing that God's faithfulness was even more important than his faith.

How Was Baptism Administered?

Whether the early Christians sprinkled or immersed candidates for baptism is not a matter of supreme importance. They insisted on baptizing in water in the name of the Trinity, but the amount of water is nowhere specified. It is not a matter that should divide Christians. Sometimes a river was at hand, and they would doubtless immerse. Sometimes it would take place in a home, like that of the Philippian jailer, where immersion was not possible. One of the early murals in the Catacombs shows John the Baptist and Jesus standing waist deep in the Jordan with John *pouring* water over the head of Jesus: both methods are depicted!

But does not the word *baptizo* mean "immerse"? Not necessarily: it can mean "wash" (Lk 11:38). The early Christians seem to have been very relaxed about the mode of baptism. The very early *Didache* says, "Baptize in the name of the Father and of the Son and of the Holy Spirit, in running water. But if thou hast not running water, baptize in other water. And if thou canst not in cold, then in warm. But if thou hast neither, pour water three times upon the head in the name of the Father and of the Son and of the Holy Spirit" (*Didache* 7:1).

Who Received Baptism?

Adult believers certainly received baptism, and they are primary in any theological reflection about baptism. But probably children, wives and slaves in the household were also baptized when the head of the household professed faith (Acts 16:31, 33). Children were sacramentally admitted to the Old Testament church (Gen 17); whole families of proselytes, including children and slaves, were baptized into the Jewish faith. The attitude of acceptance that Jesus displayed to tiny children would have helped (Mk 10:13-16). Infant baptism does emphasize the objectivity of the gospel: what Christ did for us at Calvary is marked upon us, whether we choose to respond to it or not. And it emphasizes the initiative of God, reaching out to us before we ever think of reaching out to him. But it is a practice open to gross abuse if it does not take place in the context of faith. It should not be administered indiscriminately but only with careful teaching of the obligations it calls for and the blessings it offers. And it requires personal reaffirmation on behalf of the candidate when he or she is confirmed.

Believer's baptism stresses that baptism is the Christian badge of belonging, not a social ceremony for the very young. It gives a clear, datable time of commitment. It produces far less in the way of fallout than infant baptism does, and it is a powerful evangelistic occasion.

Can You Repeat Baptism?

There is an ambiguous longing for rebaptism today. People very often feel that their baptism as an infant was deficient. There was too little faith around, too little water, too little feeling, too little chance for public confession of faith. But baptism cannot be done again, any more than birth can. It is ever to be remembered but never to be repeated.

What Is Baptism with the Holy Spirit?
There are seven references to baptism with the Holy Spirit in the New Testament: Matthew 3:11; Mark 1:8; Luke 3:16; John 1:33; Acts 1:5; 11:15-16; 1 Corinthians 12:13. The first six of these draw the distinction between John the Baptist's baptism, which was looking forward to Jesus, and the baptism Jesus would himself give "in" (or "with" or "by") the Holy Spirit. These six point forward, then, to Christian initiation. It is the same with the seventh, where Paul reminds the Corinthian charismatics and noncharismatics alike that they had all been baptized by one Spirit into the one body. So none of the New Testament references points to a second and more profound experience. That is not for a moment to deny that such subsequent experiences may and do occur. Sometimes they are the most momentous spiritual experiences in our lives. But it simply causes confusion to call them baptism. As we have seen, the Pentecostals are right about the importance of having the Spirit to come and flood your life; they are wrong to call that experience "baptism in the Holy Spirit" in contrast to "baptism in water." The Bible never speaks of it that way.

Although there are not many references to baptism in the New Testament, it was clearly critically important to early Christians as the sacrament of initiation. It sealed for them their unrepeatable incorporation into Christ. It pointed them to the dying and rising life that Christians are called to live. It joined them to brothers and sisters throughout the world. And it released in them the power of the Holy Spirit so long as they claimed in faith the gift God so generously offered them.

See also ADOPTION; CONFIRMATION; FAMILY.

References and Resources
P. R. Beasley-Murray, *Baptism in the New Testament* (Grand Rapids: Eerdmans, 1962); D. Bridge and D. Phypers, *Waters That Divide: The Baptism Debate* (Downers Grove, Ill.: InterVarsity Press, 1977); G. W. Bromiley, *Children of Promise* (Grand Rapids: Eerdmans, 1979); M. Green and R. P. Stevens, *New Testament Spirituality* (Guildford, U.K.: Eagle, 1994); P. K. Jewett, *Infant Baptism and the Covenant of Grace* (Grand Rapids: Eerdmans, 1979); L. H. Stookey, *Baptism: Christ's Act in the Church* (Nashville: Abingdon, 1982); W. Ward, "Baptism in Theological Perspective," *Review and Expositor* 65, no. 1 (1968).

Michael Green

BIRTH CONTROL. *See* CONCEPTION; CONTRACEPTION.

—BIRTHDAYS—

The Bible proclaims that everything God has made is good, which includes you! God's view of you is true and unchanging. You are a unique, unrepeatable creation; you are understood fully and beloved. This good news is important to remember on your birthday and every day.

A birthday celebration provides a special time to appreciate the unique gifts each family member or friend brings into our lives. Before making specific plans, think about your purpose. As you remember age, hobbies and talents, consider what would best suit the individual you are wishing to honor.

In many families the birthday person selects the menu for the celebration meal. Traditionally, a favorite kind of cake with an appropriate number of candles is the highlight of the party. When the cake appears, it signals the start of the "Birthday Song." The second verse is not as familiar but is an excellent addition to family traditions: "We love you, we do; We love you, we do; We love you, dear _____; We love you, we do." This simple verse provides an opportunity for family members to verbalize the words "I love you." Cards, gifts* and various expressions of caring attention help to make it a special day.

Looking Back

At a family dinner retell the story of your child's birth. Everyone who remembers joins in the telling, filling in special details. Let an older birthday person share important decisions that became turning points, changing his or her life. What are the special memories from the year or years? Others may want to speak of activities and events from the past that caused the friendship to grow.

Experiencing something together builds relationships. This is a time to share positive developments that have been observed in your loved one. Simple words of affirmation will mean so much.

Bring out the baby books, slides, movies, home videos* and scrapbooks that help to retell the birthday person's life story. Be sure to take a birthday picture!

Looking Ahead

"In everything you do, put God first, and he will direct you and crown your efforts with success" (Prov 3:6 LB). Encourage the guest of honor to share goals, hopes and dreams for the coming year. Thankful for benefits received, joyfully dedicate all of the days ahead to the service and worship of God.

In conclusion, offer a prayer asking God's blessing on your loved one. Invite everyone present to place a hand on the honoree. To bless* someone is to address God in prayer,* calling for mercy, assistance, happiness and protection. This simple ritual is a powerful way to affirm a life and for family and friends to declare their faith in God.

See also BLESSING; FAMILY HISTORY; GIFT-GIVING; PRAYER.

References and Resources

G. Gaither and S. Dobson, *Let's Make a Memory* (Waco, Tex.: Word, 1983); S. W. Shenk, *Why Not Celebrate!* (Intercourse, Penn.: Good Books, 1987).

Martha Zimmerman

—BLESSING—

Blessing is one of the most powerful ways human beings can express love,* especially in a family context. To give a blessing is to use speaking in a powerful way to express positive goodwill toward, bestow favor upon and offer some benefit to another person. Blessing can be given without words through a gift* or action, but such material blessings have greatest meaning when accompanied by words. Blessing is more than affirmation. In this article the older meanings of bless as "consecrate" or "sanctify by a religious rite" will not be explored, though, as we shall see, blessing is a holy relational ministry that takes us to the very heart of God.

Blessing in any context, but especially in the family, is good for three reasons.

First, it is one of the fundamental ways God relates to the world. God relates through dramatic intervention (deliverance) and through regular positive participation in it. Second, blessing is an expression of one's person at a very deep level so that through words or actions an individual communicates presence, peace and goodwill to another. The words are fraught with unavoidable consequences. When an Israelite pronounced a blessing, he or she did not merely offer good wishes for the future. Rather, the soul was offered and something happened (Pedersen, 1:200; compare Gen 48:15). Third, to bless and be blessed is a fundamental need of every human being, created as we are for love and to love.

Family Blessings in the Bible and Beyond

In biblical times, and in all older cultures, blessing the children was something expected; it was often attended with certain rites and ceremonies (Banks, 72-74). Israelite fathers were expected to give their blessing to their children before their own death* (Gen 27:4). This was not a fully egalitarian act. These blessings often involved appointing the future leadership of the family or tribe (the first-born male usually took over) and passing on the inheritance (again the first-born male would get twice as much as the others). Occasionally the birthright could be sold, as was the case when Esau exchanged his family leadership for a bowl of stew (Gen 25:29-34).

Parental blessing was like an unwritten last will* and testament. Job was conspicuously different from other ancients in this matter, for he gave his daughters an inheritance along with his sons (Job 42:15). Blessing the children in ancient times was, however, not merely a legal and financial act. It was a ministry that involved speaking a prayer for health, abundance, protection and peace (Gen 27:28-29). Sometimes the father would speak prophetically about the future of each child, as Jacob did in Genesis 49. Remarkably, the author of Hebrews selects this very last act of Jacob's blessing his children as his supreme act of faith (Heb 11:21). For parents, blessing our children is an act of faith in which we trust them to God,

pray for God's blessing upon them, discern God's unique gift to them (including talents and spiritual gifts) and release them to fulfill God's purpose in their lives. There is an important principle involved in this ancient and almost universal practice.

The Importance of Family Blessings

From the earliest age children crave the approval and favor of their parents and will do almost anything to get it. The less-favored son, Esau, pathetically tried time and again to get his parents' blessing (especially his mother's) by marrying women he thought they might approve of, only to find out the wives brought more bitterness to them (Gen 26:34-35). Paradoxically, the parents who withhold affirmation from their children because they fear making the children proud may assist in producing pride and self-centeredness as the children try to prove themselves. Bless children and they will grow up with good self-esteem* and will experience freedom from organizing their life around the need for approval. They may gain a measure of humility and will be freer to think about others.

Blessing a child's marriage* is another crucial ministry of parents. This blessing includes support, goodwill and expressed love. It means that the parents will never undermine the marriage even if at an earlier stage in the relationship they feared the choice was not a good one. As with forgiveness,* the parents will put the past in the past when they bless. The parents' blessing frees not just the children but paradoxically frees the parents to release their children to form a new family* while still remaining connected to the parents in a revised way. When this is not done, the parents may still be bound to their children even though the children want nothing to do with them. The parents may cling to their married children in a codependent way, a phenomenon that usually leads to a tragic emotional triangle of husband, wife and in-laws.

In healthy families, blessings of children and marriages are woven into everyday life. Daily expressions of appreciation, with or without the actual word *bless* and not always tied to performance at school or around the house, reinforce that people are valuable for themselves, not just for what they do. Parents who only reward excellent achievement at school are contributing to drivenness and workaholism.

When Blessing Is Hard

When parents are not able to bless their children regularly, it is often for reasons that signal the need for growth in the parents themselves. God gives children to parents to help the parents to grow up! Perhaps the parents were not affirmed, never had their parents' approval for their marriage or did not choose a career acceptable to their parents. Much deeper than these factors is the possibility that the parents do not themselves enjoy a profound acceptance with God.

Paul speaks to this in Ephesians 6:1-4. Parents are not to exasperate their children; this is exactly what they do when they make demands without blessing, requiring performance without acceptance and approval. Instead, Paul says, parents are to raise their children "in the training [nurture] and instruction [admonition] of the Lord" (Eph 6:4). This is commonly misunderstood

to mean that parents are to deliver Christian education to their children. In fact, it speaks about the context in which both parents and children grow—while they both experience the nurture and instruction of the Lord.

Have the parents experienced the unconditional love of Jesus? Are they aware of the Lord's instruction, discipline and nurture in their lives in such a way that even the parents have limits and are held accountable? Do they delight in the Lord's approval and the certainty that they have a future with promise? We give what we get. If parents did not get such blessing from their parents, they must seek it from the Lord. If children cannot get such blessing from their earthly parents, they must find it with their heavenly Parent. If parents do not receive the blessing from their children, they too must find this in their relationship with God. Fortunate are those who experience such compensatory blessings from God through parents and children in the Lord as part of their involvement in a familial small group or house church in the congregation.

Not only do children need blessings from parents, but parents need their children's blessing. Husbands and wives need blessing from each other, as do brothers and sisters and members of the extended family. The wife of noble character described in Proverbs 31 receives an invaluable gift: "Her children arise and call her blessed; / her husband also, and he praises her" (v. 28). Such blessing cannot be contrived or demanded. When it is, it is no blessing at all since it does not come from the heart. The words fall to the ground. But when a blessing is freely given, it nourishes the soul. Few children and few spouses understand the power at their disposal to nurture their closest neighbors in life.

See also FAMILY; GIFT-GIVING; LOVE; SHAME; WILL, LAST.

Resources and References

R. Paul Stevens, "Blessing," in *The Complete Book of Everyday Christianity*, ed. R. Banks and R. P. Stevens (Downers Grove, Ill.: Inter-Varsity Press, 1997) 72-74; J. Pedersen, *Israel: Its Life and Culture*, 4 vols. (London: Oxford University Press, 1963); M. H. Robins, *Promising, Intending and Moral Autonomy* (Cambridge: Cambridge University Press, 1984); L. B. Smedes, "The Power of Promising," *Christianity Today* 27 (January 21, 1983) 16-19; H. W. Wolff, *Anthropology of the Old Testament*, trans. M. Kohl (Philadelphia: Fortress, 1964).

R. Paul Stevens

BODY. *See* DEATH; FEMININITY; HEALTH; MASCULINITY.

—BREAST-FEEDING—

Usually a newborn babe is brought to the breast as soon after birth as possible. For the infant it is their first experience of eating* and drinking, and for the mother it is a privilege to provide sustenance. Breast milk is a vital, natural resource available in almost unlimited supply, provided demand feeding is encouraged. In the early months feeding patterns that respect the child's needs require parental altruism and stamina. Breast-feeding is a cost-effective and health-promoting activity that mothers can undertake during their children's early years of life. Through this intimate, everyday act bonding is facilitated, forming the essential foundation for relational and family health. Suckling at the breast can be the beginning of a trusting and nurturing relationship, providing the primal context in which we understand God's constancy and love.

Through breast-feeding mother and child together weave a new cord to replace the one that was severed at birth. Fathers and siblings contribute their own colorful threads, which become more significant as the infant gradually leaves the breast to explore the world independently at longer intervals. Parenting* is a lifelong task that seeks to balance dichotomous needs—drawing together and pulling apart, offering nourishment and protection as well as encouraging independence.

There are only two lasting bequests we can hope to give our children. One of these is roots; the other, wings (Carter, in Hodgson, 82). Breast-feeding helps secure the first, making the second procurable. With well-established self-esteem* and secure spiritual identity, we have the freedom to climb, putting our feet in high places where the wind invites our wings (Ps 18:33).

Breast-Feeding as Affection

Bonding is not an instantaneous event but a gradual process of claiming each other and establishing understanding, love* and loyalty. Bodily contact—the skin-to-skin exploration of the scent of babe and mother's milk—is vital for animals in recognizing each other and no less so for humans. Unique among mammals, the human mother and child nurse within distance of the eye's focal range. Like marsupials, human offspring are born "prematurely," that is, almost a year before they can eat or move independently. The almost continuous contact required during early months of breast-feeding can be regarded as a continuation of gestation. In the delivery room the breast helps to bridge the abrupt change of worlds. Arriving cold and wet into brightness, the babe can be soothed against the warm breast. Breast-feeding provides not only nutrition but vital communication of caring and affection through touch. Institutionalized infants who are seldom held fail to thrive despite seemingly adequate nutrition, indicating that as we hold babies we feed their souls. There are volunteers who visit neonatal hospital units specifically to hug needy babies.

Touch initiates a reflex, a little fist grasping around your finger and the instinct to draw the child to your breast. It becomes a healing language we all understand, smoothing the furrows in our hearts. Softening the ripples of anxiety, a mother's hand traces over her newborn's face, wrinkled and covered in greasy vernix—the ointment acquired in the womb. Common sense tells us that what we crave as infants, what is the source of our earliest sensations, is a need that continues throughout our lives, be it a healing touch, a handshake or the embrace.

Nutrition and Immunity

Parenting, like breast-feeding, involves not only protection but a translation of nutrients and information from the world to the child. Parents actively select enriching experiences and assist their children in defining emotions and in guiding responses. Interpreted and refined by the parent, nourishment and immunity are presented in an easily digestible or understandable form.

In keeping with the baby's needs, breast milk is differentiated and varied. The greater the variety of foods the mother consumes, the more tastes the newborn becomes accustomed to through the ever-changing milk. "Foremilk," received when the infant begins to suckle, is diluted and thirst quenching. For the reward of a hungry baby's persistent suckling there is the richer "hindmilk." In contrast to consistently composed formula, breast milk prevents excessive caloric intake; if the baby is simply thirsty, he or she can stop with the foremilk. The advantages of less readily digestible formula is that its use prolongs the interval between feedings. This may be convenient for the mother, but it ignores the infant's need for apt milk and frequent interaction. Breast milk is easily digested, leaving a soft stool without an offensive odor. Likewise, regurgitated breast milk is not unpleasant like formula vomitus. Diapering and laundry duties have a sweeter air about them when the infant is breast-fed.

Breast milk is ordered to human neurological growth. One of the most species-specific characteristics of human milk is the unique biochemical composition that assists the cerebral cortex to double in size in the first postnatal year. The breast also synthesizes neural chemicals that resemble placental hormones thought to influence sexual development and gender formation. At the same time, according to some studies, breast-feeding offers some protection to the mother's health by providing neurochemical and hormonal defenses against postpartum blues and depression* as well as decreasing risks of breast, uterine and ovarian cancers.

During pregnancy* and through breast milk, a mother confers to her child the wisdom of her years as an immunologic heritage. The memory of countless victories fought against viruses and bacteria are passed on as antibody artillery and houndlike white blood cells that have been programmed to act on a specific scent of a past offender. Breast-fed babies have documented healthier, more allergy-free childhoods. In addition, some forms of cancer and diabetes are rarer in children who have been breast-fed as infants, presumably through immune-mediated protection.

Breast-feeding need not be discontinued in situations of maternal or infant illness. Even in cases of infections of breast or gastrointestinal tract, breast milk continues to provide vital immunological resources and rehydration fluid. Care must be taken with regard to medication usage during breast-feeding. Chemicals in the mother's bloodstream, including alcohol and nicotine, are found diluted in breast milk and are absorbed from the baby's intestines. Because an infant's immature liver and kidneys have difficulty metabolizing and, eliminating chemicals and because few medications have been formally tested in pregnant women, nursing mothers or infants, few reassurances can be given with certainty. Motherrisk is a medical service that will provide information by phone or e-mail regarding medications for pregnancy and nursing women.

The baby can be weighed before and after feeding to reassure the mother of adequate milk ingestion. Documenting the progression of the baby's weight gain is important especially after the anticipated weight loss in the early weeks.

Bottles, Laughter and Time
A mother with a babe at the breast appears as a closed circle—two people existing only for each other. This dependency is celebrated at satisfying reunions after even brief separations are felt in swelling breasts, a hungry tummy or anxious wondering. Mother and child yearn for another, not unlike God's zeal for us or our thirst for him (Ps 42:1-2). This circle opens, allowing a father to burp, bathe and change the newborn and a sibling to bring a diaper or toy, sing a song or sit for a story while Mother nurses. As

weeks pass into months and breast-feeding is well established, the father and siblings can experience the satisfaction of giving a bottle on a daily basis. This creates an opportunity for a mother to occasionally exit without being anxious that the infant's needs cannot be met by another caregiver. Ideally a small amount of expressed breast milk in a bottle, given daily in the evening, will not appreciably alter milk supply, especially if it is part of the routine. Later, if the mother chooses to work outside the home, the infant will already be familiar with the bottle and will have fewer adjustments to make. The mother can still nurse in the morning and after work, maintaining her unique identity with the child despite the presence of secondary caregivers. Later, as the baby becomes interested in family foods, exploring tastes and finger-painting with textures, family members participate by holding spoons or umbrellas!

If "mommy" means primarily comfort, "daddy" means predictable fun. Laughter becomes as tangible as food passed between father to child. Sounds and words become invested with personal meaning even from birth, and little jokes are carried across the decades. "My little sparrow" became a term of endearment for a newborn who almost died from birth asphyxia; this reminded the new father that if God knows even when a sparrow falls, then his children are worth even more to him, so much that even our hairs are numbered (Mt 10:29-31). During feeding parents can observe their children, drinking in their beauty—the unique curve of their ears and the pattern of hairs on their head.

Time is also a food that passes reciprocally between parent and child, persisting long after weaning in the form of reading* aloud, running errands, walking, making crafts, building projects, cooking, learning computer* skills, playing sports and gardening. Breast-feeding may involve extra time, but it means time with the baby and less time mixing formula and sterilizing bottles. The positive interaction during breast-feeding also occurs with bottle feeding, provided the bottle is not propped up and the baby left alone. Breast-feeding is not a guarantee of good mothering, nor does bottle feeding rule it out.

The Case of Adoption

Adoptive* mothers with sufficient motivation and support can breast-feed. Knowing the baby's approximate due date, the receiving mother can actually induce lactation, even if she has never been pregnant or nursed a child before. If she faithfully expresses her breasts several times a day with a hand-held pump for two to six weeks before the baby's arrival, her breasts will respond by producing milk, although perhaps only in small quantities. When the baby arrives, the adoptive mother can use a nursing supplementer—a small tube taped to the breast that adds formula by gravity while the baby is nursing. The breast still receives stimulation and is encouraged to make more milk while the child receives additional nourishment. Thus it is possible for an adopting mother to experience the intimacy and naturalness of breast-feeding, which may compensate her in some way for the missed experiences of pregnancy and birth.

For the adoptive parents who carry the torch of life onward, it is a task of claiming, naming and protecting the flame. By comforting, nourishing and investing all of themselves, they complete the love that others began. Spiritual and emotional nurturing establishes a heredity that is eternal—not transient like the legacy of DNA (see Conception), which alters or is lost as a branch of a genealogy comes to an infertile end. In welcoming and attending to the needs of children, it is as if we are ministering to Christ himself (Mk 9:37).

Breast-Feeding as Pleasure

It is a curious commentary on our own society that we tolerate all degrees of explicitness in our literature and mass media with regard to sex and violence, but the natural act of breast-feeding is taboo. There is a whole generation of women who as children may never have observed their own mothers nursing and consequently have invested their breasts with exclusively sexual value. Without the necessary modeling they find themselves embarrassed with even the thought of breast-feeding and are unable to overcome their modesty.

Nursing mothers need to be sensitive to the potential embarrassment of observers. Discretion can be the better part of valor. Retiring to a private place to get the baby started it is possible to return with a lightweight blanket draped over a shoulder to conceal what might embarrass someone. Many mothers can nurse successfully with no one even surmising what is happening.

Although breast-feeding can be initially painful, especially if the nipples are infected or traumatized, over weeks and with proper latching of the baby, breast-feeding becomes a pleasurable experience. This is mediated by two hormones. Oxytocin is released during the "letdown" or milk-ejection reflex and is experienced as a "tingling," "pins and needles" or "pulling sensation" as the milk ducts contract. The "supply-demand" hormone prolactin is released in proportion to the duration of suckling. These hormones facilitate a meditative focus that for mothers who are usually whirling dervishes provides the necessary calm to hold their little one close in rapture.

Breast-Feeding as Service

Breast-feeding is an act of service as the

mother respects and responds to the baby's needs, putting aside her own agenda and enduring discomforts, interruptions, inconveniences and sleep* deprivation. What is natural may not be uncomplicated or effortless. Despite all the sentimental expectations a mother may have of the breast-feeding experience, there can be many hurdles to overcome as mother and babe settle into the early weeks. Until the nipples become tougher and desensitized, breast-feeding may be initially uncomfortable. Excess milk leaking out of both breasts during feeding or spontaneously at night may require breast pads. The initial engorgement of the breasts that occurs in the early days as the milk comes in can be uncomfortable and presents a hard, stiff surface, making it difficult for the baby to latch successfully. After expressing by hand, the pressure is relieved and the breast softens. With time the breasts settle down and produce milk only at designated feeding times without the exaggerated responses of the early weeks. Time and maturity also dampen the oscillations of parental reactions, reflecting God's constancy with us.

Many circumstances can make breast-feeding difficult to initiate. Although babies will instinctively turn toward a breast, latch and suckle, successful feeding depends on appropriate positioning. To maintain the baby's body and head in line often requires supporting the baby on a pillow and using a hand to guide the baby's head and shoulders. Breast-feeding is a learned skill, and solutions to problems that have been gleaned over generations are passed on through family, friends, lactation consultants and midwives.

Infants instinctively know when to stop, and they should be allowed to feed as long as they wish. Babies will spontaneously let go of the breast when satisfied. The first breast should be emptied before offering the second to prevent milk stasis and infections. Some babes nurse on only one breast per feed. In addition, if the babe exclusively drinks the thin, sugary "foremilk" by being switched prematurely to the other breast, colicky gas and hunger pains can be exacerbated. Routine supplementation is unnecessary, and especially in the early weeks it takes away from the infant's time on the breast, resulting in decreased milk production. Also, in the early weeks supplementation and use of pacifiers can result in "nipple confusion." Infants use quite distinctive techniques to suckle on a breast versus an artificial nipple. In the early weeks frequent feeding at the request of the baby is exhausting but essential for establishing the milk supply and preventing jaundice and dehydration.

The rigors of breast-feeding or even bottle-feeding are not to be underestimated. Responding to a newborn's needs results in sleep deprivation and exhaustion. As months pass, however, it is possible by feeding at more frequent intervals during the day and introducing solid foods, that nighttime feeding will lessen. If the baby is in a nearby but separate room, a mother will not inadvertently respond to every little noise. Making the clear distinction between day and night feedings can be accomplished by keeping lights low, voices quiet and saving play* and talk for daytime. Occasionally settling the tired babe who has been fed earlier allows it to learn to fall asleep without the breast. This learned skill can help create more restful nights for everyone. Sudden prolongations between feeds in the early months are unwise. As in weaning, gradual changes are the least traumatic for everybody.

Weaning: Taking Wing from the Breast

Weaning is a milestone in the child's development, an achievement of independence and the differentiation of self from mother. It is a transition that should be made in gradual steps to avoid not only engorged breasts but inconsolable babies, and it should not be perceived as a time of punishment or abandonment. It can be very satisfying if it progresses at the pace of the slowest member of the pair. Often children lose interest in the breast before a mother is ready to wean. Sometimes children are still very attached to the breast, relying on specific nursing times for reassurance, more so than for nutrition. Often a thumb or a soft toy becomes a more easily acquired source of comfort. It is possible to allow a toddler to breast-feed discreetly, as they are at an age when they can understand the need to wait for an appropriate time and place. Alternate forms of attention through interacting in play, reading or sharing chores* should gradually replace the time spent feeding.

Breast-feeding is not incompatible with pregnancy. The birth of an additional child does not necessarily mean abrupt weaning is indicated. Nursing two children at once is possible and egalitarian, defusing sibling rivalry. Usually the older child needs very little attention at the breast; perhaps the option to nurse is enough. Holding on to our children longer than necessary can thwart their growth, just as can prematurely pushing them out into the world before they have the necessary confidence and skills.

When considering the motivations for weaning, one needs to examine societal pressures and the need for time away as a couple. In 1 Samuel, Hannah sensitively considers the needs of her toddler when she stays back from the temple, delaying the fulfillment of her promise because he is not yet ready to wean. We can experience God in "the ever-present now" as his love* permeates daily life, flowing from breast and spoon, through laughing mouths, sparkling eyes just learning to read and in the taste of a child's tears kissed into oblivion.

Strengthened and equipped by adequate nurturing, our children are released into the world to feed each other with the fruits of their daily work, sharing monetary wealth and the gifts of health and education with the nations of the world (Is 58:10-11). As breast-feeding is a paradigm for the spiritual rooting of our identity and the nourishment we receive in God's family and by Scripture, so weaning is analogous to being launched by the strength of our own wings, lifted by love, to explore and enrich the world.

See also ADOPTION, PARENTING; PREGNANCY.

References and Resources

L. Bailey, Promises for Parents calendar (Bloomington, Minn.: Garborg's Heart and Home, 1990); B. T. Brazelton, What Every Baby Knows (Reading, Mass.: Addison-Wesley, 1987); P. Teilhard de Chardin, Hymn of the Universe (New York: Harper & Row, 1965); M. Shirley Gross, "Pain in the Breast-Feeding Mother," The Canadian Journal of CME (January 1997) 129-37. H. Hodgson, When You Love a Child (Minneapolis: Deaconess Press, 1992); La Leche League International, The Womanly Art of Breastfeeding, 5th ed. (New Market, Ont.: La Leche League International, 1991); V. H. Livingstone, "Protecting Breastfeeding: Family Physician's Role," Canadian Family Physician 38 (August 1992) 1871-76; V. H. Livingstone, "Too Much of a Good Thing: Maternal and Infant Hyperlactation Syndromes," Canadian Family Physician 42 (1996) 89-99; J. M. Vickerstaff-Joneja, "Breast Milk: A Vital Defense Against Infection," Canadian Family Physician 38 (August 1992) 1849-55; <www.motherisk.org>.

Carol Anderson

CALLING. *See* MARRIAGE.

—CHARACTER—

Character, the real essence of a person, is composed of the traits of the habituated life. Simply, character is not what we do but who we are and what we become by doing what we do. But this is never a finished business and so character development is a lifetime process. Character is more than temperament (which is a psychosomatic manifestation of the person) and more than personality (the person expressive in relationships). Temperament and personality are given to us at conception,* though they may be quenched, stunted and paralyzed through bad nurturing and bad choices. Even spiritual conversion does not necessarily change temperament and personality or remove all their perversions. Many presalvation problems—addictions, the need to control and the need to be constantly approved—may continue until they are dealt with in the process of sanctification. While temperament and personality are given, character is grown. Thus our personal biographies, and those of our children, have two tables: the first is God's providential ordering of our lives; the second is personal development through self-knowledge (Houston, 4). It is this second that is the subject of this article.

Character is forged through life, especially in the formative years, when a child is under the direct and primary influence of parents and is learning who she or he is. Our first community is the family,* but soon it includes school,* friends, the church and wider society. Ultimately we live out our lives, if we are open to this, within the love community of the triune God—our deepest family, our final home* and our perfect parent. God is at work in life, especially the hard places, as Paul says in Romans: "We also rejoice in our sufferings, because we know that suffering produces perseverance; perseverance, character; and character, hope" (5:3-4). The hardest experiences in life turn out to be the best, though it does not feel that way in the middle of them.

Character Formation and Transformation

As we explore habits, conscience formation and virtues, we will see that while character is formed in part by parenting,* socializing and schooling, the development of a Christian character involves active cooperation by means of a personal relationship with God through Jesus by which the person becomes not only "formed" but "transformed" (2 Cor 3:18). So if the highest parenting goal* is to develop a Christian character in children, this must include that your children may come to accept Christ as their savior in their own way and time.

It is undeniable that parents are teaching and children are learning from birth onward. Parents are the child's first educators, and children learn through imitation to be like their parents, including assessing and evaluating their parents' values.* Parenting involves more than discipline;* it includes discipleship. Jesus said that the disciple [or child], when he or she is fully trained, "will be *like* his teacher" (Lk 6:40, emphasis mine). This is a matter of critical importance when parents consider schooling since the school can at best cooperate with families in forming character (*see* Schools—Public and Private, Home Schooling).

As mentioned above, character is not "natural" and preprogrammed but is formed. It includes emotional, moral, relational and spiritual development. Notably in the wider community—business, professional life and politics—it is increasingly recognized that what makes a leader trustworthy and credible is not merely performance but character—the essence of the person. Qualities touted as desirable in leaders—authenticity, openness, purpose, congruence and compassion (Cashman, 43)—are remarkably close to the sevenfold fruit of the Spirit in Galatians 5: love, joy, peace, patience, kindness, goodness, faithfulness, gentleness and self-control (5:22-23). What greater goal can there be for character development than the formation and transformation of the person into a fraction of Christ's image and a person whose good works and ethical life arise from internal goodness that is a manifestation of Christian life.

Sowing Habits

Character is habituated life, and habits are formed chiefly in family life. These habits cover such fundamental daily routines as eating* and sleeping,* relational patterns such as how we treat other people (including listening,* affirming, blessing* and forgiving*), and thought patterns including how we think about our personal dignity, our sexuality,* masculinity,* femininity* and self-esteem.* Habits form around the structures of common life such as meals, spending money, vacations, play,* work and prayer.* A habit is primarily an action, an acquired pattern of behavior, which is done often and therefore easily. Some "bad" habits are hard to break because they are so well rehearsed that they appear to be automatic. Thought patterns and "self-talk" can also take on the nature of a habit due to the amount of repetition of the same thought that an individual entertains.

A way of life. Though the Bible seldom makes use of the word *habit,* it does have a great deal to say about a person's "way of life," what he or she "believes and practices." Certainly the Scriptures encourage acquired patterns of behavior that are godly and "so well rehearsed" and "done so often" as to come easily. For example, Job regularly practiced being a priest-father so that his children would walk regularly in forgiveness (Job 1:5). Near the end of his life Paul could say to young Timothy about his "habits": "You, however, know all about my teaching, my way of life, my purpose, faith, patience, love, endurance, persecution, sufferings" (2 Tim 3:10).

One can also develop negative and ungodly habits. Jeremiah speaks the Lord's mind about Jehoiakim by saying that his "way of life" from his youth was not to listen or to obey God (Jer 22:21). The author of the letter to the Hebrews confronts his audience about their getting out of the habit of meeting together and encouraging one another to love and good works; as a result, they developed a habit of not persevering in the faith (Heb 10:24-25).

Becoming what you do. By developing habits one "becomes what one does." This is readily apparent in the proverbs of Solomon. The stated purpose of this collection of wise sayings is for "acquiring a disciplined and prudent life" (1:3). A cursory reading of Proverbs 11—14 shows the acquired speech habits of the wise and the foolish. The wise have learned how to guard their tongue, keep secrets, use kind and true words (11:13; 12:17, 22, 23, 25; 13:3) while the foolish have practiced gossip, reckless and rash words, and mockery (11:9, 13; 12:17, 18, 22; 13:1, 3; 14:6). The New Testament encourages the believer to become who he or she is in Christ by the "habitual" practice of putting off the flesh and putting on Christ (compare Col 3 and Eph 4—5), of walking in the Spirit (Rom 8; Gal 5), setting the mind on the things of the Spirit (Rom 8). What a person repeatedly practices tends to become more and more an automatic part of his or her behavior.

Unlearning habits. Difficulties in developing godly habits stem primarily from three arenas: learned and acted out behaviors, whether poor, neutral, or sinful, which are left unexamined; negative patterns of thinking or belief that are not challenged and unlearned; and unrealistically high expectations that lead to continued self-defeating minimal goal achievement. Classic behavioral psychology suggests that when pleasure accompanies behavior, the behavior is likely to repeat. Bad habits usually have some form of pleasurable payoff that reinforces the continued behavior. Changing the cues that precede the undesirable behavior helps break the "automatic" behavior. The Christian who is serious about breaking ungodly habits will seek both prayer and counseling wisdom in order to assure there are not "hidden reinforcers" to the undesirable behavior. Wise parents will see this at work in their home and deal with it. As we go about establishing godly habits, we can remember the promises of Solomon's wisdom for those who find a way of life, who acquire a pattern of behavior consistent with the fear of God: prolonged life, favor and a good name in the sight of God and others (Prov 3:2-3).

Cultivating a Clear Conscience

When children exasperate their parents with forbidden behavior followed by remorse, the parents sometimes comfort themselves with the fact that "at least they have a conscience." Forensic psychiatrists sometimes deal with criminals who appear to have no conscience at all. What is our conscience? How does it work? Why does it sometimes deceive us? How is it possible to have a clear conscience?

Conscience in contemporary thought. Various theories are offered to describe the almost universal experience of having an internal monitor of thought and behavior. Social-learning psychologists link conscience development to the parenting process. Behaviorist psychologists view conscience as conditioned by rewards and punishments so that patterns of self-criticism develop and persist even when the punishers are no longer present.

In contrast to these theoretical frameworks, theologians propose that conscience is not socially developed but "inbuilt" as a God-designed capacity to put human beings in touch with the moral code of the universe. Ambiguity on the meaning of conscience is further heightened by the almost complete absence of "conscience" words in the Old Testament and the infrequent use of "conscience" in the New.

Conscience in the Bible. Conscience only became a popular concept in the first-century B.C. in the Greek world to describe "the judge or witness within" or "knowing oneself," both phrases translating Greek words for "conscience." It was part of the Greek segmentation of the human person into sections with the outer shell, the body, being the least valuable. But the Hebrew view of the human person was different. Persons are integrated wholes. In the Old Testament there are only six instances of "conscience" in the English New International Version, and in each case the word translates the general word for "soul" or "heart."

For example, the word *conscience* is not used in the text of Genesis 3:7 (when

Adam and Eve sinned) because their whole persons were alienated from God and filled with shame.* When Job declares, "My conscience [lit. "heart"] will not reproach me as long as I live" (27:6), he is claiming to be a person free from condemnation in relation to God; none of his sins can explain his suffering. It is not until the first Christians were called upon to address the Greek world that biblical authors began to use a specific word for conscience. So in Acts and the letters we find references to "good conscience" (Acts 23:1), "weak conscience" (1 Cor 8:7), "clear conscience" (1 Tim 3:9), "seared" conscience (1 Tim 4:2), "corrupted" conscience (Tit 1:15), and "cleansed conscience" (Heb 10:22).

Significantly Paul tells the Romans that his "conscience confirms . . . in the Holy Spirit" that he is speaking the truth (9:1). This is especially insightful because the New Testament authors used "conscience" to describe the whole person *in relation to God,* not an independent witness built into human nature with or without God. The author of the letter to the Hebrews elaborates on this profoundly. Human beings have a guilty and polluted conscience that cannot be cleansed by sacrificial offerings in the temple and even the ritual of the Day of Atonement offered only temporary relief (Heb 9:9). But the "once for all" sacrifice of Jesus results in a permanent cleansing that empowers us to enter the presence of God and serve all the time and everyday.

Misguided conscience. Not all condemnation is the result of the Spirit witnessing to our consciences that something is wrong. Satan "accuses" brothers and sisters day and night (Rev 12:9). Sometimes we serve Satan's purposes by doing our own accusing of ourselves. Worse still, we judge one another.

Letting our conscience be our guide is usually bad advice unless we are first sure that the conscience is properly formed. God is our guide, and conscience is only one dimension of witness to God's guidance but not a witness in isolation. Conscience gives us a false reading when we experience socially induced shame (despising our very persons) and false guilt (feeling badly for things that were not actually wrong or were not our fault). Paul deals with this in 1 Corinthians 8:4, 7-8, when Christians are inhibited from enjoying something for which they can truly thank God. In some cultures such shame is more pervasive than guilt. But it comes from people and not from God. Sometimes we feel no guilt for genuine sins of commission or omission. Or we condemn ourselves when God has already justified us. As John says, God is greater than our consciences. By dwelling in love "we set our hearts at rest in his presence whenever our hearts condemn us. *For God is greater than our hearts, and he knows everything*" (1 Jn 3:19-20, emphasis added).

Conscience formation. Here is where the spiritual formation of children (and their parents) is critical. Parents can model that God is their Guide, that God's Word is their ultimate authority, and that God's approval is more important than peer or family approval. Once again Paul's statement that his conscience confirms in the Holy Spirit that he is speaking the truth (Rom 9:1) is significant. Self-consciousness is an accurate witness when we are in the Spirit, in right relationship to God. It should not be captive to culture, to peer groups, to advertising, to our judging brothers and sisters. Conscience is not a freestanding authority within but rather dependent upon and built up through every thought becoming captured for the obedience of Christ (2 Cor 10:5) through submission to Word and Spirit, daily relying on the cleansing of Christ's forgiveness, and daily feeding our souls on the revelation of God's Word. It depends as well on the proper exercise of the virtue of prudence (justice).

The family and the church are two communities in which moral formation takes place, each nurturing our souls and giving perspective when we feel falsely accused or when we have actually sinned. When we have a guilty conscience, we should turn to Scripture and seek the mind and will of God in the company of others. But in their company we can also rejoice that we are spiritually alive, that our consciences are not "seared" (1 Tim 4:2) like scar tissue without any feeling and that we are wonderfully and gloriously forgiven.

Nurturing Virtues

Few would deny that moral education is a pressing need today. If cultivating a clear conscience is the negative part of moral education, developing virtues is the positive. Unfortunately, the concept of virtue has over the years deteriorated and, like a host of other terms ("tradition," "heritage" or even "right" and "wrong") has lost its vibrancy (Benson, 1069-72). Nonetheless, what virtue is, how we can become virtuous and why, are crucial considerations for family life, for they are the substance of being and doing good, and doing so habitually.

Virtues in the Bible. There is no equivalent Hebrew word for the Greek *arete,* even though the so-called cardinal virtues are often mentioned as part of the fully lived Christian life. Not surprisingly, in the Old Testament the righteous do justice and live by wisdom. In the New Testament the term *arete* is used only once in the writings of Paul (Phil 4:8) and four times in Peter's letters (1 Pet 2:9; 2 Pet 1:3, 5) though usually not translated in English as "virtue." Nevertheless, it is indisputable that early Christians were aware of the good

qualities found outside the family of God, and they interpreted the Christian life partly in the categories of Greek thought. The list of commendable virtues Paul gives in Philippians—true, noble, right, pure, lovely, admirable, excellent, praiseworthy (4:8)—seems reminiscent of virtues commended by the Greek philosophers. This is no more surprising than the fact that Paul frequently uses the Greek concept of "conscience," as mentioned above, to communicate our moral responsibility and accountability in the Greek world when no such word was given him from his Jewish and biblical heritage.

Nonetheless three observations can be made of the biblical treatment of this subject. First, there is nothing in the Bible comparable to the cataloging of virtues, especially the four "cardinal" virtues (justice, wisdom, courage and moderation). In fact, other virtues are offered as the "hinges" of the spiritual life. Second, all the "lists" in the Bible are ad hoc—representative and exemplary but not definitive. And third, the discussion of theoretical versus practical virtues—fundamental to Greek philosophy—finds no place in the New Testament, where doing and being are fully united in the righteous life. The reasons for these differences are profoundly theological and stem from the distinctiveness of the Christian way.

The three theological virtues: Faith, hope and love. In the New Testament the fundamental character-virtues are faith, hope and love,* often mentioned singly and sometimes as a triad (1 Cor 13:13; 1 Thess 1:2-3; Col 1:5). These are sometimes called the "theological virtues" because they are gifts of God and have God as their primary object. They are also the spiritual foundation of all the other virtues.

Education in the virtues. True education, as Augustine noted, is to learn what to desire. The gospel declares that God gives what he requires, that the grace of the new creation accomplishes what never can be obtained by reason or moral effort alone. Virtues are gifts of God that invite and even require human cooperation. That is surely what is behind Paul's exhortation to "think about such things" (Phil 4:8) in the context of a list of commendable character qualities, "get rid of" (vices like slandering, Eph 4:31), "make every effort to add to your faith goodness" (2 Pet 1:5) and "live a life of love" (Eph 5:2).

Christian living is essentially responsive and always God-centered. We owe every moment of our being to God's continuing grace and the justifying power of the Holy Spirit, a matter Thomas Aquinas emphasized in his treatment of the virtues (Cessario, 4; Pinckaers, 174, 180). Faith, hope and love keep us focused on the source—the God of all true virtue. Peter says that God's divine power "has given us everything we need for life and godliness through our knowledge of him who called us by his own glory and goodness (erete)" (2 Pet 1:3). Paul reminds the Colossians that it is as "God's beloved" they are to clothe themselves with goodness and patience (Col 3:12). The virtues may be seen as the working out of love for no one can be truly loving without being, at the same time, virtuous.

So parents cooperate with God in the moral and spiritual education of their children in the virtuous life through modeling, disciplining, discipling, teaching, interpreting life situations and nurturing faith, hope and love. Every child needs affirmation and love, limits and correction, a future with promise, and every child needs to respond to the seeking God. This is rearing children "in the training and instruction of the Lord" (Eph 6:4). Developing Christian character involves formation and transforma-

tion: sowing good habits, cultivating moral and spiritual education, and nurturing virtuous living in a lifelong process toward maturity. In the early years, parents are the primary educators and ministers.

But children are also teaching parents continuously, and parents, along with their children, are being "raised to maturity" in the crucible of family life as the parents experience with their children "the training and instruction of the Lord." Parents are confronted with their own addictions, their own compensatory emotions, their own habits of the heart through their interaction with their children and in the marriage* relationship itself. So character formation is not merely a parenting task but a family experience. Put simply, children are God's gift to help parents grow up. In the end the most probing question to be asked of family life is not how the children turned out but what kind of people the parents became!

See also DISCIPLINE; GOALS; HOME SCHOOLING; PARENTING; SCHOOLS, PUBLIC AND PRIVATE.

References and Resources:

I. Benson, "Virtues," in *The Complete Book of Everyday Christianity*, ed. R. Banks and R. P. Stevens (Downers Grove, Ill.: InterVarsity Press, 1997), 1069-75; R. Cessario O.P., *The Moral Virtues and Theological Ethics* (Notre Dame, Ind.: University of Notre Dame Press, 1991); S. R. Covey, *The Seven Habits of Highly Effective People* (New York: Fireside, Simon & Schuster, 1989); R. Guardini, *The Virtues: On Forms of the Moral Life* (Chicago: Henry Regnery, 1967); S. Hauerwas, *Vision and Virtue: Essays in Christian Ethical Reflection* (Notre Dame, Ind.: University of Notre Dame Press, 1974); S. Hauerwas, *Character and the Christian Life: A Study in Theological Ethics* (San Antonio: Trinity University Press, 1975); J. M. Houston, "The Nature of Christian Character and the Dilemma of Contemporary Ministry," (unpublished lecture notes, Regent College, Vancouver, 1989) 1-4; P. Kreeft, *Back* to *Virtue* (San Francisco: Ignatius Press, 1992); C. S. Lewis, *Mere Christianity* (London: Bles, 1956); A. MacIntyre, *After Virtue* (Notre Dame, Ind.: University of Notre Dame Press, 1984); G. C. Meilander, *The Theory and Practice of Virtue* (Notre Dame, Ind.: University of Notre Dame Press, 1984); C. A. Pierce. *Conscience in the New Testament* (London: SCM Press, 1955); S. Pinckaers O.P., *The Sources of Christian Ethics* (Washington, D.C.: Catholic University of America Press, 1995).

Iain Benson, Mike Nichols
and R. Paul Stevens

—CHORES—

Family life is full of chores. Chores include any type of responsibility, generally of a manual and repetitive nature that are basic to our everyday functioning. Because they involve work* and often seem trivial in character, most people dislike chores. When life is busy with more enjoyable or more weighty activities, chores easily become a point of contention. This may happen between husband and wife, especially where both partners work outside the home. Chores are frequently the basis of arguments or nagging between parents and children or teenagers. Few Christians look to Scripture for help in understanding or doing chores. Yet the first reference occurs in God's injunction to "take care of" the Garden of Eden (Gen 2:15). Throughout the Bible there are many other references, some of which we shall consider shortly.

Chores as Burden and Instruction

Members of a family often feel that chores are a burden we could do without, an intrusion into other more important responsibilities. Some people do seem to take them in stride and a few become obsessive about them, which is the opposite of not taking them seriously enough. What most families lack, and most churches do not teach, is insight into how chores fit into the divine scheme of things. Can they too be a service or ministry as much as anything else, or are they just a monotonous aspect of life that has to be tolerated so that we can get on with more important things? What should be our attitude toward chores, and how should we undertake them? Should they be mainly assigned to certain people while those who have more important functions to perform are exempted?

According to common wisdom, children should also do chores so that they can learn responsibility and contribute to the full life of the family. In the workplace, chores are mainly undertaken by juniors so that senior employees or employers themselves are set free for more significant tasks. Though men tend to help more with chores a little more than they once did in the home, surveys show that women continue to do far more of the work around the house.

Generally, Christians with important responsibilities view chores as mundane and as peripheral. That is, chores should be gotten out of the way as quickly as possible or left in the hands of someone else, lest they distract from the real work of ministry. In this case, chores are done when there is nothing more significant on the agenda or when it is imperative they be completed. They should be left as long as possible and done as quickly as possible. In other words, chores are an unfortunate necessity.

However, in the Bible we find reference to people doing chores as a normal part of living out their obedience to God, their discipleship to Christ and their new life in the Spirit. Just see how often there are references in a concordance to words for making meals (*see* Meal Preparation), sewing and mending, washing and cleaning. In addition to these, we only have to think how often chores come up for mention in household settings in Jesus' parables. There such everyday chores as cleaning house, organizing parties and preparing food can instantly become reflections of the way the kingdom operates.

So rather than being a preliminary to the work of ministry, chores can be an expression of it. This does not only happen through their teaching us lessons about the kingdom. It also takes place through our joining with God in caring for that part of his universe where our homes stand, also through the way our chores help us be hospitable to fellow family members and strangers. Through doing chores we learn that attention to the small details of life prepares us to perform the larger challenges God places before us.

From Conflict Over to a Spirituality of Chores
When conflict (*see* Conflict Resolution) arises over chores, families should develop effective ways of dealing with it. This can be done through

☐ clearly articulating who does what and when in a way that demonstrates the contribution of every member of the family in this area

☐ regular check-ins to ensure that everything is on track and joint discussion of what to do if not

☐ recognition that according to their personalities and other responsibilities,

family members will go about their chores in different ways

☐ occasionally, perhaps once a month, all members of the family doing chores together, turning the exercise into a social as well as work occasion

☐ setting up an appropriate system of punishments and, from time to time, gratuitous rewards, for faithfulness in doing chores

In addition, conflict can partly be avoided if from the beginning of a marriage* or from the earliest days of childhood it is assumed that everyone will take part in doing chores, in a way that is appropriate to their other responsibilities and their stage in life. While some parents offer payment to children if they will do their chores, this tends to set up a monetary and contractual view of life that is very different from the loving and covenantal one that comes before us in the Bible (*see* Allowances). We also need to help our children to see chores through God's eyes from their earliest days. We do this best of all by actually doing our chores in a timely and thorough way, out of a cheerful not grudging heart.

See also ALLOWANCES; HOMEMAKING; MEAL PREPARATION; VALUES.

References and Resources
D. Adam, *The Edge of Glory: Modern Prayers in the Celtic Tradition* (London: Triangle/ SPCK, 1985); E. Dreyer, *Earth Crammed with Heaven: A Spirituality of Everyday Life* (New York: Paulist, 1994); C. Forbes, *Catching Sight of God: The Wonder of Everyday* (Portland, Ore.: Multnomah Press, 1987); Brother Lawrence, *The Practice of the Presence of God* (Albion Park, Penn.: Hadidian, 1989); K. A. Rabuzzi, *The Sacred and the Feminine: Toward a Theology of Housework* (New York: Seabury, 1982).

Robert Banks

CHRISTMAS. *See* GIFT-GIVING; HOLIDAYS—CHRISTMAS.

CHURCH. *See* FAMILY.

—CLOTHING—

Of all of God's creation, people are the only ones who need to wear clothing. The history of clothing began in the book of Genesis when God's first man and woman became aware of their sin. Since the day Adam and Eve covered themselves with fig leaves, clothing has been both a blessing and a curse (Gen 3:7).

Clothing Is a Gift

Calvin Seerveld states that "clothing is a gift of God to humankind," given to us after our expulsion from the Garden of Eden. Even though we disobeyed God, he took pity on us and provided clothes to protect our skin and keep us warm. In the New Testament we are assured that God will provide us with the necessities of life, including clothing (Mt 6:28-30) and not just any old hand-me-downs but perhaps even designer labels, as Matthew claims even the lilies of the field surpass "Solomon in all his splendor."

Judging from the Outward Appearance

Although we know intellectually about God's promise to care for us, many of us still fret about what to wear when we get up each morning. From a very young age, children are style-conscious. They are bombarded with messages about what is cool and not cool to wear. In the way they dress, they aim for the fine line between individuality of expression and conformity to their peers, heedless of the weather conditions! Unfortunately, they also tend to judge others solely on the basis of what they are wearing. Many parents advocate school uniforms, which not only solves the problem of what to wear on schooldays but also levels the discrepancy in socioeconomic status between students and forces them to form relationships with others based on who they are, not what they wear. After instigating a school uniform policy, some schools* have reported an increase in attendance and a decrease in bullying and vandalism. It has been suggested that uniforms encourage a sense of pride and community, in much the same way that wearing a football team uniform or a Girl Scout uniform does.

Just as we may wrongly judge people from their appearance, we may also inadvertently send the wrong message to others by what we wear. In the case of adolescent girls, whose bodies are maturing sexually, parents need to be concerned that their daughters understand how dressing provocatively may put them into dangerous situations. The apostle Paul wrote to Timothy expressing his wish for the women in Ephesus to "dress modestly, with decency and propriety" and to concentrate instead on doing good deeds (1 Tim 2:9-10). The Wife of Noble Character in the book of Proverbs is praised because, above all, she is "clothed with strength and dignity." She realizes that while "beauty is fleeting . . . a woman who fears the LORD is to be praised" (Prov 31:25, 30).

Clothing as a Measure of Growth

Parents view clothing from other aspects as well. Parents are typically more conscious than their children of the protective nature of clothing, resulting in universal and repeated admonitions to use bicycle helmets, keep mittens on and wear hats. The pace at which children outgrow their clothes helps to denote the swift passage of time. A typical used-clothing store item is the almost brand-new dress that a mother had "saved" in the closet for a special occasion, only to find that when the big day arrived, the dress was too small for her quickly grow-

lives of our children are marked by articles of special clothing that gain sentimental value over time: the christening gown, baby's first shoes, first day of school outfit, first suit, confirmation dress, graduation dress or suit, or wedding clothes.

We Are Made in God's Image

"What to wear" can become a huge power struggle between parents and children, as the parent's self-image may depend on they way their children look. A mother who cultivates the Victorian ideal of girls in pink frilly dresses may despair of the blue-jean clad tomboy she has instead. The clash comes when the parent's image of the child, whether realistic or not, differs from the child's self-image. Parents need to refrain from projecting an image onto their children or from living their children's lives vicariously (see Self-Esteem). It is important to remember that as Christians our true image comes from God (Gen 1:27), who created us to have a relationship with him such as no other living creature does, one so loving that it led to his Son's paying the ultimate sacrifice for our sin (Jn 3:16).

Do Not Sweat the Small Stuff

It is important for parents to allow their children some freedom of expression in the way they dress, since when they eventually leave home,* they will have to dress themselves. While it may be tempting to try to control every aspect of the child's dress, parents and children should not get into fights about relatively unimportant matters. For example, it is reasonable for a parent to insist that their children's clothing fits properly and is clean and mended. Whether the parent likes the color of a garment or whether everything matches is less important.

Clothing as a Basis for Interesting Discussion

It is crucial, however, for children to honor their parents (Ex 20:12). By honoring parents, children show esteem for parents or give others their opinion of their own parents. Unfortunately, humans have a natural tendency to rebel against authority of any kind (Eph 2:2). Children quickly realize that they can annoy their parents by what they wear or do not wear, resulting in much friction in the home. As superficial as clothing is, it can be the basis for some interesting parent-child discussions about such topics as capitalism, advertising, peer pressure, sex* and ethics. For example, children may not realize that the high cost of designer clothes is directly attributable to the millions of dollars the designer spends on advertising, even though his clothes may not be any better quality than generic items. There may need to be a parent-child dialogue about the ethics of spending so much money on clothes while other people in the same city are going hungry (see Shopping). Children can be encouraged to be creative and resourceful in their quest to look good. Children also need to be reminded about the transience of style and the foolishness of putting a lot of money into items that will become next year's castoffs.

Some children are obsessed not with looking like supermodels but with looking as unattractive as possible. There are several reasons for such "false humility." In their quest for an identity, adolescents* love to challenge adults to "look beyond the surface and see the real me." A child from a wealthy home may feel guilty about his or her wealth and dress sloppily in an effort to hide his or her background. Children need to know, however, that any fashion statement that insults others, such as wearing ripped jeans to a wedding, or that interferes in any other way with the worship of God, needs to be reconsidered.

The Christian Paradox: Looking Good Matters

In movies and television,* Christians are often portrayed as prim and straitlaced, with no style or adornment (except a large cross pendant), wearing either paramilitary uniforms or ill-fitting, drab-colored, mismatched garments. The contrast between the joyous good news they are supposed to be spreading and their dowdy, lackluster appearance is laughably unattractive. Although this is a media caricature, it pinpoints a paradox: Christians need to have a healthy concern for what is on the surface even though God can see straight through it. This is because judging others by the way they look is a basic human characteristic. Even in biblical times dishevelment and dirtiness were considered signs of mental derangement or demonic possession! In terms of a Christian witness, therefore, we need to work with this tendency rather than to ignore it. Non-Christians are already convinced that to become a Christian means to adopt a life of restriction and mindless conformity. But when Christians present an attractive image, it is not to deceive but to demonstrate a healthy self-respect and to celebrate that each person is a unique creation of God.

Where Is Your Treasure?

Children and adults need to be cautioned that being obsessed with clothing is tantamount to worshiping clothing as a god (Ex 20:3). A Christian's daily struggle is to discern how God wants him or her to behave and to allow the inner character to shine through to the outside. Children should be encouraged to change their priorities and focus on things that do last. As Jesus exhorted his disciples, "Provide purses for yourselves that will not wear out, a treasure in heaven that will not be exhausted, where no thief comes near and no moth destroys. For where your treasure is, there your heart will be also" (Lk 12:33-34).

Put On the Full Armor of God

The fashion industry depends on planned obsolescence in order to assure itself of a steady stream of income. But fashion is fickle and unpredictable, and the happiness it brings is short-lived. We would do well to put most of our efforts and resources into dependable things, such as the love God has for us, for the Lord says, "I do not change" (Mal 3:6). Ultimately we cannot go wrong if we adopt God's own uniform as itemized by the apostle Paul: "the full armor of God," "the belt of truth," "the breastplate of righteousness," "the shield of faith," "the helmet of salvation and the sword of the Spirit" (Eph 6:13-17).

References and Resources

C. Seerveld, "Adornment," in *The Complete Book of Everyday Christianity*, ed. R. Banks and R. P. Stevens (Downers Grove, Ill: InterVarsity Press, 1997); C. Jackson, "Should Your Kids Be Forced to Wear School Uniforms?" *The Capital News*, October 10, 1999, A1-A5.

Kathryn E. Lockhart

COHABITING. *See* DATING; MARRIAGE; SEXUALITY.

—COMMUNICATION—

"We can't communicate!" is the ever-common complaint from families* that are not working well. A distraught parent says, "That kid of ours just wants to go hang around the mall all night long. He never says anything to us without a sneer." A rejected wife complains, "I have to phone my husband's secretary to remind him about my birthday. And then when we go out for dinner, he talks more on his cell phone than to me!" Bad scenarios are numerous. Tragic examples are the content of books, cartoons, sermons, and late-night heartaches and tears.

However, family theorists have a different interpretation of broken communication. They argue that not communicating is a powerful expression of information as well as an editorial comment about the relationship. Not communicating is an effective expression of rejection that has the intended result—rebuffing the other member of the family. We cannot *not* communicate. In fact, all verbal and behavioral interaction is by definition some sort of powerful and purposeful communication.

All family communication is a message that is communication plus some evaluative comment on the quality of the family relationship (metacommunication). For example, a teenage boy with acne stutters to his library study partner, who is a supermodel look-alike, "I need to study for my math test a l-l-little bit l-l-longer. I'm going to come back after dinner. What about you?" She smiles and replies, "I guess I could do some more research on history." The facts are obvious: both are serious students! The metacommunication is also clear—another opportunity for being in psychosexual proximity has been achieved without rejection. Victory on all counts!

Levels of Communication

There are various message levels of communication. At the least intimate level of conversation, speaker and listener repeat expected clichés. These may be anything from stereotypical greetings ("How ya doin'?") to preprogrammed discussion to avoid intimacy (e.g., talking about the weather). These are clichés because the communication is designed to avoid human contact rather than embrace intimacy. While superficial contact between people does occur

and may have some value (acknowledging that you are there), these transactions are so predictable as to be exhausting, frustrating and depressing within families. Why? Because the emotional message is "You are not worth my commitment to really talking." The metacomment (the comment about the comment) is greater than the comment.

The next level of interpersonal communication is what might be called *stranger communication* or *conversation*.* It is essentially the exchange of cognitive information (or reporting of facts) without much meaning or emotion. This kind of reporting interchange is typical in business meetings. Families will occasionally choose to suffer with this kind of "facts transmission" rather than face the consequences of an emotional encounter—perhaps anger or blaming. In marriages and families lacking in respectful intimacy, much of the communication deteriorates to the level of reporting facts. Couples talk about the kids' schoolwork or the price of cabbages. This information might be true and important, but it does not build what is essential to family life. Many therapists, however, recommend that families who persistently fail at communication begin at this fairly inoffensive level. The injunction to "talk like strangers to each other" is good advice to those whose communication spirals down to blaming and hurt.

The next level of communication has to do with expressing values* and central emotional convictions. It is much deeper and more powerful than conversation. I remember talking to my preadolescent daughter about her fears in starting at a new school the following day. In tears she said, "But Daddy, what if they do not like me?" Her life was caught up in that brief explosion of worry and dread. Afraid of being left out when she had not yet had the chance of being accepted, she was expressing one of her central emotional convictions—"I need to be loved." Psychologists talk about the *teachable moment* in parenting.* This is the time when the parent can communicate some essential virtue or value to the child. When a family member is expressing the central value of her life, much emotion is experienced. The communication is palpable. It is the same between husband and wife. Here the most effective communication may be active listening* and not talking at all.

The deepest level of communication has to do with the personal and emotional commitment of your life to another. In wholesome marriages and families it is the joyful explosion of an unrequired "I love you!" The communion level of communication is also the experience of being accepted by the God who accepts us. No verbal communication goes on—it is more spirit to Spirit. And this communion fills both with joy! Also, the tentative glance of a single mother to her awkward teenager who is caught doing something right, and the reluctant smiles that this produces, speak of years of communication that can only mean that they have communed many miles together. Communi-

cation of this sort is often called *communion communication,* and it expresses belonging and acceptance.

Digital or Analogic?

Family communication is done in two modes: digital and analogic. *Digital communication* is verbal and conveys the content of the message. *Analogic communication* is nonverbal and carries most of the relational aspect of the message. For example, when I was a child, I often asked my father to bring me half an apple when I went to bed. I was not hungry; I was not making excuses to stay up late. I was asking my dad, who couldn't seem to speak his warm emotions, to say what he thought of me. After walking up to my room he would place two corners of a green apple into my sleepy hand. He was saying that he loved me, though he could never say it in words. Analogic communication expresses without the use of words acceptance or rejection, hope or despair, confidence or worry, and a future with grace or a future of failure.

Target the Heart

In the family and in the church it is important to target our communication well. Blessings* and curses are powerful forms of communication. In 1 Corinthians 14:3 Paul says that "everyone who prophesies speaks to men for their strengthening, encouragement and comfort." In our family communication we need to be aware that we are constructing the future of our listeners, guaranteeing the outcome of our lives together. We can do this by targeting the heart. Communication is always more than the exposition of facts or the persuasive preaching of information. It needs in addition to be a declaration of our commitment and affection one to another. Effective families do more than have superficial conversations; such families express a wholesome blessing that calls for an imperative response.

For example, when my children were little, I would ask them questions such as "What are you going to be like when you grow up?" They would answer, "I do not know, Daddy." Then I would gaze down my outstretched arm to my pointing finger and say, "I think that I can see." Inevitably they would gaze off in the horizon of my imagination. And I would describe a life full of down-to-earth faith and practical romance with God. Theirs would be the pleasure of being fully alive. They would make a difference to the world. We would talk about the Holy Spirit sneaking into their lives with special gifts to give to others who needed what they had. I told them about the creativity that it takes to risk failing in the pursuit of God and that success might occur too. I spoke of the importance of doing well in life.

In the family we target the things of the heart. But we also need this quality of communication in the fellowship of the church family. To his church family in Thessalonica Paul says, "We loved you so much that we were delighted to share with you not only the gospel of God but our lives as well, because you had become so dear to us" (1 Thess 2:8). In both family and church we are conscripted to live emotionally and vulnerably and commitedly with one another, giving ourselves willingly.

Listening Hard and Speaking Hard

The last recorded exchange between Peter and Jesus (Jn 21) is a paradigm for wholesome family communication. Peter and some of the other disciples had quit the family business to follow Jesus. Now they were defeated in this venture and had returned to fishing. They were depressed and felt like failures. As they came to shore, dawn was breaking, and they saw Jesus cooking over an open fire. Peter was beside himself with craziness

that this dead Savior had come to life again! Clothed, he threw himself into the Sea of Galilee, swimming through his tiredness to be with Jesus. And Jesus asked him three times, "Do you love me?" After each query, Peter replied, "Yes, you know that I love you."

We are told that Peter was grieved to have had to repeat himself for something that seemed obvious to him. Jesus had a reason for such perseverance. In Matthew 4:4 Jesus said, "It is written: 'Man does not live on bread alone, but on every word that comes from the mouth of God.'" Peter had denied Jesus three times and now needed a word that came from the mouth of God. Jesus was giving Peter the opportunity to express his love* three times, creating an opportunity for intimate communication. We have no way of knowing whether he asked Jesus for forgiveness.* Perhaps, as in the case of the prodigal son, he did not ask for forgiveness because that expressive family affection was all he needed. Peter needed to say that he loved his Lord and to hear that this was sufficient. Because Jesus loved Peter, he created a perfect opportunity for Peter to say that he loved Jesus. With this experience Peter changed from an intimidated coward during Christ's crucifixion to a fearless witness after Jesus' ascension. In the same way, Jack and Judith Balswick point to the power of family communication: "People struggling today to find intimacy in an impersonal society need to realize that they, too, can change by expressing love" (210).

See also BLESSING; CONFLICT RESOLUTION; FAMILY; FAMILY SYSTEMS; LISTENING; LOVE; PROBLEMS; VALUES.

References and Resources

R. Anderson and D. Guernsey, *On Being a Family: A Social Theology of the Family* (Grand Rapids: Eerdmans, 1985); J. O. Balswick and J. K. Balswick, *The Family: A*

Christian Perspective on the Contemporary Home (Grand Rapids: Baker, 1989); W. M. Brody, *Family Dance: Building Positive Relationships Through Family Therapy* (Garden City, N.Y.: Anchor, 1977); E. H. Friedman, *Generation to Generation: Family Process in Church and Synagogue* (New York: Guilford, 1985); R. Richardson, *Family Ties That Bind* (Vancouver: Self-Counsel Press, 1984); V. Satir, *Conjoint Family Therapy* (Palo Alto, Calif.: Science & Behavior, 1967).

Paddy Ducklow

COMMUNION. *See* EATING; HOSPITALITY; MEAL PREPARATION.

—COMPUTER—

Some parents watch the way their children take to computers with a mixture of admiration and fear. The children seem to relate immediately to computers and use them with ease. But the ease that our children often have with computers is a mixed blessing. It gives them access to incredibly wide varieties of information and vivid experience of people and places we hardly dreamed of at their age. But it also gives them a power that sometimes quickly grows outside of our own capabilities as parents. Our children (sooner than we expected) have a facility with computers that we lack and can do things that we sometimes only dimly understand. Sooner then we expected, we are face to face with their skilled manipulation of ideas and information that we do not really grasp. What are they doing on that computer? Mostly, they are using computers in one of three different roles. Our children use computers to remember and access information, communicate with other people and explore alternate worlds.

Computers Are Rememberers

Humans have used computing devices for millennia. The abacus is an ancient example. Through the years we have invented an amazing array of machines to help us compute things more rapidly and accurately. But our digital computer (what we now mean by "computer") is not simply another computing device. Though computation is at the core of what computers do, they are really not computers but rememberers. Computers act as devices to remember information.

From the invention of writing and before, humans used the means at their disposal to record information in hopes that it would be remembered. But merely recording is itself insufficient. In order to remember and reuse information, it must be retrieved as well. Computers excel at this.

As more information becomes available to us over computer networks, the role that computers play as rememberers has become ever more significant. They are not merely a means by which we store and retrieve information; they are tools that allow us to navigate around the world's enormous information stores to find just the knowledge we need.

Our children have learned how to use computers this way. They are able to discover information that is stored in computers—information that we may prefer they not have just now—in ways that are beyond us.

For parents the way computers can remember information and deliver it easily to our children gives us one of our basic challenges. The information that is available via computer is immense and so is largely unsorted, unedited and unverified. Our children can discover anything from the location of Jupiter in the sky tonight to instructions for making a pipe bomb. It's all "on the Web" somewhere. With this vast amount of information, we parents need to provide what the computer cannot—guidance through the sea of information.

The guidance can take a variety of forms, but most important is giving our children a context to understand the vast information riches (and wrongheadedness) available via computers. They need to know, at an appropriate age, that we understand about pornography or about revolutionary manifestos and that we have come to see that drenching yourself in this kind of information only stymies the soul. They need to know that we have struggled to gain a framework of life that understands that focusing in other places will feed them and make them strong. Giving them this context and guidance is not a single instruction but an ongoing conversation.* We've always had this responsibility; computers have just made it more critical that we exercise it soon and wisely.

The second part of our role here is to act as editors. The information available in printed encyclopedias has been honed and edited and subjected to purification by many hands—not so the information available via computers. Much of it is straight from a single mind onto the Web. As a result, much of the information available to our children via computers is thoughtless and immature. We need to help them sort through this if we are to grow our children into thoughtful and discerning adults rather than into victims of the latest rant and foolishness.

Computers Are Communicators

Our computers aren't just rememberers though; they are also communicators. Far from being a modern version of a worldwide encyclopedia, a "read-only" information store, they are two-way devices. They allow our children to produce feedback rather than receive input only. This aspect of computers as communicators has allowed our children to revive some skills that were nearly lost to us. We nearly lost, for instance, the ability to write a personal letter. As we became more dependent on telephones,* letter writing fell into disuse throughout our culture. Our children discovered e-mail, however, and letter writing has seen a resurgence.

Yet computers present problems for our children that other media do not. Communicating via computers allows the recipients our children write to, potentially, to be not who they seem to be. Internet* chat rooms, for example, are well known for the elaborate disguises of their denizens. Electronic communication* allows this duplicity in ways that other forms of communication do not.

Our children are sometimes too trusting. They can accept these disguises at face value. And without the social context that has built up around other forms of communication, they run significant risks. We all know the horror stories. Letting our children know that there are predators in the woods is not alarmist; it's prudent. The majority of the people they "meet" communicating with computers will be interesting, friendly and harmless. A small number will not be harmless.

The challenge we face here is to teach our children not to believe all they read in other people's e-mails to them. These may seem to be straightforward, friendly communications, but they need to exercise the same discrimination they use with advertising or other common forms of potentially deceptive communication. Everything is not as it seems. Learning this lesson is an important part of growing up. The facility that computers have given us in communication have only made our job of helping our children learn this lesson more pressing.

Computers Create Other Worlds

It's a scene acted out a thousand times a day. A child is "glued" (so a parent thinks) to a computer screen: unresponsive, concerned only with the search or flight or battle being played out in a computer game.* The fascination is real. In fact, one of the most addictive aspects of modern computers is that they can create such engrossing simulations and renderings of other worlds.

Many of the simulations and alternate worlds that computers provide via games give many of the pleasures associated with travel—exploring a new place and never quite knowing what you'll find—and with traditional fiction—compelling characters and situations. But they do all this in an interactive and highly involving way. And so we worry that our children are glued to the computer in these games.

Our parents had similar concerns about us with television.* We were glued to it, and they worried that we were somehow being warped by it. But television gave us access to other worlds, both synthetic (movies, situation comedies, cartoons) and real (travel and documentaries). What computers have added to this is the interactive dimension. Television never responded to you, no matter how much you wanted it to. Computers respond constantly. The alternate world the game provides is malleable to your touch. You can explore alleys or try moves, and they have a "real" effect inside the synthetic reality of the computer.

This addition makes the world of computers much more engaging and engrossing than the flat and unresponsive worlds of television. But there are some obvious cautions parents need to apply.

The first is to pay attention to the content. Interactive, simulated violence has the same numbing character as graphic violence in other media. It's not that violence should be completely excluded from these worlds (as if it were not a part of the real world); rather, just as we do not live our real lives for and through mayhem, so our simulated worlds shouldn't reward such living. We need to help our children understand that drenching themselves in simulated worlds that require routine and indiscriminate killing, especially of obviously human creatures, are nasty and brutish worlds and not worth the engagement. They provide little or nothing that nourishes the soul and much that numbs it.

The second thing we can do is play along with our children. Many adventure style games have puzzles that are complicated enough to reward several minds working together to find their solutions. Watching our children play, praising their capabilities (which are sometimes quite amazing) and helping them solve problems they face in the simulation can be very rewarding. And they help our children know that we care about their activities. In this area, there is no substitute for playing with your children.

Being Guides

Providing our children with guidance is difficult. Our childhoods do not contain many experiences that help us, so it is easy to feel helpless. But computers really give our children the same kinds of capabilities we have had historically—access to information, communication and fantasy. Computers provide it immediately, vividly and interactively. But these are capabilities we do know and must teach our children to deal responsibly with in any case.

Our challenge is to provide guidance as our children discover the new worlds and capabilities that computers provide. We do have the raw materials to provide this guidance. Our task is to guide them in ways similar to the guidance we provide in other areas. Computers do the same things so much faster and so much more compellingly, but they require the same guidance we're used to providing for our children in many other areas.

Christian Reflection

Several things can be said to help us respond to the gift and challenge of the computer and the information superhighway.

☐ As with all advances in technology, this one is a mixed blessing, facilitating our communication and exchange and at the same time extending some present imbalances. On the one hand, the information superhighway opens up possibilities of improving access to a wide range of sources and democratizing discussion of them. On the other hand, it may reinforce the dominance of data and information over interpretation and wisdom, and increase information overload and induce people to spend more time on their computers than with people.

☐ Although the cost of computers continues to decrease, it still costs money to obtain equipment and use a provider to get on the information superhighway. Thus poorer and more marginal groups in society may still to some extent miss out and become further disadvantaged. Also, people with poor relational skills may be tempted to feel that they are achieving intimacy through electronics when there is no technical fix for these. While using the Internet may help some to grow in confidence in their ability to communicate, relationships mainly grow through speaking and listening* to actual others, preferably when eye contact can be made and feelings "read."

☐ Parts of the net are in danger of being co-opted by advertisers looking for fresh ways to get customers. It is also already being used to solicit a wider audience for pornography. There is a need for users of the net to monitor both their own and their children's use of it. In some cases technical devices can be used to block children gaining access to certain services. While legislated regulation of suppliers is one course of action here, unlike television, net providers are more information exchanges than prepackaged senders. As with other technologies, all dimensions of grappling with the principalities and powers are involved in using, developing and harnessing this new tool.

☐ All power-based technologies offer an implicit temptation to idolatry. This is part of the "technological illusion" (Ellul). Many people spend too much time on the net and direct their major energies to exploiting its potential. Computer addiction is a serious alternative focus for daily life. It is important to keep the information superhighway in its place, as a servant. One way of doing this is to "fast" from its use on a regular basis, so as to keep it in proper perspective.

☐ At the same time, the information superhighway allows for some level of communication between members of family and colleagues separated geographically. This "small talk" is not to be despised, especially if the new technology allows generations to communicate (grandparents and grandchildren, e.g.). Relationships are partly built on regular small talk, and the latter can also lead to big talk, the full sharing of personhood in community,* family,* church* and in spiritual friendships.

As private citizens, churches, businesses, and government increasingly turn to the information superhighway, there will be undoubtedly be an ever-deepening hunger for the personal and warm human relationships. Since persons are always at the center of the kingdom of God, God's people face an unparalleled opportunity to humanize the world for God's glory.

See also COMMUNICATION; COMPUTER GAMES; INTERNET.

References and Resources
N. Negroponte, *Being Digital* (New York: Knopf, 1995); <http://home.netscape .com/home/internet-search.html>; <www .yahoo.com>.

Hal Miller

—COMPUTER GAMES—

Though most computers are actively used for activities like accounting and word processing, a remarkable amount of their resources is devoted to simple diversion. Games* account for a significant portion of younger people's interactions with computers.

Similarities to Traditional Games

With some important exceptions, computer games fall into all the categories of traditional games. There are games of skill, usually called *arcade games* from their origins in pinball arcades. While these games are hardly aerobic, in other ways they are very much like traditional games of skill such as athletic contests or pocket billiards. Arcade games generally require speed and coordination in the use of input devices from their players. Current arcade games couple these demands with the color and sound distractions used to complicate pinball games for decades. Common examples of arcade-style games include various chase games and flight and driving simulations.

Related to arcade games are the *action games,* which require arcadelike skills but use those skills in a more or less continuous series of battles. The violence of these battles may be quite graphic at times. Indeed, the excesses in violence and gore of some action games led to the current system of voluntary rating of computer games by the industry.

A third category of computer game is *solitaire games* or puzzles. In these games, computers bring a fresh capability that revitalizes the game itself. Computers selflessly shuffle the cards or set up the pieces, leaving only the play to the human partner. Computer versions of crosswords allow you to erase the same word an unlimited number of times without making the paper illegible. In these cases, the difference of medium is an enhancement to the game itself.

We have also developed computer versions of *traditional games* that use boards or manipulatives. Chess and checkers, for instance, are based on relatively simple sets of determinate rules. But both games are endlessly rich in their strategic and tactical variety. In these cases, computer versions provide portable partners but also do something more significant. Here computer games can become serious contests between people and machines.

A final category of computer game is *adventure games,* including the newer interactive story. These games have fewer counterparts among traditional games, although the scavenger hunt is a reasonably close analogy. Adventure games require players to follow a thread (or one of several threads) through a story. Along the way problems arise that the players need to solve, often using materials they have gathered in the course of the adventure.

Adventure games run the gamut in

their premises and plots. Some require fights of various kinds; some are set in magical fairy tale* worlds. The themes may be overtly sexual or romantic, or black magic or warfare may dominate them. Overall, adventure games are much like novels or movies and cover the same range of themes. They also require similar guidance from parents.

Significant Differences in Computer Games

Although in most ways computer games are simply traditional games thrust into a new medium (with all the changes in speed and dimension that they bring), they are qualitatively different from traditional games in three important ways.

First, computer games have strongly contributed to blurring longstanding distinctions between gaming and education. In the past few years we have begun to hear this described by the neologism *edutainment*. Edutainment—and many computer games, especially those aimed at preteenagers, are excellent examples of edutainment—is shorthand for the loss of easy differentiation among the so-called content industries, such as schools, media companies and publishers.

Twenty years ago it was easy to distinguish music from movies and learning from playing. Now MTV and video gaming have made those conventional distinctions less compelling. Skillful teachers have always known that their job was at least part entertainer. That knowledge is now mainstream in the sense that it is often difficult to tell which part of an activity is the instruction and which the entertainment.*

Edutainment presents information or drills on skills in the context of a game or, alternatively, creates a game that requires players to master certain information or skills to succeed. Contemporary analyses of edutainment are also hobbled by the fact that the widespread use of computers has revolutionized the types of skills required for success in the working world. In some sense just being "computer literate," a skill players on standard desktop machines often develop merely to tune their gaming environment, is itself an important educational achievement. The edutainment phenomenon has been driven in large part by the evolution of computer gaming, but its influence on traditional educational goals is far from complete.

A second way that computer games are qualitatively different from traditional games is the way they can transport the player's senses. Unlike almost all traditional games, many computer games give the player a change of scenery. Computer games give you travel opportunities. The ability to explore strange buildings or cities or worlds is one of the novel fascinations of the computer game.

In a computer game the cities of the world (Where in the World Is Carmen San Diego?), a fantasy island (Myst) or a post-holocaust building complex (Doom) is yours to explore. Computer games allow, and often reward, simply poking around in unknown places. In this way they correspond much more to other rewarding human endeavors like natural science than do any traditional games.

Third, computer games are qualitatively different from traditional games in their graphic portrayals. A most instructive comparison here is between traditional chess and a computer version called Battle Chess. Chess is of course about war, and war is about killing. Yet chess hides all that carnage behind stylized game pieces and their moves. When a pawn is captured by a knight, what has "actually" happened in the reality represented in the game is that the foot soldier has been slaughtered by the horseman. Yet in the game, the wooden pawn is bloodlessly removed from the playing surface. Battle Chess, however, does away with this antiseptic distance between the game and what it represents. When the queen captures the bishop in Battle Chess, you watch on the screen as she slips out a stiletto and slides it between his ribs. The other pieces are no less violent in their activities.

Part of the "realism" of computer games, and the violence and gore that sometimes come with it, is a mere change of aesthetic. Photorealism has its seasons in art of all kinds, as do less representational forms. Traditional games were forced to stylize what they were portraying. With the computing resources currently available to games, this limitation is no longer in force.

Partially, however, the change from mere representation to more graphic realism is in the social role of the game. Traditional, less representational games are played at a distance of abstraction from their theme that computer games deliberately avoid. Chess may be about war, but it is a very abstract kind of war. Many action games are simply about killing, and the closer they come to the sensory reality of killing (it seems) the better. This difference gives traditional games a refinement and finesse that many computer games do not even try to achieve.

This change in portrayal may be only a stage in the evolution of computer gaming, but it has the same net effect as the evolution from screen kisses to graphic sexual encounters in movies. When mysteries like these are unveiled, a certain innocence is lost that cannot easily be recovered. The ultimate effect this will have on computer gaming remains to be seen, but it is an important development to watch.

See also COMPUTERS; ENTERTAINMENT; GAMES; INTERNET; PLAY.

Hal Miller

—CONCEPTION—

When a sperm and ovum unite, they become "one flesh" literally as a unique conceptus, "fearfully and wonderfully made" (Ps 139:14 KJV; see Ps 139:13-16; Eccles 11:5). New reproductive technologies* now allow conception to occur outside the confines of the human temple, creating ethical dilemmas and evoking the need to restore reverence to our idea of conception and dignity to personhood.

Evolving Ideas of Heredity and Origins
Biblically there is a rich tapestry of philosophies that dovetail with science. When Genesis describes the creation of Adam, the material of his body is completely and utterly earthy (Ps 90:3; 103:14). This contrasts with creation myths where humankind is extrapolated from blood or tears spilled from the gods. In the Bible the first man is the result of clay formed by the hands of God and invested with spirit and life through the transforming breath of the potter. In life man works this soil in intimate relatedness, returning to it in death (Eccles 12:7). There is speculation and some evidence that humble clay crystals may have served as the original catalysts for the formation of the hereditary molecule of life, deoxyribonucleic acid (DNA), in the first simplest life forms.

DNA has the unique ability to replicate itself, dividing and preserving a blueprint from one cell division to the next, maintaining the form and function of the cell and communally the organism. During replication the DNA spiral staircase cleaves equally, like a zipper parting. Components of the ladder rungs reassemble based on strict *exclusive* pairing in a lock-and-key fashion analogous to male and female union in marriage (Gen 2:24). It is this monogamy that preserves the sequence and meaning of the code, ensuring the faithful replication from one generation to the next (Ps 100:5).

That moment of divine spark in which matter was brought to life is in no way demystified by progress in the understanding of origins. Science serves to enhance, not diminish, the wonder of God's signature in matter. Biblically, *semen* and *seed* are used interchangeably and intersexually. Note the allusion to the female seed made in Leviticus 12:2, "to sow a seed," and in Hebrews 11:11, "Sarah received power to have [literally] a seminal emission."

Historically views were often opposing. The traditional notion that the mother was not the begetter but only the nurse of the newly sown embryo conflicted with observable patterns of heredity whereby children resembled both parents. In Job 10:10 we are given the image of human creation as the pouring out of milk that curdles into cheese: the development of a firm embryonic body from milky semen. From the sixth-century B.C. women were known to possess ovaries, although they were referred to as testes. Pre-Socratic philosophers defended the view that female semen is also necessary for procreation; hence menstrual blood was regarded as the female contribution to embryogenesis. The ancient principle that the seed of either parent can be "overpowered" is preserved in modern understanding of sex* determination and gene dominance over recessiveness.

The ovum and sperm each contain half of the genetic material necessary for human life. The male has two varieties of the sex-determining chromosome, designated X and Y. Thus there are two forms of sperm existing in the semen with regard to this one characteristic. Ovum, however, contain exclusively an X chromosome; the mother has a pair of X chromosomes from which to donate, one originating from each of her parents. It is the type of sperm, then, that engenders the sex of the conceptus. The Y "maleness" chromosome overpowers the X, resulting in a male offspring. Alternatively, the presence of another X chromosome from the sperm complements the X that is already in the ovum to produce a female offspring. In Genesis the creation of Eve from the rib of Adam has been metaphorically linked to the taking of the X chromosome to create out of man "flesh of his flesh and bone of his bone."

As the thread of life, the DNA molecule suggests metaphors for contemplation. An impossibly simple molecule, DNA contains the language to flesh out such diverse creatures as the towering cedar tree spanning a millennium and the transient intricate mouse, attesting to the universality of a spiritual language that knows no bounds of race or religion. If DNA is the self-propagating molecule of life, then love* is the expanding universal message of the spirit. Simple in concept, but indomitably extensive, it forms a genetic fingerprint. From only one cell, a strand of unwound DNA would stretch to the moon and contains the equivalent of three billion bytes in a computer program.

The double helix of DNA spirals cyclically (or seasonally) but directionally counterclockwise in defiance of time's entropic and decaying forces. The Creator's nudgings are acknowledged even in the scientific community as "creative explosions" that occurred "against all odds" in the evolutionary saga. God's sovereign hand has prompted us toward mindfulness of Creator and is beneath us despite threat of extinction and genetic deterioration (Deut 33:27). The consequences of mutations (errors in replication of the DNA molecule as a result of radiation or toxins) is usually disease and only very rarely an improvement. Life as we know it is precariously balanced on a knife edge between order and chaos, a grand compromise between structure and surprise. With increasingly specific knowledge about our genes and how they manifest themselves in sickness and in health (see New Reproductive Technology), the wonder of our innate complexities magnifies as we attempt to discern "God's creative thoughts after him" (Isaac Newton).

Conception Evokes Consummate Wonder

Consider the sperm, an enveloped package of DNA that has a means to propel itself through the female reproductive tract. Its limited energy resources give it a decidedly finite timeframe of several days to complete the task of navigation and penetration. The sheer number of sperm provided (five hundred million) demonstrates the magnitude of the undertaking and the competitive strain that ensures the best is rewarded with success.

In contrast, the ovum is the nutritive home for the woman's genetic material, "frozen" in time from her own intrauterine life. Sensing the monthly hormonal prompting, it will ripen and be released (see Menstruation). Once penetration by that first sperm has occurred, there is a change in the outer coating of the ovum. Instantaneously it changes its structure, preventing another sperm from entering even before the two nuclei have fused—

a paradigm of betrothal and monogamy. Hence, the exact amount of genetic material necessary to make up a new human individual is present and preserved from the moment of conception as the two halves become a whole.

It is interesting to explore symbolically the spherical ovum, roughly the size of the dot of an *i*, an hospitable planet for the sperm's delving, a refuge for the conceptus and the initial provider of nutrients to flesh out the designs held in the DNA. As the already fertilized ovum is propelled by hairlike cilia through the fallopian tube, it becomes a spherical clump of dividing and differentiating cells that plunges into the fertile soil of the womb. Putting down placental roots that absorb nutrients from maternal blood, the conceptus sends chemical messengers to lull the mother's immune system to accept its intrusion and signal the presence of the pregnancy, now detectable by lab tests.

The Soul of Personhood

Although the onset of personhood eludes us, the scientific knowledge we have confirms our deepest conjectures that soul, spirit and body are integrated in some wondrous way from the moment of conception of a genetically distinct individual, even prior to implantation, even prior to acquiring full consciousness and rationality. T. W. Hilgers is correct when he asserts that "once conception has occurred an individual human life has come into existence and is a progressive, ongoing continuum until death ensues" (quoted in Hui, 6).

Soul—that dimension of personhood that makes us God-conscious and expressive—and body (or physicality) are so interdependent that one cannot think of a person having a body without a soul. Contrary to Greek philosophy, which created a schism between spirit and matter, the Judeo-Christian view is that we are fully integrated as ensouled bodies or embodied souls. Understood in this way, conception is not merely the formation of physical shells for persons but is the cocreation with God of a person.

The element of development and "unending becoming" is a distinctive quality of human experience throughout life. When children begin to grapple with the notions of death* and spirit, they find the concept of eternity as simple and understandable as the circles they draw in the sand—a universal symbol of infinity, no beginning and no end. In contrast to these truths "revealed . . . to little children" and "hidden . . . from the wise and learned" (Mt 11:25), consider technology's liberty in controlling the origins of persons through the new reproductive technologies.

We are more than DNA living on in our offspring. What is this pearl that persists beyond flesh's fragility, the élan,

the part of us that smiles and sings, worships and loves? God has "set eternity in our hearts" (Eccles 3:11, author's translation). We are more than energy transformed into matter and nudged into consciousness. Our identity and hope is with the eternal God.

See also FEMININITY; MASCULINITY; NEW REPRODUCTIVE TECHNOLOGY; PREGNANCY; SEXUALITY.

Resources and References

P. Teilhard de Chardin, *The Appearance of Man* (New York: Harper, 1965); E. C. Hui, *Questions of Right and Wrong* (Vancouver: Regent College, 1994); M. J. Nash, "How Did Life Begin?" *Time*, October 11, 1993, 42-48; M. J. Nash, "When Life Exploded," *Time*, December 4, 1995, 38-46; L. Nilsson, *A Child Is Born* (New York: Dell, 1993); P. van der Horst, "Did Sarah Have a Seminal Emission?" *Bible Review*, February 1992, 35-39; H. W. Wolff, *Anthropology of the Old Testament* (Philadelphia: Fortress, 1974).

Carol Anderson

—CONFIRMATION—

The practice of confirmation has a complex history. In the earliest days, initiation into the Christian faith was through baptism,* anointing with oil and the imposition of hands. Thus baptism and confirmation were all part of the same rite. This was usually done by a bishop, when the church was young and bishops had only a little area to oversee. But by the fourth century confirmation was a separate rite. The (infant) baptism was done by the priest and the confirmation subsequently by the bishop. In the East they tried to maintain the original unity of the rite by having the oil consecrated by the bishop, the baptism conducted by the priest, and the infant being given Holy Communion—all in the same service. In the West confirmation was deferred until there was an opportunity for the candidate to be personally confirmed by the bishop. The Roman Catholic Church normally confirms shortly after the seventh birthday; Anglicans and Lutherans later, when young people are able personally to undertake the promises made for them at infant baptism.

There is no justification for seeing confirmation as a supplementary rite to baptism. And there is no scriptural justification for regarding confirmation as

imparting the gift of the Holy Spirit.

Confirmation is a profession of personal faith by those baptized in infancy. They take upon themselves and "confirm" the promises of Christian allegiance made for them by their sponsors. Then the bishop lays his hand on the their heads in the context of prayer to God "to certify them by this sign of thy favor and gracious goodness towards them. Let thy fatherly hand ever be over them. Let thy Holy Spirit ever be with them," as the Anglican Book of Common Prayer expresses it. Confirmation has a double dimension: the candidates confirm their faith in Christ, and we trust that the Lord, through the bishop's prayer and action, confirms (lit. "strengthens") them for the battle of the Christian life ahead.

Confirmation is, second, a domestic rite bringing the candidate into full accreditation and recognition within a particular branch of the Christian church. A person is baptized into Christ and made a member of the universal church, but confirmation is used (by some churches) in a divided Christendom to bring a person into full standing within a particular denomination. In baptism the person is made a member of Christ and his one holy, catholic (i.e., universal), apostolic church.

Third, confirmation is a commissioning for service. It contains a prayer that the candidate may remain Christ's forever and daily increase in his Spirit. It is a commissioning service. When adult candidates are baptized, confirmation and Holy Communion normally take place in the same service, thus retaining something of the original unity of baptism and confirmation.

See also BAPTISM.

Michael Green

—CONFLICT RESOLUTION—

Conflict is a natural part of life. Many people think "family conflict" means open controversy. However, a more biblical definition might be "the absence of the complete unity, mutual peace, love and understanding between family members together before God" (Jn 17:20-23). Persistent lack of the "peace that passes all understanding" (Phil 4:7) may be due to old conflicts, behavior patterns, expectations, resentments and sins. This is particularly true in families, where the emotional stakes are higher and escape difficult.

In American culture today, even within Christian families, an adversarial approach to "winning" a conflict has become a common substitute for direct personal discussion, reconciliation and personal ministry to others with whom we disagree. This focus on individual rights and needs sometimes supplants concern for the good of the whole family or community. Conflict itself can become an idol of the heart, diverting our energies from what God would have us do with our lives (Jas 3:14).

In some cultures there continues to be reliance on the judges at the gate (Ruth 4:1-12), but in America's increasingly anonymous society the perceived emotional cost-benefit of resolving conflict personally and amicably, even between family members, may work in favor of keeping the conflict unresolved. In extreme cases Christians seek conflict resolution through divorce,* child custody, support and other legal proceedings in civil court, with the aid of lawyers. This approach sometimes is necessary but rarely desirable, as it never reconciles personal relationships and provides a poor witness for Christ (1 Cor 6:1-8).

Common Christian Attitudes Toward Personal Conflict

Christians may be more vulnerable than other people to sin in conflict. This vulnerability arises from a misunderstanding about what it means to be Christlike. For example, some Christian spouses believe they always should "turn the other cheek," without realizing that unless one does so freely, without resentment, this is no true reflection of Christ's peacemaking character. Such actions are like the Pharisees' caring more about the letter of the law than its spirit (Lk 6:6-11). Further, giving in may be inconsistent with God's Word, which includes also the concepts of caring for others (Phil 2:4), justice (Acts 16:36-38; 22:25), restitution (Num 5:5-7) and personal accountability (Prov 19:19).

Other mistakes result from a misreading of Scripture. For example, some Christians imagine that it is up to them personally to carry out God's justice (1 Sam 25:28) in a manner that others experience as antagonistic. They may appoint themselves as God's avenging angel in the neighborhood or at the local school board, even though Jesus instructed us not to do so (Mt 7:1-2). Although God indeed may want to use us in these situations for his purposes (Esther 4:13-14), an adversarial attitude is precisely the opposite of how God approaches discipline,* which is with a loving and expectant heart (Heb 12:1-13).

Finally, some Christians appropriately spend a great deal of energy on broader social matters of global peace and justice, all in God's name (Lk 4:18-19). Although these are important concerns (Mt 25:34-40), some people who focus on these pay scant attention to resolving their own interpersonal conflicts, failing to recognize the broader community implications of individual discord (Phil 4:2-3).

All these attitudes can lead to confusion, abuse* or pent-up anger. In contrast, to seek resolution of disputes according to biblical principles means seeking both personal reconciliation and the just settlement of substantive issues (Acts 15:1-35). This should be done not only for the purpose of Christian unity but also to bring praise and honor to God (1 Cor 10:31). Jesus specifically urged peacemaking among his followers as a personal attitude that brings blessing* (Mt 5:9). Paul considered "the ministry of reconciliation" to be a universal call for believers (2 Cor 5:20), essential to following the Great Commandment (Mt 22:37-40; 2 Cor 5:11).

God's Interest in Conflict Resolution

As well as giving us the ultimate model of reconciliation—Jesus Christ (Heb 10:10)—Scripture is full of direction from God on the reconciliation of persons to himself and each other. There are many pictures of unilateral forgiveness* (Gen 50:19-21) and provision for sacrifice as a substitute for judgment (Is 53:6; 2 Cor 5:21). It is obvious that complete, direct, personal reconciliation is one of God's major preoccupations (Heb 2:1-4). God's method of resolving conflict serves both as a model for our own behavior and as a reminder of our own utter dependence on him as the source of all good we hope to achieve in his name (Eph 2:8-10).

By studying the ultimate conciliator at work, certain guidelines emerge for dealing with conflict in our daily lives:
☐ Conflict is an opportunity to grow to be more like Christ (2 Cor 12:7-10).
☐ Peacemaking starts with our own personal attitude, which in turn comes from a focus not on the conflict but on God (1 Pet 3:13-15).

□ It is possible to reconcile oneself unilaterally, but only if the past is forgiven completely (Phil 4:2-9), without resentment or bitterness (1 Cor 13:5).

□ Resolving conflict may require different methods at different times and places (1 Sam 25:26-35; Esther 7:1-6; Prov 6:1-5; Acts 16:22-24; 22:22-23, 29). Prayerful reliance on God's direction is crucial (Prov 3:5-7).

□ Differences of opinion on all but essential matters are inevitable and usually are acceptable (Acts 6:1-7; 15; 1 Cor 12).

□ Reconciliation does not necessarily require giving up or giving in, especially when someone is being hurt by ongoing conflict; loving confrontation may be preferable (Gal 6:1-5).

□ God reconciled all to himself through sacrifice and forgiveness, but we must pass this gift on to others to realize its full benefits (Eph 4:29-32).

□ Resolving conflict God's way may require us to accept consequences and to alter our own behavior (Eph 4:22-32).

□ Justice is God's, not ours (Lk 6:27-39).

Biblical peacemaking involves an active commitment to restore damaged relationships and develop outcomes that are just and satisfactory to everyone involved (1 Jn 3:18). A spirit of forgiveness, open communication* and cooperative negotiation clear away the hardness of hearts left by conflict and make possible reconciliation and genuine personal peace (Is 32:17-18). True biblical vulnerability, honesty and forgiveness can restore a person's usefulness, both to God and to others, and lead to complete restoration of relationships (Gal 6:1-3; Eph 4:1-3, 24).

Resolving Conflict as Believers

The Bible contains two basic messages about how believers should seek to resolve conflict in their daily lives. First, God's Word contains promises, principles and practical steps needed for resolving conflict and reconciling people (Is 30:18; 48:18; Mt 7:12). Second, it is clear that peacemaking is an essential discipling ministry of the local church, not a task reserved exclusively for professional clergy, counselors or lawyers (1 Cor 6:5; Eph 4:1-16).

Biblical principles and practical steps. The Bible helps to consider conflict resolution as an opportunity for personal obedience and witness (Jn 14:15-31). Sometimes we wonder why God has allowed a certain difficult family member or other person into our lives (2 Cor 12:17). Instead of viewing conflict with such a person as a painful burden, Christians can learn to see the situation as an opportunity to please God and to draw attention to God's wisdom, power and love* (1 Cor 10:31-33).

Always examine your own part in the conflict first (Mt 7:3-5). This includes not only your actions but also your attitudes, motives and omissions (Jas 3:13-16; 1 Jn 2:15-17). Focus especially on your reactions once the conflict began. Because it reveals our sinful attitudes and habits, conflict provides an opportunity for us to grow to be more like Christ (Ps 32:3-5; 139:23-24; 1 Jn 1:8-10). This growth takes place when we follow Jesus' command to accept responsibility for our own contributions to a problem-before pointing out what others have done wrong (Mt 7:5).

Look for steps you can take toward resolution of the issues. Each of us is commanded to make the first move when in disagreement with another (Mt 5:24). In this way the conflict provides an opportunity to serve others. Sometimes this can be done through acts of kindness and mercy (Prov 19:11), but at other times it requires constructive confrontation (Mt 18:15). Recall that Jesus confronted people not simply by declaring their sins to them but by engaging them in conversation* designed to help them arrive at the same conclusion on their own (Mt 7:12; Lk 5:27-28; Jn 4:7-26).

Accordingly, if someone is angry with you, go to them immediately (Mt 5:23-24), even if you believe the other's anger is unjustified. If you are angry with someone else, first ask yourself if the issue really is worth fighting. If an offense cannot be overlooked (Phil 2:3-4), go privately and express your concerns. But do not assume that the other knows or understands your perspective; explain what you are concerned about but also why (Mt 18:15). Be sure to affirm the relationship and your desire to work things out lovingly before launching into a discussion of the issues (2 Cor 2:5-8).

Making the first move does not mean that someone else has done something wrong or bad. An otherwise innocent word or act can cause an unexpected negative reaction in another, leading to serious disagreement (Jas 3:5-7). One can apologize for the trouble such miscommunication has caused simply because one regrets the result. Too often, however, our own sins have played a part either in creating the conflict or in escalating it (Jas 4:1-3).

The discipling ministry of the church. Call on the church for help if necessary. Private, gentle confrontation is a preferable first step, so long as we speak the truth in love (Eph 4:15). However, if after sincere good-faith efforts to work things out you are unable to resolve the issue or to mutually forgive each other (Prov 19:11; 1 Jn 3:16-20), then seek out the assistance of a few "witnesses" (Mt 18:16). These are present not to provide evidence or accuse the parties but to act as supportive advisers to both sides and help restore peace (Phil 4:3). This can be done informally with a respected relative, friend or other adviser trusted by both parties or more formally with a pastor, elder or deacon, church-appointed committee or trained conciliator.

If someone will not listen to you and the witnesses, and the issue is too serious to overlook (Prov 17:14-15), then, as we are instructed, "tell it to the church" and allow the church to decide (Mt 18:17). This is preferable to filing lawsuits in civil court (1 Cor 6:1-8). Today, as in Paul's time, our churches (and most believers) have abdicated this authority to the legal system; yet the courts do not focus on restoration of personal relationships, only on the disposition of tangible assets and liabilities. The church should model God's view that discipline* is an act of love and shepherding (Heb 12:6).

Finally, going to court is a possible last resort in cases where real harm (e.g., to a child or physically threatened spouse, or to property or a business) must be prevented. Whether or not the civil authorities can assist, if a party will not listen to the church, then we are commanded to treat such a person as an unbeliever (Mt 18:17). Does this mean that now we are free to sue in court or to press criminal charges? Yes, but again our decision to do so should depend on the nature of the dispute and the consequences to us, to others or to property in our care if we do not pursue our claims (Phil 2:3-4).

Beware. Some believers involve the church in following the Matthew 18:15-20 steps as a substitute for civil legal processes, demonstrating the same vengeful zeal and advocacy as if in court. The key to effective use of Matthew 18 is to appreciate it as God's detailed direction to us on how to keep peace on earth. Our attitude should be one of caution, prayerfulness and thanksgiving.

Conflict with Unbelievers

Even though Paul's admonition to the

Corinthians about lawsuits (1 Cor 6:1-8) is directed at believers suing believers, it only makes sense to tie God's conflict-resolution principles back to witness through reflection of Christ's character. Christ's approach was to lead with mercy, hoping for repentance, even while directly confronting a harmful attitude or act (Lk 15:3-7; Jn 8:1-3). Whatever the choice, our attitude needs to remain one of obedience to and reliance on God, and the aim should be peace with others, even unbelievers (Rom 12:17-18; 1 Cor 10:31—11:1).

Because Jesus loved and sought out unbelievers even as he tried to both correct and heal them, we can at a minimum attempt to work out differences with unbelievers using the same progression of steps as we would with believers (1 Pet 2:12). Mailing an angry letter, gossiping about or even suing an unbeliever, before trying to work out things another way, may not be the other person's best introduction to God's redemptive plan (Jas 3:18)!

See also COMMUNICATION; FAMILY PROBLEMS; FORGIVENESS; LISTENING; STRESS.

References and Resources
D. Allender, *Bold Love* (Colorado Springs: NavPress, 1993); D. Augsburger, *Caring Enough to Forgive/False Forgiveness* (Scottsdale, Penn.: Herald Press, 1982); E. Dobson et al., *Mastering Conflict and Controversy* (Portland, Ore.: Multnomah, 1992); R. Fisher and W. Ury, *Getting to Yes: Negotiating Agreement Without Giving In* (New York: Penguin, 1991); J. Hocker and W. Wilmot, *Interpersonal Conflict* (Dubuque, Iowa: Wm. C. Brown, 1991); Institute for Christian Conciliation, 1537 Avenue D, Suite 352, Billings, MT 59102, (406) 256-1583; B. Johnson, *Polarity Management: Identifying and Managing Unsolvable Problems* (Amherst, Mass.: HRD Press, 1992); S. Leonard, *Mediation: The Book—A Step-by-Step Guide for Dispute Resolvers* (Evanston, Ill.: Evanston Publishing, 1994); Peacemaker Ministries, 1537 Avenue D, Suite 352, Billings, MT 59102, (406) 256-1583; <www.HisPeace.org>; K. Sande, *The Peacemaker: A Biblical Guide to Resolving Personal Conflict* (Grand Rapids: Baker, 1991); C. Sande, *The Young Peacemaker* (Philadelphia: Shepherd Press, 1997).

Robbie E. Monsma

CONSCIENCE. *See* CHARACTER.

—CONTRACEPTION—

Contraception has been a matter of theological and ethical debate, largely among Christians. Contraception, or birth control, is the voluntary prevention of the conception of a child by human intervention. In this article we will explore the matter scientifically, scripturally and theologically.

Methods of Contraception
Today there are a number of methods of contraception available. The most primitive method is coitus interruptus, in which the male withdraws before ejaculation. This method has a 20 to 30 percent success rate in avoiding pregnancy. Next are the barrier methods, which employ creams, foams, jellies, caps, diaphragms or condoms to prevent the sperm from reaching the ovum. These methods are about 75 percent effective in pregnancy prevention. Hormone-based contraceptives include oral contraceptives, which contain fixed or variable doses of synthetic estrogen and progestin, Depo-Prov-

era injection, and Norplant, which is a sustained-release contraceptive system implanted under the skin that acts continuously for five years.

The hormonal contraceptives all work through one of the following mechanisms: (1) by thickening the viscosity of the cervical mucus, making it hostile to sperm, (2) by inhibiting ovulation via interruption of a crucial feedback loop between the pituitary gland and the ovaries, or (3) by making the lining of the uterus hostile to the implantation of any newly fertilized ovum that "breaks" through the first two lines of defense. The current low-dose pills most likely operate through this third mechanism, making them in fact *abortifacient* (i.e., they achieve birth control through early abortion). Other examples of abortifacient methods are surgical abortion,* IUDs and RU-486 (mifepristone); these are not considered contraceptive devices because a new human life in the form of an embryo is being destroyed. The use of low-dose hormone pills does carry high moral risks. Hormonal birth control has a theoretical effective rate of 99 to 100 percent and a 97 percent user-effective rate.

Permanent sterilization procedures are often performed for contraceptive purposes. For the female, two procedures are available: (1) tubal ligation, in which the fallopian tubes are tied and severed so that the sperm will not reach the ovum, and (2) hysterectomy, which makes conception impossible by removal of the womb. For the male, the method of permanent sterilization is vasectomy, tying the vas deferens (a small tube that transports the sperm from the testes to the prostate gland) to block sperm from entering the ejaculate. Tubal ligation, vasectomy and hysterectomy have a 99 to 100 percent pregnancy prevention success rate. Tubal ligation and vasectomy can be surgically reversed

with a 30 percent and 50 percent success rate, respectively, in achieving a subsequent pregnancy.*

Recently a new educational approach to birth control called natural family planning has been advocated primarily by those who do not want to engage in pharmacological or surgical contraception. It is a day-to-day method based on self-diagnosing the day of fertility in the woman's cycle, giving the married couple the choice to abstain from or enter into sexual intercourse at that time depending on their intention with regard to possible pregnancy. This is considered a true method of family planning in that it can be used to achieve or to avoid pregnancy. Some couples report a recurring honeymoon effect with this method. Four studies in the United States and two in the Two-Thirds World claimed a 96.4 percent and 99.2 percent effectiveness rate, respectively, in using these methods to postpone, delay and avoid pregnancy.

Attitudes Toward Contraception

Even though contraception was known throughout the ancient world some four millennia ago, it was not widely practiced. The question of the legitimacy of the use of contraception arose in the early church, when Christian free women who married Christian slaves wanted to avoid pregnancy in order not to bring more slaves into the world. The church responded by condemning contraception as sinful while affirming the basic equality of all human beings in the eyes of God, in whose image every man and woman is created. Historically, opposition to contraception has basically been the position of the church until the twentieth century.

The change in attitude toward contraception came at the same time that people gained better understanding of the physiological processes involved in reproduction. Prior to the nineteenth century most people thought that new life was transmitted in the male semen and the role of women was to receive and nurture it. The ovum was discovered in 1827, and the relationship between ovulation (the production of a fertilizable egg) and the menstrual* cycle was completely worked out in the late 1920s. As a result, the calendar rhythm method was introduced in 1932. This coincided with the growth of the birth control movement, which grew due to the perceived imbalance between population growth and available resources. For some Christians the break with the traditional opposition to contraception began at the Anglican Lambeth Conference in 1930, when the bishops recognized a moral obligation to limit parenthood and allowed for the use of contraception in certain limited circumstances.

The Roman Catholic Church responded with "On Christian Marriage" (1930) and "Of Human Life" (1968). These affirmed that the *unitive* meaning of the sexual act (in which the married couple grows in love* and fellowship) and the *procreative* meaning of the sexual act (in which the potential of childbearing is actualized) are both inscribed by God into the very act of sexual intercourse and cannot be separated without serious moral consequences. Periodic abstinence is the only permissible course of action for couples who wish to delay conception.

Protestant writers, on the other hand, see "the completion of marital fellowship" as the "first essential meaning" of sexual intercourse; from the standpoint of this fellowship, then, it may not be generally and necessarily required that it should be linked with the desire for or readiness for children (Barth, 269), and readiness for children should include both procreation and education

of offspring. Contraception is therefore acceptable as a means to achieve "responsible parenthood," especially in cases where the mother's physical and psychological welfare may be jeopardized as a result of getting pregnant or where other problems exist, such as an already overcrowded family.* Such factors are held to preclude a decent environment to ensure a proper upbringing of the child.

Contemporary Responses of Christians
Ninety percent or more of modern Christian couples favor temporary contraception or permanent sterilization. This response emphasizes the importance of human responsibility and takes stewardship seriously. It tends to downplay God's sovereignty in this matter and clearly believes that the unitive and procreative meanings of the marriage covenant and act need not be maintained in every sexual intercourse.

A tiny minority, less than 1 percent of Christians (both evangelical and Catholic), rejects every form of contraception, sterilization and even natural family planning. These Christians insist on God's sovereignty in procreative matters and do not accord human responsibility and freedom any significant role in procreation within the sexual/marriage act. They do not see the unitive and procreative meanings of the marriage covenant and act as two separable aspects.

A small number (3 to 4 percent) are practicing natural family planning. This approach combines respect for God's sovereignty and human responsibility. When sexual intercourse is experienced, it does not contravene the total openness of the marriage act but trusts in God's providence for any outcome. And when sexual intercourse is abstained from for good reasons, the couple's sacrifice and self-control are considered a gift of the Holy Spirit and an integral component of Christian life.

A Christian Evaluation of Contraception

Undoubtedly, contraception has brought many positive benefits. Many women have been able to relax during sexual intercourse without the fear of annual pregnancies. It has helped some couples take more responsibility for bringing children into this world. But there has been a downside as well. Contraception has not solved the population problem nor made happier marriages. In fact, the divorce* rate skyrocketed from 25 percent in 1960 to approximately 50 percent in 1975, when contraception had reached saturation levels in North American culture. Furthermore, contraception has not decreased the demand for abortion. In fact, every country that has accepted contraception has had to pass abortion laws, as there are no 100 percent effective contraception methods.

There are many factors involved in the alarming statistical trends we observe in today's Western world. Universally available contraception is certainly one. There has been an explosion of abortion from below 50,000 per year before 1960 to 1.5 million per year in the United States today. The reality of unwanted children has not been eliminated. It is well known that the advent of contraceptive technology coincides with the devastating social consequences of adultery, sexually transmitted diseases, value-free sex education and teenage pregnancy. Furthermore, many believe that contraception, by separating the unitive and procreative dimensions of the marriage covenant, has managed to reduce women and men to mere objects, seen as means of giving pleasure rather than as total persons with their fertility intact. This objectification of women is at the root of the increased abuse* and violence against women in our society.

Toward Responsible Contraception

First, even if we do not agree with the Catholic Church's position on artificial contraception as intrinsically immoral, it must be admitted that contraception has contributed a great deal to the immorality of our society. Any Christian endorsement of the use of artificial contraception must be accompanied by condemnation of those immoral consequences that run against all fundamental Christian teachings on humanity, sexuality* and marriage. Teenagers especially must be taught that parental use of contraceptives does not mean justification of premarital sex.

Second, throughout the Bible children are considered a great blessing. In the Old Testament barrenness is considered to be a lamentable state. In Genesis 1:28 the command to be fruitful and multiply is seen to be integral to the meaning and stewardship (responsible parenthood) of the marriage union in creation. Every birth is a sign of God's ongoing commitment to creation, work in redemption and extension of the kingdom.

Third, other concerns, such as service to God's kingdom, can take precedence over marriage and family (1 Cor 7). The biblical injunction to be fruitful and multiply (Gen 1:28) need not be interpreted to mean that parents always have to bear the maximum number of children. Rather, the objective of marital partners must include cultivating an environment that is conducive to the growth of partner-fellowship between the couple and an optimal number of children who may receive adequate nurturing, attention and education. If this involves the assistance of artificial contraception, we should use it responsibly and with caution.

Fourth, it is a different matter if a Christian couple decides at the beginning of their married life to be permanently childless by the use of contra-

71

ceptive devices. Here caution must be exercised. Some argue that the decision to be childless is similar to the decision to be celibate in order to be freed for a higher calling and thus the use of contraceptives should be allowed. Others link sexual intercourse to the kingdom of God. "The line of reasoning goes this way: Families are for the Kingdom of God. Marriage is for families. And therefore, since sex is for marriage, sex is for the kingdom of God" (Smedes, 167). Even though the reproductive meaning of sexuality need not be fulfilled in every instance of the sexual act, the link between the unitive and procreative aspects of sexual intercourse should be respected by insisting that all marriages should be open to the hope of bearing children at some point.

See also ABORTION; CONCEPTION; FAMI-LY; MENSTRUATION; MISCARRIAGE; PARENT-ING; SEXUALITY.

References and Resources
C. Balsam and E. Balsam, *Family Planning: A Guide for Exploring the Issues* (Liguori, Mo.: Liguori, 1986); Karl Barth, *Church Dogmatics* 3/4 (Edinburgh: T & T Clark, 1961); R. A. Hatcher et al., *Contraceptive Technology* (New York: Irvington, 1994); J. T. Noonan Jr., *Contraception: A History of Its Treatment by the Catholic Theologians and Canonists,* 3d ed. (Cambridge, Mass.: Belknap/Harvard University Press, 1986); Pope Paul VI, *Of Human Life (Humane-Vitae)* (Boston: St. Paul Editions, 1980); M. Pride, *The Way Home: Beyond Feminism, Back to Reality* (Westchester, Ill.: Crossway, 1985); C. D. Provan, *The Bible and Birth Control* (Monongahela, Penn.: Zimmer, 1989); L. B. Smedes, *Mere Morality* (Grand Rapids: Eerdmans, 1983).

Edwin Hui and Michael Maloney

—CONVERSATION—

Conversation is basic to daily life. Throughout the day, in a wide variety of settings, we relate to others through talking informally with them. Originally the word referred to "a way of life"; now it means "a type of discourse." Conversation overlaps but can be differentiated from discussion. Though one can easily move into the other, discussion is generally more focused and structured.

The Complexity of Conversation
Though conversation appears to be a simple activity, it is actually quite complex. First, not all conversation is the same. It is governed by unwritten conventions or codes particular to the settings in which it is taking place. We talk about conversations as being formal and informal, polite and frank, freewheeling and directed. What we talk about with a friend and the way we talk differs from the way we converse with a client or boss. Face-to-face conversation differs in certain respects from that conducted over a telephone or a modem.

Second, women and men tend to converse differently. Men tend to discuss matters more abstractly, women more concretely. Women tend to discuss in order to connect with other people, men to express their point of view. Men tend to be more preoccupied with ideas about which they sometimes feel strongly, women with the cognitive content of their feelings. Women tend to listen* and ask questions better, men to give answers and cut off others.

Third, cultures as a whole have different conventions governing how people converse. Among Australian aborigines, members of a group wait to speak until the most respected person among them has spoken or indicated that others may do so, women will wait until the men have spoken or given them the permission to do so, and each one will pause before speaking to examine whether he or she has something worthwhile to say. Even between Western societies there are noticeable differences. Most Americans speak more loudly and in a more uninhibited way than most Canadians.

In spite of these various conventions, conversation is the most spontaneous, versatile and open-ended way of communicating that we have. We enter into conversations with our partners, children and friends, as well as with colleagues, salespeople and strangers, sometimes even ourselves! We do it one on one and in small groups, casually and by arrangement. We chat about trivial matters, yet also about personal or social concerns. In prayer we converse alone in company with God.

The Importance of Conversation
Conversation is fundamental to social life. It is central to (1) acquiring the necessary information to help us find our way around places or carry out our daily activities; (2) relating to other people in order to develop an understanding of who they are and how they function; (3) resolving problems that we find difficult to deal with individually; (4) enjoying the company of others and, through the "play"* of conversation, just having a good time; (5) helping to determine our basic worldview, commitments and priorities. Conversation is so pervasive and common that it is easy to overlook its importance. This is especially true in relation to learning or teaching.

We seldom regard conversation as having educational value. We assume that serious or substantial learning can take place only in a formal teaching situation. Interestingly, studies of lecturing suggest that a speaker is mainly effective when there is a conversational element or style in the address. In fact, it is through conversation that infants primarily come to know and cooperate with others. Older children prepare for adult life by "playing grownups." Spending time "hanging out" with their peers or talking over the telephone help teenagers formulate their views and develop their relationships. Popular television* and radio programs reflect life more than we acknowledge. As adults, many of our views on work, social issues and politics are formed by conversation with others. Studies suggest that the most effective evangelism also flows from informally sharing our experience with people we know.

Conversation in the Bible and History
In the Bible, conversation is not only central to the way people relate to each other but also characteristic of the way we learn about God. The Old Testament contains a number of conversations between God and key figures in the divine drama. For example, God converses at length with Abraham (Gen 18:22-33), Moses (Ex 3:1—4:17), Jeremiah (Jer 14:1—15:2) and, in a more one-sided way, with Job (Job 38—42).

In these writings conversation is also central to the way the people of God were to pass on their faith. For example, the people of Israel should not only recite the Ten Commandments to their children but "talk about them when you sit at home and when you walk along the road" (Deut 6:7; compare 6:20-25). At the Passover the meaning of this basic ritual was to be discussed with children during the meal (Ex 13:1-10). In fact, conversations were to take place within families about the whole range of God's instructions to Israel (Deut 6:20-21).

The Bible also contains numerous conversations that consciously or unconsciously reveal people's motives, attitudes and intentions; their beliefs, standards and practices; their problems,* fears and longings. Others focus on God's character, actions and purposes. In many of the psalms we find a combination of the two (explicitly in Ps 32; 81; and implicitly in many others, e.g., Ps 85; 89); sometimes we also come across the psalmist having a conversation with himself as well as God (Ps 42; 77). Elsewhere people fulfill God's wider purposes through engaging in conversations with influential people (compare Neh 2:1-8; Esther 5—7).

In the New Testament we often find Jesus talking with his disciples as they ate a meal together or journeyed from place to place. Sometimes outsiders generate a discussion on some important topic (Mt 19:1-12); sometimes one or more of the disciples generate it (Mt 20:20-27); sometimes Jesus himself generates the conversation (Mt 16:13-28).

In the early church purposeful conversation continued to play an important role. The only narrative we have of an early church meeting describes Paul as first dialoguing with (not preaching to) the people at length and then conversing with them after their common meal (Acts 20:7, 11). In those days both the sermon and the Lord's Supper had a strongly conversational character, one that was lost in the following centuries as churches got larger and clergy emerged as a separate group. Paul also trained people such as Timothy, Titus, Priscilla and Aquila for missionary service largely through working and talking with them on his various journeys.

Although in subsequent Christian history more formal approaches to learning and teaching tended to predominate, key figures continued to affirm the role of conversation in Christian formation and education. In the third century Clement of Alexandria instructed his students through both informal conversation and more structured discussion. Augustine taught mainly through dialogue with his students in informal surroundings. Martin Luther's collected *Table Talk* shows how he supplemented his formal lectures with regular theological and practical conversations over meals. Dietrich Bonhoeffer followed a similar pattern at his underground seminary in Germany during the Nazi era, as reflected in a discussion of the ministry of listening and communicating in his book *Life Together.*

During the Reformation influential converts in the universities were won over to the Protestant cause initially through conversation in taverns and pubs. In the eighteenth century it was through conversations initiated in one household after another that John Woolman induced Quakers throughout America to abandon slavery, just as later in England regular and lengthy conversations over many years in the homes of William Wilberforce and other members of the Clapham Sect formed the basis for the antislave movement there.

The Demise of Conversation

For at least two main reasons conversation today has fallen on difficult times. It is a victim of the increased busyness and noise that afflict modern society. We have less time for others generally, whether extending hospitality* to them or visiting with them, and so less time for simply talking together in a regular or leisurely way. Settings where we could talk have become too noisy with traffic or background music. The individualism and fragmentation of people in the West are also a problem. A century and a half ago the French social commentator Alexis de Tocqueville commented that Americans do not so much converse as speak to one another as if they were addressing a meeting. Instead of conversation there is either a discussion with a particular shape and goal or a series of individual presentations by people more interested in expressing their own ideas than participating in a genuine group experience in which people take their cues from one another.

Busyness, noise, individualism and fragmentation make it all the more important to recover conversation in significant areas of life. In this matter we can learn from those who are marginal in our society. For different reasons African Americans, women and children all seem to converse easily with one another: the first perhaps because they have become skeptical of discussions, the second because they are less linear and more person-oriented, the third because they are so unselfconscious.

Recovering Conversation

Restoring conversation to a central place in life has many advantages.

For repairing marriages and families. Psychologists suggest that the main problem in marriages* today is the lack of communication. This stems partly from people's inability to talk with and hear from one another, partly from issues arising in which highly emotive factors take control, and partly because people do not spend enough time talking with one another (less than twenty minutes a week in meaningful conversation, according to one Australian study). Time spent by parents with their children has also decreased, as the preoccupation with spending *quality* rather than *quantity* time testifies.

Behind such problems lie poor modeling and training during people's upbringing, the overly volatile place financial matters occupy in our lives and the emphasis on achievement in both school and workplace at the expense of personal and relational growth. When families reorder their priorities, and where necessary learn some communication skills, the threat of marriage breakdown and of the generation gap diminishes. One step in reordering is to restore the evening family meal to its rightful place, free from the intrusion of television and telephone. Also helpful are regular opportunities for partners, while walking or relaxing, to talk about their dreams and frustrations, ideas and feelings.

For understanding and relating the Christian faith. When people engage in conversation about an interesting book or film, they tend to become enthusiastically caught up in discussion. They talk about how wonderful, exciting, or moving it was, what part they liked most or least or just didn't understand, who or what they really identified with. They may also talk about the values* or ideas it was projecting and how it challenged or confirmed certain attitudes or convictions. The same degree of involvement and excitement can be generated in studying the Bible or learning about the Christian faith.

Though not as ordered an approach to learning as more formal study of the Bible or theology, good conversation does lead to greater understanding and self-challenge. It can bring to life stories and figures from the Bible, as well as ones that come out of the pages of church history. Even the lives and writings of Christian thinkers, past and present, can come alive in people's minds and wills if they are approached in this way. Formal classes or structured programs are not necessarily the best way for most people to learn and apply the basic elements of the Christian faith.

For deepening and extending the church. Small groups have brought into church life a more relational, supportive and practical dimension. But in comparison with early Christian meetings and our own contemporary needs, they are still structured and limited. Some groups are led and directed by one person and do not always provide opportunities for all to share with and care for one another according to their God-given gifts and experience. Building into such gatherings a full meal—preferably carrying the full significance of the Lord's Supper—during which conversation on a wide range of concerns, small and large, to individuals and to the group as a whole, can take place can have tremendous effects. Recovering the importance of a meal, this time with unbelievers rather than believers as guests, is central to the task of extending as well as deepening the church. The early church grew largely through the act of ordinary Christians extending hospitality to others in their homes.* It was around the dining room table in a conversational way that the gospel was most effectively shared. This is a challenge and a direction for all Christians and churches that are serious about evangelism today.

Conversation is a multisided phenomenon with multiple uses. Though often familiar or standardized, and in turn both comfortable and comforting, it is also full of the most extraordinary possibilities and consequences.

See also EATING; HOME SCHOOLING; LISTENING; MISSION; SPIRITUAL FORMATION.

References and Resources

W. R. Baker, *Sticks and Stones: The Discipleship of Our Speech* (Downers Grove, Ill.: InterVarsity Press, 1996); E. Goffman, *Forms of Talk* (Philadelphia: University of Pennsylvania Press, 1981); R. Hattox, *Coffee and Coffeehouses: The Origins of a Social Beverage in the Medieval Near East* (Seattle: University of Washington, 1985). G. Lakoff and M. Johnson, *Metaphors We Live By* (Chicago: University of Chicago Press, 1980); C. Lasch, *The Revolt of the Elites and the Betrayal of Democracy* (New York: Norton, 1995) 117-28; D. Roger and P. Bull, *Conversation: An Interdisciplinary Approach* (Philadelphia: Multilingual Matters, 1988); D. Tannen, *You Just Do Not Understand: Women and Men in Conversation* (New York: Ballantine, 1990).

Robert Banks

—CREDIT CARD—

More than half of North Americans have a credit card in their wallets or purses. It is a handy way to obtain consumer credit for the purchase of goods or services without carrying cash or making payments instantly, especially while traveling. The debit card, a variation on this, instantly withdraws the money from one's bank accounts and does not extend the usual thirty-day credit. Credit cards produce profits to the institution granting them by direct user fees, by high interest rates on unpaid balances and through payments from retail establishments, or some combination of these. Many cards now offer further incentives by giving points that can be redeemed for airline travel and penalizing, so it seems, the use of cash or checks.

As with all forms of credit, the credit card is based on the trust expressed in an individual by a bank or lender. An individual's credit rating is a measure of trust placed in him or her by a financial institution. Thus, the process of getting and maintaining a credit card is a form of financial testing, proving that one is a reliable person who will pay his or her bills. As with all forms of credit, this one facilitates the transfer of money in a way that increases its productivity by placing it where it will work. At the same time, it economizes on the use of currency.

As with many technological advances the use of credit cards has changed the way we live and think. We now carry "plastic money." We can make large purchases quickly without a penny in our pockets or guarantee a hotel room halfway around the world by simply using our number. Instead of providing a large cash deposit to guarantee a car rental, we simply use the line of credit provided with the card.

But there are several disadvantages. It is well known that credit cards make theft and fraud quite simple. The more serious problems are less obvious. We no longer have to wait, for we can buy it now, even if we are not carrying cash. We can afford it because we have thirty days to pay, even if we do not have the money in the bank ("It will come!"). It is undeniable that easy credit feeds consumerism and stimulates impulse buying. Many people are tempted to live beyond their means, accumulating debt* beyond their ability to repay. Young people in particular are tempted to abuse credit and are filing for bankruptcy in distressing numbers.

So the use of a credit card is in one sense a test of our maturity. Put differently, it is an invitation to grow to an increasing maturity. We can do this by determining not to make purchases unless we actually have the money or a clear and workable plan for repayment of the debt (see Debt). We can reduce the number of credit cards we have to one or two to resist spreading credit— really debt—over multiple institutions.

Further, we can take our credit card invoices as statements not only of purchases made but values held and carefully reflect on how we should exercise stewardship by preparing a budget and living by it. The last place we should look for help in setting our own credit limit is the institution granting it. Sometimes it is good to fast from credit card buying and to use only cash. This gives a more accurate experience of the flow of money.

The book of Proverbs speaks to the use of money and credit. It takes wisdom from God to possess money* without being possessed by it (Prov 1:17-19). Without wisdom we can have wealth but no true friends, food on the table but no fellowship around it, a house* but not a home,* the ability to buy things but no financial freedom. Without wisdom we will use a credit card to indulge ourselves (Prov 21:17) and still never be satisfied (Prov 27:20; 30:15-16). Credit card in hand, the unwise person "chases fantasies" (Prov 28:19) and so comes to ruin, but the wise, accumulating as stewards "little by little" (Prov 13:11), "will be richly blessed" (Prov 28:20).

See also DEBT; MONEY; SHOPPING; TITHING.

References and Resources

R. N. Baird, "Credit Card," in *The Encyclopedia Americana* (Danbury, Conn.: Grolier, 1989) 8:166-67; J. Barnett, *Wealth and Wisdom: A Biblical Perspective on Possessions* (Colorado Springs: NavPress, 1987).

R. Paul Stevens

CRISIS. *See* CONFLICT RESOLUTION; FAMILY PROBLEMS; STRESS.

CULTS. *See* ALTERNATIVE RELIGIONS.

—DATING—

A recent article titled "Is Dating Dead?" in a Canadian magazine observed that dating has changed. In the Western world a person tries a succession of sexual partners prior to cohabiting. Understandably some refuse to use the word *dating* at all, preferring instead such an innocuous phrase as "going out." Even "having a relationship" unfortunately now connotes a sexual liaison. The much older English words *courting* and *wooing*—similar in meaning to the terms "speak to the heart" and "allure" found in the Hebrew Bible (see Is 40:2; Hos 2:14)—suggest the sensitive persuasion with which a man will plead to a woman's heart for her hand in marriage,* thus raising the crucial question of whether dating and mating should themselves be married!

Must dating be practiced with a view to finding a suitable marriage partner? Should Christians participate in recreational romance or romantic networking—whether or not one has any interest in or calling to marriage? Can dating be a ministry to not-yet Christians, a form of romantic evangelism? Should dating be restricted to finding a spouse? Is there a place in dating for relationship enhancement, the enjoyment of other persons, a form of neighbor love* without marriage in view? Is there an explicitly Christian approach to dating? Is there a place for dating after one is married? Are there initiatives a person can take when no dating prospects loom on the horizon?

Dating Through the Ages

All cultures have found ways of allowing people to meet members of the opposite sex with a view to finding a suitable marriage partner, though in most cases these have been tightly controlled by social taboos, such as "no dating without the presence of a chaperon," and in others there simply was no opportunity for relational experimenting. In most ancient societies, marriages were arranged by parents, and there was virtually no social contact prior to engagement (except through observation in village life or shared survival activities) and no sexual contact until marriage.

In some cultures today it is assumed that a man or woman cannot be alone together without having sexual intercourse. So the arranged marriage survives in a few places, and where there is wisdom exercised by parents, family and friends, this system may be preferred to the romantic networking of the Western world, which is usually focused on falling in love or infatuation—a temporary phenomenon. The Christian church has entered various cultures all over the world, but where it has brought the Christian view of marriage, it has not always eliminated the system of arranged marriages. But one thing Christianity has always brought is the requirement of consent, which is based on theological reasons relating to God's covenant with God's people. No covenant can be formed without the willing heart agreement of the bride and groom—hence the questions asked in a Christian marriage ceremony ("Do you take this man to be . . ."). Consent is implicit in making promises and vows.

Some African tribes offered socially acceptable ways for young people to explore relationships with the opposite sex by permitting limited sexual affection in a very controlled situation, especially for couples that were predisposed to marry each other. This was not unlike the *bundling* or *binding* (in bed for an exploratory night together with a physical barrier between!) formerly practiced by some Christian sects. Festivals and harvest celebrations were natural contexts in which people in agrarian societies would experimentally explore special relationships with others of marriageable age, sometimes indicating interest through socially learned signals such as making repeated eye contact.

The older systems assumed a stable social network of families,* tribes and peoples in which the parents and the children knew each other. A young man and woman would observe each other at work, home* and community activities over years. This prolonged exposure cannot easily be accomplished in the modern city, especially in a mobile society (see Mobility). In fact, there is no possibility for prolonged exposure in most of the world, careening as it is toward global urbanization. Only a disciplined approach to the modern dating system can replicate the advantage of long-term relationships in the same social network.

Jewish Betrothal

The Jewish system of Jesus' day did not allow dating. There was simply betrothal—the arrangement, much more than the modern engagement, by which two people were pledged to each other. Through the betrothal ceremony the couple formally partnered, so much so that betrothal could be broken only by divorce* (as the case of Mary and Joseph in Mt 1:19 poignantly illustrates). Betrothal was presexual marriage—covenant without covenant consummation—and therefore Scripture views betrothal as an illuminating analogy for our relationship with Christ as we wait for his second coming when we will "know" as we are now known (1 Cor 13:12; 2 Cor 11:2). Until then we belong unconditionally, but we do not have full union.

In the Jewish context betrothal might last for up to a year and was concluded with the wedding feast, sometimes lasting a week, during which the couple would consummate the relationship. Both virginity before marriage (Deut 22:13-21) and regular intercourse within marriage were assumed.

North American and Western Dating

There has never been a dating system like the modern Western one. At the same time, there has never been a more fragile marriage system than the modern Western one. Indeed, researchers on family life suggest that the greatest problem in North American marriage may well be North American courtship, that is, the dating system (Sell). From the earliest age children are taught and socialized to prepare for an extended period of relational experimentation in which each presents his or her best self to potential girlfriends or boyfriends and marriage partners. Long before dating became industrialized through dating services, voice mail, e-mail and newspaper advertisements, an entire industry supported this social expectation through providing dress (see Clothing), cosmetics, mass media (especially Hollywood movies) and endless environments in which to meet people such as singles bars, which do not encourage honest self-disclosure and true friendship.

Dating, as currently practiced, is a staged play in which each person presents his or her outer "ideal" self to the other. Inside, both he and she are insecure and weak, but they each see in the other the external image of what they have always wanted in a friend/partner of the opposite sex. They fall in love, in which judgment is suspended and people live in a dream world of ecstasy. Some research suggests that hormones in the body support this delightful derangement, though eventually the chemical balance of the body is restored. Without revealing their private selves, couples become entangled sexually sometimes as early as the second or third night, believing that touch, feel and fondle are quick ways to intimacy, whereas, in reality, the conversation* they have shut down would better serve the purposes of intimacy.

This romantic relationship is promoted in ideal circumstances—restaurants, theaters, leisure spots—with scant exposure to one's family and with rare openness to being seen without being made up, dressed up and presentable. Psychologists call this a collective defense mechanism. If two people marry at this point, they are doomed to disillusionment, as when he (in his insecure, private self) realizes he has married not a Barbie doll but another insecure person who is saying, "Please fill up my emptiness." Couples often divorce at this point, at the very moment when they could get married at a deeper level and when sensitive counseling could serve them well. If they are cohabiting or just spending weekends together in each other's apartments, they will probably move on to another "ideal" relationship and fall in (and out) of love once again.

Can Dating Be Redeemed?

But both the arranged-marriage system and the dating system can be redeemed. People have found suitable partners and made lifelong companionship covenants through private arrangements. Some people who have found very suitable partners by anonymous, computerized dating services (including some Christian couples). In the same way, the dating system can be redeemed, but this will require deep and costly measures.

Shrinking from the to-bed-the-first-night culture, and sometimes reacting to a promiscuous past, some Christians refuse to date at all. In its place they enjoy fellowship and pursue ministry with people of the opposite sex, all the while praying that God will deliver that one special person in the world who is God's choice. Some of this amounts to group dating and has the advantage of mutual exposure to others in contexts that are not idealized. There are, however, severe drawbacks, especially since any resulting relationship can be founded exclusively on mutual interest in Christian service and is not a well-rounded friendship.

The advice not to marry until you find someone with whom you can better serve God together as married rather than as single people is problematic and probably dangerous. Marriage is for companionship (Gen 2:18), not to get God's work done on earth. Further, many Christians think that if they pray, God will magically deliver a spouse from heaven. But in reality there are only two ways to get married: have an arranged marriage or arrange one yourself! God can work through both, and the church has a crucial role to play in both.

What the Family and the Church Can Do

Arranging marriages. Mature couples in a church could sensitively introduce people to each other. Such arrangement must be followed by a period of friendship and mutual self-disclosure in a variety of settings and assumes that a couple will not marry until they are substantially without reservations and are able to give their full consent. Romance will follow and usually does, contrary to the mythology of Hollywood. Marriage does not destroy romance but is the normal garden for its cultivation. As Walter Trobisch once observed, the Western system of marriage is like taking a hot bowl of porridge and letting it cool down on the table, while the arranged-marriage system is more like putting a pot of porridge on the stove to cook and turning up the heat (56).

Arrangement is implicit, or at least envisioned as a possibility, in the promises and vows that ask "Will you love . . . ?" not "Do you love . . . ?" Arrangement is also consistent with the view of marriage as a vocation or calling. Two biblical examples of such arrangement are Abraham's servant finding a wife for Isaac (Gen 24) and Naomi's guiding Ruth to take the initiative with Boaz (Ruth 3:1-6), though Ruth may be one of the few biblical examples of a woman who took an initiative in finding a marriage partner (Stevens 1990, 32).

Interestingly, psychologists now say that in one sense all of us have marriages arranged by our parents, since our families to a large extent determine whom we choose to date and marry, even in a healthy home and especially in one that encourages fusion and codependence. The process of leaving one's father and mother (Gen 2:24), which is so crucial to cleaving and becoming one flesh, turns out to be a lifelong process rather than a single wedding event.

Developing a congregational dating and mating ministry. As well as offering sensitively and confidentially to make some matches, leaders in the church can teach and model a family style of dating by encouraging kinship relationships in the church and the development of significant friendships in the context of service. Couples can open their homes to young adults to let them discover models of marriage other than ones in their families of origin. An environment can be created in which young adults can meet one another in the context of hospitality,* perhaps even through a spiritual friendship weekend. The church should offer seminars on sexuality* to help people cope constructively with the sexual pollution of our culture.

As members of the church we can encourage group dating to take the pressure off one-to-one pairing. We can encourage people to seek preengagement counseling with trusted older people in the Lord's family to discern the marriageability of the relationship (this is generally a more teachable moment than after the engagement is announced and the wedding date is set). We can teach biblical love and help people learn how to love one another with all the languages of love (from practical caring to verbal affirmation). We can empower laypeople to be involved in marriage ministry by linking mature married couples with engaged couples to do marriage preparation in the context of a home. Above all, we can work in the church to develop covenantal relationships, a for-better-or-worse type of church membership that is implicit in house churches and small groups, and so to communicate and foster covenant formation in marriages. We should not yield to the tendency in the Western world to reduce church life (and the marriages within that church) to a contract basis amounting to an exchange of goods and services for pay by agreed-upon terms. If the church can prayerfully assist in the redemption of the arranged-marriage system, it can also minister toward the redemption of the dating system.

Arranging Your Own Marriage

For Christians, a number of significant strategies are implicit in preparing for marriage and redeeming the dating system: (1) put the Lord's kingdom first; (2) pray to know God's will, whether it is to be single or married; (3) develop friendship relationships; (4) make a success of singleness, (5) become a marriageable person by developing the betrothal qualities of Hosea 2:19-20 (Stevens 1990, 47-55; *see* Character); (6) be open to special relationships; (7) build these relationships on social and spiritual friendship, expressing minimal physical affection and avoiding sexual entanglement; (8) keep your ministry priorities but do not regard the building of a relationship as a diversion from ministry or the spiritual life; (9) go out for a long time, preferably one to three years, spending as much time as possible in the home and with the family of your friend; (10) seek the counsel of mature believers and your parents, who know you better than most others; (11) speak your heart to your beloved; (12) wait for marriage for intimate sexual expression but prepare for it (see Stevens 1990, 63-75). Indeed, this last point may reveal the need for sexual healing before one can anticipate a life of sexual companionship and mutual sexual enjoyment. While the Bible does not offer specific directions on dating, it does provide a theological context in which to rethink it.

Toward a Theology of Dating
Dating relates to two great theological themes: friendship and marriage. On the latter, dating serves as one, though not the only, way to discover your marriage partner and discern marriage readiness in both yourself and your friend. Therefore all the following theological dimensions of marriage call us to see that dating becomes a relational ministry to the glory of God.

Marriage is part of God's creational design (Gen 1:27; 2:24); dating, while culturally determined in its present form, is potentially a means of conforming to God's law. God's creational design is leaving, cleaving and one flesh (Gen 2:24), the experience of which led to the first hymn of praise in the Bible (Gen 2:23). Dating one's marriage partner after marriage can strengthen the cleaving and continue, albeit in a more mature and changed way, the romance that is meant to be lifelong. Because of the ex-

clusivity of the marriage covenant, datinglike relationships with persons other than one's spouse are highly problematic, dangerous and usually an offense to the covenant.

Sexuality—and its call to relationality, complementarity and community—is part of what it means to be made in the image of God. Dating can be a way of experiencing Godlikeness—though not, of course, by experimenting with full marriage sexual communication. Each person dated is potentially someone else's marriage partner, so one must behave in a way that will not mark that person as one's spouse. Even an engagement can be broken.

Marriage is "Christian" through conformity to God's plan and intention in marriage (Gen 2:24; Hos; Mal 2:14; Mt 19:1-12), not simply because of the presence of two Christians or a church wedding; dating must be understood covenantally as a progressive preparation for covenant making and filling. Marriage is an exclusive, lifelong covenant in which there is total sharing of one's life; dating someone without faith is therefore highly problematic (though divinely ordained exceptions exist). A Christian should marry a person of the same faith (see 2 Cor 6:14-18, though it was originally written about a different subject).

People in dating relationships will struggle with the tendency of men to rule and control and of women to revolt or comply, neither of which is a good basis for marriage. Under the new covenant the curse is substantially reversed as Christ empowers couples to live with mutual submission (Eph 5:21); couples enjoying a dating relationship will need the continuous infilling of the Spirit in their relationship to learn mutual submission (Eph 5:18, 21).

The mystery of covenantal marriage is that God joins a couple together (Mt

19:6). Couples preparing for marriage through dating are called to reverence, prayerfulness and humility. This raises the question of the spirituality of dating as a preparation for marriage.

Toward a Spirituality of Dating

Because marriage is a parable of Christ and the church (Eph 5:32), the experience of unity through difference links us with God and makes sexuality contemplative (Gen 1:27). Dating therefore is a process of learning to cultivate gratitude for unity through difference.

Marriage is a vocation or calling, an all-embracing investment of ourselves in response to the summons of God that involves realignment of our relationship with parents (leaving), exclusive focusing on one special relationship (cleaving) and a private celebration of the covenant (one flesh). Dating that prepares for this is a process of spiritual discernment about the call and leading of God, not merely a process of making the best choice.

Marriage is a ministry through which all believers becomes actualized in mutual husband-wife ministry and in which we touch God through our spouse (Eph 5:21-33). Dating that prepares for marriage will be regarded not as recreational romance but as a form of ministry, even in playing* together. Further, all the issues of ministry are raised by marriage and dating: accepting someone else's spirituality, affirming God's work, refusing to play God, being interdependent, being spiritual friends (which can happen only between equals), trusting a loved one or friend to God and interceding on behalf of another.

Marriage is a spiritual discipline because it invites us Godward by requiring a level of cooperation humanly impossible. Marriage calls us to lay down our life daily for our spouse as to Christ (Eph 5:21-33). It constantly proposes that our

spirituality has to be down to earth (paying bills, raising a family, trying to say "I love you" and having sex). Marriage raises the question whether we are truly justified by faith and not by works by calling us to enjoy our spouse and not merely work with him or her. It calls us to renounce power and control and to become equippers of our spouse through empowerment. Marriage forces us to come to grips with ourselves—a person cannot role-play a marriage for very long—for our spouse is a mirror! Because of all this, dating that prepares for marriage is a school of Christian living.

Dating Without Marriage in View

Single people should be marriageable people, cultivating those qualities that make for both stability and quality in a marriage covenant: faithfulness, loving loyalty, compassion, justice and righteousness (Hos 2:19-20). Given the parameters outlined above, namely, that dating must be conducted in such a way that if one does not marry this person, no violation of the person sexually or emotionally would have taken place, then dating need not, in every case, be an active search for a partner. Indeed, some potentially vital friendships are spoiled by the pressure to head in the direction of marriage. Provided that both friends understand well the level of commitment (a very sensitive matter when one is anxious to find a mate), and provided that dating is not used for recreational sex, a series of dating partners may be a valuable way to learn about ourselves, the opposite sex and the ways of our God. Dating, like betrothal, can place us in a truly spiritual posture: learning, waiting, expecting and growing toward covenant readiness.

See also LOVE; MARRIAGE; SEXUALITY.

References and Resources

R. S. Anderson and D. Guernsey, *On Being*

Family: Essays in a Social Theology of the Family (Grand Rapids: Eerdmans, 1985); A. Fryling and R. Fryling, *A Handbook for Engaged Couples* (Downers Grove, Ill.: InterVarsity Press, 1996); J. Harris, *I Kissed Dating Goodbye* (Sisters, Ore.: Multnomah Press, 1997); J. Huggett, *Dating, Sex and Friendship* (Downers Grove, Ill.: InterVarsity Press, 1985); J. H. Olthius, *I Pledge You My Troth: A Christian View of Marriage, Family, Friendship* (New York: Harper & Row, 1975); C. M. Sell, *Family Ministry: The Enrichment of Family Life Through the Church* (Grand Rapids: Zondervan, 1981); R. P. Stevens, *Getting Ready for a Great Marriage* (Colorado Springs: NavPress, 1990); R. P. Stevens, *Marriage Spirituality: Ten Disciplines for Couples Who Love God* (Downers Grove, Ill.: InterVarsity Press, 1989); R. P. Stevens, *Married for Good: The Lost Art of Remaining Happily Married* (Downers Grove, Ill.: InterVarsity Press, 1986); R. P. Stevens and G. Stevens, *Marriage: Learning from Couples in Scripture*, Fisherman Bible Studies (Wheaton, Ill.: Harold Shaw, 1991); W. Trobisch, *I Married You* (London: Inter-Varsity Fellowship, 1971); E. L. Worthington, *Counseling Before Marriage* (Waco, Tex: Word, 1990); N. Wright, *The Premarital Counseling Handbook* (Chicago: Moody Press, 1992).

R. Paul Stevens

—DEATH—

My (Paul's) father died of pneumonia in my brother's arms after being unable to speak or eat for two years. He was not afraid to die, but he seemed to be lingering, hanging on, for reasons we could not discover. His wife had died months before, and there was no unfinished business known to us. My brother embraced him and said, "Dad, it's all right to go." And within minutes he died peacefully. But he left us wondering about the mystery of death, its timing, its meaning and the strange way that we are created by God to hang on to life, sometimes even longer than we need.

This article considers death as an occasion for theological reflection and spiritual contemplation and deals with letting go of ourselves. Grief is the process of letting go of others. Grief is an emotion of intense sadness resulting from loss. But death and grieving are related; the experience of losing others can teach us how to die and, because of that, how to live today in the light of eternity.

The Last Unmentionable Topic

Death is rarely discussed in polite company and has been tragically separated from everyday life. Instead of dying at home,* surrounded by relatives and friends, we normally die in a hospital surrounded by machines. Death has become institutionalized. Before medical science became capable of prolonging life by two or three decades, people expected death at any time, if not from disease, then from childbirth, famine, plague or war. But now people do not expect to die. Few people, except for those in the medical profession, actually see someone die, and dying for them is often surrounded by a sense of failure.

Death has also been sanitized. Instead of washing the person's body and digging the grave themselves, the family arranges for a mortician to prepare the body to be as "lifelike" as possible and displayed for all to see, though rarely in one's home. The funeral service takes place in a mortuary chapel, and the body is delivered hygienically to the flames or the soil. The cemetery is not likely to be found in the courtyard of the family church but in a place apart. It may never, or only rarely, be visited. To gain a theology and spirituality of death will involve recovering the connection between this once-in-a-lifetime experience and everyday living. To do that, we must also try to understand just what death is.

When Is Someone Dead?

Clinically, death is defined as "the cessation of heartbeat, breathing and brain activity." Yet it is widely recognized that a person as a body-soul-spirit being may have died hours and perhaps even months earlier. The ambiguity of the matter is highlighted by the intrusion of technology. Life can be artificially prolonged on machines, sometimes with the purpose of "harvesting" organs for transplants from a dead-yet-still-living being who will die in all respects once the machines are turned off. Or will he? Does the soul remain near for a while to be reunited should the person be resuscitated by starting the heart and breathing again? Did the person actually die when brain activity ceased, perhaps in a traumatic car accident, even though clinically the person remained living? Is it possible to die months before clinical death by becoming incapable of giving and receiving love, perhaps through a debilitating disease that puts the person in a "vegetative" state? If so, there are many walking dead in this world.

There were two trees in the Garden of Eden, the tree of life (presumably offering immortality; Gen 2:9) and the tree offering godlike knowledge of good and evil. Adam and Eve could live forever only if they accepted their creaturely limitations, eating from the first tree and refusing to eat from the second. If they took from the knowledge tree, they would die (Gen 3:3). But there were other dimensions of that than simply returning to the dust (Gen 3:19). They died to oneness with God (spiritual death), intimacy with each other (rela-

tional death) and trusteeship of the world (vocational death).

Could Adam and Eve, had they not sinned, have died of old age, perhaps in a transition like Enoch's that led to fuller life with God? We do not know. Significantly, the first death in the account was not God-inflicted but brought by humankind on itself: the murder of Abel. Equally significant is the growing consciousness of sin-cursed death by the characters of the drama exemplified in Cain's plea for protection from a violent death (Gen 4:14-15) and Eve's plea for a replacement son to fill the emptiness left by death (Gen 4:25). So whatever might have been possible in Paradise before human sin, death has become something terrible, something fraught with spiritual consequences, something to be feared.

The Right to Inflict Death

The judgment of Cain (Gen 4:1-16) shows that God does not want human beings to inflict death, either by taking the life of another through murder (Ex 20:13) or by ending life by one's own act through suicide. The time and manner of death are to be left in God's hands, whether death comes by disease, accident or some natural process. Consider the distinction between artificially prolonging a life and actively ending a life (euthanasia). While murder by an individual or group is prohibited in all of its forms, including physician-assisted death, execution by the state or nation (as a just penalty for a grievous sin) was prescribed by the Old Testament. Some Christians arguing from both testaments claim that capital punishment is state murder, though in contrast to this view, Luther maintained that even the hangman is God's servant bringing God's justice into this world.

We have much to learn about death from Jesus' own fate. It was a murder by the sinful religious establishment (expressing the violence in all human hearts against God), it was a state execution by the Roman government, but it was a voluntary death without being suicide. "No one takes it [my life] from me," he said, "but I lay it down of my own accord" (Jn 10:18). The voluntary aspect of his death is most deeply indicated by the statement that he committed his spirit to God (Lk 23:46) and "gave up his spirit" (Mt 27:50)—a powerful hint that while death is ultimately in God's hands, we may be permitted a part in relinquishing ourselves, something we observe happening with many people at the point of death. While Jesus' death has some unique dimensions as a sacrificial death for all, it is also "typical" in this way: it involved his whole person, not just his body.

Death of the Whole Person
Jesus tasted death for everyone (Heb 2:9), clearly indicating that whatever death has become through sin—in all of its psychological and spiritual consequences (Mt 27:46)—it was experienced by Jesus on the cross. Death is more than the mere stopping of the heart, breathing and brain activity.

Understood biblically, persons are not souls with bodily wrappings but ensouled bodies or embodied souls, a psychopneuma-somatic unity. The body does not "contain" a soul to be released through death—a fundamentally Greek notion that has permeated European culture. The body is the expressiveness of soul and soul the heart of body. But these are so interdependently connected, indeed interfused, that to touch either is to touch both—hence the seriousness of sexual sin. We do not "have" bodies and "have" souls but *are* bodies and souls. So death, to the Hebrew mind, cannot strike the body without striking the soul, a connection that is not clear in many translations that substitute "person" for "soul" or "body" (Pederson, 1:179). For example, "the soul that doeth aught presumptuously . . . shall be cut off from the people" (Num 15:30 KJV). However much we may qualify this in the light of passages like "today you will be with me in paradise" (Lk 23:43; see Cooper), we must still deal with death as death *of a person,* not just of a person's shell.

More than our bodies die: emotions, personality, capacity for relationships, for giving and receiving love.* Do our spirits die or at least "taste" death? We simply do not know whether we enter into a "soul-sleep" until the day of resurrection or persist in some kind of intermediate state, as it is called in theological texts, until Christ comes again and the dead are raised. What we do know is that death is more than a merely physical phenomenon. The whole person dies. We are obviously dealing with a mystery, but it is a mystery with windows.

A Vanquished Power
In all of this we admit we are facing a formidable power. Death holds people in slavery to lifelong fear (Heb 2:15). The fear may have multiple sources: fear of pain, the unknown, having to experience something we cannot control or predict, losing all that is familiar and dear to us. Many older people fear increasing withering, loss of dignity and independence. A profound fear is that we will plunge into nothingness. Deeper still is the fear of unpredictable consequences after the grave if there is a God. We are ultimately accountable to God, and the happy continuation into the "next" life is contingent on our performance in this life. Death is fraught with eternal consequences.

The fact that human beings cannot simply treat death as a way of recycling people illustrates what Scripture proclaims: death is one of the principalities and powers. Paul spoke of death as the last enemy (Rom 8:38; 1 Cor 15:26) because it seems death has a "life of its own," making its pretentious claims on human hearts and holding them captive to their mortality. This last enemy was destroyed by the death of Christ, this death of death being certified by the resurrection of Christ. For the Christian, death is not fraught with temporal fear or eternal consequences, as it is for those who have not yet heard the gospel. Yet we still must die.

Come Sweet Death

The epicenter of our hope for life through death is the resurrection of Jesus. Only one has come back from the dead to tell us about the other side. The Gospels record all we need to know about Jesus after his death: (1) he had a real body that could walk, cook, eat and speak—this was no mere phantom or angelic presence; (2) there is a continuity between the body in this life and the next, so much so that the disciples recognized him—a powerful hint that we may recognize one another in the New Jerusalem; (3) there were continuing evidences of things experienced in bodily life in this world, namely, the scars; (4) the scars were not now the marks of sin but a means of grace as Jesus invited Thomas to touch and believe.

In other words, our works done in this life are transfigured rather than annihilated. Even the creation itself will not be annihilated but transfigured (this being quite probably the meaning in 2 Pet 3:10). Ezekiel envisions the land "radiant" with the glory of God (Ezek 43:2), a prophetic announcement that the earth will become "a new earth" (Rev 21:1) just as the psychological body (literal Greek; "natural" NIV) will be transfigured into a "spiritual body" (1 Cor 15:44). In other words, the Christian hope is not the survival of the spirit after the death of the body or even the continuation of immortal (but disembodied) soul in a nonmaterial "heaven" or the provision of another body, soul and spirit to be given us through reincarnation.

Christian hope promises a renewal not a replacement. Our bodies, souls and spirits are transfigured and "will be like his [Christ's] glorious body" (Phil 3:21). Christians see death in a sacramental way: a physical experience through which a spiritual grace is mediated. In this case the spiritual grace is located in the promise of resurrection. Even personality defects in this life get healed, but not by our becoming *different* persons. In Christ we more than survive the grave; we triumph over it.

The Art of Dying

First, we must repudiate the death denial of Western culture. Deaths of relatives and friends provide good opportunities in a family context to discuss what death means and to declare the Christian hope. The thoughtful preparation of our last will* and testament helps us prepare and contemplate what inheritance, material and nonmaterial, we leave behind.

Second, living Christianly involves the idea of dual citizenship: living simultaneously in this world and the next. We are equidistant from eternity every moment of our life from conception* to resurrection. We treasure life as good and flourish on earth, but it is not the highest good. We resist death as evil but not the greatest evil, because it is the way to a better world.

Third, we can number our days. This is not done by calculating our expected life span and then squeezing all we can into the remaining years because there is nothing more (or because eternity is just more of the same). This view unfortunately treats time as a resource to be managed rather than a gift. Rather numbering our days means treating every day as a gift, being aware that it may be our last, yet investing ourselves, talents and all in a world without end (compare Mt 25:1-13). We do not live "on borrowed time" but on entrusted time. So we live one day at a time, not bearing tomorrow's burdens and anxieties today (Mt 6:25-34) but trusting that God will be sufficient for each day that we live.

Fourth, everyday hardships give us an opportunity to learn to "die daily." Through these pains, persecutions and weaknesses that we suffer, we are able to live in the resurrection power of Christ, dying to self, living in him (2 Cor 4:10-12, 16-18).

Fifth, we can practice progressive relinquishment. As we go through life, we relinquish childhood and youth, our friends and parents through death, our children as they leave home (see Empty Nesting) and eventually our occupations and health. Most people will discover the hard words of the marriage vow, "until death do us part." Ultimately we must relinquish life in this world. We are left with the one treasure of inestimable value—the Lord. One of the Ignatian exercises invites us to contemplate our own death using our imaginations and doing so prayerfully in the Lord's presence: people gathering around our bed, the funeral, the burial, the gradual decomposition of our body until all that we were as a person in this life has dissolved and we are ready for full transfiguration. Are we ready to die? Are there broken relationships to be mended, persons to be forgiven, debts to settle? Is there something we can do for someone that we have been putting off?

The philosopher George Santayana said, "There is no cure for birth and death save to enjoy the interval" (quoted in Jones, 30). This accurately expresses the practical theology of a generation that denies death, fails to believe in a new heaven and earth and therefore is preoccupied with fitness, health* and pleasure. But the Christian approach, as J. I. Packer once said, is to "regard readiness to die as the first step in learning to live" (quoted in Jones, 30).

See also DEPRESSION; FAMILY SYSTEMS; WILL, LAST.

References and Resources

D. Augsburger, "Grieving," in The Complete Book of Everyday Christianity, ed. R. Banks and R. P. Stevens (Downers Grove, Ill.: Inter-Varsity Press, 1997) 469-71; J. W. Cooper, Body, Soul & Life Everlasting: Biblical Anthropology and the Monism-Dualism Debate (Grand Rapids: Eerdmans, 1989); O. Cullmann, Immortality of the Soul or Resurrection of the Dead? (London: Epworth, 1958); C. D. Exelrod, "Reflections on the Fear of Death," Omega 17, no. 1 (1986-1987) 51-64; T. K. Jones, "Death: Real Meaning in Life Is to Be Found Beyond Life," Christianity Today 35 (June 24, 1991) 30-31; G. Meilaender, "Mortality: The Measure of Our Days," First Things 10 (February 1991) 14-21; K. Mitchell and H. Anderson, All Our Losses, All our Griefs (Philadelphia: Westminster Press, 1982); J. Moltmann, Theology of Hope, trans. J. W. Leitch (New York: Harper & Row, 1967); R. Neale, The Art of Dying (New York: Harper & Row, 1974); J. Pedersen, Israel: Its Life and Culture, 4 vols. (London: Geoffrey Cumberlege, 1964); W. Perkins, "The Golden Chain," in The Work of William Perkins, ed. I. Breward (Appleford, U.K.: Courtney, 1970); E. Trueblood, The Common Ventures of Life: Marriage, Birth, Work and Death (New York: Harper & Row, 1949); G. Westberg, Good Grief (Philadelphia: Fortress, 1962).

Gail C. Stevens and R. Paul Stevens

—DEBT—

While debt has been a subject of considerable discussion in Christian circles for a long time, it was probably the explosion of business and personal bankruptcies in the 1980s that brought unusual attention to the topic and even caused some Christians to doubt their standing before God.

Many Christian commentators were quick to condemn Christians who took this avenue of escape from their debts. American businessperson and author Albert J. Johnson suggested that those considering voluntary bankruptcy to resolve debt problems should read Psalm 37:21, "The wicked borrow and do not repay." He argued that a person considering bankruptcy was in financial trouble because of past violations of scriptural principles (Johnson, 82, 85). Financial and business adviser Larry Burkett is similarly outspoken, as is evident in one of his taped addresses:

Now isn't that amazing to you, that somebody would actually default on a debt that they created legally, morally, ethically, and then they would default on it? See, it ought to never happen with Christianity, or it should happen so rarely that we would take that person, and we would admonish them according to Matthew 18, and bring them before the church to restore them back to the faith.

This hard-nosed attitude toward bankruptcy is sometimes held toward taking on debt generally. Some commentators have argued that debt is a substitute for trust in God and that to be truly effective a Christian must be financially free. Furthermore, debts are viewed as lifelong obligations, ruling out any possibility of their being forgiven via the bankruptcy process. Taken to its extreme, financial success is, in some circles, linked with divine favor and right standing before God, while debt problems are seen as an indication of a Satan-defeated life.

Given the fact that North Americans have taken so readily to consumer and business credit and that indebtedness has become a normal aspect of life for many Christians, it is crucial to know just what the Bible says, and does not say, about the topic of debt. This will enable us to come to sound conclusions about the use of credit.

Is Debt Evil?

The biblical message concerning debt appears at quick glance to be a mixed one. On the one hand, many times God's people are urged to lend to the needy. Deuteronomy 15:7-10 is particularly forceful:

If there is a poor man among your brothers . . . do not be hardhearted or tightfisted toward your poor brother. Rather be openhanded and freely lend him whatever he needs. Be careful not to harbor this wicked thought: "The seventh year, the year for canceling debts, is near," so that you do not show ill will toward your needy brother and give him nothing. He may then appeal to the LORD against you, and you will be found guilty of sin. Give generously to him and do so without a grudging heart; then because of this the LORD your God will bless you in all your work and in everything you put your hand to.

Our Lord takes a similar view with one's enemies: "Love your enemies, do good to them, and lend to them without expecting to get anything back. Then your reward will be great, and you will be sons of the Most High, because he is kind to the ungrateful and wicked" (Lk 6:35) and "Give to the one who asks you, and do not turn away from the one who wants to borrow from you" (Mt 5:42).

On the other hand, in the Bible we see borrowers, desperate to avoid the exactions of hardhearted creditors, attempting to persuade a third party to act as a guarantor for their debts. The Old Testament frequently warns against this practice (Prov 6:1-5; 11:15; 17:18; 22:26-27). In fact, being in debt is sometimes linked with being in a hopelessly vulnerable situation, as Proverbs 22:7 suggests: "The rich rule over the poor, / and the borrower is servant to the lender" (see further Deut 15:6; 28:12, 44). We also have the Pauline injunction: "Avoid getting into debt, except the debt of mutual love" (Rom 13:8 JB).

Given the many times that God's people are urged to lend, compassionately and generously, to the needy, it would be ridiculous to assert that borrowing, and therefore debt, is evil. However, it is realistic to conclude that incurring debt can be dangerous. This two-edged characteristic is typical of most aspects of material life from the biblical point of view. For example, wealth and property can be seen as gifts from God and even as a reward for obedient living (Deut 28:1-14). Their value is in the opportunities that they provide for increased service to humanity (2 Cor 9:11), rather than for self-indulgent use (Lk 8:14). But material wealth, at the same time, is one of the chief obstacles to salvation (Lk 12:13-21; 16:19-31; 18:24-25).

One cannot arbitrarily conclude, then, that debt is inherently evil. God would not command his people to proffer help that was wrong to receive. But debt, like so many other aspects of economic life, can be abused by the lender and borrower alike. Thus, care must be taken to use debt wisely.

What Was the Purpose of Debt?

In Pentateuchal times Israelites were involved almost exclusively in agriculture. The most common commercial participant in those days was the traveling merchant, called simply a "foreigner" (Deut 23:20) or sometimes a "Canaanite" (Zech 14:21). While Israelites were to lend to their fellow Israelite farmers interest free, making loans with interest to foreigners (or traders) was permissible.

It was with respect to the interest-free loans to covenant brothers and sisters that the lender was urged to be compassionate, taking minimal collateral and forgiving unpaid debts by the sabbatical year. Loans would have typically been solicited not for commercial investment purposes but as a result of economic hardship (Judg 6:1-4). Borrowing was an indication of serious financial trouble, imperiling the well-being of the family unit, which was the fundamental building block of society. Thus, while the debtor was to be treated with great compassion, he or she was usually in debt not because of self-indulgent motives but because of the inability to meet the basic needs of life.

Commercial debt is mentioned but with very little comment. Clearly it was not wrong for God's people to be involved in commercial investments. They had to recognize, of course, that a loan carried with it not only responsibilities but also dangers, whether of loss or of exploitation. (This is evident in the many warnings about unwise involvement with lenders that could bring a borrower to the point of losing personal independence.)

So we see two kinds of debt in the Old Testament: interest-bearing loans to foreigners and interest-free loans to fellow Israelites. It was with respect to fellow Israelites that more well-to-do Israelites were enjoined to be generous and forgiving. So important was this principle to God that it even appears in the Lord's Prayer as the perfect example of godly forgiveness (Mt 6:12: "Forgive us our debts, as we also have forgiven our debtors"). Neither of these types of debt is condemned. But the former tends to be discussed within the context of risk and the need to avoid being exploited. The latter is found within the context of generosity and forgiveness and the requirement not to exploit.

Are Debts Forgivable?

According to biblical teaching, borrowers were obliged under normal circumstances to repay their debts. This responsibility to meet one's financial obligations is vividly illustrated by a provision recorded in Leviticus 25:39. Here a debtor in default could go so far as to sell himself into slavery. However, the possibility of those debts being canceled (or debt-slaves released) was not ruled out. In accordance with sabbatical-year legislation, debtors were automatically relieved of their obligations every seventh year, whether or not they deserved compassionate treatment.

Compassion of this sort—the setting aside of the legitimate rights of lenders—was typical of all economic relations envisioned in the covenant community. God's desire for his people was that they would enjoy economic stability and security as family units. Wealth was viewed as a divine blessing (Deut 8:11-18; 28:1-14). This blessing was associated with God's people living in obedience and was based totally on God's compassion. Such financial mechanisms as the poor tithe* (Deut 14:28-29; 26:12), gleaning in the field (Deut 24:19) and interest-free loans (Ex 22:25-27; Lev 25:35-37; Deut 23:19-20) were tangible ways by which God's people could show compassion for each other. God provided the sabbatical year and

Jubilee to ensure that temporary misfortune barred no family from full participation in economic life (see Ex 21:2; 23:11; Lev 25:1-7; Deut 15:1-15).

It is important to keep two points in mind. The cancellation of debts in the Old Testament was done at legislated intervals—every seventh year (sabbatical year) and every seven sabbaticals (Jubilee year)—regardless of the performance of the debtor. In addition, these borrowers were not involved in commercial life. They were usually poor farmers borrowing to preserve their ability to make a living and feed their families. But the principle that can be legitimately extracted from the biblical model and applied to our modern free-market economies today is that while taken seriously, debt could be canceled to achieve some higher purpose, such as the preservation of the family* unit. No desirable goal is achieved when unscrupulous debtors are allowed to escape from their financial obligations. But the Old Testament did provide for the cancellation of debts as an act of mercy, with no stigma attached.

Conclusion

Debt is a morally neutral concept. Never are God's people told that debt is wrong—quite the opposite! In fact, one of the reasons that God entrusts his people with material means is because "there should be no poor among you" (Deut 15:4). Loans were one way of restoring the poor to economic stability, especially if the lending was accompanied by a merciful and forgiving attitude. Well-off Israelites could also participate in commercial ventures provided that they made careful allowances for the risks involved. But access to loans brings with it all of the temptations associated with material life: self-indulgence, riskiness and exploitation. Debt is a two-edged sword to be handled with care.

See also ALLOWANCES; CREDIT CARD; MONEY; TITHING.

References and Resources

L. Burkett, *God's Principles for Operating a* *Business* (Dahlonega, Ga.: Christian Financial Concepts, 1982), audiocassette; A. J. Johnson, *A Christian's Guide to Family Finances* (Wheaton, Ill.: Victor, 1983).

John R. Sutherland

—DEPRESSION—

Depression is the most common and often most misunderstood of all the painful emotions. Despite the fact that Scripture presents clear examples of depression (Elijah, Saul, David and Paul) and in the history of great preachers (Luther, Wesley and Spurgeon), Christians have tended to hold to the belief that to be depressed is a sign of failure or spiritual weakness. We have failed to grasp the naturalness of depression and the fact that often it has biological origins. Even the severest of depressions can have healing benefits if we strive to understand its purpose. Because so many do not understand the depressive process, they feel like spiritual failures.

How common is depression? One out of every eighteen adults suffers from a clinical depression at any one time. In a church of 250 members this means that at least fourteen parishioners could be suffering from an incapacitating depression. One in five adults will experience a severe depression at least once in their lifetime. This reality about the commonness of depression cannot be avoided. What people need is clear guidance on when it is a normal process that should be left to take its course and when it is necessary to seek treatment.

Current Progress in Understanding Depression

Progress has been made in providing relief for this debilitating condition. We have gone from virtually no effective treatment for the biological depressions (electroconvulsive shock treatment was the only help available for a long time) to a rich armament of effective medications that are not addicting and have minimal side effects. Yet many Christians turn their backs on this help, fearing that they will be stigmatized, become drug addicts or, worse, find that their problem is spiritual and not psychological or biological. The result is unnecessary suffering by millions of Christians, as well as by family members who must stand by and try to cope with a dysfunctional loved one.

Why Is Depression So Common?

While the more serious depressions are essentially biochemical in origin with a strong genetic tendency, stress seems to be a major aggravating cause. The frantic pace of modern life combined with a breakdown of traditional values* is causing many to feel hopeless, uncertain and disappointed. This stress aggravates the genetic factors that predispose to biological depressions. It also sets the stage for an appalling sense of loss, which is the primary cause of psychological depressions. Demoralization is rampant in our modern culture and can turn an even minor setback into a major depression in a body overextended by stress.

Many losses in our modern world are tangible and material. More significant, however, in causing psychological depression are such losses as insecurity,

92

uncertainty, rejection, lack of job fulfillment and a general sense of the meaninglessness of life. These are losses that were not as prevalent in earlier times. As a culture we may well have entered our own emotional "Great Depression."

The Cost of Depression
Estimating the emotional and human costs of serious depression, in the lives of both those who are depressed and the family members and friends who must suffer alongside, is almost impossible. Major depression always disrupts, and sometimes disintegrates, otherwise healthy families* whose lives are turned topsy-turvy by the emotional devastation of one member unable to function normally (see Family Systems). Should the depressed person commit suicide, the consequences can continue for the rest of a family's lifetime.

In times past, depression was always associated with a major mental breakdown and seemed to be restricted to a few poorly adjusted, usually anonymous persons. Now it has assumed a common, familiar and very personal identity for all of us. It is found with frightening regularity in ourselves, our relatives and friends. There is hardly a family today that is not touched by depression.

Who Is at Risk?
Depression is no respecter of age, sex, socioeconomic status or occupation. In fact, the dramatic increase in depression in both the very young and the elderly is among the most frightening features of modern-day depression.

Women, however, are significantly at greater risk for depression than men (a two to one ratio). The reproductive biochemistry of the female body implicates depression more often. At various times during the menstrual cycle, as well as in the lifecycle of reproduction, depression results from hormonal changes. Prob-

lems with depression just before menstruation* (premenstrual syndrome) as well as later in life (menopausal depression) are extremely common.

Dealing with Depression
Nothing is as tough to fight as depression. It robs you of the energy and motivation to do anything about it. Untreated biological depressions are often debilitating and can last up to three years during each attack.

For some the depression hits with an alarming, unannounced suddenness. For others it stalks up insidiously and may go unrecognized for months or years.* When sufferers finally realize that they are in its grasp, it has already sapped their strength and fogged up their mind so that they do not believe anything can be done to help.

Alarmingly, only about one-third of those seriously depressed will actually seek treatment. Some do not know they can be helped. Some are afraid to admit they need help because it might stigmatize them. Some are callously told by their pastor or Christian friends that they should just pray harder or try to find the sin that is causing the depression. Most do not seek treatment because they are too depressed and feel too hopeless to believe they can get better; they try to "tough it out." Unfortunately, this can have serious consequences not only for the sufferer but for all those connected to him or her. They do not realize that with the right sort of treatment they could probably bounce back in a matter of weeks and, more important, prevent any recurring episodes of their depression later in life.

How Can You Tell If You Are Depressed?
One of the most unfortunate secondary effects of depression is that it often causes the sufferer to be oblivious to the de-

pression. Depression eludes recognition, especially in the less severe types. Some people can be depressed for a long time, therefore, and not realize it. Depression can also mask itself in irritability, fatigue and workaholism. Many who overeat do so as a form of "self-medication" to ease their dejected state (see Eating). Even when someone vaguely knows he or she is depressed, there is a tendency to deny the depression. Depression is often mistakenly viewed as a weakness, and people fear that even acknowledging their emotional pain to themselves is an admission of defeat.

So a large percentage of people with depression do not get appropriate treatment because they do not recognize their depressive symptoms. Religious sufferers tend to spiritualize their condition and want to blame God, Satan or some spiritual failure for their malady. The first step, then, in getting help is to recognize the symptoms and acknowledge that one is depressed.

What Are the Symptoms?
The following are among the most common symptoms of depression: persistent sadness, anxiety or an "empty" mood; a sense of hopelessness and pessimism; feelings of guilt, worthlessness, helplessness; crying at the slightest provocation; loss of interest or pleasure in ordinary and pleasurable activities, including sex,* sleep* disturbances such as insomnia, early-morning waking or oversleeping; eating* disturbances (either loss or gain in weight); fatigue; thoughts of death* or suicide; restlessness and irritability; difficulty in concentrating, in remembering and in making decisions; and physical symptoms (headaches, digestive disorders and chronic pain).

In all depressions, fatigue is a prominent symptom. This is particularly true for the biologically based depressions that tend to drain energy. There is also a general lack of interest in normal activities. Sadness or crying may or may not be present. In some, sadness is the least important sign of depression.

Getting Help
How one copes with depression depends on its cause. Since all depressions fall basically into two categories, endogenous (or biological) and exogenous (or psychological), this discussion will focus on each in turn and provide some treatment guidelines.

Endogenous depressions. Endogenous literally means "from within." Since there are many biological causes for depression, treatment must be directed primarily at the underlying disease or biochemical disorder. Besides obvious serious illnesses such as cancer or heart disease, disruption of the endocrine system is a particularly common cause of many depressions. So whenever a biological depression is suspected, a thorough evaluation of the endocrine system, particularly the thyroid gland, is warranted.

When endocrine dysfunction is ruled out, attention turns to the nervous system and the brain's chemistry. The cause of two of the most common forms of endogenous depressions—major depression and bipolar disorder (the sufferer alternates between mania and depression)—lies clearly in a deficiency of a neurotransmitter within the brain's nervous system. Fortunately, there are now very effective antidepressant medications available that can correct these deficiencies.

While a complete discussion of these medications is not possible here, the following important points need to be stressed:

☐ Not everyone benefits from the same antidepressant. Individualized treatment is therefore essential.

☐ Antidepressant medications do not act

immediately; they take between two and four weeks, or even longer, after the appropriate level of treatment has been reached before relief is experienced. Persistence in treatment is therefore essential.

☐ Modern antidepressant medications have far fewer side effects than earlier ones and are perfectly safe when taken under supervision for long periods of time. Do not be in a hurry to stop them.

☐ Antidepressant medications are not addicting. They may be taken without fear of becoming dependent on them.

Exogenous or reactive depression. While these depressions are not usually as serious as the biological ones, they can be much more difficult to cope with. There is no medication to speak of that treats them. Besides, since they are a reaction to loss, medication is most times inappropriate. What is needed is the more painful work of grieving.

Reactive depression is essentially a call to let go of whatever it is we have lost. God has designed us for grief, so that whether the loss is the death of a loved one, the departure of our first child to college, getting fired from a job or a business venture that has gone bad, we have to face this loss with courage and allow ourselves to grieve. Ecclesiastes tells us that "to every thing there is a season" (3:1 KJV) and that there is "a time to weep" (3:4). This is what reactive depression is all about. It is a healing time to help us cope with loss.

The grief work needed for a major loss can seldom be accomplished without talking it through with someone else. Consulting a professional counselor, preferably a Christian, is almost es-

sential in more severe depressive reactions. However, an understanding pastor, lay counselor or friend can also be tremendously helpful.

Whatever resource is used, the following important points must be kept in mind:

☐ Grief work takes time, so do not be hurried. The more significant the loss, the longer it will take to get over it and the deeper will be the depression.

☐ Do not try to short-circuit your depression by rushing to replace your loss. Sooner or later your mind will bring you back to complete your grieving for past losses.

☐ Invite God to be a part of your grieving. Do not blame him for your loss, and there is certainly nothing to be gained by getting angry at him. He knows your pain and longs to be your comforter, so do not turn your back on him.

☐ Within every grief experience there is great potential for spiritual and personal growth. Embrace your experience with the full confidence that when you come out of the fire you will be a little better for it (Job 23:10).

See also DEATH; FAMILY SYSTEMS; PROBLEMS.

References and Resources

Dean Foundation for Health, Research and Education, *Depression and Antidepressants* (Madison, Wis.: Dean Foundation, 1995); A. D. Hart, *Counseling the Depressed* (Waco, Tex.: Word, 1987); A. D. Hart, *Dark Clouds, Silver Linings* (Colorado Springs: Focus on the Family, 1993); U.S. Department of Health and Human Services, *Depression in Primary Care: Detection, Diagnosis and Treatment* (Washington, D.C.: U.S. Government Printing Office, 1993).

Archibald D. Hart

—DISCIPLINE—

Many parents, when they think of the word *discipline,* think of punishment directed toward changing the behavior of their children. When children misbehave, parents are understandably concerned about how to change such behavior and prevent its reoccurrence. Larger issues, such as their children's character* development, are also important to parents. These more abstract goals, however, can easily be overwhelmed by the more concrete worries that surround problem behavior.

Popular Approaches

Many parenting manuals from the 1970s to the present are based on concepts that derive from a limited number of theoretical approaches. Those based on behaviorist and social learning principles give the most explicit direction on how to modify children's behavior. Adopted by both Christian and secular writers (e.g., Dobson, Peters), these principles show parents how to manage child behavior through a carefully orchestrated system of reward and punishment. Rewards can be tangible (e.g., some desired object or activity) or social (e.g., praise). Punishment also takes many forms (e.g., removal of privileges, time-outs, physical pain, disapproval).

Opinions are divided as to the advisability of these strategies. Behavioral techniques succeed at changing behavior, but questions have been raised regarding longer-term consequences. Some studies, for example, demonstrate that kids who are physically punished become more aggressive. A more fundamental issue, however, is whether behavioral methods teach the lessons that parents want their children to learn. Parents do not simply want to control their children's behavior; they want them to learn self-control. Parents want their children to do what is right for the right reasons and not simply because they are made to. Research, however, suggests that in many cases it is the rewards and punishments that children remember, and not the moral or social lessons that parents wanted to teach.

Nevertheless, advocates of behavioral approaches argue that long-term changes in behavior will change a child's attitudes.

Other approaches make the learning of self-discipline more central than behavior change. The humanistic approach of Thomas Gordon, as well as advice based on the psychology of Alfred Adler, insists that self-discipline cannot be imposed from without.

Adlerians substitute the concept of *logical consequences* for punishment. Touching a hot stove has immediate consequences, and the lesson usually does not need to be repeated. These are called *natural consequences.* By extension, logical consequences are those set up by parents and must have a logical and explainable relationship to the behavior in question. Telling a child who behaves aggressively with other children that she will have to be sidelined until she is ready to cooperate is logical; spanking her is not. In this view, then, the child readily learns self-discipline if the connection between behavior and its consequences is clear.

Gordon, however, views even logical consequences as a form of punishment because it relies on coercion by the parent, who sets the rules and enforces them. Gordon prefers a more egalitarian relationship between parent and child, where parental authority lies in areas such as superior life expertise more than in their ability to control. He emphasizes creating the right kind of relationship, a way of communicating with children that is both respectful of their feelings and honest, and trusts them to come up with their own solutions to problems.

How does a Christian parent respond to the broad range of advice presented in these books? There is more at stake in discipline than just the correction of troublesome behavior. For Christians, the theme of discipleship encompasses the larger issues of character development raised earlier and helps to provide a context for a more comprehensive understanding of the parenting role.

Discipline and Discipleship

It is important to observe that the Bible does not make a clear distinction between discipline and punishment, for example, "the Lord disciplines those he loves, and he punishes everyone he accepts as a son" (Heb 12:6). The structure of the verse suggests that discipline and punishment are parallel concepts. Furthermore, though the words translated here as "disciplines" and "punishes" are distinct in the Greek, they are used by Luke and John respectively to refer to the same incident: the flogging of Jesus by the Roman garrison (Lk 23:16, 22; Jn 19:1).

This does not mean, however, that parents should equate discipline with simple punishment. The larger biblical context of passages emphasizes God's relationship of covenant love with his people. God's demands for obedience are based on this covenant relationship, not on an arbitrary exercise of power over creation. An appropriate way to capture this more relationally oriented understanding is through the notion of discipleship.

A diverse array of parent advisors (e.g., Bettelheim, Nelsen, Rosemond) have already recognized the connection between discipline and discipleship. Understanding parenting* as discipleship emphasizes the quality of the teaching relationship between parent and child, rather than focusing on punishment and behavior change. As columnist John Rosemond writes, "Discipline is the process by which parents make disciples of their children, a child-disciple being one who pays close attention to his parents and follows their lead" (170).

How might the concept of discipleship change the way Christians think about discipline? Although many insights are possible, at least three areas deserve mention: the personal discipleship of the parent, a foundation of respect for children, and the importance of understanding and empathy.

The Parent as Disciple

When we are frustrated with our children, it is easy to focus almost exclusively on their misbehavior. This severely limits any discussion of discipline. Whether or not a parent lashes out in anger and name-calling is first a matter of the parent's own discipleship to Christ (cf. Mt 5:22).

In an important sense, children are already disciples of their parents, learning more from what they do than what they say. Children are very sensitive to hypocrisy and will know quickly whether or not parents who claim to follow Christ truly believe what they profess.

The discipline that we apply to our children should always be considered in light of God's discipline of us—with grace and mercy. The proper stance is one of humility. The question of how we might change a child's behavior must be subjected to the larger question of how we might tangibly demonstrate to them the reality of God's covenant love.

Respecting Our Children

Throughout history, children have been relatively powerless in the face of adults. Our own age is probably more tolerant and indulgent of children's needs than any that came before, due in large part to theories that were interpreted to support "permissive" child-rearing methods. Nevertheless, Christian parents must ask themselves if they identify more with Jesus, who embraced and blessed children, or the disciples who were ready to dismiss them as having little significance in a world of adults (Mk 10:13-16).

What does this mean for discipline? Christian parents who quote, "Children, obey your parents in the Lord, for this is right" are often less aware of the verse that comes shortly thereafter: "Fathers, do not exasperate your children" (Eph 6:1, 4). Many parenting experts would agree that much child misbehavior is a product of their frustration that their own feelings, ideas and opinions are not taken seriously.

Approaches to discipline that encourage a more authoritarian, power-assertive stance are more likely to lead to violations of respect. This does not mean, however, that the opposite style of permissiveness is the answer. What some experts call "authoritative" parenting successfully steers a middle course, combining a warm, nurturing style with the consistent and reasonable limits that children need (Baumrind). For Christians, the key is in the attitude with which we approach our children when matters of discipline arise. Remembering our own discipleship means approaching our children with humility. More than this, we respect our children because we know that they are the objects of God's love,* even when needing correction.

Understanding and Empathy

Finally, Christian parents should reflect on the fact that God does not simply deal with human rebellion "from on high." In the ultimate act of love, God became one of us, serving humanity to the point of dying in humiliation on the cross. As Paul interprets discipleship, it is this attitude of service that Christians should emulate (Phil 2:5-8).

What might this mean in practical parenting terms? If respect entails that we remember that God takes children seriously and commends a childlike heart to all his disciples, empathy takes this one step further. In empathy we attempt to understand our children, to see the world from their perspective. We were all children once; though sometimes painful, we can remember what it was like. To do this opens the possibility of greater compassion for what it means to be a small person in a world of a grown-ups.

An empathetic understanding of children may have many components. First, a basic knowledge of child development is important. Such knowledge helps ensure that parental expectations are appropriate to a child's age-related capabilities. Second, it is also helpful to know the ways in which children differ from one another from the moment of birth. The concept of *temperament* is useful here. What may appear to be sheer disobedience or willfulness on the part of a child may be related to biologically rooted differences in how children experience the world and express themselves.

More generally, we can recognize that we ourselves frequently feel misunderstood and would not listen well to someone who declared that we were simply wrong or acting immaturely. This is just as true of parents and children as it is of any other relationship. Children only gradually come to see the world from an adult perspective. In our own impatience, however, we often assume that they *should* understand much more than they already do or can.

Empathy for others is a crucial character quality we want our children to develop. The ability to understand how others feel, particularly as a result of one's own behavior, is a key element of moral development. Family researcher John Gottman argues that emotional empathy is the foundation for creating the kind of relationship in which children learn to adopt the values and limits set by their parents.

In summary, coercive discipline methods can succeed in making children comply with parental standards, at least temporarily. In some cases, if the methods used are not overly coercive, changes in behavior may indeed lead to positive changes in attitude. Christian parents, however, must look beyond behavior change and seek intentionally to create a climate of discipleship with their children. While parents should set and enforce reasonable limits, and actively teach standards of right and wrong, they should do so from a posture of humility, respect and empathy.

These goals, of course, do not apply only to Christian parents. If, however, discipleship is the proper context of discipline, then Christian parents will strive to embody the character appropriate to one who follows Jesus, as they in turn guide the children who are following them. Good discipline requires patience and understanding, and a consistent focus on the long-term character goals we have for our children.

Reading the Gospels we are struck by Jesus' patience with his disciples. He had high expectations of them, even knowing their shortcomings. Occasionally he resorted to rebuke. Above all, however, he led by example. The character of the disciples was formed in the crucible of their daily interaction with their teacher, watching how he responded to the challenges of life. Similarly, discipline informed by discipleship

takes time, far beyond the moments in which we hurriedly try to determine how to handle misbehavior, when we are pressured with conflicting and highly charged emotions. Discipleship also cannot be relegated to brief segments of "quality time." All of our time belongs to God, and if we are serious about discipleship, we must adjust our priorities regarding discipline accordingly.

See also CHARACTER; COMMUNICATION; CONFLICT RESOLUTION; GOALS; LOVE; PARENTING; SELF-ESTEEM; SHAME; VALUES.

References and Resources

D. Baumrind, "The Development of Instrumental Competence Through Socialization," in *Minnesota Symposium on Child Psychology*, ed. A. D. Pick, vol. 7 (Minneapolis: University of Minnesota Press, 1973); Bruno Bettelheim, "Punishment vs. Discipline," *Atlantic Monthly* (November 1985) 51-59; S. Chess and A. Thomas, *Know Your Child* (New York: Basic, 1987); R. Coles, *The Moral Intelligence of Children* (New York: Random House, 1997); W. Damon, *The Moral Child* (New York: Free Press, 1988); D. Dinkmeyer Sr., G. McKay and D. Dinkmeyer Jr., *The Parent's Handbook: Systematic Training for Effective Parenting* (Circle Pines, Minn.: American Guidance Service, 1997); J. Dobson, *Dare to Discipline* (Wheaton, Ill.: Tyndale House, 1970); R. Dreikurs and V. Soltz, *Children: The Challenge* (New York: Duell, Sloan, and Pearce, 1964); T. Gordon, *Parent Effectiveness Training* (New York: Wyden, 1970); T. Gordon, *Discipline That Works* (New York: Times Books, 1989); J. Gottman, *The Heart of Parenting* (New York: Simon & Schuster, 1997); J. Nelsen, *Positive Discipline*, rev. ed. (New York: Ballantine, 1996); R. Peters, *Do Not Be Afraid to Discipline* (New York: Golden Books, 1997); J. Rosemond, *A Family of Value* (Kansas City: Andrews and McMeel, 1995).

Cameron Lee

—DIVORCE—

Divorce is a tragic dimension of life. With so many marriages ending in divorce, many people are skipping marriage* altogether and are simply cohabiting. Others want to get married "until death do us part," as the vows state, but enter marriage with a deep fear that they may become a statistic. Still others, influenced by a culture of "throwaway" relationships, enter marriage with an emotional loophole, thinking (often unconsciously), *If it doesn't work out we can always get a divorce.* Rather than being a covenant for lifelong companionship, marriage today is frequently reduced to a contract for the mutual meeting of needs. "So long as we both shall live" has become "so long as we both shall love." Taken in its best light, divorce is regarded by many as part of the process of personal growth. But the negative consequences for children, families,* society, morality, mental health and education are well documented.

Approaching the Divorce Question

This article is concerned with the theology and spirituality of divorce: how we are to think about it, how divorce affects our relationship with God, and how we are to relate to this phenomenon in the world today. It must be said at the outset that nobody likes divorce (except some who profit financially from it), and few want to get divorced. Further, those people who have been divorced have not committed the unforgivable sin and are in deep need of love* and acceptance.

A theology of divorce must rest on the Bible rather than on statistics, social mores or expediency. When it comes to divorce, taking the Bible as authority is a complicated matter. The church has tried to understand the divorce question in at least three ways: (1) through a legalistic interpretation of Scripture to find the permissible grounds, (2) by interpreting Scripture to find out whether the hard passages are really for today or some other age and (3) through biblical theology that considers two realities—Scripture and contemporary culture.

It is difficult to speak of divorce and marriage at the same time. That seems to have been Jesus' dilemma when he was pressed with questions about the legality of divorce by his contemporaries (Mt 19:3-4). In effect, he said, "I can't speak about divorce until I have brought you back to God's intention in Genesis, which takes us beyond culture into the paradise of God. When two are united by God and have become one, you would be tearing apart a God-given unity if you divorced them." While Jesus does not say that divorce causes polygamy (or polyandry), he implies this by stating that "anyone who divorces his wife, except for marital unfaithfulness, and marries another woman commits adultery" (Mt 19:9). Simply put, someone who already belongs to someone should not, perhaps cannot, also belong to another. Whether the practice results in multiple wives simultaneously (as in some cultures) or multiple wives sequentially (as in our culture), the effect is the same. Modern practice and biblical truth require treating the divorce question as a case study in serial polygamy and polyandry, as unpopular as this might be.

The Textual/Legal Approach

Those who approach the subject of divorce from a legal perspective are concerned to find the correct grounds for permissible divorce. This necessitates dealing with the absolute statements against divorce in Mark 10:11-12 and Luke 16:18. These must be considered in light of the clause "except for marital unfaithfulness" found in Matthew 5:32 and 19:9. On the assumption that Mark and Luke knew of this clause, some argue that a person can be divorced if he or she is the innocent party of a marriage that has been destroyed by adultery. If death permits the physical survivor to remarry (Rom 7:3), adultery may permit the "moral survivor" to remarry.

Peter Davids argues, however, that when Jesus was asked for an interpretation of Deuteronomy 24, Jesus rejected this passage as a permission for divorce. Davids's point centers on the argument that one cannot really divorce. The parties involved have sinned, but they have not ended the marriage. The relationship can be negative, distant and cold, but it has not been annulled. These two cannot be as they were before marriage. The passage ceases to have relevance for us in Christ except in the case of a woman or man desiring to return to a former spouse after a remarriage to a second spouse had terminated, for that is what Deuteronomy 24 deals with. Even then, the full light of forgiveness in Christ might make us reconsider this as legislation applying to the Christian today.

A further problem Davids explores concerns the language found in Matthew 5:32 and 19:9: the Greek word *porneia* is used rather than the usual term for adultery, *moicheia*. This suggests that Jesus is dealing not with marital adultery but with premarital sexual sin. While the Old Testament called for stoning to death one who committed such sexual sin (*porneia*), divorce would have been more likely in the New Testament period. Joseph's predicament with Mary, and his intended righteous action, is a case in point. Frequently, those who try to uncover the legal grounds for divorce in the New Testament fail to notice that in the Gospels adultery is grounds for forgiveness,* not divorce. They also fail to note that according to Jesus, the lust-ful eye—intending adultery—is as evil as the deed. This makes almost everyone divorceable.

What about the second ground for divorce in the Bible, desertion by an unbelieving partner? "But if the unbeliever leaves, let him do so. A believing man or woman is not bound in such circumstances" (1 Cor 7:15)? In this case one partner has become a Christian, and the other demands either renunciation of faith or the end of the marriage. Where one must make such a choice, Paul advises that the believer is not bound to his or her partner. But, he is careful to note, the believer does not deny his Lord (or defile the marriage) by remaining married to an unbeliever, if this is possible.

In fact, no sooner has Paul said that the believer need not restrain the unbeliever from leaving (though the believer is not to take the initiative) than he reminds the believer that a believing husband may even save the wife (1 Cor 7:16). Previously Paul had said that an unbelieving husband is already sanctified through his believing wife (7:14). The use of the term "not bound" in verse 15 emphasizes the freedom of the Christian spouse, and it is possible that Paul would give cautious permission for remarriage of the believer in those cases where the unbeliever has contracted another marital union. But it is highly unlikely that Paul is counseling divorce and remarriage for the believer when the unbelieving spouse remains unconnected with another marital partner.

There is no New Testament legislation concerning persons divorced and remarried before becoming Christians. The gospel covers that possibility, and every other one as well, by proclaiming a new start in Christ. The New Testament does not deal with the situation of an abused woman (or man). Presumably, Paul would have said that a woman

101

should not submit to abuse* even if her husband leaves her. But Paul would also say that while they may separate for peace or even for personal emotional survival (assuming that all other means of dealing with it have temporarily failed), they are not granted the right to divorce and find another partner. Grace holds out the hope of reconciliation and never gives up hope that the fractured covenant could be healed.

It is difficult to believe that Paul was more lenient than Jesus on the matter of divorce, even though Paul had to legislate, whereas Jesus did not. The burden of Paul's teaching, as it was for Jesus, is the divorceless covenant, not the grounds for permissible divorce. As a realist within the grace of God, Paul dealt with the difficulties in which believers found themselves, but he refused to reduce marriage to a contract with terms that, through being violated, would annul it. It is impossible to legislate for every possible situation in extremely strained marriages by appealing to the teaching of either Jesus or Paul.

The Dispensational Approach

This view takes seriously the existence of different stages in the story of God's dealing with the human race. Christ taught the ethics of the kingdom and, as the King-in-person, introduced God's reign into this age. The new age of the kingdom overlaps with the old. And the ethic of the kingdom, it is argued, is too high to be lived out in a partially saved world. According to this view when Jesus spoke about divorceless marriage, he was speaking about life in his ideal kingdom, not about life in this mixed reality we now have of kingdom and flesh. So, for example, Dwight Small argues that we must balance Jesus' ideal teachings with the realities of the overlapping kingdoms (this age and the next). While he does not call this dispensational thinking (differ-

ent parts of the Bible deal with different seasons of God's saving activity), the effect is the same. It divides the New Testament into parts that apply now and parts that do not. The problem with Small's approach is that Jesus says it is the foolish person who does not build his life on obedience to his teaching now (Mt 7:24-27).

P. T. Forsyth takes a slightly different approach worth considering, arguing that the legislation for divorce regarding "hardness of heart" (Mt 19:8) is not a concession to individual weakness and human nature but a reflection on the incomplete development of God's society on earth. Even if we must recognize divorce as a reality, and perhaps even a gracious reality in the case of an innocent victim, we should never lose sight of God's intention. God's design is a divorceless covenant, and no marriage should be conceived on any other foundation. Forsyth notes, however, that a move from basing marriage on covenant to consent would change the very idea of marriage. This has now happened. What we are losing today are not marriages but marriage itself—the whole covenant idea.

Biblical Theology

A third approach emphasizes the teaching of Jesus that "what God has joined together, let man not separate" (Mt 19:6). Until now I have assumed that God is normally pleased to join together those who will enter into a covenant with all its dimensions: leaving, cleaving and one flesh (Gen 2:24) (see Marriage). But we must ask whether God joins everyone who gets married. Are there people whose marriage is neither blessed nor founded in God (whether they believe in God or not), and for these people is divorce right, if not necessary? Perhaps no one has thought more comprehensively on this subject than Karl Barth in his work *Church Dogmatics*. The following discussion summarizes Barth's theology on the subject.

Marriage (covenant) is an indissoluble union. According to Barth, "the marriage which rests upon the command of God and therefore upon his calling cannot be dissolved by man even if he wishes" (Barth 1968, 34). Such a marriage, he argues, makes the indicatives "I am yours" and "you are mine" into imperatives. We must accept this until death us do part. The little key to the exit door is lost. Whoever would enter marriage must renounce the thought of ever leaving it.

Even a well-married couple should not presume on God's grace. Such a couple, he says, should not rely on the encouraging indications of their marriage but "can only hold fast the mercy of God without any merit of their own" (Barth 1968, 35). Beware if they think they stand by their own effort! This is an important corrective to the pragmatic approach today that if you go to enough marriage-enrichment seminars, you can guarantee a good marriage.

Can you know for sure your marriage is not blessed by God? Barth says no. Even though there may be many indications of an unsuccessful marriage and people suspect that their marriage lacks God's blessing, this blessing may simply be hidden from them for the moment. Barth calls them to consider "whether there may not be indications that its malady can finally be healed and its union given permanence" (1968, 36).

No matter what, we are to cling to God's yes. Covenant marriage is based not on external indications but on the provision of God. Therefore, since the Word of God is primarily a word of promise and only secondarily a word of judgment, a believer is called to cling to God's yes rather than his no. For "no negative indications, however bad, can engender the certainty that a particular

marriage is without promise and stands finally under the judgment of God because [it is] not . . . 'made in heaven' " (Barth 1968, 38).

But in an extreme case we may painfully conclude that a couple should not remain married. We must be cautious in assuming that we can discern whether or not a marriage is blessed by God. The saying of Jesus cannot be reversed to say "what God has *not* joined together, let man separate." Divorce may be permitted where God has evidently condemned the marriage as a noncovenant. Divorce applies only to the legal institution of marriage and not the divine covenant, which is indissoluble. Therefore the covenant is not dissolved, because there never was one.

The church must show compassion to the divorced. Barth asks rhetorically, "May it not be that those who are joined in a 'good' marriage are supremely characterized by the fact that they can manifest toward those to whom this boon has not been granted something of the divine mercy which they themselves may enjoy in this respect?" (1968, 36). Often couples with "good marriages" tend to flock together and avoid those with "bad marriages," each group developing its own support network.

Divorced persons must not be refused remarriage. In Barth's view, divorced persons know themselves as judged by God in their (noncovenant) marriages, but the church "will not regard them as polluted, or scandalously . . . refuse them the church's benediction in the case of a second marriage" (1968, 41) if they turn in repentance to Christ and the gospel. The ministry of the gospel is to create a new beginning, whether in a single life or to be married again.

The big question is not divorce but marriage. "Legal divorce," according to Barth, "is not part of the divine command concerning marriage; for this proclaims and requires its indissolubility. It belongs only to the institution of marriage. The human institution takes into account the possibility of marriages which have no divine foundation and constitution . . . and which therefore can be dissolved" (1968, 40). In other words, marriage is dissoluble (i.e., marriage as a human institution), but the covenant is indissoluble.

Divorce and the Spirituality of the Church

What does divorce do to our hearing (see Listening) of God's voice in Scripture and our knowing God's presence in everyday life? The pastoral approach to divorce has more than one dimension. There is the obvious pastoral concern of how to prevent divorce if possible and care for those going through a divorce. But what does easy and widespread divorce do to our spirituality?

First, the marriage covenant takes us to the heart of God, who is a covenant-making and covenant-keeping God. Second, if we cannot believe that God will work a miracle in our hearts to keep covenant with our spouse, even in a difficult marriage (indeed, what marriage is not?), how can we believe that God could work the greater miracle of raising Jesus from the dead? Like Hosea in the Old Testament, we may seek a solution to a difficult marriage beyond the institution of marriage itself. Hosea called his wife Gomer into court and spoke of her as divorced (and perhaps would have gone through a legal divorce) in order to win her back! Third, the essence of being a child of God is obedience. If we obey what we already have from God, we can be given more. As we do the truth, God reveals more. Finally, a hard heart is both the cause and usual consequence of divorce (Mt 19:8). If we harden our heart to our spouse, we will be dead to the voice of God.

A church where couples can exchange partners freely, where divorce is accepted as normal, and where marriage is entered lightly as something less than a lifelong covenant is a church that will soon have no real spiritual power. But when a church does not stand beside divorced people and offer grace and hope if they turn in repentance to Christ but instead offers judgment, condemnation and exclusion, the church will soon not hear the voice of God. Of the three Christian virtues that should be offered by the people of God today (faith, hope and love), especially in relation to marriage, the one most urgently needed is hope. And hope is what the gospel of Jesus brings.

See also CONFLICT RESOLUTION; DEPRESSION; FAMILY PROBLEMS; FORGIVENESS; MARRIAGE; SEXUALITY; SINGLE PARENTING; STRESS.

References and Resources
K. Barth, *Church Dogmatics* 3/4, *The Doctrine of Creation*, trans. A. T. Mackay et al. (Edinburgh: T & T Clark, 1961); K. Barth, *On Marriage* (Philadelphia: Fortress, 1968); P. Davids, "Divorce: The Biblical Data" (Vancouver: Equippers, 1985, unpublished); P. T. Forsyth, *Marriage: Its Ethic and Religion* (London: Hodder & Stoughton, n.d.); D. H. Small, *The Right to Remarry* (Old Tappan, N.J.: Revell, 1975); J. H. Olthius, *I Pledge You My Troth: A Christian View of Marriage, Family, Friendship* (New York: Harper & Row, 1975); R. P. Stevens, *Getting Ready for a Great Marriage* (Colorado Springs: NavPress, 1990); R. P. Stevens, *Married for Good: The Lost Art of Remaining Happily Married* (Downers Grove, Ill.: InterVarsity Press, 1986); J. S. Wallerstein and S. Blakeslee, *Second Chances* (New York: Ticknor & Fields, 1989); M. Weiner-Davis, *Divorce-Busting* (New York: Simon & Schuster, 1992); R. Weiss, *Marital Separation* (New York: Basic Books, 1976).

R. Paul Stevens

—DRUGS—

Many believe that drugs like heroin and cocaine are at the heart of the drug problem because they are illegal, powerfully addictive and ruinous. Yet their use is minor compared to legal drugs like alcohol and tobacco. Millions of Americans are problem drinkers, and tens of thousands of deaths* are directly attributed to alcohol each year. Furthermore, alcohol is considered a factor in most fatal car accidents, homicides, suicides and child abuse* cases. Consider as well the harmful effects of tobacco with over 50 million smoking Americans, many of whom will succumb to lung cancer, emphysema or other ailments. One should also consider the negative effects resulting from prescription and nonprescription drugs that are sufficient to hospitalize over 1.5 million Americans each year.

A drug is any substance that can influence one's mind, body or emotions and, when misused, can harm oneself or others. Most people use drugs for some purpose, and given that our bodies manufacture drugs like endorphins and adrenaline, everyone is a drug user. Our society clearly has a love-hate relationship with drugs—sending mixed messages of benefit and harm. We advertise the potential harm of drugs and the importance of just saying no. Yet we glorify celebrities who model drug use as a means of popularity and success. Drug abuse shakes the very foundations of our society by negatively influencing our homes,* our schools,* our political and law enforcement systems, and our economy.

Why Do People Use Drugs?

Attempts to seek a single cause for drug use and abuse are futile. The causes of drug abuse vary with the type of drug and involve interactions of biological, psychological, sociocultural and spiritual conditions. However, four major reasons or risk factors for substance abuse have been identified: personality, family,* friends and crises (Newcomb, Maddahian and Bentler).

First, those who are angry, impulsive or depressed* or who have achievement problems are more apt to abuse drugs. Second, individuals whose family relationships are distant, hostile or conflicted, whose parents use or abuse drugs or whose parents are permissive, ignoring or rejecting will more often abuse drugs. Third, those who abuse drugs have friends and peers who use or tolerate the use of drugs. Finally, a person is more apt to abuse drugs when in transition or crisis, for example, when experiencing problems with school, family or romantic relationships, or during times when questioning values* or religious commitment.

What Can Be Done to Limit Drug Abuse?

Strategies to curtail drug abuse generally focus on limiting supply or demand. It is popular to wage supply-side war on the sale and distribution of illegal drugs. However, strategies that focus on the demands of users are more promising. If we consider the factors that put people at risk for drug abuse, there are several logical strategies. For example, as we raise an individual's self-esteem,* promote meaningful achievement, improve family life and provide safer alternatives for gratification, escape or relief, we help to mitigate drug abuse. Also, prevention is definitely preferable to intervention or postvention. Children need to receive helpful skills and information before they develop drug habits and dependencies that are difficult to break.

Thinking Christianly About Drug Use and Abuse

A Christian should view drugs in the context of God's creation of human persons affected by the Fall, redeemed by Christ and patiently sanctified by the Holy Spirit. This involves integrating a comprehensive biblical view with what God enables us to learn through inquiry and observation.

In Genesis 1:28-31 we read that God blessed woman and man in connection with the created order and called the whole relationship "very good." In other words, God created us with needs and created elements in our environment to meet those needs. Undoubtedly our human capacities to develop drugs like analgesics, allergy relief agents, antibiotics and laxatives are part of God's creational design. Yet we must struggle to discern proper and improper uses for the drugs we discover. Some drugs should not be used at all, some are good only in moderation, some should not be used too early in life, and some are intended for good but produce great harm (e.g., thalidomide). One might also question whether instant chemical relief is preferable to building character* through exploring and coping with root causes of anxiety, depression* or pain.

The major goal of the Christian is not the pursuit of self-interest but the well-being of all people and the glory of God. Short of complete abstinence from drugs, perhaps a good general principle is to consider the personal results of drug-related activities in light of the works of God's Spirit and the works of the flesh. The work of the Spirit is to produce such qualities as love,* joy, peace, patience, kindness, goodness, faithfulness and self-control (Gal 5:22-23). Does a particular form of drug use help to develop or maintain such quali-

ties, not just as transitory personal emotions but as concrete actions in our relationships? Does another form of drug use associate with works of the flesh such as fornication, uncleanness, enmity, strife, jealousy, wrath and envy (Gal 5:19-20)? We are to love God with all our heart, mind, soul and strength (Mk 12:30). Does drug use open a person's heart to God, clear her mind, deepen her relationships with others and increase her strength? Or does the use of a given drug harden a person's heart, cloud his thinking, close him in on himself or dull his reactions?

Drugs and Child Abuse

Drugs are allegedly involved in 60 percent of all child abuse cases. Victimization for many of these children begins in prenatal life when indiscriminate use of drugs and alcohol during pregnancy condemns some children to a "bio-underclass"—children whose physiological damage and underprivileged social position may doom them to a life of inferiority (Rist). Some children are removed from their families and placed in foster care because one or both parents are incarcerated for drug-related crimes. Drug abuse may shatter the lives of some parents to the extent that effective supervision of and provision for their children are severely compromised. Parents under the influence of alcohol or other drugs may torment, batter or sexually exploit their own children. A cigarette may ease a parent's frustration but may also be used to inflict telltale circular burns on a child's arms, legs or buttocks.

Summary

One child may be devastated by her father's indiscretions while under the influence of too much alcohol. Another child's aberrant development is greatly assisted by regular use of a prescribed drug. One may consume a moderate amount of a fine wine at a wedding reception while remaining clear-headed and deeply appreciative of God's gifts of love, friendship and commitment. Another individual's hallucinogenic trip may lead her to think of herself *as* God. The drunken stupor that clouds one's perception and judgment, taxes one's liver and alienates one from family, friends and work is anything but a proper state for any human being, let alone a follower of Christ. There are no simple answers that hold for all forms of drug use and abuse. We must use biblical truth and the minds God gives us to discern proper from improper forms of drug use.

See also ADOLESCENCE; DEPRESSION; HEALTH; FAMILY PROBLEMS; SELF-ESTEEM.

EASTER. *See* HOLIDAYS—EASTER.

References and Resources
D. Kandel and R. Logan, "Patterns of Drug Use from Adolescence to Young Adulthood: I. Periods of Risk for Initiation, Continued Use and Discontinuation," *American Journal of Public Health* 74 (1984) 660-66; M. Newcomb, E. Maddahian and P. Bentler, "Risk Factors for Drug Use Among Adolescents: Concurrent and Longitudinal Analyses," *American Journal of Public Health* 76 (1986) 525-31; M. Rist, "The Shadow Children," *The American School Board Journal*, January 1990 19-24; J. Van Wicklin, "Substance Abuse," in *Christian Perspective on Social Problems*, ed. C. DeSanto, Z. Lindblade and M. Poloma, 2d ed. (Indianapolis: Wesley, 1992) 376-97.

John F. Van Wicklin

—EATING—

There is perhaps a no more taken-for-granted part of family life than the business of eating. From hurried breakfasts to comforting bedtime snacks, from elaborate family celebrations to the daily routine of packed lunches or hamburgers from the local drive through, we eat so routinely that to stop and consider its deeper significance is an unusual task. The accepted traditions of yesterday are often seriously challenged—even squeezed out—by the realities of family life today. So what can we say about eating from a Christian perspective? How do we approach the daily routines of eating in the family context as those committed to the values* and the callings of the Christian faith? First, we will first explore some of the cultural meanings associated with eating. Second, we will consider the significance of eating in the Bible. In light of these discoveries, we will then consider how the Christian faith can, in practical ways, impact the daily eating habits of today's families.

Eating from a Cultural Perspective
There are many cultural meanings associated with eating.

Eating and culture. Eating is a transmitter of culture. This is true for a society as a whole and for each family within it. Such basic matters as who sits where at the family table, who prepares the meal, who serves, who is served first, what is served and what is not, who dominates or directs communication* and who cleans up after the meal—all of this communicates a wealth of information about social obligations and customs, authority structures, gender roles, history, prejudices and priorities. Some of these reflect the broader culture of society or of a particular religious or ethnic heritage. Others are the unique expression of an individual family.

Eating and relationships. In all societies of the world eating is a primary way of entering into and sustaining relationships. Eating plays a central role in almost every social and family gathering. Every time a family sits down to a meal together, it routinely affirms the unspoken solidarities of a group of people inextricably linked to each other. Inviting an "outsider" into such an event communicates a welcome of that person into the intimate life of the family. Business and collegial relationships, friendships both intimate and casual, romantic ties, political alliances—all these and more are recognized, ritualized and celebrated through the sharing of food.

Eating and covenant. In the ancient Near East, sharing food with a guest was equivalent to establishing a covenant. The host was obliged to offer protection and shelter to a guest who had eaten at his table. This concept of food as the seal of covenant is not confined to the ancient world. Today the Bantu of southern Africa regard exchanging food as the formation of a temporary covenant they call a "clanship of porridge." In Chinese society the giving and sharing of food is considered to give flesh to relationships. And in the West most major business deals are sealed with the mandatory business lunch. Various family celebrations are, in their own way, routine affirmations of family covenants. Those annual events that draw together extended families in one place are a key way families reaffirm their ties.

Eating and celebration. Celebration is incomprehensible within any society or family without the activity of eating. So central is it that certain food items are associated with particular rites of celebration. To a North American, Thanksgiving* would not be Thanksgiving without the turkey, cranberry sauce, giblet gravy and pumpkin pie. For the English, a Christmas* without plum pudding is hard to imagine, as it is for the Danes without the traditional rice dessert with almonds and whipped cream. In the West weddings are celebrated with an elaborately decorated cake and a birthday with a cake and candles. Wedding anniversaries, retirements, engagements and graduations are often the cause for a celebratory feast. Even funerals are marked by the sharing of food and drink.

Eating from a Biblical Perspective
When the biblical ties between eating and Christian faith are discussed, often it is the subjects of fasting and gluttony that get the attention. While the Bible has much to say on both issues, there is so much more in both Old and New Testaments that can enrich our appreciation of eating from a Christian vantage point.

Eating in the Old Testament. From the very beginning, in the story of creation, God's role as the Creator and Sustainer of life culminates in his provision of food for "everything that has the breath of life in it" (Gen 1:30). There is an obvious note of celebration as creation flourishes in the abundance of God's provision. As we continue through the Old Testament, the imagery of eating consistently signifies the presence, promises and blessings of God. As the people of Israel wandered in the desert, it was God who rained down manna from heaven every day for forty years (Ex 16). Gathering the manna each morning and eating it served as a daily reminder of God's presence with them. The Promised Land itself was repetitively described as "a land flowing with milk and honey" (Ex 13:5; Num 13:27; Deut 6:3). For the people this description came to symbolize the richness of what lay ahead of them. The Old Testament imagery of blessing and judgment is often tied to food. Satisfaction in eating was a picture of God's blessing (Deut 6:11; 8:10-12; 11:15), as lack of satisfaction was a picture of judgment (Lev 26:26; Is 9:20; Hos 4:10). Just as these more temporal of God's blessings were tied to eating, so the ultimate deliverance of the people is described in terms of God's invitation to an open table laden with an abundance of good food (Ps 23:5; 36:7-9; Is 25:6; Joel 3:18; Amos 9:13-14).

In the Old Testament world, eating was an important step in the establishment of covenant. As two parties sat down together, their common meal indicated reconciliation, enabling oaths and agreements to be entered into (Gen 26:28-31). It was by God's initiative that covenant relationship was established with Israel (Gen 12:1-3; 15:9-21; 35:9-15). The complex rites and rituals of sacrifice (Lev 1—7), and later establishment of feasts that played host to these sacrifices (Lev 23), were essential to the establishing and renewing of this covenant relationship. Sacrifices and feasts were moments in which God and the people would sit at table together and celebrate the ties that bound them together.

Eating in the New Testament. Around almost every corner of the Gospel accounts, Jesus can be found eating and drinking. He was labeled by some as a "glutton and a drunkard" (Mt 11:19). In a society that drew very clear and precise social and religious boundaries through the customs of the meal table, Jesus demonstrated a blatant disregard for protocol and tradition. His willingness to eat with anyone, regardless of class, race, profession or moral record was deeply threatening to those who saw it as their duty to enforce such customs. Through time influential Jewish groups had constructed a complex set of rules and regulations designed to protect their racial and religious purity.

Jesus' habit of sharing his meals with "tax collectors and 'sinners' " (Lk 5:30) was threatening, for it demonstrated that his new kingdom order had little to do with religious customs and regulations. The kingdom of God was now symbolized by an open table to which all were invited to come and feast, an invitation without boundary or exclusion (Mt 25:1-13; Lk 14:15-24; 15:11-32).

Jesus also used eating imagery to define his own mission.* He calls himself the "bread of life" (Jn 6:35-59) and the "living water" (Jn 4:10-14). As he met with the disciples for the Last Supper, he established that until the kingdom of God is fully come, his presence will be made tangible through the shared meal. Jesus established this meal as a time of remembrance when he said, "This is my body given for you; do this in remembrance of me" (Lk 22:19; cf. Mt 26:26; Mk 14:22), a time of covenant renewal; "This cup is the new covenant in my blood, which is poured out for you" (Lk 22:20; cf. Mt 26:28; Mk 14:24). It is also an anticipation of the messianic banquet that is to come: "For I tell you, I will not drink again of the fruit of the vine until the kingdom of God comes" (Lk 22:18; cf. Mt 26:29; Mk 14:25).

Eating and the Christian Family

In the light of these cultural and biblical perspectives, the question remains: how do we allow our Christian faith to affect and inform our eating habits, especially in the context of the family? We will address this question by way of five images—each one a window into, and an expression of, the Christian faith: providence, sacrament, community, service and mission.

Eating and providence. Central to the prayer that Jesus taught his followers is the petition "Give us today our daily bread" (Mt 6:11). Every time family members "break bread" together, whether in an overtly religious ritual or simply the daily routine of breakfast, they are gathered up into the mystery of God's providence. Food is the stuff of life, and the creation and sustaining of life are God's business. This dependence on God as Provider is not altogether obvious for the majority of families in the developed world. In the West only 3 percent of the population is needed to produce more than 100 percent of the required agricultural products. Yet for those who still plough the earth, await the rains, milk the cows, cast nets into the ocean and nurture the grapevines, dependence on a power outside of themselves is a daily experience. Whether we are aware of it or not, every time we eat we express our complete dependence on a power outside ourselves. For those who bow to pray before eating, dependence is articulated; those who do not so pray are still unavoidably dependent.

Eating and sacrament. As Jesus broke bread and shared it with his fellow travelers on the road to Emmaus, "their eyes were opened and they recognized him" (Lk 24:31). While every meal we participate in is not overtly religious in nature, each time we sit down to a meal, God is present. It is an expression of the principle of incarnation.

In the celebration of the Lord's Supper we articulate a spiritual truth: life is dependent on death.* In order that we might enter into the fullness of life, life had to be surrendered. Jesus surrendered his life to death in order that we might live. In a sense, that same principle of "life for life" is at work in every meal we eat. Every time we swallow, we enact that principle. Whether we are eating a bowl of porridge, devouring a sirloin steak or sipping a glass of orange juice, life had to be laid down for us. It is part of the order of things. It is so ordinary, and yet in this ordinariness is mystery.

Nurturing a conscious awareness of God's presence at the meal table is crucial if we are to develop an integrated family spirituality. It will call for a degree of creativity as we seek to establish mealtime rituals that make God's presence a daily experience. It will mean consciously watching for incarnational moments when God's presence and purposes can be named and celebrated.

Nonetheless, one cannot afford to be too idealistic about such things. The realities of family mealtimes do not always lend themselves to deeply "spiritual" encounters. Those who have small children, for example, will know that the family mealtime is a more often a struggle than a heady religious experience. Similarly, the often tense and even angry encounters that occur at the family table make this business of being aware of God's presence a challenge indeed. Regardless, the reality persists. God *is* present—as profoundly present in the midst of chaos or tension as God is in the midst of peace and harmony. The simple act of lighting a candle at the table can be an acknowledgement of the fact even when the sentiments of the spoken word feel empty and strained.

Eating and community. It has been said that to be human is to belong. The need to belong is a need that has been central to our humanity from the beginning. As we have already discovered, Jesus extended the boundaries of belonging to the community of God's people. He proclaimed God's kingdom open to and inclusive of all those who respond to God's invitation to eat with him.

Wendy Wright has written, "When we break bread together, we symbolically enact the basic truth that we are most complete when we are together." A family is that group of scattered individuals who come together at the end of the day, most commonly around the meal table. They may or may not be related, but every time they meet there, they acknowledge their identity as a family and reaffirm together their sense of belonging. There is a sense in which our meal table defines the boundaries of our community. Occasionally, or regularly, an outsider is invited to the table. In welcoming him or her we communicate that, for the period of the meal at least, this person is no longer a stranger but belongs with us.

In a society that increasingly values individualism, where families are sacrificing their common identity in pursuit of individual interests, the common meal time is disappearing or shared around the television* set. Our task is to reinvent the household mealtime as a time to value relationships, listen* to each other, extend welcome to the outsider and reaffirm our need for community. Guarding the sanctity of the shared mealtime is crucial. Finding ways to make meal preparation* a communal event will only deepen the experience.

Eating and service. Through his words and actions Jesus painted a picture of a kingdom in which love* and self-giving are central. His proclamations were, and still are, radical. It is in the kingdom distinctive of service that we discover the greatness for which we were created. Jesus' example shows that there are few places where this can be so demonstrated as at the meal table. Whether a ministry of compassion or of simple hospitality,* it is clearly a ministry of service that is offered at the table.

Ernest Boyer Jr. calls what we offer at the meal table "the sacrament of care." Care is offered most often in the routine and the ordinary activities of the day—washing dishes, peeling vegetables, making beds and so on. Is the one who selflessly prepares meals for a family, week in and week out, year in and year out, conscious of it as a sacrament of care? Probably not. Yet if we take Jesus' words

seriously, then what this provider offers to the family is as significant and valued in God's kingdom as any glorified act of service offered by prophet, priest or king.

As a church we should be looking for ways and opportunities to recognize and celebrate these "sacraments of care" being offered daily by often unrecognized members of our church communities. As household members we can nurture those who serve us by regularly voicing our thanks for revealing to us more of God's nature and character.

Eating and mission. In a sense, Jesus' eating habits embodied his mission. His sitting at table with the despised and disenfranchised was a clear indication that the kingdom of heaven is a place of welcome, refuge and healing for all. It indicates that the mission of the church is not merely proclamation of the "good news" to those outside the kingdom, nor is it limited to the clothing* and feeding of the outcasts. It is a mission that calls for both of these and yet more. It calls for intimate investment in the lives of those we call to the table. Jesus could have limited his ministry to the proclamation of the kingdom from the mountaintops and the synagogues. Instead, such moments were the exception. More commonly Jesus was to be found brushing up against all manner of people in the most domestic settings and very often eating with them. The mission of the early church clearly reflected this pattern. Mission for Jesus and the early church involved initiating relationships and clearly demonstrating the nature of God's inclusive kingdom. According to Jesus, welcome into the kingdom will be extended to those who extend to others the same open hospitality of the table: "For I was hungry and you gave me something to eat, I was thirsty and you gave me something to drink, I was a stranger and you invited me in" (Mt 25:35).

111

Being invited into a private home for dinner is becoming the exception in Western societies. Increasingly today such an invitation of intimacy and commitment is avoided. In an uncertain and fearful world, perhaps the family home is valued more as a refuge—a place to close the door on the world—than a place of community and welcome. Of course, there is an important role for the family home to play as a refuge. Protecting, nurturing and healing of those within—these are all important to the mission of the Christian home. However, if we intend to model the inclusive nature of God's kingdom for our children and for each other, yet fail to invite even those who are like us to the dinner table, then how in the world do we begin to address the call to the stranger and the alien? The mission of the church is about more than a distant proclamation or a free handout at the soup kitchen. It is about intimate investment in the lives of those around us. It is about securing our identity as a family and then opening the table to those who need the open embrace of Jesus.

While our eating may always be a very routine and ordinary part of our lives, essential to keeping us physically healthy and whole, it should not be forgotten that it is significant at much deeper levels. In the Christian family, eating provides one of the most immediate and daily opportunities to nurture one another in the faith, to live together in the awareness of God's presence and goodness, and to practice the call of God to holiness, service and mission.

See also CHORES; HOMEMAKING; HOLIDAYS—CHRISTMAS, EASTER, THANKSGIVING; HOSPITALITY; MEAL PREPARATION; MISSION.

References and Resources
S. S. Bartchy, "Table Fellowship," in *Dictionary of Jesus and the Gospels*, ed. J. B. Green, S. McKnight and I. H. Marshall (Downers Grove, Ill.: InterVarsity Press, 1992); E. Boyer Jr., *Finding God at Home: Family Life as Spiritual Discipline* (San Francisco: Harper, 1991); J. A. Brillat-Savarin, *The Physiology of Taste* (London: Penguin, 1970); A. C. Cochrane, *Eating and Drinking with Jesus: An Ethical and Biblical Inquiry* (Philadelphia: Westminster, 1974); S. C. Juengst, *Breaking Bread: The Spiritual Significance of Food* (Louisville: Westminster John Knox, 1992); R. J. Karris, *Luke: Artist and Theologian* (New York: Paulist, 1985); J. MacClancy, *Consuming Culture: Why You Eat What You Eat* (New York: Henry Holt, 1992); M. Visser, *Much Depends on Dinner: The Extraordinary History and Mythology, Allure and Obsessions, Perils and Taboos of an Ordinary Meal* (New York: Grove, 1986); W. M. Wright, *Sacred Dwelling: A Spirituality of Family Life* (New York: Crossroad, 1990).

Simon Carey Holt

EDUCATION. *See* HOME SCHOOLING; PARENTING; SCHOOLS, PUBLIC AND PRIVATE.

E-MAIL. *See* COMMUNICATION; COMPUTER; INTERNET.

—EMPTY NESTING—

An expression that pinpoints the moment when grown children are out of the home* and the parents face a new lifestyle, empty nesting is the time in a marriage* between launching the children and retirement. Even in intact marriages it is a time of crisis, for it is usually the lowest point of marital satisfaction. The good news is that if the marital partners reinvest in their marriage, there is a dramatic upswing in their sense of joy.

Understanding the Transition

One reason why empty nesting is a high-stress time, especially at its immediate onset, is that it marks the completion of a couple's investment in what they may have seen as the primary purpose of the marriage, the rearing of children. There are additional reasons.

There is a tendency for men and women to be going in opposite directions psychologically at the point where their children move out on their own. Men, perhaps realizing that they have missed most of the intimacy of their children's development, may begin to seek closeness, whereas women, after years of focusing on caring for others, begin to feel energized about developing their own lives—careers, friendships outside the family and other activities (Carter and McGoldrick, 52).

At this point the marriage is often viewed by both partners as sterile. There is often a switching of roles: the distancer becomes the pursuer, and the pursuer becomes the distancer. Further, in the more traditional marriage, the man has invested his life in his career and the woman in her children. Even if he is successful, the career seems less attractive. For the woman her reason for living, as she perceives it, has disappeared. The danger is that they will both blame the marriage for their dissatisfaction when it is not the prime culprit. Indeed, if they reinvest in the marriage, they will gain back some, even all, of the intimacy they have lost. Sadly, many couples who are unaware of the dynamics of the marriage give up on the marriage at a time when a minimum reinvestment could pay significant dividends.

If there are complications for intact marriages, there are greater ones for those for whom divorce* and remarriage have been a reality. Complications generated by the unhealed wounds of spouses and children affected by the divorce are a considerable challenge emotionally and spiritually. A support/accountability system is not just desirable but a vital necessity. There is a further complicating factor. The empty nest is experienced mainly by the "sandwich generation." During this time the marital partners are torn between the demands of their adolescent* children and those of their elderly parents, to say nothing of their own urgent needs.

Even if the children (young adults) have physically left home, their psychological, spiritual and financial demands often do not cease. They can continue to dominate the marriage unless the couple has agreed on how to handle their young adult offspring. When the increasing needs of elderly parents are added to this, the pressures of life can easily affect the quality of the couple's marriage. They will need to make space for their own relationship and for themselves and see this as a legitimate Christian decision.

Coping with the Transition

How any couple negotiates this point in their lifecycle will be a function of how they have handled their relationships over the previous years. If they have empowered their children and each other, they will come into this period feeling good about the family,* the marriage and themselves. If they have a deepened spiritual life individually and together, there will be a high degree of intimacy. If their church relationship is significant, they will not need the kind of emotional support from their children that encourages unhealthy dependence.

Empowered children and parents,

113

deep spiritual lives and strong church ties are particularly important if the children decide to return home, a not uncommon event in our day. Parents who are not good at setting healthy boundaries will find this a major crisis. It is imperative that if it is acceptable for children to land in the nest again, there is a clear understanding of how this is to be managed. Issues such as privacy, financial contributions, responsibility for chores,* presence or absence from meals and general use of the premises need to be clearly spelled out.

Betty Carter and Monica McGoldrick maintain that the key emotional process at this stage in the life cycle is "accepting a multitude of exits from and entries into the family system" (15). They go on to list what they describe as "Second Order Changes in Family Status Required to Proceed Developmentally" (Carter and McGoldrick, 15): (1) renegotiation of the marital system as a dyad, (2) development of adult-to-adult relationships, (3) realignment of relationships to include in-laws and grandchildren, and (4) dealing with disabilities and death of parents (grandparents*).

Preparing for the Transition

The time to get ready for empty nesting is long before it arrives. Marriages and families that are built on what Jack and Judith Balswick propose as a theological basis will do much more than survive; they will thrive. The Balswicks argue for four biblical themes on which family should be based. First, commitment is to be based on a mature (i.e., unconditional

and bilateral) covenant. Second, family life is to be established and maintained within an atmosphere of grace that embraces acceptance and forgiveness.* Third, the resources of family members are to be used to empower, rather than to control, one another. Fourth, intimacy is based on a knowing that leads to caring for, understanding, communicating* with and communing with others. The Balswicks see these as a continual process. Each feeds on and reinforces the other. The result of so building one's family is that each member has a sense of worth along with "deep levels of communication and knowing" (Balswick and Balswick, 33).

Empty nesting is a deeply challenging period. If the couple come into it with a healthy and godly commitment, it will bring them a deeper bonding and contentment. For David in the Old Testament it was an unmitigated disaster. It can be the opposite for those who, unlike David, have cultivated good marriages and families and see them both as an adventure in service of the kingdom.

See also FAMILY PROBLEMS; FAMILY SYSTEMS; GRANDPARENTING; PARENTING; STRESS.

References and Resources

J. O. Balswick and J. K. Balswick, *The Family: A Christian Perspective on the Contemporary Home* (Grand Rapids: Baker, 1991); B. Carter and M. McGoldrick, *The Changing Family Life Cycle*, 2nd ed. (New York: Gardner Press, 1988); F. Minirth et al., *Passages of Marriage* (Nashville: Thomas Nelson, 1991).

Roy D. Bell

—ENTERTAINMENT—

Today entertainment is virtually synonymous with leisure,* since entertainment is the major form of leisure. People seek entertainment as a means of relieving boredom, a diversion from the difficulties of everyday life, and a vehicle for courtship or friendly socializing. Most entertainment has two characteristics: (1) it is offered at a financial cost, and (2) it is consumed or used up by the people being entertained. In other words, entertainment is a leisure-oriented commodity produced by industry and used by consumers.

Electronic Forms of Entertainment

Since World War II one form has increasingly dominated entertainment time—television,* which includes broadcast and cable TV, satellite television, the videocassette recorder (see Videos) and video games (see Computer Games). In the United States, for instance, television represents more leisure time than all other entertainment activities combined. Adult females view over five hours daily, while males watch four hours and children average approximately three and one-half hours. The phenomenal popularity of TV is undoubtedly partly the result of the medium's seemingly low cost to consumers, who often bear the indirect expense through the cost of advertised products, government subsidies or monthly cable-TV charges.

Many other popular forms of entertainment are also influenced by electronics. Radio, for example, is combined with sophisticated audio circuitry for higher fidelity and greater realism. Musical concerts often rely on electronic sound reproduction and rely increasingly on high-tech visual "effect." Movies also take advantage of special effects created by electronic fabrication of image and sound. New amusement parks are even started in conjunction with the entertainment industry, which creates exhibits and rides based on successful movie, television, computer* or musical products.

It appears that the electronic revolution in entertainment products may be affecting the perceived value of other forms of leisure. Reading,* exercise sports, participatory sports, companionship (e.g., conversation* and socializing) and some hobbies are not as appealing to many people in a high-tech world. Some of these low-tech activities are being combined with electronic technologies (e.g., reading computer files or conversing via computer bulletin boards), but the overall shift in industrial societies is toward electronic entertainment.

Entertainment as a Public Event

One of the unfortunate impacts of electronic entertainment is the decline of valuable public events. Electronics tend to make entertainment an individual and private activity instead of a social and public event. Electronic reproduction enables industry to manufacture inexpensive copies of entertaining products, thereby permitting individual consumers to enjoy the entertainment whenever and wherever they wish. Videotape, for example, delivers movies and even some plays and musical concerts directly to the home. Why should a consumer bother with the effort involved in attending a public performance?

The answer is that public events generally provide opportunity for social interaction and collective discernment. When small groups attend concerts, for example, they typically discuss the quality of the entertainment. At home individual consumers shift almost effortlessly from one entertainment product to another, whereas at public events the entertainment is connected to the shared relationships of the attending groups. As a result the public event is selected more carefully, taken more seriously, enjoyed more deeply and discussed more fully.

Christians can avoid the loss of public entertainment in two ways. First, they can spend more leisure time attending public events and less time consuming personal entertainment products at home. Alternatively, Christians can practice hospitality* (1 Pet 4:9) by inviting friends and relatives to their homes* to enjoy entertainment together. This type of event-oriented hospitality has considerable potential in a media-oriented society, in which so many people live relatively shallow, insignificant lives. Post-entertainment discussion and fellowship are appealing to relationally hungry consumers. Even among families* this kind of media event can help break the cycle of personal, selfish entertainment use, as well as enhance familial discernment about the broader culture.

Producing Our Own Entertainment
Another disadvantage of the overindulgence in consumer-oriented electronic entertainment is people's underdeveloped gifts and talents. Nearly all personal satisfaction comes from the act of consumption and very little comes in the joy of production. In other words, industrialized entertainment tends to disenfranchise the public, which is relegated to the status of audience, viewer or purchaser. Industry becomes the playground of professional entertainers, while the public is transformed into a fickle, often irrational market. People may spend much time watching professional sports on televi-

sion, for example, but little or no time themselves participating in entertaining sports activities.

The church can encourage people to experience the joy and satisfaction derived from producing entertainment for their family and friends, including their church family. One possibility is for local congregations to sponsor more of their own homegrown entertainment. Some of this entertainment can be integrated into worship services in the form of dramatic presentations, music and readings. This technique certainly has its limits, given the appropriateness for worship, but it also has the advantage of transforming entertainment into something more than relief from boredom or diversion from the hardships of life.

Another use of gifts and talents in Christian circles is service-oriented entertainment. Comedy, drama and music can help people inside and outside the church who suffer from stress or the fears and pains attendant to physical illnesses. Entertainment can also help individuals to see more clearly the spiritual dimensions of their lives.

Even within the family there are possibilities for teaching children to exercise gifts and talents as entertainers. We should encourage children to make their own games* and not just to rely on commercial products for entertainment. We should similarly invite our offspring to participate in the planning of social events, including family vacations,* birthday* parties, holiday celebrations and neighborhood gatherings. It might be helpful for some children if parents simply limit the availability of manufactured entertainment during particular hours or on given days. Especially for children, spontaneous play* is often the most entertaining, creative activity.

Family Entertainment
Unless parents consciously promote

family-oriented entertainment in their homes, the marketing of popular products will tend to isolate family members. The vast majority of entertainment products are sold to particular taste groups represented largely by demographics such as age. Teenagers, for example, tend to consume television shows, movies and music that are marketed to their own generation. An age difference of even five years can make an enormous difference as to which radio stations and movies teenagers prefer.

Parents would do well to offset this generational segmentation with cross-generational, family-oriented entertainment. It may require a bit of give-and-take on the part of each family member, but there are worthwhile entertainment products and events that all ages can enjoy. Local theaters and video stores are among the best options.

Family-oriented entertainment also gives parents an opportunity to transcend some of the highbrow versus lowbrow distinctions that separate many children and adults. Unless parents provide interesting fine-art entertainment for their offspring, children will gravitate almost exclusively toward popular art. And many parents will not appreciate any of their children's popular art unless they take the time to view and listen with their offspring. Therefore, parents should be encouraged to share entertainment time and money* with children, especially adolescents.*

Entertainment and Identity

Finally, contemporary entertainment frequently becomes a status symbol for people to establish a meaningful identity. Like other consumer products, entertainment says much about the individuals who purchase and display it. Entertainment often has a status value that transcends the mere entertainment value.

Teenagers are most susceptible to this type of identity formation. They compare themselves on the basis of who has seen the most popular movies or been to the biggest musical concerts. Stereo systems are not just a means of listening to music, but for many teens they are also a symbol of cultural power and personal cultural relevance. In fact, access to adult-oriented videos or movies, such as R-rated films, is often an important sign of a teenager's coming of age.

In contemporary consumer cultures, however, the identity value of entertainment extends across the generations. Individuals and even entire families define their social standing partly by access to entertainment products and, increasingly, by the purchase of entertainment technologies. Every new technological frontier, from personal CD players to enormous television screens, advances the requirements for membership in the electronic status clubs. As soon as one identity is "purchased," the status frontier has shifted to a new arena, casting a shadow over the old identity. Even young children play this status game, comparing themselves on the basis of TVs, video games, DVD players, telephones* and beepers.

From a Christian perspective the whole concept of consumption-oriented identities is problematic, and entertainment-based status competitions may be among the most troubling of all. Christ looks not at our external consumption—what we are pretending to be by what we purchase and display—but at the heart of the individual believer (1 Sam 16:7). When our hearts focus on acquiring entertainment products, we define our value by the standards of the world, not by heavenly standards. In some cases this misplaced identity actually represents the love of entertainment rather than the love of God and neighbor.

The Discernment of Entertainment

Entertainment is an important area of life for Christians to exercise discernment (Ps 119:125). Such discernment should take three forms: (1) stewardship of one's time, (2) wise selection of entertainment and (3) critical use of entertainment.

Godly use of entertainment first requires a stewardship of leisure time. It is too easy to fill nonwork time with personal entertainment, thereby living without deep and rewarding relations with God, family and friends. Entertainment should have an important but carefully limited place in the lives of Christians.

In addition, it is imperative that Christians select the most worthwhile entertainment to fill this limited time (Phil 4:8). People often feel the need to consume entertainment with a kind of thoughtless frenzy, for fear they will miss out on enjoyable products. Video stores, record shops, cable TV, broadcast TV and movie theaters encourage this frenzy by regularly changing their products. Instead of being duped easily by the consumerist onslaught, Christians should seek helpful, critical information about entertainment products before investing time or money.

Finally, Christians are called to be on guard against the false prophets of every age, even as those prophets are represented in the seemingly benign forms of entertainment (2 Pet 2:1). Popular art is never culturally neutral but is instead an expression of values* and beliefs usually forged by audience-minded entrepreneurs. Our task is not to enjoy this entertainment uncritically but to help ourselves, our children and our communities see it for what it really is. Then we may truly celebrate the best and the most entertaining of the lot.

See also COMPUTER GAMES; GAMES; LEISURE; PLAY; SABBATH; TELEVISION; VIDEOS.

References and Resources

A. M. Greeley, *God in Popular Culture* (Chicago: Thomas More Press, 1988); K. A. Myers, *All God's Children and Blue Suede Shoes: Christians and Popular Culture* (Westchester, Ill.: Crossway, 1989); N. Postman, *Amusing Ourselves to Death: Public Discourse in the Age of Show Business* (New York: Viking, 1985); Q. J. Schultze, *Winning Your Kids Back from the Media* (Downers Grove, Ill.: InterVarsity Press, 1994), also available in a five-part video series with Gospel Films; Q. J. Schultze et al., *Dancing in the Dark: Youth, Popular Culture and the Electronic Media* (Grand Rapids: Eerdmans, 1991).

Quentin J. Schultze

EXTENDED FAMILY. *See* FAMILY; SINGLE PARENTING.

—FAIRY TALES—

For some, the term *fairy tales* conjures up visions of wand-waving ballerinas; for others, the term is simply used for any fanciful story that could not be true. But though traditional fairy tales, with their "once upon a time," edge us into "another world" of wonder and magical possibility, that world can open us to truths we have forgotten—or refuse to see in our own world. "These tales," writes G. K. Chesterton, "say that apples were golden only to refresh the forgotten moment when we found that they were green. They make rivers run with wine only to make us remember, for one wild moment, that they run with water" (*Orthodoxy*, 257).

Since the umbrella of "fairy tale" spreads so widely that at times it covers everything from ancient myths and legends to Saturday-morning cartoons, we do well to get a good grip on its handle—the traditional fairy tales. These stories, such as "Cinderella," "Little Red Riding Hood" and "The Frog Prince," not only contain the basic patterns—story types and motifs—of literature but also help us understand the ability of literature to move us in profound ways. As Christopher Morley has often been quoted as saying, "When you sell a man a book, you do not sell him just twelve ounces of paper, ink, and glue—you sell him a whole new life."

The power of great literature, of stories, to change our lives—to shake heart, mind and soul to the core of our being—is itself embedded in traditional fairy tales.

Characteristics of Fairy Tales

"Once upon a time"—agelessness. These stories are sometimes called "nursery tales," implying that they are best read to toddlers. While many can be appreciated by very young children, the prime age for most fairy stories is anytime from ages six and up. The bare bones of plot are there for all, including the very young, but these bones are a sturdy skeleton for the whole human story. As we grow older, we flesh them out more and more with our own experience, and we clothe that flesh with interpretations and understandings that we weave with the warp and woof of our own needs and longings.

These bones of human story in fairy tales have the ability to hold the flesh of our own stories—no matter how old we are or who we are—because they have weathered the storms of historical and cultural change. The story of Cinderella, for example, comes in over fifteen hundred versions from sources as spread out over time and place as Egypt's first-century B.C. "Rhodopis," China's ninth-century A.D. "Yehshen," North America's Algonquin Indian "Rough-Face Girl" and Germany's "Aschenputtel." And the German and English names reflect the tales' inherent universality of both character and theme, for *Cinderella* and

Aschenputtel describe a very lowly state—a "girl in ashes"—rather than a distinguishing name.

Through all the variations of detail and development in these versions of "Cinderella," the essential story of a young maid's rise from ashes to royalty has remained remarkably intact—complete, in most cases, with a focus on footwear. As G. K. Chesterton points out, "The lesson of 'Cinderella' . . . is the same as that of the Magnificat *exaltavit humiles* ['he exalted the humble']" (253). The great truth underlying the story of Cinderella can be a door to the scriptural truth of Mary (herself another such humble handmaid) and of her song (the Magnificat), and of the Gospels—the good news: our God "has lifted up the humble" (Lk 1:52).

Fairy tales have a habit of making heroes of the humble: the rejected daughter becomes a princess, the youngest son becomes a king, the ugly duckling becomes a graceful and beautiful swan. These old stories can cut through our despair and disillusionment, enabling us to remember that we can be a son or daughter of the King and that through his life-giving love* we look forward to the great end-celebration of hope we call heaven.

"Do not stray off the path"—moral truthfulness. "The Ethics of Elfland" is the title G. K. Chesterton gave to his fine and deeply Christian treatise on fairy tales. There he claims that a great principle of the fairy philosophy is "the Doc-

trine of conditional Joy" (258). In these old stories "happiness depended on *not doing something* which you could at any moment do and which, very often, it was not obvious why you should not do" (260).

The condition is usually simple obedience to a seemingly arbitrary command. As Robert Farrar Capon puts it in *The Third Peacock,* his book on the problem of evil, "After entering the garden go straight to the tree, pick the apple and get out. Do not, under any circumstances, engage in conversation with the third peacock on the left" (27). We all remember the childhood lessons of Little Red Riding Hood: "Stay on the path; do not talk to strangers."

Nevertheless, the heroes and heroines of these tales are reassuringly like us—they fail to meet the condition. As Chesterton reminds us, in the biblical story "an apple is eaten, and the hope of God is gone" (259). And so these tales teach us the lessons of character* we need to pick up and keep on going. They teach us persistence and faithfulness, the ability to keep trying against all odds and in spite of repeated failure; they teach us kindness and compassion, the ability to forgive* others' failings and weaknesses; and, above all, they teach us love,* the willingness to sacrifice our own happiness for someone else's. In fairy tales, the burden of these lessons for living is lightened by the wings of story.

"And they lived happily ever after"—good (and bad) endings. The greatest wonder of the fairy tale world is the "happily ever after." Yet the hope offered to Cinderella, and vicariously to us, is more and more rejected as wishful thinking. But to endure the ups and downs of life we *need* hope, and these tales offer hope of a perfect end. These good endings are not cheap grace: as Chesterton makes clear, "In the fairy tale an incomprehensible happiness rests upon an incomprehensible condition" (259). The scales of justice tip on this "if" from which hangs the balance between gloom and glory, between death* and life, between dancing to death in red-hot shoes and a wedding celebration of great splendor. The good endings are glorious intimations of heaven; the bad endings are sometimes so harsh and hellish that fairy tales are accused of both black-and-white rigidity and violence that is too much for children.

Yet we need these tales to clear our clouded consciences and sharpen our moral sensitivity. "For children are innocent and love justice, while most of us are wicked and naturally prefer mercy" (Tolkien, 66). Mary's Magnificat promises that God lifts up the humble, but, as both the Magnificat and the Cinderella story remind—warn—each of us, he also brings down "those who are proud in their inmost thoughts" (Lk 1:51). The good ending of a fairy tale is, like the good ending of all time, always bought with a price. In his great essay "On Fairy-Stories," J. R. R. Tolkien affirms that familiar refrain "and they lived happily ever after": "The Evangelium has not abrogated legends; it has hallowed them, especially the 'happy ending.' The Christian has still to work, with mind as well as body, to suffer, hope, and die; but he may now perceive that all his bents and faculties have a purpose, which can be redeemed" (Tolkien, 89).

Some Suggestions for Reading Fairy Tales

1. We should begin reading these stories in the nursery, but we must not leave them there. *All* of us need these stories. Perhaps, however, the prime time for them is ages seven to ten. During these years the doors of the soul can start to swing shut on the possibility of that larg-

er world—the heart of Faerie—that includes not just the realities we see and touch every day but the spiritual realities of God and of that "Perilous Realm" of the human soul where choices lead to heaven or hell.

2. We should remember that fairy tales were originally told, not read, and that much of their value comes from the embellishments we add with our mind's eye. Illustrated or extensively rewritten versions often fill blanks best left open to the imagination and perceptions of the listener.

3. We must try to resist finding allegories and lessons in these old stories. And we must certainly resist pointing out such possibilities to children. They will grow into a continually richer and fuller understanding on their own. Sometimes our interpretations can block out what children need to discover on their own. We must, however, listen to their interpretations. Through the connections they discover and tell us about, we may learn much about the concerns of our children (or of our friends).

4. We need to avoid worrying that our children will confuse the "other world" of Faerie with the world of the biblical story—or with the everyday world. Recently this fear has escalated into a panicky association of these old tales with the New Age movement (see Alternative Religions), leading to a rejection of not only fairy tales but also, in extreme cases, such imaginative literature as the Narnia books of C. S. Lewis. Fairy tales are accused of being nightmarishly scary, of leading to fantasizing and unreal expectations and longings or, increasingly, of being remnants of ancient satanic rituals. But fairy tales, like all stories, rise from longings to know who we are and what we are about—and these are spiritual questions. Any good literature is dangerous and often fright-

ening because it forces us to deal with these questions—and thus more deeply with spiritual issues. The "other world" of fairy tales tells us truths that help us recognize patterns of spiritual truth—and even God *himself*—better in our own everyday world.

5. We *must* immerse our children and ourselves in the "other worlds" of C. S. Lewis's Narnia, J. R. R. Tolkien's Middle Earth and George MacDonald's Princess books. We should read them out loud and often. Their worlds were created by a wide reading of both fairy tales and the biblical story.

But we need to keep coming back, all our lives, to the old, traditional tales. Fairy tales that insist on wonder and magic can enrich our reading of the biblical accounts—for deep through that ocean of fairy tale runs the warm, rich current of God's full and final truth.

See also ENTERTAINMENT; PLAY; READING.

References and Resources

R. F. Capon, *The Third Peacock* (New York: Image Books, 1972); G. K. Chesterton, "The Ethics of Elfland," in *Orthodoxy,* vol. 1 of *The Collected Works of G. K. Chesterton* (San Francisco: Ignatius, 1986); M. T. Donze, *Touching a Child's Heart* (Notre Dame, Ind.: Ave Maria, 1985); R. Haughton, *Tales from Eternity: The World of Fairy Tales* (New York: Seabury, 1973); C. S. Lewis, "On Three Ways of Writing for Children," in *Of Other Worlds* (New York: Harcourt Brace Jovanovich, 1966); C. S. Lewis, *The Voyage of the Dawn Treader* (New York: Harper, 1980); G. MacDonald, *The Princess and the Goblin* (New York: Books of Wonder, 1986); I. Opie and P. Opie, *The Classic Fairy Tales* (New York: Oxford University Press, 1974); J. R. R. Tolkien, "On Fairy-Stories," in *The Tolkien Reader* (New York: Oxford University Press, 1974).

Where to Begin

P. C. Asbjornsen, I. D'Aulaire and E. P. D'Aulaire, eds., *East of the Sun and West of the*

Moon (New York: Viking, 1969); W. Gag, ed., *Tales from Grimm* (New York: Coward, Mc-Cann & Geoghegan, 1981); W. Gag, ed., *More Tales from Grimm* (New York: Coward, Mc-Cann & Geoghegan, 1981); V. Hamilton, *The People Could Fly: American Black Folktales* (New York: Knopf, 1985); A. Lang, *The Blue [Gray, Purple, Red, Pink, Brown, etc.] Fairy Book* (New York: Airmont, 1969); M. Twain, *The Arabian Nights* (New York: Grosset and Dunlap, 1981).

Mary Ruth Wilkinson

—FAMILY—

Family applies to any group of people that claim to belong together, including same-sex couples. It is a freely contracted relationship between individual consenting adults. Traditional families (father, mother and children) are under attack not only from the option of many alternatives but also from erosion of confidence within those families. Some argue that the nuclear family (mother, father, children) is dead except for the first two or three years of child rearing. In the light of this many Christians are appealing for a return to "family values"* and family goals* without realizing that *family* has no common, shared meaning.

Does Scripture point to a common core meaning of this basic and first human community? What is the Christian's experience of family of God (the church) and how does this relate to one's biological family? As we shall see, the "biblical family" looks much more like an African extended family than the stripped-down Western nuclear family. Companion articles explores the idea that for Christians the family is a place of spiritual formation* and mission.*

The Fragmented Family

Tremendous forces have conspired to re-shape the family in the Western world. The rise of wage labor and industrialization took work out of the household into the factory and office. The family changed from a unit of production to a unit of consumption. Children came to be treated with new tenderness and removed from the family for education; family roles were reduced once again. Political changes have had their effect as well. The feudal system dealt with households, but later political forces tended to abstract the individual as a political unit. Indeed, the basic unit of society in the Western world has become the individual—a truly revolutionary change. Not surprisingly, family is understood in this cultural context as an arrangement between individuals rather than the way people experience a corporate identity.

Whereas the bourgeois family (composed of a master of a craft, his wife, children, other blood relatives, a fluctuating number of tradesmen, and apprentices all living together) functioned as a shared economic enterprise (Berger and Berger, 87-104), the modern family is a stripped-down version with mother, father and children, moving from place to place, having few vocational roles other than the mutual meeting of emotional needs. Many modern families are single-parent* families. Blended families with children from various previous marriages* have convoluted and interlocking circles of belonging. Taking this trend to the logical extreme, the post-modern West, having shorn its roots with the Judeo-Christian faith, now wants to have family without risk. So what has emerged is no-fault divorce,* cohabiting couples, both parents working outside the home, the demise of vocational homemaking,* and the professionalization of parenting* in care centers and schools.* All this is aided and abetted by the church, which has successfully moved Christian education from the home* to the church. What Marx attempted by social revolution (the replacement of home education by state and of families by collectives) the church has assisted by neglect.

The Changing Family

In spite of the popular misconception, the "nuclear family" (a household consisting only of a married couple and their children) has a long history. Research has shown that in North America and Western Europe the nuclear family is not a modern invention arising from industrialization and urbanization but predates these trends by centuries, at least as far back as the High Middle Ages, though in Eastern Europe something closer to the extended family was more common (Berger and Berger, 87). Nuclear families in previous generations, however, did contain servants (now replaced by machines). Brigitte and Peter Berger argue that modernity did not produce the nuclear family; the nuclear family produced modernity through a closer relation between parents and children, greater parental influence and greater individuation (91). All of this, however, is under serious attack and subject to bewildering forces of change.

People in other cultures are wrestling with their own changing family forms. The African family, once experienced as concentric circles of family, clan, tribe, often with polygamy at the center, experienced the disintegration of its core through colonization and urbanization (separating father and mother to gain remunerated employment) and a changed value of children (once a sign of wealth, now a major cause of poverty). In spite of all this, even first-generation city dwellers retain profound ties to the family land. Asian families, characterized by hierarchy and power structures, now face their own pressures of modernity and postmodernity.

The Extended Family

In all cultures most of us belong to multiple families: our family of origin, the family created through marriage, the spouse's family we joined through marriage, and, in the case of multiple marriages, overlapping relationships with children and former spouses (because we cannot divorce family members). The extended family is one way of speaking of this wider network of relationships among people who belong by blood, adoption or covenant. Add to this the Christian's experience of entering the family of God through faith in Jesus, and we have one more family experience— this one less provisional, as it lasts forever! While mobility* has taken its toll on the extended family in the Western world, communication by the Internet,* e-mail and travel has made it wonderfully possible to have significant family experiences with uncles and aunts, cousins, grandparents,* nieces and nephews. Many grandparents now have regular contact with their grandchildren in distant cities through e-mail. Parenting, as we have elsewhere seen (see Character; Parenting; Single Parenting), is too large a task for one or two parents, and this extended family, including brothers and sisters in the church, has a crucial role, especially where the nuclear family is fragmented. Many children of divorced parents, or children suffering the death of a parent, have found real family nurture and support in uncles and aunts, as well as nonblood relatives through the church.

123

Relating to in-laws through marriage is never without its difficulties. Making the transition of "leav[ing] father and mother" (Gen 2:24) for those becoming married, and letting go on the part of the parents, is a difficult, often painful transition. Marrying couples are advised to make the process of separating themselves gradual rather than abrupt, to accept the spouse's concern for her or his parental family and that parents cannot automatically stop being interested in their children; nor should they be. At the same time, couples need to present a united front to any attempt by parents or in-laws to interfere, affirming the priority of the marriage relationship.

Family Theology

All of this raises an important question. Is there a continuous core meaning to our nonchurch family that is not culturally crafted but divinely ordained?

Family is a permanent human community that one enters by birth, covenant (marriage) or adoption.* The simplest and smallest family unit was the Adam and Eve covenant (dyad), through which persons not actually "next of kin" became closest relatives. This is the meaning of Adam's outburst: "This is now bone of my bones and flesh of my flesh" (Gen 2:23). While Adam and Eve were commanded to "be fruitful and increase in number" (Gen 1:28), they were a God-imaging community even before Eve brought forth a man "with the help of the LORD" (4:1). Even a childless couple is a core family, though they will continue to experience other levels of family life with their birth families, thus extending the family experience to other generations. So at the heart of the family experience are a man, a woman and child; this calls into serious question whether same-sex couples can ever be truly "family" in a divinely approved way (see Homosex-

uality). Cohumanity is central to the family experience.

Family is marked by covenant, that binding personal agreement by which a man and woman belong to each other "for better, for worse" (see Marriage). Covenant communicates the relational genius of family: each lives for the other and all live for the one. This unconditional belonging extends to our parents even when we "leave" them to "cleave" to our spouse (Gen 2:24); the new core family is thus prioritized over the extended family. Even though we have left father and mother, however, we do not divorce our siblings and parents. When we have children, we extend covenant belonging to them unilaterally, even before they can respond. But that covenant becomes bilateral when children are able to reciprocate. The covenant may, much later, become unilateral again as we become dependent parents needing care from our children (Balswick and Balswick, 21).

There are theological reasons for restricting the idea of family to the covenant community. First, in the Bible the first community on earth was the family, predating the church or the nation. Family is not a human invention but a divine creation, a matter of vocation or calling rather than convenience and human choice.

Second, God is family. God exists communally as a triune God marked by covenant love (Jn 17:1) in which each person is for the other and all for the One. Thus every family in heaven and on earth derives its nature and dignity from God as family (Eph 3:14-15).

Third, Old Testament legislation dealt with family-plus-land units, as is graphically illustrated by the story of Ruth. These families were more like what we would extended families and constituted the basic social, kinship, legal and religious structures of the people of God. God ultimately owned the land but entrusted it to families, to whom it would be returned in the Jubilee (Lev 25:4-18). God deals with families under the Old Covenant.

Fourth, even under the New Covenant, God continues to work through families. God's kingdom works through families as whole households (including servants and resident aliens) become Christians (Acts 16:32-33). Spouses are sanctified by their believing partner (1 Cor 7:14), and children grow up in the nurture and admonition of the Lord (Eph 6:1-4). Church leaders are expected to prove their ministry first at home (1 Tim 3:4-5). So we may speak of the family as a domestic. But there is another family for the Christian.

Church as First Family

Jesus creates a new family. It is the new first family, a family of his followers that now demands primary allegiance even over the biological family. Those who do the will of the Father (who, in other words, live under the reign of God) are now brothers and sisters of Jesus and one another (Mk 3:31-35). Jesus can speak even more challengingly: the advent of the kingdom means brother will turn against brother, children against parents and parents against children (Mt 10:21-22). So far as biological family is concerned, "I have not come to bring peace, but a sword" (Mt 10:34). Those who love father or mother more than him, Jesus says, are not worthy of him (Mt 10:37).

The sense of church as first family is also clear in the letters of Paul. His most significant language for describing the church is the language of family. For Paul, Christians are children of God and brothers and sisters to one another (see, e.g., 1 Thess 1:4, 6). The phrase "my brothers" occurs more than sixty-five times in his letters. Paul can also call members of a church "my children" (as in 1 Cor 4:14 or Gal 4:19). Both the number and intensity of these familial phrases make Paul's letters remarkable in their time and place.

Such greetings were not merely pious niceties. The church Paul knew met in households. Paul expected and depended on Christians' opening their homes (and thus their biological families) to Christian brothers and sisters (Rom 16:5; 1 Cor 16:15; Col 4:15; Philem 2). Such hospitality* extended to a wide network of Christians, including missionaries and those on business trips (2 Cor 8:23). By opening their homes these Christians recognized and welcomed "relatives" near and distant.

On a more basic level Paul links familial language with baptism.* The Gospel of John recognizes a need for the disciples of Jesus to be "born again," to know a second birth that redefines identity and admits the disciple to a family-community that will nurture the new identity. Paul has similar concerns but addresses them with the language of adoption rather than birth (Rom 8:15-17; Gal 3:26—4:6). He reminds believers that they have a new identity because they have been baptized into Christ. When children are adopted, they take on new parents, new sisters and brothers, new names, new inheritances. And those who have been baptized into Christ have been adopted by God. This new baptism means Christians' new parent is God the Father ("Abba," cries Paul). Their new siblings are other Christians. Their new name or most fundamental identity is simply "Christian"—one of those who know Jesus as Lord and determiner of their existence. And their new inheritance is freedom, community and resources provided a hundredfold (Gal 3:26—4:6; Mk 10:28-31, see Adoption; Godparenting).

New Testament scholar N. T. Wright affirms the centrality of what is here called first family. Noting that "from baptism onwards, one's basic family consisted of one's fellow-Christians," he writes:

> The fact of widespread persecution, regarded by both pagans and Christians as the normal state of affairs within a century of the beginnings of Christianity, is powerful evidence of the sort of thing Christianity was, and was perceived to be. It was a new family, a third "race," neither Jew nor Gentile but "in Christ" (Wright, 449-50).

The Synergy of Family Life

It is important to notice that Jesus did not destroy the biological family. He did create a new first family and call for allegiance to the kingdom to precede the biological family. Yet he also spoke strenuously against divorce (Mt 19:3-12) and welcomed and blessed children (Mk 10:13-16; Lk 18:15-17). So Jesus did not expect biological family to be denied or eliminated. What he did was decenter and relativize it. He did not see it as the vehicle of salvation. He expected first family, the family of the kingdom, to grow evangelistically rather than biologically (Mt 28:19-20). Entrance to the kingdom in fact required a second birth, this time of water and the Spirit (Jn 3:5-6). For those who would follow Jesus, the critical blood, the blood that most significantly determines their identity and character, is not the blood of the biological family. It is the blood of the Lamb.

So in one sense, the church becomes the family for the follower of Jesus; in another sense, the biological family is a form of church. In reality, the Christian's family experience is both enhanced and complicated by being a member of two families. It is enhanced by the gift of an extended family for parenting, personal growth, character*

development, service and mission. But it is complicated when there are competing loyalties.

Jesus lived with the complexity of competing loyalties to his "birth family" (Mary, Joseph and his siblings) and the family of Father, Son and Holy Spirit, as evidenced in the sensitive way he fulfilled his mother's request to work a miracle without betraying the Father's timing (Jn 2:1-11). At the cross he provided for his mother as a good son would (Jn 19:25-27). Apparently Jesus regarded family as an appropriate context in which to practice discipleship (Mk 5:1-20) and even called siblings into his disciple community (Mt 10:2-4).

So family—both the biological and the ecclesial—are places of spiritual formation (see also Character), parenting and mission. For the Christian family is vocational, a calling.

See also CHARACTER; FAMILY SYSTEMS; GODPARENTING; MISSION; PARENTING; SINGLE PARENTING; SPIRITUAL FORMATION.

References and Resources

R. S. Anderson and D. B. Guernsey, *On Being Family: A Social Theology of the Family* (Grand Rapids: Eerdmans, 1985); J. O. Balswick and J. K. Balswick, *The Family: A Christian Perspective on the Contemporary Home* (Grand Rapids: Baker, 1989); B. Berger and P. L. Berger, *The War over the Family* (Garden City, N.Y.: Doubleday, 1983); R. Clapp, *Families at the Crossroads: Beyond Traditional and Modern Options* (Downers Grove, Ill.: InterVarsity Press, 1993); M. Eastman, *Family, the Vital Factor: The Key to Society's Survival* (Melbourne: Collins Dove, 1989); J. A. Henley, *Accepting Life: The Ethics of Living in Families* (Melbourne: Joint Board of Christian Education, 1994); C. J. H. Wright, *God's People in God's Land: Family, Land and Property in the Old Testament* (Grand Rapids: Eerdmans, 1990); N. T. Wright, *The New Testament and the People of God* (Minneapolis: Fortress, 1992).

Rodney Clapp and R. Paul Stevens

—FAMILY HISTORY—

What is it about doing a family history that interests people? Why are more people pursuing their family history now than in years gone by? What is the place for this in the Christian scheme of things?

Sometimes people begin pursuing their family history because they have retired and want a hobby to give some structure to this period of transition in their lives. For others, friends got them involved, and they sensed the pleasure and excitement their friends experienced as they delved deeper into the past. Others begin because they have developed a medical problem and want to see if it has its genesis in their family. Sometimes it is the names inscribed in the front of a family* Bible that start the search.

The Value and Risk of Undertaking Family History

Viewed from one perspective, the Bible is a family history. It records the genealogies of many individual families (Gen 10:1—11:32), but it also records the story of the family of God through the ages. It contains not just Jesus' genealogy but the social and religious history that fleshes that out. We cannot fully understand the impact of Jesus' birth, death and resurrection without understanding the overall scheme of God's relationship with Israel through the years. Precisely because the Bible contains the sagas of numerous families, there is much psychological, as well as spiritual, truth in it that speaks with deep insight to our own families today.

Just as an understanding of the Bible story gives us an appreciation of our spiritual roots, so an understanding of our family history can help us to understand who we are as families and individuals. With communities now so dispersed, and the family folklore no longer readily accessible through grandparents* or other members of the older generation, we find ourselves digging into the past to discover our roots and link up with our heritage. The 1977 television* series *Roots* provoked an unprecedented desire on the part of many to trace their own family's origins.

This could all sound like selfish preoccupation, and for some it is. But those writing up their family history are also making a significant contribution to the wider culture, especially local culture. Demographers have realized that family historians have a fund of knowledge to offer about members who moved from place to place, what occupations they pursued, and how often they relocated. Social historians, as well as medicos, also raid the findings of family historians to glean useful information for their own research.

One danger is that it can become addictive. It is easy to get consumed with the dead to the neglect of the living. Like a giant detective novel, there are many mysteries to be solved. Why did Grandmother leave Ireland when she did? Why did one great-grandfather leave his first wife and family in Germany when he emigrated? What happened to those other children listed on your great-grandmother's death certificate that you never heard of? Why does it say on this certificate that she was born in Canada when family folklore says she was born in New York?

We also must be ready for surprises. Sometimes those surprises are good ones, such as discovering we are related to some famous person; we may also discover skeletons in the family closet. Unraveling some of these puzzles can lead to a greater appreciation of why our family relates or makes the choices it does. This brings with it the possibility of healing memories buried deep in the family's past or of reestablishing relationships with estranged branches of the wider family. In many families there are secrets buried in the past that need to see the light of day so that forgiveness can take place and peace between family factions be restored.

Ways of Researching Your Family History

How and where do you make a start on researching your family history? You begin with the most recent piece of accurate information that you have—perhaps the date of your grandfather's death. Armed with that, you can visit your local library and talk with the person who looks after the local history section. You can visit a bookstore and pick up something written on the topic, usually with "family history" or "genealogy" in the title. You can contact your local family history or genealogical society.

There is an amazing amount of information available now to assist you in your research. This includes birth, death* and marriage* registers, shipping records, census results, military records, land sales registers, letters, journals, diaries, wills, ships' logs, government records, local histories and newspapers. Because of their particular interest in genealogy, the Mormons have established a remarkable collection of resources at their headquarters in Salt Lake City as well as resource centers throughout America and overseas. Joining the nearest family history association or genealogical society is another positive step. There you will meet people keen to share what they have learned who will put you in touch with others who may be able to help.

It is also important before you begin to work out a way of organizing your research and its findings. Without this you will spend many fruitless hours trying to remember where you put something, what the name was of that book you read some fact in, or rereading records consulted five years earlier. There are many ways of doing this, but without doubt a computer* is best and easiest, especially with materials stored on CD-ROM and on the Internet.*

While most people want to research the history of their family of origin, others are keen to research the part of a different kind of "family" to which they belong, whether it be an organization such as a bowling club or a local church. Not so many years ago congregations had annual "anniversaries" where they celebrated their life together and rehearsed various aspects of their history, often inviting a previous minister to preach at the event. These occasions probably ceased as they became a meaningless ritual, but they fulfilled an important function—providing an opportunity for the church to rehearse its story under God. Perhaps this kind of "family" history will help congregations to find fresh ways of celebrating their life together.

See also FAMILY; FAMILY PROBLEMS; FAMILY SYSTEMS.

References and Resources
A. Eakle and J. Cerny, *The Source: A Guidebook to American Genealogy* (Salt Lake City: Ancestry, 1984).

Julie Banks

—FAMILY PROBLEMS—

All families* have problems. Living together through the thick and thin of everyday life, family members will encounter struggles and stressors all along the way. Whether it is a major problem like substance abuse, serious illness, natural disaster or economic failure, or a minor difficulty like sibling rivalry, unhealthy coalitions in the family or personal conflicts between family members, it will take a toll on family relationships. Since the external problems are usually beyond the control of the family, this article will focus on relational problems that family members can change.

Four common problems that lead to internal family disharmony are conditional love,* shame,* control and distance. If a family is to function effectively, members must first recognize and then learn to change these disruptive patterns. Four antithetical healing principles that can bring harmony between family members are covenant (commitment and faithfulness), grace (acceptance and forgiveness*), empowerment (competence and growth) and intimacy (closeness and communication*). Knowing the difference between harmful and healing relationship dynamics will point families in the direction of health.* And, embracing these healing principles, family members will be able to combat the relational problems that cripple their functioning. Healing relationship principles will move family members toward well-being, whereas repeating the hurting patterns will move them toward further strife.

Loving That Is Conditional

Conditional love says a person is loved if, because or when he or she behaves a certain way. Love that depends on external behavior places an enormous burden on a family member to earn love rather than to be loved. Conditional love becomes a leverage: love is withheld or withdrawn when a member's behavior is "unacceptable." This perpetuates the "try harder" compulsion to please others in order to feel acceptable. Family members who live under the dominating influence of conditional love begin to believe they have an internal flaw that makes them unworthy of being loved. Without the assurance that their family will "love them forever," even when they make mistakes, they become insecure. Conditional love leads to a pattern of distrust and untrustworthiness that spirals in a negative direction.

The exact opposite of conditional love is unconditional love. A compelling picture of God in the Bible is that of one who faithfully initiates and persistently pursues people through unconditional covenant love, even when they pull away and turn their back on him. Jehovah God of the Old Testament is the model parent who loves the children of Israel with a love that will not let go. A family that can keep on loving, even when members behave in unlovable ways, provides a basic trust and security for its members. Because it is inevitable that family members will disappoint and fail each other, it is absolutely essential that they experience the security of unconditional love. Trust is the foundation that makes connection and growth possible. Just as God's unconditional love is demonstrated through grace that accepts us just as we are, so family life needs to be lived in an atmosphere of grace.

Shaming One Another

To forgive and be forgiven is the hallmark of the Christian family. Unfortunately, families often live under the cloud of shame* rather than grace. In shaming

129

homes, family members set up a standard of perfection that is impossible to achieve. The strong focus on external behavior impedes that person's internal development. Members not only fear making mistakes, but they believe they are a mistake, thinking they can never be good enough. In the innermost part of their being, they are ashamed of who they are. Totally discouraged by failing to live up to unreasonable standards, they give up! Though it may be their only defense, blaming themselves or others for their predicament leads only to further problems and irresponsible behavior.

The discouragement incurred in a shaming home defeats the hopeful message of God's grace! For God so loved and cherished each unique created person that he gave his only Son for them. The intent was to restore and reconcile. Likewise, a family of grace will embrace each member as a unique, cherished creation of God. While they acknowledge human failure, they also take hope in people's capacity to learn from mistakes and recover from imperfections. Repentance and forgiveness become the ways to reconciliation, hope and life. It is only when family members are loved, accepted and forgiven that they have the courage to begin anew.

Using Power to Control Others

Parents who control and coerce their children give the message that "might equals right." With this perspective, one inevitably tries to get more power in order to lord it over others. This interpretation of power leads to serious problems of physical and emotional abuse.* Mostly it is the people who have very little power who resort to physical and mental punishment. In controlling families, members respond out of fear rather than respect, cowering under the more powerful members. The question of what they do in the controller's absence ("out of sight is out of mind") is another serious problem. They may rebel and strike out in destructive ways. This "law and punishment" model keeps abusive systems perpetuating themselves from one generation to the next.

But Jesus radically redefined the notion of power. The model in the New Testament is one of empowerment or of using power for others. Just as the Holy Spirit empowers Christians to live out the life of faith, family members are called to nurture, equip, instruct, confront, encourage and assist one other in personal growth. Jesus announced that he came to serve and not to be served. The idea of laying down one's life for another family member is the extraordinary way of the cross. It is possible to turn the other cheek or go the second mile only if there is the strength of character to do it. When parents come alongside their children as moral and loving leaders who affirm their children's strengths and build up their potential, they empower them to become responsible members of society.

Keeping Emotional Distance

Families today are besieged by activities and conditions that keep them removed and distanced from each other. If the family is a place where members experience rejection, the best way for family members to protect themselves from that kind of pain is to pretend they are okay when they are not. In addition, if members are loved only when they do acceptable things, or shamed when they make mistakes, or harshly punished when they fail, they will look for ways to anesthetize themselves from these condemnations. Addictive behaviors, such as drinking, eating,* overwork and so on, promise relief by taking one's mind off the self-defeating messages, but they only intensify the problem. These addictive substitutes are not only self-destructive but are destructive to relationships within the family. When denial and cover-up become a way of life, they keep family members emotionally distanced from each other and are a barrier to intimacy, which is the healing force in family relationships.

Adam and Eve were described as being "naked and not ashamed" when they encountered each other. They were completely open and vulnerable in their relationship. The psalms give a similar picture of intimacy when they express the psalmist's deepest thoughts and emotions of pain, joy, anguish, anger, victory and love to God in prayer. The scriptural truth that "there is no fear in love . . . perfect love drives out fear" (1 Jn 4:18) is a compelling reason to come before God naked and not ashamed. There is safety in being loved unconditionally, being gracefully accepted and empowering others. In healing families, there is no need to hide or deny what one feels because all thoughts and feelings are honorable and listened to with compassion. In fact, conflicts offer us an exhilarating capacity for constructive growth when family members are able to hear and respond with appropriate understanding. Resolutions are sought in order to bring harmony and closeness between members. Intimacy is the fruit of vulnerable sharing and working through family problems together. It is the time a family spends together that deepens their level of interaction and emotional connection.

Finding Solutions

Once problems are recognized, the family has a great opportunity to deal effectively with them. If your family is operating under the four disruptive relationship patterns, it is necessary to reverse them. The family must do something different to break the hurting patterns and add something new to put the healing relationship principles in place. Here are some ideas for moving toward solutions.

One must declare the problem and commit to the solution. Admitting the inadequate past way and then indicating the desire to replace it with a more effective way is illustrated in the following statements: "I withhold my affection when you do not do what I say, and I scold and shame you when you do something I do not like, but I'd like to extend grace and acceptance instead"; "I've been trying to force you into my way of doing things, but I know your way is equally good, and I will affirm you rather than criticize you"; "I realize I keep my distance by blaming you, and I will accept responsibility for my actions. It's important to me to find good ways to connect." The confession initiates the process. The vulnerable, "about-face" change of attitude opens others up in a way that will make a real difference. It is important to give some idea of what family relationships are when members are operating according to the four healing principles.

It is crucial to pay attention to the things family members already do that contribute to the four healing principles. You may want to ask all members to talk about the specific times when they have felt loved, accepted, empowered and emotionally close. Recognizing family strengths and particular activities that contribute to positive interaction provides specific behaviors to emulate. Discovering what the family is doing *right* is an important clue as to how the problem will be solved. By fostering positive behaviors, the family will be able to eliminate negative ones.

Choosing to empower rather than to control, or deciding to accept rather than to shame, automatically reverses the negative trends. Eliminating unrealistic expectations means a person is free to discover what he or she can do well and to learn what is appropriate for a particular age and situation.

It is especially helpful for family members to make a list of all the behaviors they can think of that lead to the four healing principles. Then every member has the chance to make a conscious decision to incorporate these specific actions to get things rolling in the right direction.

An approach that focuses on solutions brings hope. Sometimes, however, a family cannot get to future solutions until it has paid sufficient attention to past hurts. In this case, repentance is a necessary part of the solution so they can begin to reestablish trust. After reconciliation they can put forth the remedial effort to make the desired changes.

A problem solved is a point of growth and celebration for the family. The solutions lead to a deeper level of intimacy in the family, which brings about more capacity for unconditional loving, acceptance and empowerment. Round and round it goes, one positive relationship principle contributing to another in an ongoing cycle of family unity.

See also COMMUNICATION; CONFLICT RESOLUTION; FORGIVENESS; LOVE; SHAME; STRESS.

References and Resources

J. O. Balswick and J. K. Balswick, *The Family: A Christian Perspective on the Contemporary Home* (Grand Rapids: Baker, 1989); R. Campbell, *How to Really Love Your Child* (Wheaton, Ill.: Victor Books, 1978); R. Campbell, *How to Really Love Your Teenager* (Wheaton, Ill.: Victor Books, 1980); N. Stinnett et al., eds., *Family Strengths: Positive Models for Family Life* (Lincoln: University of Nebraska Press, 1979).

Judith K. Balswick

—FAMILY SYSTEMS—

In this article, family life is understood as a system, that is, as a whole composed of interconnected and interdependent members that are all the time influencing one another. No one lives entirely by himself or herself. This is true not only within the smallest family unit, sometimes called the *nuclear family,* but also between generations as family systems influence each other. The term *family of origin* refers to the family or families in which one is reared. Virginia Satir stresses the importance of the family of origin as "the main base against and around which most family blueprints are designed." She suggests that "it is easy to duplicate in your family the same things that happened in your growing up. This is true whether your family was a nurturing or a troubled one" (124). This foundational insight, so often observed by psychiatrists and family counselors, was expressed centuries ago in the Bible where God says, "I, the LORD your God, am a jealous God, punishing the children for the sin of the fathers to the third and fourth generation of those who hate me, but showing love to a thousand generations of those who love me" (Deut 5:9-10). The promise of intergenerational grace in this last phrase is restated in Deuteronomy 5:29, which indicates that people are to live in harmony with God's ways "so that it might go well with them and their children forever." While family systems theory is less than fifty years old, it is essentially in harmony with the biblical revelation of how families, communities and the people of God function (Collins and Stevens, 92-107).

Family of Origin

The problem with us as people is that we had parents, and of course so did they. While parents are sometimes a problem for us, it is a good thing that we had parents—and a good thing that they did as well. In our families we not only duplicate the lives from our families of origin, we sometimes potentiate (i.e., increase the intensity of) the problems.* To be a healthy member of a family, we need to practice forgiveness,* which permits us to free our parents from the resentments we have accumulated about them. Forgiveness also frees us to determine our own way of living without the burden of the demands from our family of origin. This is a key to growth and maturity in thinking about the family as a system.

Through our family histories* we can view the relationship dynamics and values transmitted through generations. Virtues and values can be embraced, and curses and criticisms can be challenged. This is the understanding of covenant making. Throughout our growing-up years we learned how to make and keep covenants and the value of promises. We learned this from our parents, or we noticed the lack of this and promised to ourselves that we would be promise keepers. Through forgiveness, promise keeping and covenant making we are empowered to bring health* and grace to the next generation.

We did not choose our parents, nor did they choose us. Further, none of us had the opportunity to choose how to live in our families of origin. We adapted to pressing circumstances as best we could with the skills and experiences we had, just as they did. However, all of us can choose how we will live in our current families and interact within our various systems or communities. We do not need to replicate the unhealthy patterns of our families of origin, nor do we need to overadapt and do the opposite.

Wholeness

Virginia Satir uses the image of a mobile to explain how a system works. In the family mobile, every part of the family is understood in terms of the whole family and how individual parts affect the whole. Each part is considered to be interdependent, not autonomous. A movement or change in one part of the mobile affects the system throughout. Picture a mobile that hangs over an infant's crib as having people instead of animals or stars hanging from it. Envisioned in this way, events that initially touch one member of the family mobile cause other family members to reverberate in relationship to the change in the initial member. Thus, if a member of the family marries a person from another race, graduates from medical school or is fired, the surrounding family system is affected. The family mobile is altered, not just the individual member.

For example, Barry (not his real name), a fourteen-year-old boy in a single-parent family from my counseling practice, stayed away from home for several weeks and made no contact with his understandably frantic mother. At a loss as to what to do, she became depressed, and the younger kids began to suffer as she drank from morning till night, ignoring their basic care. When Barry finally came home, he vowed to God that he would stay. His mother gave up drinking, and the family mood improved greatly. The siblings were delighted at this change and blessed their older brother for doing what was right in their eyes. As the mom became more functional and pleasant, Barry figured the family problem was solved and he could now live his own life again without the presumed obligation to be the "designated father." (Barry's father had divorced his mother when Barry was just six years old.) Since life was now okay, Barry began to skip some school and

133

stayed out late at night. Barry's mother then became upset and was soon as depressed as before, precipitating a crisis in the younger children, who began to display their own symptoms of depression.* Barry again saw the cost of his behavior on the family and promised anew that he would be a "good kid." The family resumed functioning as normal until the cycle repeated itself again. Barry's growing up affected both his mother and his siblings, and he felt trapped into being the absentee father that all people long to have and resent missing. His feeling of being trapped was felt by each of the other members of the system.

In the analogy of the family mobile, every time one part of the family changes position, the entire mobile shifts. All parts are unbalanced until the changed part returns to its original place. Barry feels impelled to "do good" for the good of the family. When Barry eventually moves out permanently from his family and creates his own independent life, the other parts of the family will adjust themselves to a new form of stability and security. Until then the family will require that he stay and function in ways that permit their stability and security. In family life each person is part of the whole. We are linked together invisibly in a relational, emotional and even a spiritual unity. But change within the system is not all bad.

Good Trouble

Shifts in the family mobile can be considered family crises and are potentially good trouble through which positive change can come. Think of the crises that would be induced in the following examples: the middle son of a solid Orthodox Jewish family becomes a Christian; the workaholic father rolls the family minivan over a cliff and nearly dies; the ultrastable mother does not come home after work until 9 p.m. and

looks a bit like a floozy; another child is conceived although the couple had agreed that "two is enough"; two families blend, resulting in two fifteen-year-old stepsisters; a younger brother suffers a prolonged death from leukemia while the older sister does not feel understood; a middle-aged dad buys a sports car and begins wearing a jogging suit. All of the changes caused by these events can result in greater satisfaction and security. It would be a shame to waste such terrific crises.

Boundaries and Subsystems

Mother and father (wife and husband) together are a family subsystem. Their children are another family subsystem, as are the grandparents* and other extended relatives. In our family, our dog and two cats are a significant subsystem that precipitates some growth-producing tension between father and daughter! We would not be the same family without each competing system within our larger system we call with much affection "our family." Our family dinner table is a cacophony of information about other systems that are affecting our family: what happened at school,* what craziness Tim did on *Home Improvement*, the CD sale at the mall and other families who are reported to be in greater crises than ours. Some of this information enters into our family and affects us; some stays out or is kept out. This has to do with how our family is defined and the values and structure of our family unit. In systems thinking this is referred to as family boundaries, or the openness of the system to other systems.

The peer groups of both parents and children are systems that affect the experience of the family. Teenage kids may have friends who wear their caps turned backwards. Being their peers, they influence the kids and thus the family. The parents' peer group may be other middle-agers on the sideline of a soccer game or prayerful adults in a church fellowship group. When these peer groups interact, there is a good chance of a crash at the intersection. Imagine the cap-wearing teen with his Bulls jacket coming to church one morning to meet a "suit" carrying a well-worn Bible who asks him to remove his hat out of respect. It should be said again that subsystem collision can result in growth for each subsystem. The issue of boundaries is whether we will permit what is outside of our understanding and experience to change us so as to help us grow.

Conclusions

Family systems show that family life sets us up to know God and gain Christian maturity right at home. We were built for relationships, and family life helps us to see that isolated individuals simply do not exist. Further, we were built for covenant making and promise keeping—two graces we may experience in our lives whether our family experience has been good or bad. Even very hard experiences in family life can be experienced as God's good invitation to make changes for the better and to practice the grace of forgiveness. The influence of subsystems and other systems on our family system causes us continuously to define our family goals* and family values—once more seeking God's mind in prayer and Scripture. Through it all the multigenerational impact of our behavior, whether bad or good, mentioned in Deuteronomy 5:9-10 is not just a curse but a blessing*: God's love extends "to a thousand generations."

See also BLESSING; COMMUNICATION; FAMILY PROBLEMS; GOALS; FAMILY HISTORY; PARENTING; VALUES.

References and Resources

R. Anderson and D. Guernsey, *On Being a Family: A Social Theology of the Family* (Grand Rapids: Eerdmans, 1985); J. O. Balswick and J. K. Balswick, *The Family: A Christian Perspective on the Contemporary Home* (Grand Rapids: Baker, 1989); W. M. Brody, *Family Dance: Building Positive Relationships Through Family Therapy* (Garden City, N.Y.: Anchor, 1977); P. Collins and R. P. Stevens, *The Equipping Pastor* (Washington, D.C.: Alban Institute, 1994); E. H. Friedman, *Generation to Generation: Family Process in Church and Synagogue* (New York: Guilford, 1985); R. Richardson, *Family Ties That Bind* (Vancouver: Self-Counsel Press, 1984); V. Satir, *Conjoint Family Therapy* (Palo Alto, Calif.: Science and Behavior Books, 1967).

Paddy Ducklow

—FEMININITY—

Femininity has diverse meanings to women as well as men, depending on cultural, economic, political and religious factors. Western cultural notions of femininity have focused on outer body image, femininity being something that one can even acquire through using various products. Even Scripture does not give a universal definition of femininity and masculinity,* concentrating instead on what it means to be a godly woman or man. The biblical text does, however, give a consistent picture of the notion of the feminine, particularly in relation to the intimate love of God. So this article focuses on the metaphorical language of feminine bodily imagery in the biblical text, its relevance in shaping our knowledge and experience of God, and its significance for family life.

In Scripture God has feminine as well as masculine attributes. As God-imaging creatures, intricately woven by an incredible Creator, we have both masculine and feminine aspects within us, though as gendered human beings we respond differently to the movement of the Spirit in our lives. This biblical invitation to experience full personhood in relation to God stands in stark contrast to the stereotypes of popular culture.

Cultural Notions of Femininity

Many cultures emphasize outer bodily qualities as the substantive foundation for femininity. This has been critiqued within academic, popular, secular and sacred circles. The heart of the criticism is the linking of the concept of femininity with a beauty image. This secular critique is congruent with the biblical notion that femininity is not an outward but an inward phenomenon—a state of being more than a state of doing.

Unfortunately femininity has been used to sell cars, vacuum cleaners and makeup and has been used to the detriment of women. The feminine body image becomes a standardized size or shape, and women, not cherishing their whole body-soul, are relegated to lives of dieting, discouragement and eating* disorders. It is a tragedy that a specific cultural definition of beauty has become the primary focus for definitions of femininity. Not surprisingly, there is a crisis in what it means to be feminine in this day and age.

Biblical Notion of the Feminine

There is no escaping the impact of what the media has fabricated and marketed as femininity. An unintended consequence of this is that "the cultural image of women, the public image, is distorted by patriarchy. We are more than victim or sexual plaything, and it is out of that 'more than' that we search for the face of God" (Proctor-Smith, 16). This search for a divine perspective on femininity and masculinity focuses more on who God is than who we are as feminine or masculine. To say that we are made in the image of God (Gen 1:27) is not to say God is like us; rather we are like God in ways we will now explore.

There are many models in Scripture of what it means to be a godly woman or man but fewer statements about what it means to be feminine or masculine. For example, the woman of Proverbs 31 is both strong and gentle, wise and vigorous, compassionate and resourceful, creative and businesslike. Deborah, a vigorous woman leader in the book of Judges, exemplifies remarkable leadership skills. These godly qualities are visible in both men and women, and it is difficult to categorize them as only feminine or masculine. One thought worth exploring is that living fully in the image of God is living fully as feminine and masculine.

In stark contrast to equating femininity with bodily image, the biblical text gives a notion of the feminine that includes the body as a metaphor of God's love. Fundamental to this is the scriptural witness that God has masculine and feminine attributes. Jesus is obviously male, yet both Jesus and God the Creator have feminine attributes. For example, Jesus refers to himself as a mother hen (Mt 23:37), and God is referred to as one giving birth (Is 42:13-14; 46:3), a midwife (Ps 22:9-10; Is 66:9-13) and an eagle in whom we take refuge (Deut 32:11-12; Ps 57:1).

Jesus includes both masculine and feminine examples in his parables, challenging the assumption of the male-centered world of New Testament times. When Jesus includes women in his parables, he reveals a down-to-earth God working through everyday life. The parables of the yeast (Lk 13:20), the woman and the lost coin (Lk 15:8-10) and the persistent widow (Lk 18: 1-8) speak of the mystery of God's breaking through the most ordinary moments of human life. Furthermore, the Hebrew word for *wisdom* is grammatically feminine. In the book of Proverbs *wisdom* expresses a feminine image of God, present from the creation and to be cherished now (Prov 8:11, 22-31). These verses are samples of many biblical passages that express the feminine and deserve our attention if we want to fully comprehend the nature of God.

Considering these aspects of femininity and masculinity gives us a clue to the relational aspect of living. Texts in the Scriptures attributing feminine qualities to God show how God has an intimate, relational life with us. These metaphors give visual and symbolic ways to grasp the text and invite the readers to experience the wide love of God bursting through their whole beings.

The cultural emphasis on the outward body as defining of femininity contributes to a dualistic understanding: body separated from heart, soul and mind. In contrast, the biblical notion of the body affirms and even celebrates the person as an interconnected whole. The feminine bodily imagery embedded throughout the biblical text illuminates an image of God as identifying with the bodiliness of a woman and communicating love through bodily metaphors. This is in opposition to historical formulations of a woman's body or bodily functions as associated with sin and evil or the idea that "women are misbegotten males" (quoted in Clanton, 39).

Living Inside the Feminine Metaphors for God

For women, our bodiliness is central to our being. We cannot escape the cycles of being women, whether we give birth or not. We are keenly aware of the cycles of menstruation,* hormonal fluxes, premenopause and menopause. Change, birth, death* and letting go are built into our bodies as females. This pull to our bodies is one that organically gives us a *cyclical* understanding of the world rather than only a *linear* one. This, in turn, will affect a woman's perspective and the way she articulates the spiritual life, theology and ministry (see Carr; Fischer).

It is in bodily imagery that the feminine attributes of God are primarily visible in the Bible. These bodily images do not focus exclusively on the mothering or nurturing qualities of God but impart a wider understanding of the spiritual life: intimacy with God, rhythms of life, waiting, suffering, joy, receptivity and responsiveness. One of the words in the Old Testament used to convey God's immeasurable mercy and compassion for the Israelites has the same root that is used for womb: *raham*. This word conveys a deep love, akin to the natural bond of a child in the womb: "As a father [or mother] has compassion [*raham*] on his [her] children, / so the LORD has compassion on those who fear him" (Ps 103:13, emphasis added). Womb love is God's love—a love that no force can break , a strong, deep love woven with the threads of grace and mercy. This is echoed by the prophet Jeremiah when God says, "Before I formed you in the womb I knew you" (Jer 1:5). God knows us like that, providing womb love from a gentle and strong Creator. When we experience God's love for us as womb love, we profoundly enter the compassion of God and truly experience the scope of *raham*.

Another feminine metaphor in the biblical text that models for us something about the intimate relationship between God and ourselves is that of breast-feeding.* The Old Testament exhorts the people to "nurse and be satisfied at her [Jerusalem's] comforting breasts" and to "drink deeply and delight in her overflowing abundance" (Is 66:11). Literally, the Hebrew expresses the passage with a more accurate reading: "For you will *suck* and be satisfied." Pondering this metaphor gives a glimpse of a God who is tenderly compassionate, intimately involved with life: breast-feeding at the heart of God.

Another potent feminine image in the biblical text is the eagle. The beautiful words in the Song of Moses remind us of this image combining strength and gentleness:

As an eagle stirs up its nest,
and hovers over its young;
as it spreads its wings, takes them up,
and bears them aloft on its
pinions. (Deut 32:11-12 NRSV)

The image of the strong eagle soaring across the weather-beaten sky, protecting and nurturing her young, is liberating. As women, we need images of the feminine that also include strength. Through this image men and women can be strengthened by God's love as both take refuge in God's wings and mount up with eagle's wings (Is 40:31).

But femininity in the Bible is not limited to motherhood. The biblical text redefines the body as something wholesome and good that is even likened to the fierce love of God. God suffers, gives birth, creates and continues to love us into existence and relationship. One learns more about who God is than what God does through the feminine dimension. This complements the masculine imagery of God, which focuses more on God's action in history. So through the feminine dimension of God, we are wooed back to the womb of God, to become God's beloved daughters and sons.

The Feminine and Family Life

The focus of this article has been on the relational aspect of the biblical metaphor of the feminine. The significance of this metaphor is its capacity for intimacy, which is at the heart of family life, of marriage* and of raising children. This is not an intimacy of sentimentality but a rugged intimacy of meeting the holy in the ordinary; the sacred in the midst of busyness. It is incarnational and relational love in the midst of hectic schedules.

Before anything, we need to experientially comprehend the fullness of intimacy with God. This intimacy is one that encompasses both a masculine and feminine understanding; one not dependent on either/or, but on both/and! We need it all: gentleness and firmness, circular thinking and rational thinking, intentionality and spontaneity, body and soul, wide and narrow, creative and logistic. When we defer to engaging in a life predicated on only one image of God, we limit the fullness and depth of God in our life. We cannot grasp the breadth, length, height and depth of the love of Christ (Eph 3:19) steeped in our bones, in the recesses of our gender and in the love of Christ. The resources that God has given to us to sustain intimate relationships are diminished, and in the process so are we. There is a direct relationship between how we experience being daughters and sons of God, and how we treat our own daughters and sons. We need to continue to be parented by a God who can be both mother and father to us, a God who sings for joy with love so deeply that we cannot grasp its beauty without these tangible metaphors becoming a reality in our lives.

This concept is even far more important today when a significant number of families do not come in the same shape as they did many years ago. In fact, it could be argued, the father who could not access the feminine within his psyche, one where emotion and intimacy did not have a central role in life, contributed to the "absent/distant father" so characteristic of the second half of the twentieth century. This has had huge ramifications for the development of male sexuality and spirituality (Nelson). No longer is the two-parent, stay-at-home mother or distant father the norm. More and more there is a commitment to coparenting and single parenting.* Families come in all shapes, sizes and cultural configurations. It is vital that as parents we can access both the feminine and masculine qualities within our own personhood and within our experience and knowledge of our Creator.

It is therefore imperative that we are able to thoughtfully deconstruct cultural notions of both femininity and masculinity that actually minimize our potential to live into the fullness of how God intended us to be as both men and women. We have too long put our values on outer concepts of femininity that have minimized our ability to access the deep feminine so needed for cultivation of soulfulness within family life. For example, if I cannot personally access my own feminine personal rhythms of life, which create balance and harmony within myself, it is certain that I cannot cultivate a soulful focus within my own family. I will be swept by the more masculine demands of performance and achievement, and I will drive my children with the same determination that drove me for years in a culture that emphasizes doing over being. The key to cultivating both the feminine and masculine within family life is balance. If this is not cultivated within each parent, it will be hardly done for our children. Our children

echo who we are, both the good and the bad. In an age where we have every resource available for parenting—skills, classes, books and every lesson imaginable—nothing can teach us the importance of wholeness in our gender unless we actively allow the God of healing to bring a balance of feminine and masculine within us. These are the riches available to us as children of God, for not only intimacy with the Beloved, but also for intimacy with ourselves, with children and with spouses.

See also BREAST-FEEDING; MASCULINITY; MENSTRUATION; PREGNANCY; SEXUALITY.

References and Resources

K. A. Callaghan, ed., *Ideals of Feminine Beauty: Philosophical, Social and Cultural Dimensions* (Westport, Conn.: Greenwood, 1994); A. E. Carr, *Transforming Grace: Christian Tradition and Women's Experience* (San Francisco: Harper & Row, 1990); J. A. Clanton, *In Whose Image: God and Gender* (New York: Crossroad, 1990); K. Fischer, *Women at the Well: Feminist Perspectives on Spiritual Direction* (New York: Paulist, 1988); J. B. Nelson, *The Intimate Connection: Male Sexuality, Masculine Spirituality* (Philadelphia: Westminster Press, 1988); M. Proctor-Smith, "Out of the Silences: Feminist Resources for Knowing God," *Perspectives* 8, no. 3 (1993) 15-17; C. S. Schroeder, *In the Womb of God: Creative Nurturing for Your Soul* (Liguori, Mo.: Triumph/Liguori, 1995; portions quoted with permission); M. S. Van Leeuwen, ed., *After Eden: Facing the Challenge of Gender Reconciliation* (Grand Rapids: Eerdmans, 1993); N. Wolf, *The Beauty Myth: How Images of Beauty Are Used Against Women* (New York: Anchor/Doubleday, 1991).

Celeste N. Snowber

—FORGIVENESS—

Forgiveness is excruciatingly difficult. There are a hundred reasons why one cannot forgive and a thousand easier, more appealing alternatives. Many of these alternatives will accomplish something worthwhile. Some will enable us to forget the pain, others will help us to understand our feelings, and still others will enable us to transfer our hurt or anger onto something or someone else. But none of them will totally heal or restore the broken relationship.

In family life, forgiveness is the solvent of relationships. Without forgiveness, intimacy is impossible in marriage. When there is no forgiveness, even parent-child relations become political. But whether healing or restoration is even possible has been questioned by some, especially in cases of extreme hurt as in sexual abuse* or rape. Are there not some cases where traveling the road of forgiveness simply raises more problems and opens more wounds than if the journey had never begun? Before examining the dynamics of forgiveness, it is important to establish what forgiveness is not.

Some Misconceptions

Understanding. Forgiveness is not dependent on our understanding everything about the person or the situation, nor is greater understanding a guarantee of forgiveness. We are being unrealistic if we expect to understand everything before we forgive. Situations and people are so complex and their depths are so unfathomable that we cannot afford the luxury of waiting until we understand before we forgive. On the other hand, people may understand all about a situation but still remain unforgiving. Greater understanding may facilitate forgiveness and may flow from forgiveness, but forgiveness is not dependent on it.

Forgetting. Similarly, forgiving is not forgetting—for three reasons. First, if hurts can be easily forgotten, no forgiveness is necessary. The hurts in question are no more than mere annoyances, here today, gone tomorrow. Second, forgetting may be no more than avoidance or suppression, a defense mechanism to avoid the demands of real forgiveness. Third, where true forgiveness is needed, and even after it has been achieved and experienced, forgetting does not happen automatically. We cannot forget on demand. Forgiving can still be sincere even

if we remember. Forgetting must happen naturally as part of the longer forgiving process. Indeed with serious and deep sins, forgiving is a process of relinquishing revenge every time we do remember. And remembering itself can become an opportunity for faith, hope and love.

Avoidance. Forgiveness is not a way of avoidance. It is an alternative to revenge and retaliation, but it is not a way of opting out. On the contrary, because it gets to the root of the problem and refuses to exacerbate the hostility by multiplying the hurts, it is the only way of truly dealing with all aspects of the conflict situation.

Toleration. To forgive is not simply to accept or tolerate. Acceptance can be selective: it can be a way of looking at the good that is in each one of us, no matter how evil many of our actions may be, but it does not deal with the bad. It concentrates on the sober generosity of the drunkard, the family commitment of the terrorist or the conscientiousness of the adulterer. But it is the bad—the drunkenness, the murder, the adultery—that is unacceptable. That is what forgiveness tackles.

Getting away with it. Finally, to forgive is not the same as saying that "it doesn't matter." Those who have wronged will still have to pay and bear the consequences of their actions—legally, socially or personally. A wrongdoer can be truly and completely forgiven, yet prosecuted. Forgiveness complements justice; it does not replace it.

Forgiveness in Scripture

The Old Testament deals mainly with divine forgiveness. From the very beginning of salvation history God has been active in forgiveness. The promise of Genesis 3:15, Noah's ark (Gen 6:13—9:17), the subsequent covenant (Gen 8:21-22) and the story of Abraham (Gen 12:1—25:10) are all early examples of God's determination to save and restore people into fellowship. There is no single word for forgiveness in Hebrew but rather a series of images. There is the image of paying a ransom price (*kipper;* Ex 30:15-16; Num 5:8; Is 6:7); taking away (*nasa';* Ex 32:32; Job 7:21; Mic 7:18); pardoning (*selach;* 1 Kings 8:30-39; Jer 31:34); and even passing over, overlooking (*'abar;* Mic 7:18; Prov 19:11). These are powerful and significant images. Initially, through the old covenant provisions of the scapegoat (Lev 16:20-22) and the general sacrificial system, God illustrated his willingness to overlook the sins of his people because they had been paid for by someone or something else. God therefore has no call to remember their sins, for they are irrelevant (Ps 25:7; 103:9-12; Mic 7:19). Isaiah uses identical language as he looks forward to the ultimate scapegoat sacrifice who will bear the sins of the people (Is 53:8-12).

The New Testament makes it clear that this was Christ and that his sacrifice was sufficient for all time (Acts 8:32-33; Heb 10:10). It is in the light of Christ's sacrifice and our hope of eternal reconciliation with God that the New Testament writers employed the image of letting go *(aphi-h-mi)* to describe divine and therefore Christian forgiveness. As God has taken leave of our sins in Christ, so too we should let go of the sins committed against us (Mt 6:12; Eph 4:29-32). This is brought out most powerfully by the parable of the unforgiving servant (Mt 18:21-35), where an unforgiving spirit is portrayed starkly as nothing less than blasphemous. One of the reasons we find forgiveness so difficult is that we are offended by God's love,* which can forgive those who have so spitefully abused us. We are like the elder brother (Lk 15:28-32), resenting the grace of God and living unfree lives, bound by our own self-righteousness and prejudice. The key to forgiveness is to understand how much we ourselves have been forgiven by God. Like the woman in Luke 7:36-50, those who truly understand the depth of God's forgiveness are driven to love, not judgment (see also Mt 7:1-5).

Forgiveness in Family Life

Crimes of violence take place mostly in domestic contexts. There are seemingly endless opportunities to wound and hurt those with whom we live day in and day out through words and actions. Since we cannot divorce* our family, we cannot simply move on to another group of friends. Those closest to us in life know where we are most vulnerable and can wound us repeatedly. It is this kind of repeated sin that Jesus had in mind when he answered Peter's proposed limit of seven offenses per person with "seventy times seven," clearly beyond calculation (Mt 18:22).

In family life we can use words as weapons to compare one child with another or our spouse with someone else's. Tempers flare and physical actions wound someone's body. Sexual sins are in many ways the most damaging and the most difficult to forgive since, as the apostle Paul said, other sins are outside the "body," but this one affects the personality (1 Cor 6:18). But the miracle of forgiveness is that through this relational action we not only release someone else from an unpaid moral or relational debt; we also free ourselves from the prison of resentment and revenge. Even the chain of multigenerational sin, passed on from generation to generation, can be broken through forgiving our forefathers and mothers, though some may no longer be still alive.

In marriage* forgiveness must be current (do not let the sun go down on your anger—Eph 4:26); it must also be specific, using words such as "I have hurt you; please forgive me;" and it is not complete until someone says "I forgive you," not denying the offense or excusing it with words such as "we are all human and make mistakes." Children need to learn to ask for forgiveness from the parents and siblings. They are most likely to do this when parents ask their children for forgiveness for inappropriate or anger-based wounding actions or words. But there is an intrapersonal aspect that is often overlooked.

Forgiving Oneself

If we need to forgive ourselves and are unwilling to do so, this will hinder our forgiving others. Often the greater the sin, the less we are able to forgive ourselves: "Sin and self-forgiveness assume inverse proportions in our minds" (Stanley, 141). This is fundamentally a theological problem. We have not really understood or experienced the forgiveness of God, which is free, unmerited and unconditional. By refusing to forgive ourselves we betray a self-centered obsession that undermines the completeness of Christ's atoning work. We claim we do not forgive ourselves because we are unworthy, yet that is the whole point of the cross. Christ died because we were unworthy. We claim we have disappointed God, yet in reality it is only ourselves we have disappointed. How can God be disappointed when he knows us exactly as we are and yet forgives us?

Two of the "pillars" of the early church had to learn to forgive themselves. Peter, because of his denial of Christ, had possibly counted himself no longer a disciple (Mk 16:7; Jn 21:15-17), and Paul had to come to terms with atrocities he had personally inflicted on Christians before his conversion (1 Cor 15:9-10). Once we have grasped the extent and manner of God's forgiveness, we are without excuse in withholding forgiveness from anyone, and that includes ourselves.

Problems with Forgiveness

The main problem with forgiveness is that on the surface it appears to ignore or take lightly an incident of gross personal injustice. An injury has been inflicted, physically or emotionally, and someone has been hurt. The automatic human tendency is to hate and desire to get even. Forgiveness demands that we come to terms with such desires and gradually seek to be released from the power that the wound (and therefore the other person) has over us. Forgiveness is not about ignoring the injury. On the contrary, the forgiver acknowledges it and confronts it openly. Nor is the injury treated lightly. Rather, the forgiver treats it differently by freeing himself or herself from the endless consuming cycle of bitterness, hatred and retribution. God did not ignore our sin or treat it lightly. The death of Christ both dealt with the problem and made forgiveness possible.

Another problem with forgiveness is that it may remain forever incomplete. The other party may not accept or experience the forgiveness because of circumstances such as death* or the continued hardness of their own heart. However, this does not mean that the forgiveness is any less real. As far as the forgiver is concerned, the act of forgiveness has achieved its purpose in freeing them from the hurt of the incident, even though full mutual reconciliation requires the cooperation of the other party. It is a temptation to shirk the task of forgiveness on the grounds that the other person does not wish to be forgiven. This is to misunderstand the purpose of forgiveness. Forgiveness is not dependent on repentance, nor cheapened by a lack of repentance. In fact, forgiveness is an offer, and an offer is an unsolicited act of initiative.

The Practice of Forgiveness

David Augsburger (1981) has highlighted five stages of forgiveness: realizing the wrongdoing, reaffirming love, releasing the past, renewing repentance and rediscovering community. Smedes (1984) approaches the subject from the "inside," highlighting four possible experiences of the forgiver: hurt, hatred, healing and reconciliation. Hurts must be differentiated from forgettable oversights, insensitivities or mere disappointments. Hurts penetrate deeply and involve betrayal, disloyalty or personal injury. "Hatred is a compliment" (Smedes, 24), for we are not treating the perpetrator as irredeemable but as a free, rational person who has behaved unacceptably. It is on the unacceptability of their actions that our hatred is focused. These, however, are stages we must pass through. We cannot hate forever, or it will consume us, and forgiveness will never take place. Alongside these two approaches to the practice of forgiveness, I offer a third that deals with past, present and future.

1. *A new attitude.* This concerns how we deal with the past. We make a choice to deal with festering hurts and to embark on the journey of forgiveness. We decide neither to perpetuate the hostility nor to suppress the hurts and allow them to eat away inside us. A refusal to forgive binds us eternally to the past. In some cases we need to admit our contribution to the breakdown in relationship. In other cases, where we have been passive victims, we need to confess that we have allowed the event to hinder our spiritual growth and that righteous anger has become self-righteous bitterness. By choosing the way of forgiveness we are prepared to change our attitude toward those who have hurt us. We are prepared to forget and to acknowledge that someday we may be able to love them. Loving Christians, if they are to model God, must keep no record of wrongs (Ps 103:3-4; 1 Cor 13:5).

2. *A new perspective.* This concerns how we cope with the present. We begin by viewing people differently. We attempt to get outside the hurts and ragings of our present brokenness and see our enemy as God sees them (2 Cor 5:16). The temptation will be to view those who have injured us in a reductionist manner, seeing them totally in terms of their sin, when in reality they are normal people, a mixture of the image of God and sinful humanity. We are blinded to their true identity because of the sin they have committed against us. A test of whether our anger is righteous and directed against the sin, or unrighteous and directed against the sinner, would be to ask ourselves whether we would find greater pleasure in the conversion or restoration of the sinner than in their destruction (ECONI, 10). Or can we imagine a situation where we would actively wish the person well (Smedes, 1984, 29)?

3. *A new determination.* Forgiveness opens the door to new possibilities in relationship that would have been unthought of at the start of the journey. That is why forgiveness must be unconditional. If we lay down conditions, it means we are choosing the future and

seeking to manipulate the other person into satisfying our unrealistic demands. "We make our new beginnings, not where we used to be or where we wish we could be, but only where we are and with what we have at hand" (Smedes, 37). We can only forgive today with today's circumstances.

The Power of Forgiveness

No one can force us to forgive. Yet in spite of our culture's preoccupation with strength and getting even, to forgive is to exhibit the greatest strength of all. Self-deception, avoidance and grudge bearing are all easier options than loving confrontation, realism and forgiveness. When we forgive, we are acting as free persons and treating others as such. The strength of the love that inspires forgiveness derives from respect and commitment. We see the other person as worth the respect and are prepared for the energy, time and disappointment that may come. No greater example is needed than that of Christ. It was he who, as he bore the physical ag-ony of crucifixion, the emotional torture of the taunts and insults of passersby, and the spiritual weight of the sins of the world, found the strength to say, "Father, forgive them" (Lk 23:34).

See also COMMUNICATION; CONFLICT RESOLUTION; FAMILY PROBLEMS; LOVE.

References and Resources

D. Augsburger, *Caring Enough to Forgive* (Ventura, Calif.: Regal, 1981); D. Augsburger, *The Freedom of Forgiveness* (Chicago: Moody, 1988); Evangelical Contribution on Northern Ireland, *Forgiveness* (Belfast: ECONI, 1992); L. G. Jones, *Embodying Forgiveness: A Theological Analysis* (Grand Rapids: Eerdmans, 1995); J. Patton, *Is Human Forgiveness Possible? A Pastoral Care Perspective* (Nashville: Abingdon, 1985); L. B. Smedes, *Caring and Commitment: Learning to Live the Love We Promise* (San Francisco: Harper & Row, 1988); L. B. Smedes, *Forgive and Forget: Healing the Hurts We Do Not Deserve* (San Francisco: Harper & Row, 1984); C. Stanley, *Forgiveness* (Nashville: Thomas Nelson, 1987).

David J. Montgomery

—GAMES—

Games are like complex toys that people can play.* They are invitations to be playful and therefore can open people to God.

God Enjoys Play

Whether the voice of Wisdom in Proverbs represents the Holy Spirit or Jesus Christ, it is striking that Wisdom was playing before God's face at the creation of the world, having fun (Prov 8:31; *meshaheqeth* JB). God's wild beasts and Leviathan also frolic in creation (Job 40:20; Ps 104:24-26). Integral to the promise of the Lord's restoration of God's people as caretakers of creation on the new earth is that boys and girls shall be able to play in the streets without getting hurt (Is 11:6-9; Zech 8:1-8).

Today joy is the primal gift of the Holy Spirit to those who receive the gift of salvation (Gal 5:22-23; 1 Thess 1:2-7). Joy, however, is deeper than pleasure, for there is a more outgoing, imaginative character than the satisfaction of merely being pleased. So joy, fun and glad exuberance are the normative traits of playing around and therefore form the clue to the meaning of games.

A Game Is Organized Play

There is always an element of surprise in playing, such as the wonderful excitement experienced when riding a swing hung from the branch of a tree. This unpredictable element epitomizes play and other aspects of this dimension of life. So playfulness explores the unexpected ambiguity that inheres all human activity and sometimes comes to the fore, especially in games.

More complex than simple play, games always have rules and usually demand a certain amount of skill from those who participate. Further, everything in the game happens in the realm of a make-believe reality. The players have to imagine somebody as "it" to play tag and must decide whether or not a player can tag back immediately upon becoming "it." Games thrive on uncertainty and usually involve some kind of guessing on what to do next. Should you aim for the wicket in your croquet shot or knock somebody else's ball into the rough? Every player strives to reach the end or goal of the game first, even though the elusive prize is imaginary. A great thing about games is that everyone, technically, begins evenly, and that evenness is recovered every time the game is restarted. So children can occasionally win over their parents, and the stronger may lose to the weaker thanks to the wonderful uncertainty that always goes with a real game, such as when the marble or soccer ball just happens to hit a piece of uneven ground.

Do Games Have a Purpose?

Educators have long understood that children learn through playing games and that play is work for a nursery school child. So games serve a social purpose. Jean Piaget (1896-1980) traced the development of games played by children (sensory-motor, then make-believe, finally symbolic games with rules) and found

they adhered very strictly to stages of a child's preverbal and postverbal accommodation and socialization toward external reality. Games for Piaget are indices of human maturation; full-grown, well-adjusted humans outgrow them. And many a Christian moralist has excused games only if they help Christians take themselves less seriously or help them work more efficiently afterward: Learn to relax and lose—it's good for you. Enjoy games as pleasant lessons in humility, perhaps even as a foretaste of a heaven free from drudgery.

A biblically directed conception of games takes us beyond the mere instrumental value of games. We should not miss the peculiar glory and blessing built into the play that God created us to enjoy, and we should not apologetically twist games into becoming a means for nonplayful ends. It is true that games generally help us discharge pent-up surplus energy, and games do prepare us to exercise competencies in nonthreatening situations—strength, agility, decisiveness or willingness not to be a poor loser. But games need to be reconceived as a service for mature people through which they thank God as the games invigorate the players' imagination. Games are not something particularly childish or remedial, nor are they a middle-class luxury or a waste of time. The refusal to play games or the indulgence in a life of constant game playing—each is an indication of an imbalanced and unhealthy spirituality.

The Rich Variety of Games in God's World

There are many games for children and adults to play. The following games appear in order of their complexity, with the most elementary appearing first:

☐ basic movement and control (kite flying, roller-skating, swimming, bicycling, skiing, gymnastics)

☐ testing physical properties (making mud pies, molding clay, sawing wood)

☐ chase and capture, and lost and found (hide-and-seek, blindman's buff, fishing, hunting)

☐ display (dressing up, participating in parades)

☐ skill competence (catching a ball, spinning tops, shooting marbles, horseshoes, ring toss, darts, group juggling, spelling bees)

☐ guessing (Who am I? charades)

☐ puzzles (fitting shapes in holes, jigsaw pictures, crosswords, anagrams)

☐ get-acquainted (passing grapefruit from neck to neck)

☐ chance (dominoes, card games, board games with dice, mahjong)

☐ combative strategy (checkers, chess, tennis, squash, pickup team sports)

☐ trust-relationships (blind fall and catch)

☐ sheer pretense (masquerade party)

One can turn almost any fascination or activity that has flair into a game so long as there is an obstacle to overcome or something whimsical that eludes straightforward calculation and implementation. There is much to be said for inventing our own games. Games that are no longer homemade but are standardized and manufactured, as with board games, remove the congealed play of a homespun game. Boxed games are like secondary sources, and one needs to be wary of the imported spirit hidden in the prefabricated game. Is the game inherently ruthless, fact-ridden, ingenuous or fantastically extravagant? During the 1960s there was a rise in noncompetitive group games, such as "mixers" made up for occasional social gatherings (see *The New Games Book* and *More New Games*), which were wholesomely critical of the overly intense, win-at-all-costs mentality that followed World War II and hurts genuine play. Computer games* also are a mixed blessing, as they teach us to interact with a machine in a socially isolated context.

Games of chance, such as card games or games with dice, have often been stigmatized by Christians as evil pastimes (or been co-opted by the church for charitable purposes—e.g., bingo). Rather than approach games of chance as a violation of belief in God's providence or suppose that the element of chance is playing loosely with God's will, we should view hidden cards in bridge and unpredictable dice as simply a handy way to bring the play in reality to the fore. Picking up six vowels and only one consonant during a turn in Scrabble or throwing a double six so you land on a penalty square in a board game is "accidental," but the chance draw or throw calls upon all your human ingenuity to achieve more with less—precisely the imaginative challenge amid the laughable surprises of any game.

When Games Go Bad

Game theorist Roger Caillois (1913-1978) puts his analytic finger correctly on what corrupts games: when the very real boundary of imagination that defines their terrain and structure is violated, the play of players and games is ruined (Caillois, 43-55). Godless indulgence in sportive amusement that is licentious and idolatrous is clearly wrong (Ex 32:1-6; 1 Cor 10:6-13). Further, games themselves can be denatured. To cheat at hopscotch or even to play marbles for keeps is to end the playfulness. Gambling is always the murder of a game, because gambling violates the allusive play of the God-created game world and enslaves fun in the straitjacket of mammon. Lotteries are an illicit turn to games, even if they are legal tender.

A dubious quality of computerized virtual-reality games is their conjuring of decorporealized illusions that appear more real than ordinary imaginative reality in which one enjoys throwing Frisbees and knows the laughter of touching bony backs in a game of leapfrog. To call professional sports a game is a misnomer. The gladiatorial contests of professional sports worldwide bank on the thrill of God's gift of play and honed acrobatic human skill, but in our days, so close in temper to those of Noah (Mt 24:36-44), professional sports have corporately adulterated the game element into an abnormal, fascinating play-for-pay spectacle.

Redeeming the Time by Playing Games

Game opportunities bear a redemptive slant when they awaken and stretch the players' imagination to rejoice in the miraculous surprises God has created for us to experience together. The best games may not be those one can become ever more skilled at, sharpening the competitive edge, but those that most generously spread around communal good humor and a refreshing playfulness based on feeling at home in God's world despite the secularized brutalization of all things bright and beautiful. Games that lean toward bonding younger and older generations in good fun, that tickle smiles to the faces of those who have been abused or wasted, that cement friendship because the playing time were as holy as good prayer—such games carry a coefficient of the Lord God's grace and offset both an obsession with pleasure and a workaholic mania. When Christ returns, one could do worse than be found with a foster child visiting a zoo of God's fantastic animals or playing checkers with a lonely widow or widower in a convalescent home, letting them be imaginatively useful and take initiative in joyfully jumping your king.

See also COMPUTER GAMES; ENTERTAINMENT; PLAY; SABBATH.

References and Resources

J. Byl, "Coming to Terms with Play, Game, Sport and Athletics," in *Christianity and Leisure: Issues in a Pluralistic Society,* ed. P. Heintzman, G. Van Andel and T. Visker (Sioux Center, Iowa: Dordt College Press, 1994); R. Caillois, *Man, Play and Games,* trans. M. Barash (New York: Schocken, 1979); A. Fluegelman, *More New Games* (Garden City, N.Y.: Doubleday, 1981); A. Fluegelman, *The New Games Book* (Garden City, N.Y.: Doubleday, 1976); B. Frey, W. Ingram, T. McWhertor and W. D. Romanowski, *At Work and Play, Biblical Insight to Daily Obedience* (Jordan Station, Ont.: Paideia Press, 1986); J. Piaget, pt. 2 of "Play," in *Play, Dreams and Imitation in Childhood,* trans. C. Gattegno and F. M. Hodgson (New York: Norton, 1962); H. B. Schwartzman, *Play and Culture,* vol. 4 of the proceedings of the annual meeting of the Association for the Anthropological Study of Play (West Point, N.Y.: Leisure Press, 1980); T. Visker, "Play, Game and Sport in a Reformed Biblical Worldview," in *Christianity and Leisure: Issues in a Pluralistic Society,* ed. P. Heintzman, G. Van Andel and T. Visker (Sioux Center, Iowa: Dordt College Press, 1994).

Calvin Seerveld

—GIFT GIVING—

Gift giving is a thermometer of the soul. It reveals what we think we possess and whether we can love.* Ironically, the rich are sometimes less generous because their gifts often come with strings attached as a form of control. The poor, with apparently little to give away, may give their last loaf of bread, like the widow who gave all she had to the temple (Lk 21:1-4).

Gift receiving is also a thermometer of the soul. It is "more blessed to give than to receive," as Jesus says (Acts 20:35), but receiving is usually harder. Sometimes the reluctance or refusal to receive a gift indicates the fear of being under obligation to perform some duty in return. In the case of the dependent poor, gift receiving often means enduring the demeaning experience of being the object of someone else's patronage. Charity is not always love. The refusal of the receivers to say thank you—so distressing to some givers—may be a symptom of this internal struggle or a silent statement that the relatively rich benefactor really owes this support. In other words, it is not a gift but a duty.

Both giving and receiving gifts are also barometers that indicate which way the soul is changing. Over a lifetime our experience of gifts indicates whether our soul is shriveling into hard-heartedness or heading toward the eternally generous environment of heaven. Some people are perpetually giving because they are hungry for relationships and addicted to people, but there is less true generosity in this than is immediately apparent. So gift giving is both a spiritual discipline and an arena requiring spiritual discernment, especially when we consider the great range and meanings of gifts.

A Lifetime of Giving and Receiving
Usually our first gifts are received before we are old enough to say thank you. The first gift is a name, an act that establishes a child's identity. Then follows a host of other gifts, such as a baby outfit, then birthday* gifts, Christmas gifts or gifts from relatives. Infants and children sometimes give gifts during this period, often to the delight of their parents—a smile, a kiss and laughter—but these are given unconsciously. Perhaps this very unconsciousness, so natural to a child, is the very thing most needed to be cultivated in adult life so we can give without our left hand knowing what our right is doing (Mt 6:3; compare Mt 25:38).

Early on many children learn that gifts may be used as a form of manipulation. In some families all gifts received are implied obligations or explicit rewards. "Giving" allowances to children may be a gift or may be a form of remuneration, depending on the philosophy of the parents (see Allowances). Christmas trees are surrounded by exchanges of mutual obligations (carefully balanced to the dollar). "Favors" by a boss are messages to perform. Politicians can be influenced by gifts. Flowers are a way of saying, "I'm sorry." The final gift of our parents, expressed in their last will* and testament, may turn out to be no gift at all but rather a posthumous form of control.

Gift giving comes only with a struggle. It starts in the sandbox, sharing a toy with a neighbor, or in the home when we use our precious savings as a child to buy Mom a birthday present. Giving does not come easily and does not seem to come spontaneously. Jesus was able to descriptively note, "You then, though you are evil, know how to give good gifts to your children" (Lk 11:13), but he was commenting on the basic goodwill parents feel toward children, something that Paul referred to much later (2 Cor 12:14). Part of the Christian education of the family is learning how to give and receive, but this starts with the parents' ability to model this.

Cultures vary on this matter, and we learn very quickly what is expected, such as a small gift when arriving to have dinner in someone's home, a large gift in advance of making a business deal with favorable terms to your own company (a bribe?), a present to the parents of the woman you intend to marry, or a "gift" (sometimes euphemistically called a "user fee") expected by officials in government offices in many countries. But learning what is expected is not learning how to give.

Gifts and Nongifts

Some gifts are *commercial transactions* or *fulfilled contracts*. These are negotiated exchanges of valuable items (money or things) according to a written or unwritten contract. Much that passes for Christmas "giving" is a series of carefully managed mutual exchanges, often with goodwill and generosity but, nevertheless, under obligation. It is a social shame* to receive a gift at Christmas from someone to whom you have not given. Real Christmas gifts, like the gifts presented by the Magi (Mt 2:11), are not expected and are sacraments of appreciation.

Other gifts are *instruments of manipulation*. A donor contributes a large sum to a Christian organization knowing that her votes on the board will carry more weight than those of lesser givers. Sometimes, when the donor's will is thwarted, financial support is withdrawn, a barometer reading of what is happening in her soul. Proverbs notes that "a gift opens the way for the giver" (18:16). Jacob's psychologically contrived gift to his estranged brother is an example of this (Gen 32:13-21). Bribes openly state the intention to influence and control even when they are given secretly. In the parallelism of Proverbs "a gift given in secret" is the same thing as "a bribe concealed in the cloak" that "pacifies great wrath" (21:14). Sometimes the control factor is not so much a direct appeal for power as it is a matter of manipulating opinion—a form of personal advertising. Ananias and Sapphira pretended to have given more than they did to the church, thus lying to God

(Acts 5:4). They did this because they wanted status in the Christian community. Both the book of Proverbs (25:14) and Jesus (Mt 6:2) warn against trumpeting our giving.

In their purest form, gifts are sacraments of goodwill. They are relatively free of the desire for personal gain, either in a material sense or in public approval. Such gifts see a need and give from the heart, not expecting anything in return, not even thanks. The Antiochian Christians, hearing of the famine in Judea, sent gifts to the Christians there (Acts 11:29-30). Later Paul expanded on this generous gift by raising funds throughout the Gentile churches in aid of the poor Jewish Christians in Judea as a sacramental expression of love, equality and mutual ministry between Jews and Gentiles in Christ (2 Cor 8:12, 20; 9:5). Especially commendable (from God's perspective) was the generosity of the Gentile Cornelius before becoming a Christian. The angels told him, "Your prayers and gifts to the poor have come up as a memorial offering before God" (Acts 10:4).

The greatest gift of all is the gift of salvation in Jesus Christ (Eph 2:8). This gift above all others is undeserved, unexpected and comes with no strings attached. It is an expression of God's unconditional love for humankind (Jn 3:16) and can never be repaid. It is precisely because of the poverty of our souls in giving and receiving that we have trouble receiving forgiveness,* atonement, access to God, membership in God's family and eternal life as free gifts. We misinterpret the gift as an exchange in which God gives salvation because of our good works (Rom 4:4) or as a contract in which we owe God a lifetime of sacrificial service. In fact, there is nothing we can do to make God love us or stop loving us. It is precisely the offense this gift causes to human pride

149

that makes so many people unwilling to enter into the joy of salvation.

The Theology of Giving and Receiving
Everything we have, receive and give ultimately belongs to God. So giving and receiving must be considered as part of stewardship. We are trustees of God's possessions, never absolute owners. That should make giving easier, more thoughtful and generous. But there is something even deeper in this ministry of giving and receiving.

God is the ultimate giver and receiver. Some of Jesus' words are sacred inspired windows on the generosity in the heart of God. The Father gives the Son into the world (Jn 3:16) but not without giving him his power, authority, glory (Jn 8:54), people (Jn 6:37) and love (Jn 17:24). The Son gives praise (Lk 10:21) and glory (Jn 17:4) to the Father. Jesus is the perfect model of selfless impoverishment to enrich others (2 Cor 8:9). The Spirit is given into the world (Acts 1:4) but also gives deference, love and glory to the Father and the Son (Jn 16:13-15). God not only continually gives within the loving communion of the Godhead but also continuously receives. When Paul says, "God loves a cheerful [literally a 'hilarious'] giver" (2 Cor 9:7), one who gives in an uncalculating and spontaneously generous way, he is saying that we are most godlike when our giving is least calculated, reciprocal, contractual or laced with ulterior motive (*see* Tithing). So both giving and receiving are spiritual disciplines.

The Spirituality of Giving and Receiving
Giving and receiving are both delightful and dangerous. Offering a gift to the Lord's servant, as Naaman did when he was healed by God through Elisha (2 Kings 5:15), is a holy act communicating gratitude and praise to God. Refusing the

gift, as Elisha wisely did (2 Kings 5:16), communicated something essential: this ministry was God's ministry and could not be hired or remunerated. In contrast, Elisha's servant, Gehazi, went after the gift and destroyed his own soul (2 Kings 5:19-27). Chasing after gifts is the special temptation of public servants of God who earn their living by ministry (Is 1:23). Paul steadfastly refused to do this (Phil 4:17), primarily so he could offer ministry as a free gift and not hinder the gospel (1 Cor 9:12). He quoted the words of Jesus, "It is more blessed to give than to receive" (Acts 20:35), in the context of giving ministry without obligation.

Giving to God is also dangerous. Jesus says we should make sure we are right with our brothers and sisters first, leaving our gift-giving incomplete at the altar until relationships are straightened out (Mt 5:23-24). God is not impressed with vertical generosity that is not expressed horizontally. Nor is God impressed with generous giving to the church at the expense of family* (Mt 15:5-6). Paradoxically, giving to our neighbor turns out to be giving to God, as the parable of Jesus indicates (Mt 25:40). But one form of giving is not approved anywhere in the Bible—displayed giving. Those who give so that all may see already have their desired reward—to be seen by people. Instead, says Jesus, let "your giving . . . be in secret. Then your Father, who sees what is done in secret, will reward you" (Mt 6:3-4). The delight of giving is the pleasure it brings God.

If giving is a spiritual discipline, so is receiving. It invites gratitude to God, receiving what we are given as from God himself. This frees us from an unhealthy sense of obligation to the donor and makes each gift, as it was for Paul, something that gives praise to God (Phil 4:18). Refusal to receive anything from others is both a negative spiritual symptom (we insist on being autonomous) and a spiritual invitation (to grow in healthy interdependence). Giving and receiving are thermometers and barometers of the soul.

The Practice of Giving and Receiving

Many practical matters emerge from this discussion. First, holy gift-giving and receiving begins with giving ourselves to God (2 Cor 8:5) and then to others. Generosity starts with the self-sacrifice that, paradoxically, leads to being rich in the things that matter. This is the source of all other giving and receiving. Second, offering ministry free of charge is especially commendable. Christian service is essentially a volunteer matter—done for love. The temptation of greed is especially serious in matters dealing publicly with God and the gospel. Third, giving to the poor and needy requires special sensitivity on the parts of both giver and receiver. Anonymous giving is one way, but not the only way, of avoiding patronage and dependency. A better way is to allow for mutual giving, as Paul encouraged between the Jewish and Gentile Christians, though with a difference in kind (Rom 15:27). Fourth, we can be creative in gift giving. Time is one of the most valuable gifts, especially in family life. Handmade gifts, thoughtfully crafted to suit the intended receiver, can communicate the message intended: you are special and I appreciate you. Fifth, we can prayerfully cultivate hilarious giving and spontaneity, even when the cultural context requires giving as a social obligation. Finally, we can turn receiving—usually harder than giving—into prayer* for gratitude to God and the joy of giving. In the end our giving and receiving tells as much about our spirituality as our prayer life; indeed they are each a reflection of the other.

See also ALLOWANCES; BLESSING; HOLIDAYS-CHRISTMAS; TITHING; WILL, LAST.

References and Resources

C. Brown, "Gift, Pledge, Corban," in *New International Dictionary of New Testament Theology*, ed. C. Brown (Grand Rapids: Zondervan, 1989) 2:39-44; G. D. Fee and R. P. Stevens, "Spiritual Gifts," in *The Complete Book of Everyday Christianity*, ed. R. Banks and R. P. Stevens (Downers Grove: InterVarsity Press, 1997) 943-49; A. A. Kass and L. R. Kass, "What's Your Name?" *First Things*, November 1995, 14-25; R. Titmuss, *The Gift Relationship* (London: Allen and Unwin, 1970).

R. Paul Stevens

—GOALS—

Setting goals is the way to make sure you will achieve what you want to have happen in your family life. A family* without a sense of direction wavers to and fro as external circumstances determine its future. A proactive family, in contrast, will make long- and short-term goals to turn their dreams into reality.

We invest ourselves in what we hold precious. Parents who value the spiritual growth of their children will make principled efforts to attend church and Sunday school. In addition, they will find ways to incorporate devotional rituals within family life, celebrate the traditions of their faith and make special efforts to discuss current events in the context of their religious beliefs. Although these activities may not be written down anywhere as specific family goals, these behaviors emerge out of clearly formed values* in the hearts of the parents (*see* Spiritual Formation). But most families need more than a desire to convert their values into action. In fact, unless these values are specified in terms of goals and subgoals, they will most likely be left by the wayside.

A purposeful goal not only helps family members identify what is important but also helps them implement concrete ways of attaining their values. Good intentions are never enough! A family needs to agree on specific objectives that will help accomplish what its members hold dear. Family researchers (Delores Curran, Nick Stinnet) have discovered that families who work together toward common goals have a sense of meaning that enriches their common life. Whether it is making plans for a birthday* celebration, solving a family problem* or accomplishing a specific task, a family reaches a deep sense of satisfaction when it joins together in this common effort. As each family member contributes to the family as a whole, they are appreciated for the unique part they play. The family that works together for common goals reaps the rewards of closeness and unity.

Goal-Setting Helps
Establishing a family council is a good place to go about setting family goals. This involves setting aside a time for members to share their ideas about family needs, values and desires. Each member is encouraged to contribute any ideas that come to mind. There are no right or wrong ideas, and even the most outrageous suggestions are warmly received. Every member, from oldest to youngest, is taken seriously and treated honorably in this information-gathering process. This exercise assures that each family member is involved individually and corporately in the creation of family goals.

Next, the family chooses by consensus one particular goal from among the ideas. Although difficult, it is necessary to prioritize. Once the main goal is established, the family can begin to brainstorm about the specific behaviors needed to accomplish this goal. The family formulates subgoals (specific objectives) that will help them execute the greater goal. Subgoals need to be both realistic and "doable." Once all of these are listed, each one must be evaluated in terms of whether it is reasonable and desirable for the whole family. In other words, it is a question of whether the family will be successful in following through.

Take the example of a family who wants to develop a deeper spiritual life. One subgoal may be to have devotions every night after supper at 5:30. Now it is time to evaluate. The teenagers may express objections because it interferes with activities after school.* A younger child complains that it will be boring. Mother says she wants the devotions to include creative activities, but Father prefers a simple Bible reading each night. As members express their thoughts, feelings and ideas, the family becomes more realistic about what needs adjusting. Often a compromise is made, such as having devotions at 5:30 on the three days a week that everyone is home.* The family decides to add variety by having everyone take turns presenting the devotion. The bonus that emerges out of this compromise is that it extends the responsibility to each member. All these modifications serve to increase the likelihood of success. The family now has a plausible way of reaching its ultimate goal that works for it at this particular time in its life stage.

An essential part of goal setting is for family members to make a commitment to keep part of the bargain. When the goal and subgoals have been evaluated together, it is relatively easy for individuals to cooperate. Clear, written objectives help everyone know exactly what is expected of them. Now it is time to clinch the deal.

Make a Contract
Once the long-term goal and the short-term behavioral objectives are estab-

lished, members promise, in front of others, that they will make every effort to do their part. This can be done by having a simple ceremonial handshake or by signing a written contract made up by the family at the end of the family council. The essential thing is that each person agrees to the conditions set forth and gives his or her word to keep the contract.

It is also vital to specify a timeframe for this contract. Whether it is after one or six months, it is best to periodically review the progress made toward the goal. Meeting each week for family council is a good place to evaluate the effectiveness of the contract. The family asks itself, "How are we doing?" "Are the objectives helping us meet the metagoal?" and "Is there anything that needs to be changed?" These questions allow for needed correctives and innovative suggestions. An ongoing fresh perspective will continue to improve or reshape the subgoals.

When problems occur, the family must also agree to come back to the family council to renegotiate. This is not to be a time for blaming but a chance to make things better and figure out why a breakdown occurred. Recognizing barriers (were the goals too high?), considering various courses of action (what can we change?) or looking to alternatives (what haven't we tried?) helps the family figure out a new course of action. Since goals can be reached in a number of ways, changing immediate small steps is often the best way to assure achievement of the long-range goals. Minor set-backs are to be expected, and failure is not viewed as a catastrophe; both are only opportunities to regroup and try again. Flexibility is the key! Listening* is the best path to ingenious solutions. It may be that encouragement, instruction or equipping is needed.

Summary

Family goals are only as effective as its members' commitment to each other. Steps of action toward long- and short-range family goals require that everyone reach beyond individual goals. Family members must work together to be a family unit. As the apostle Paul explains, each part has something essential to offer the whole body, and no one part can function effectively without the others. When we give of ourselves, set time apart, put forth effort and contribute our special giftedness, we serve the whole. Converting our values into goals requires a vision. Family members must play their unique part in making their ultimate family dream a living reality.

See also CHARACTER; COMMUNICATION; FAMILY; FAMILY PROBLEMS; SPIRITUAL FORMATION; VALUES.

References and Resources

D. Curran, *Traits of a Healthy Family* (Minneapolis: Winston, 1983); D. Dinkmeyer and G. McKay, *Raising a Responsible Child* (New York: Simon & Schuster, 1973); R. Dreikurs and V. Soltz, *Children: The Challenge* (New York: Dutton, 1964); S. Simon, *Meeting Yourself Halfway: Thirty-One Values Clarification Strategies for Daily Living* (Niles, Ill.: Argus Communications, 1974).

Judith K. Balswick

—GODPARENTING—

Godparents are adult Christians who act as sponsors at the baptism* of an infant or small child, answering the questions addressed to the child by speaking the church's statement of faith on the child's behalf. This is understood to be the beginning of a lifelong calling for the godparent, who takes on a responsibility, along with the parents, for the spiritual nurture of the child (see Spiritual Formation). Today there tends to be little significance attached to godparenting as a spiritual calling. Why do we have godparents in the first place? What does it mean to be a godparent? How might one live out that role as the child grows up? These questions are rarely addressed, with the result that godparenting tends to become a purely ceremonial role, like that of a bridesmaid or groomsman. Yet the concept carries great potential. This potential is being fulfilled by members of ethnic traditions that emphasize godparenting and by individuals who find their own ways to connect with their godchild in an enduring relationship with a spiritual focus.

Godparenting

How Did the Role of the Godparent Develop?

In the earliest centuries babies or small children were usually brought to the baptismal font by a parent who answered the creedal questions for the child. By the sixth century there is evidence from both the East (Pseudo-Dionysius) and the West (Caesarius) that persons other than the parent are "receiving the child from the font."

We do not know exactly why this shift in practice away from parent sponsors occurred. There is no record of any official church pronouncement urging nonparental sponsors. Only centuries after the custom was established would there be a rule to that effect. It seems to have been the choice of the parents themselves to involve another adult in their child's life in this way, thereby ensuring that adult's interest in the child's welfare—a sacramental role in the Christian tradition created by and for the people! When theologians first mention it, it is already an established custom, and the role of the sponsor is understood to be one of moral guidance and teaching, especially teaching the child to pray.*

In the Middle Ages godparenting became important as a social institution in Western Europe, a nonbiological extension to the kinship structure. By asking someone to sponsor your child, you formed a quasi-familial bond between that person and your family,* a bond that had important social and economic, as well as spiritual, aspects. The godparent was bound to the child in a reciprocal relation of duties and responsibilities. The godparent was expected to give gifts, throw the baptismal party and provide protection for the child. In return, the godchild owed the godparent a special kind of lifelong respect.

Protestant Reformers who supported infant baptism maintained the role of godparent, though with varying degrees of enthusiasm. Luther, while noting that sponsorship was a human addition to the sacrament, commended it as an ancient and pious custom. Calvin downplayed the godparental role in order to place the emphasis on the parents' own responsibility.

Since the sixteenth century godparenthood as a social institution has gradually decreased in importance. Today in the United States the practice of godparenting is continued in Presbyterian, Lutheran, Episcopal, African Methodist Episcopal, Roman Catholic, Eastern Orthodox and some United Church of Christ and United Methodist churches, as well as in some Baptist churches, where the godparents are involved in the dedication service. The social significance and definition of that role varies according to ethnic and regional background more than denominationally. Some Latino and African American godparents have a clear sense of the nature of their continuing obligation to the godchild (which can include financial support and rearing the child if the parents die), while many people of northern European extraction have little social guidance as to the nature of the godparent's role.

Why Should We Care About the Godparental Role Today?

Bringing a child up in the faith is the responsibility of the whole Christian community. The parents (see Parenting) have the primary responsibility, but they cannot do it alone. This communal responsibility is taken on by Sunday school teachers, pastors, youth leaders, godparents and others who take a personal interest in children and their spiritual nurture. Of all such relationships, that between godparent and godchild has the distinction of not being locale dependent, so that it can last throughout a child's growing up.

The need of children for concerned adults in their lives in addition to their parents is harder than ever to meet in our cultural setting. Mobility,* the isolation of the nuclear family, the decline of community ties in neighborhoods and the increase in single-parent* families are all factors that make this need more acute.

The liturgical movement has brought a greatly increased focus on the lifelong centrality of baptism to Christian identity. Baptism is not just an entry rite and certainly not just a lifecycle rite for Christian babies. Baptism is seen as incorporation into the death of Jesus and, through the cross, into the promise of the resurrection. Churches that practice infant baptism teach that in baptism the child is adopted into God's covenant people

and called into ministry for the sake of the world, an identity and a mission that are lifelong. Helping godparents understand and live out their calling is one way to raise awareness of baptism as the enduring core of Christian identity. If godparents can come to see their role as one of remembering with the child that she or he is baptized, the institution of godparenthood can be a key part of baptismally focused renewal.

Churches that do not have godparents as part of their tradition might consider adopting the practice, even if it would not have a baptismal focus. Some churches that do not practice infant baptism have adapted the godparental role to their situation, letting parents choose godparents who participate in the service of dedication, agreeing to share with the parents the responsibility for the child's spiritual nurture.

How Can Godparents Live Out Their Calling?

The calling of a godparent is to help the parents raise the child in the faith. This means finding ways to share with the child about God, faith and values.

One of the responsibilities of the Christian community is to teach adults how to listen to children and share the faith with them. For centuries godparents have been told, "Be an example to the child, and pray for him"—advice that did little to help them form a relationship with the child where the faith might be nurtured. Godparents need more concrete advice about ways to dialogue with children about the things that matter, ways to form a long-distance relationship with a child, ways to remind a child that he or she is baptized and explore what that means.

Here are some of the things that godparents might do as ways to share the faith with their godchildren: Draw pictures together about Bible stories, or holidays* such as Christmas or Easter. Mark the child's baptismal anniversary, rather than just the birthday.* Give presents that recall baptism symbolically, like bath or pool toys. Let the child designate some of your charitable giving. Play games* that allow for discussion of feelings and values. Make a bedtime tape where you sing a Christian lullaby. Talk together about what to pray for. Make a personalized Advent calendar. Go together to a synagogue's sabbath* service or to a Greek Orthodox Easter midnight service. Give (or read on tape) well-written children's books that address religious issues: the nature of God, the problem of evil and suffering.

It is important to note that many of these things can be done by long-distance godparents. One of the main ideas the church needs to get across to people in our mobile society is that it is possible for an adult to form and maintain a significant relationship with a child who is far away. Long-distance godparents could find helpful ideas on relationship forming in how-to books written for long-distance grandparents or noncustodial parents.

Godparents who faithfully live out their calling cannot help but grow in faith themselves. There is no better spiritual discipline than learning to listen* respectfully to a child; after all, Jesus said we should look to a child as a model of faith and should become like children ourselves. There is no better way to have the stories and images of the faith come alive in a new way than to hear them in a child's telling, to see them in a child's drawing. The adolescent's* driving demand for honesty can challenge us to face up to theology's unanswerable questions, to admit our limits and our compromises. These opportunities for growth in faith should not be restricted to parents alone. As children need other caring adults in their lives besides parents, so adults need the chance to become a soul friend to a child.

See also BAPTISM; CONFIRMATION; FAMILY; PARENTING; PRAYER; SINGLE PARENTING.

References and Resources

J. G. Fitzpatrick, *Something More: Nurturing Your Child's Spiritual Growth* (New York: Penguin, 1991); J. M. Hull, *God-Talk with Young Children* (Philadelphia: Trinity, 1991); J. H. Lynch, *Godparents and Kinship in Early Medieval Europe* (Princeton, N.J.: Princeton University Press, 1986); E. Ramshaw, *The Godparent Book* (Chicago: Liturgy Training Publications, 1993).

Elaine J. Ramshaw

—GRANDPARENTING—

Grandparenting has changed today. Age and the attitude toward age are certainly one difference. Another is style—from the grandparent who acts like a teenager to the grandparent who appears never to have enjoyed life. Marital status is a further factor. One set of grandparents may have retained an intact marriage,* while others have had more than one partner. Likewise the grandchild may possess either no acknowledged grandparents or several, depending on the definition of marriage and family* and how the stresses have been processed.

Values* and convictions of grandparents vary considerably. The grandparents may be people of faith. On the other hand, it may repel all who are affected by them. Or they may be grandparents whose lives are consumed by their own self-absorbed lifestyle. The attitudes with which grandparents approach life also differ enormously. Some grandparents embrace life, deal constructively with their losses, and maintain a sense of optimism and hope. Others become negative, are critical of the oncoming generation, and cover life, family and community with a blanket of darkness.

Changes in family and society are obviously affecting the experience of grandparenting, especially the amount and nature of support and the degree to which it is reciprocal. Robert O. Hanson (13) points out factors that affect the ability of a family to support grandparents. These include the reality that multigenerational families are becoming more common, partly because of the declining birth rate and increased longevity. There is a much greater generation span, and there is a lack of siblings in the younger generation to share the burden of support. Longevity means that adult caregivers are likely to spend more years caring for their parents than providing support for their own children.

All the other problems that arise from how family is constituted today complicate the issues. These include the increase in divorce,* blended and single-parent families, the large number of women entering the work force, and geographical mobility.* These factors, added to improved health* care, mean that age-related disabilities happen much later in life. Family caregivers are assuming that role later in their own lives, at a time when they may themselves be vulnerable both physically and financially.

Nevertheless, grandparents can and often do play a highly significant role in family life today.

The Importance of Grandparenting
Margaret Mead believed that it takes three generations to rear a child. Mead also made the acute observation, "From grandparents children learn to understand something about the reality of the world not only before they were born,

but also before their parents were born. . . . Experiences of the past gives them means of enjoying the future" (quoted in Fowler and McCutcheon, 201). How can they do this if they are constantly "out of the picture"?

Grandparents are a significant influence on the future generation, for both intact and broken families: "Grandparent access visits can be a vital factor in the well-being and development of children of divorced parents—often essential role models for absent or missing mothers or fathers" (Wells, 35). But if grandparents are good for children, the reverse is also true. Rosemary Wells lists what it means to have a grandchild: (1) your family will live on into the future; (2) you are given a second chance to be a better parent; (3) you can enjoy helping the children (with schoolwork and at playtime); (4) your grandchild may achieve things you or your child did not (35). This may seem a modest list, but in a world where both parents work, an available grandparent can make a huge difference even with a modest investment of time.

Grandparenting does other things for the grandparent as well. Because losses are common and cumulative at this point in life, depression* and self-absorption can very quickly devour the grandparent. So can self-indulgence. Caring for one's grandchildren without making favorites is one way of escaping the domination of one's moods and feelings. Finding a support system in the local church and in one's relationship to God will further enable the grandparent to cope better with these challenges. In extreme cases where the grandparent takes over the parenting role, a support

157

system within the local church is absolutely essential.

The Pitfalls of Grandparenting

In normal circumstances grandparents do best when they have boundaries, keep out of destructive triangles and do not engage in "cutoffs," to use the language of family systems. Good boundaries mean that they are up front about what they will do for the family members and are generous and loving in their support but do not allow unreasonable demands to be made on them. This does not refer simply to gross demands that come close to elder abuse.* Grandparents must respect their own persons and legitimate needs and find a balance between their own needs and those of others, including their grandchildren. Expectations that are clear and negotiated without emotional blackmail are healthy for all the parties.

Grandparents can very easily get triangled in a way that is tough on the actual parent. For example, very few adolescents* think highly of their parents. Being a gentle advocate for the parents may be necessary and even occasionally desirable. Being a coconspirator is not. Some families are conflict ridden. They are quick to quarrel and slow to reconcile. People get cut off. Grandparents can make a large contribution to the family by refusing to engage in cutting off people from their emotional support system. They can listen, reflect, refuse to be judge and jury, and keep doors open. They must never undercut parents.

Indeed, grandparents should learn not to volunteer advice unless it is requested. The less initiative they demonstrate here, the more likely they are to be asked and the advice heeded. Some grandparents may end up as surrogate parents for all kinds of reasons, but the grandchildren do not need to be the pawns in any family disputes.

The Contribution Grandparents Make

Grandparents can model what long-term commitments produce. Even if a marriage falls apart, they can still demonstrate that revenge, hatred, guilt and shame* also need not dominate. Grandparents can demonstrate respect for others. As the keeper of family history, grandparents also need to be careful not to overindulge in anecdotes. As grandchildren get older, they will want to know more about their family story. Family secrets may need to be handled carefully but not buried.

The most important contribution a grandparent can make is in terms of imparting and modeling faith. No other responsibility comes close to this; when it is effective, no other joy exceeds it. Of course, it includes praying for grandchildren (see Prayer); it must also involve a lifestyle that affirms anything that is said. It means taking advantage of teachable moments, which should be natural, not contrived, and joyful, not legalistic.

Grandchildren need grandparents. Grandparents need relationships with their children and grandchildren. There comes a day when it changes from giving support to receiving it. The capacity to do both with grace is not always easy. But when it is done with grace, the rewards for everyone are exceptional. To be an active, godly grandparent is more satisfying than being a self-absorbed senior citizen. If a person's chief aim is to glorify and enjoy God forever, grandparenting offers a significant role in fulfilling this objective.

See also COMMUNICATION; FAMILY; FAMILY SYSTEMS; PARENTING; PRAYER.

References and Resources
B. Carter and M. McGoldrick, eds., *The Changing Family Life Cycle,* 2nd ed. (Boston: Allyn & Bacon, 1989); M. Fowler and P. McCutcheon, eds., *Songs of Experience* (New York: Ballantine, 1991); R. O. Hanson, *Rela-*

tionships in Old Age (New York: Guilford, 1994); R. Wells, *Your Grandchild and You*

(Oxford, U.K.: Sheldon Press, 1990).

Roy D. Bell

GRIEVING. *See* DEATH; DEPRESSION; STRESS.

HABITS. *See* CHARACTER; DISCIPLINE.

—HEALTH—

Health is one of the most precious assets a person can possess, yet there is no consensus as to what health is. Some want to restrict the meaning of health to "a state of physical well-being without significant impairment of function." But modern psychosomatic theories, which relate our physical well-being to a whole host of psychosocial factors, render this narrow definition of health inadequate. If we accept humankind as essentially a multidimensional unity consisting of mechanical dimensions, then any attempt to define health in terms of physical well-being is to reduce it to one dimension or to dissociate one's body from one's unified self—something is essentially misguided.

Health as Shalom

The Hebrew word *shalom* is translated as "peace" 172 times out of 250 times in the Old Testament. Peace in this case means much more than an absence of strife. It is used in various contexts to express the idea of totality, completeness, soundness, welfare, well-being, prosperity, wholeness and harmony. It refers to all areas of life: personal, mental, physical, corporate and national. In this sense, *shalom* is probably the closest word in the Old Testament to health. Implicit in the word *shalom* is the idea of unimpaired relationships with God, self, others and nature. *Shalom*, therefore, incorporates and integrates the concepts of holiness and righteousness. In practice it means living a covenanted life, set apart for a morally committed existence in relationships. To be healthy, then, includes being holy and righteous.

Shalom also strongly implies the idea of fulfillment that comes from God. God is the one who speaks *shalom* to his people (Ps 85:8). The one to whom God

has given *shalom* is identified as the one who is blessed, guarded and treated graciously by Yahweh. *Shalom* is fulfillment through divine presence, specifically through the Messiah. In the New Testament, Paul identifies Christ as the messianic prince who through self-sacrifice brought redemption, righteousness, fulfillment, wholeness and *shalom* to humankind. It is for this reason that the meaning of health in both the Old and New Testament includes such themes as blessedness, wholeness, maturity and holiness. God's ultimate focus is on spiritual health rather than physical or even psychological health. The quality of our personal relationship with God is the cornerstone to all other health issues.

Health as Wholeness

We take on more holistic perspective of humankind when we broaden our definition of health to include all dimensions of life. Thus, whenever one dimension is affected, so are all other dimensions. The concept of *savior* embraces the idea of a

159

healer that makes people healthy and whole. The ideal healer is the one universal healer, Jesus Christ, who has come to bring in God's kingdom in which we are restored to wholeness.

Understanding health in this way provides a different perspective on well-being. While physical health is good, it is not necessarily the only good and certainly not the ultimate good. We do not deny that our physical infirmities are real or should be removed, but in some special circumstances they may actually make a contribution to our flourishing. Some secular medical social scientists have also developed a health-within-illness perspective, which sees an illness as an event that can accelerate human growth (Jones and Meleis). Indeed, a healthy life includes an ability to cope with disease, suffering and death* and to integrate them as part of one's life. It is for this reason that Paul thinks that his lack of physical well-being is more than compensated for by his participation in the suffering of Christ (2 Cor 12:7-10). Many biblical figures and believers throughout church history have considered that their physical health could be sacrificed at times for the sake of God's cause in the world.

Health and the Family

Families are often described as being either healthy or dysfunctional. However, since no family is without sin, it is more accurate to think of family health as being on a continuum, with some families experiencing greater or lesser degrees of health than others. In accordance with the above holistic understanding of health, family health can be broken down to include three main elements.

Physical health. All families have to deal with disease of one kind or another during the family lifecycle. Some are forced to deal with chronic illness and physical/mental handicaps on an ongoing basis. Thus, what constitutes physical health and how it is achieved varies broadly among families. Regardless of individual circumstances it is important that families promote physical health among members. A holistic understanding of health means that we must take responsibility for our well-being. Paul teaches that our body is God's temple (1 Cor 3:16; 6:19), holding us responsible for some of its maintenance. In this regard, social scientists have also highlighted personal responsibility by defining health as a personal virtue and a task that each person and whole families cultivate through awareness and discipline. Yet it is not enough merely to attend to the physical as an end unto itself. The Bible teaches us "that [our] bodies are members of Christ himself" (1 Cor. 6:15). Thus, how we use our bodies, as well as our sexuality,* is an important component of a Christian understanding of physical health.

Psycho-social health. Several factors both measure and promote the emotional and psychological well-being of individual family members. Foundational to emotional family health is the strength of the marriage* bond. A marriage that is stable, committed and growing in love* provides the kind of atmosphere of safety and love that is optimal for raising children. Undergirding such relationships are strong communication* skills where there is a great deal of sharing, openness and emotional safety. Though often not well understood, conflict is an inevitable and even necessary part of family life, and healthy families do not shy away from it but instead use it to teach conflict resolution* skills with their children.

Healthy families display a balance between connectedness and individuality: members have a sense of their uniqueness and their personal boundaries, yet also feel part of the whole family and are willing to compromise for the sake of others. With regards to discipline,* it is neither too harsh nor too lax, and parents are clearly united and in control. The one constant in family life is change, and families who master the demands of change are those who exhibit a balance between order within the family. They provide stability and flexibility that allows them to adapt to new circumstances. Empathy, care and concern are hallmarks of families where emotional health is nurtured. Such families are attuned to one another's needs and respond in ways appropriate and developmentally accurate. The goal of parenting is not to get children to do what the parents want them to do; it is to get children to do what they need to do in order to grow, develop and follow Christ. In summary, healthy families are those families living out the Bible's teaching on respect, concern and love for one another.

Spiritual health. The spiritual health of a family is dependent on its relationship to Christ. The Bible teaches that even if only one member of the family knows Christ, the whole family's spiritual well-being is positively affected (1 Cor 7:14). Again, it is up to the parents to set the spiritual tenor of the home. Children are most impacted not by what the parents teach them verbally but by what is modeled for them. Because of the intimacy of family life, there can be no faking the importance of one's relationship with Christ. When children see that their parents' lives match what they proclaim they believe in, this makes a profound and lasting impression. Though parents cannot make their children accept Christ, they can provide optimal conditions in the home by having family prayer times, reading the Bible or other Christian literature to their children, involvement in church and participating in family ministry. Despite all that fami-

lies can do to foster spiritual health, ultimately faith is inspired by the leading of the Holy Spirit. That is why upholding one's family in prayer* and entrusting them to the care of the Savior is the most important part of helping our families find spiritual health in Christ.

Cautions

Two points of caution should be noted. First, personal and family responsibility does not mean that we must pursue health to the point of obsession. Contemporary society has become addicted to health. To idolize health is to confuse God with his temple. Second, personal responsibility includes accountability not only to oneself but to others—especially family members. An interpersonal and social understanding of health insists that we assume some responsibility for other people's sickness. We all contribute to the social conditions in which we live. Sexual permissiveness, media violence, consumer culture and environmental pollutants have adversely affected public health. The line between personal and public health is not well demarcated. Christians must take to heart our share of social responsibility in health as an expression of loving our neighbors. It is not enough to teach our children to care for themselves. By our words and our actions, as part of our commitment to Christ, we must teach them to care for the world around them.

See also BLESSING; DEATH; FEMININITY; MASCULINITY; SABBATH; SEXUALITY; SPIRITUAL FORMATION.

References and Resources

J. Balswick and J. Balswick, *The Family* (Grand Rapids: Baker, 1991); I. Illich, *Medical Nemesis* (New York: Pantheon, 1976); P. Jones and A. I. Meleis, "Health as Empowerment," *Advances in Nursing Science* 15, no. 3 (1993) 1-14; S. E. Lammers and A. Verkey, eds., *Moral Medicine* (Grand Rapids: Eerdmans, 1987); L. Larson, W. Goltz, and C.

Hobart, *Families in Canada* (Scarborough, Ont.: Prentice Hall, 1994).

Edwin Hui and Mark Davies

—HOLIDAYS—CHRISTMAS—

About two thousand years ago God gave his one and only son, Jesus, to the world. He chose a young woman named Mary to bear this unblemished child: "And she gave birth to a son" (Lk 2:6 NEB). The Redeemer was presented in the humble setting of a shepherd's cave and was laid in a manger, where animals went to be fed. It was the perfect place for the Savior to appear.

Some from the village of Bethlehem may have gone to see Jesus, but the Bible, for a significant purpose, mentions only two groups of visitors: humble shepherds and, later, foreign kings. The prophecies concerning the Messiah focused on his dual mission, redeeming us from our sin and returning to reign in glory.

From the very moment Adam and Eve stepped out of perfection and walked into the darkness of the world, they needed to be redeemed. Israel lived with God's promise that he would send a savior. The period of waiting must have seemed endless. People of faith continued to assure the Israelites that one day the Messiah would come. Certainly there was enough evidence that God always keeps a promise!

Advent

The word *advent* is derived from a Latin root meaning "to come." Early Christian leaders recognized the need to set apart a special time to remember those long years of waiting and to provide time for people to prepare spiritually for the coming of Christmas. They acknowledged that getting ready for Jesus' coming has more than one meaning. Not only is it an annual celebration of an event that took place many years ago; it is a celebration of his coming to us each day as well as each year during the holy season. It is also a time to remember Jesus' promise to come again.

The celebration is to begin on the fourth Sunday prior to Christmas Day, allowing four weeks for spiritual preparation. This decision was in keeping with Old Testament festivals, which often included a number of days of preparation prior to the holy day.

The Festival of Christmas

No one knows the exact day when Jesus was born. December 25, the date assigned to remember the birth, was introduced to counter the pagan feast of the sun god—the popular winter solstice festival held in Rome—the birthday of the Invincible Sun. This was a significant celebration in the cult of Mithras, the Persian god of light who was often identified with the sun. The Christian celebration was intended to be a theological corrective. The season was chosen to recognize and proclaim that Christ was born into a dark world and that he is the true source of light.

The theological corrective and observance of the birth of Jesus did not happen immediately after his life and death. For three hundred years after the ascension of Jesus to heaven, people remembered his death and resurrection. It was not until the early part of the fourth century that Christians felt a need to honor the birth of the Savior. In keeping with Old Testament feasts and festivals, it was designated a feast day, called the Feast of the Nativity. The celebration featured a special mass in honor of the remembrance of his coming. It was thus called *Christ's Mass,* known later as simply *Christmas.* This in itself is significant, for it was Christ who was being celebrated, not Christmas.

The Twelve Days of Christmas
In the sixth century Christian leaders declared Christmas a twelve-day festival. December 25 to January 5 were designated feast days to remember the birth of Immanuel, which means "God is with us." The incarnation, God's becoming human in order to be at one with us, is a worthy reason to continue the celebration beyond December 25.

Epiphany
The focus of Christmas is on Jesus, the Lamb of God. Epiphany celebrates Christ the King. The word *epiphany* comes from the Greek and means "appearance," "manifestation" or "showing forth." Epiphany, January 6, remembers the arrival of the kings who journeyed a long distance, guided by a special star, to honor the birth of the Christ Child. They said,

"For we saw His star in the east, and have come to worship Him" (Mt 2:2 NASB). The adoration of the Magi represents the manifestation of Christ's glory to the Gentiles. The wise men clearly recognized who he was and worshiped him.

Celebrating Christmas
If you had never practiced any tradition in relation to Christmas, how might you celebrate the good news of the birth of the Savior? What might you do to show your appreciation for God's gift? An old Hebrew proverb is helpful as you contemplate your answer: "Put something where you can see it so your eye will remind your heart." The Christmas season is filled with myriad visual opportunities. Carefully choose the images you want your heart to remember.

See also HOLIDAYS—EASTER; HOLIDAYS—THANKSGIVING.

References and Resources
G. M. Nelson, *To Dance with God* (New York: Paulist, 1986), pp. 59-126; R. E. Webber, ed., *The Services of the Christian Year,* vol. 5 of The Complete Library of Christian Worship (Nashville: Star Song, 1994) 157-222; M. Zimmerman, *Celebrating the Christian Year* (Minneapolis: Bethany House, 1993) 19-91.

Martha Zimmerman

—HOLIDAYS—EASTER—

The resurrection has been the central celebration of the church from its beginning. For centuries people have gathered annually on hilltops, beaches and open meadows to greet the rising sun, a visual reminder of the risen Son of God. Easter is observed during the season of the Jewish Passover, within which Christ was crucified and rose again. Resurrection Day is the first Sunday following the first full moon on or after the first day of spring. If the full moon is on a Sunday, Resurrection Day is celebrated the following week.

History
The original Christian celebration was

called *Pesach,* a name borrowed from the Hebrew word for "the Passover." For the first three centuries Christian believers reserved only one or two days for prayer in preparation for the celebration. The festival was not idolatrous, it was not called *Easter,* and it was not preceded by Lent.

The origin of Easter is found in Chaldean paganism. Astarte, or Ishtar, was a Babylonian goddess dedicated to a fertility cult, which spread to Europe and was adopted by Teutonic people, who called this fertility goddess *Eostre* or *Oster.* Many pagan religions worshiped her with religious ceremonies. The festival was celebrated on the spring equinox with rabbits and brightly colored eggs. In ancient Egypt the rabbit was a popular fertility symbol because of its reproductive record and was the obvious choice for a fertility festival.

The period for this pagan worship was called Easter Month. *Lent* comes from the word *Lencten,* which means "spring" and marks the lengthening of days in the spring. This was the dominant celebration devoted to the pagan worship of Astarte, or Eostre, and was marked by forty days of abstinence.

Christian leaders tried to change the emphasis by blending biblical themes with existing pagan practices. They established a forty-day fast to remember the forty days Jesus spent in the wilderness preparing for his earthly ministry (Mt 4:1-11) and the forty days Moses spent on Mount Sinai preparing to receive the Ten Commandments (Ex 34:28). The forty days of the pagan lent were stretched to forty-six days in the Christian calendar, with Sundays thus reserved for weekly celebrations of the resurrection.

Astarte worship was not easily suppressed by the new Christian Lent. A further attempt by church leaders in the sixth century to require the observance of the Christian season was met with resistance, violence and bloodshed. To se-

cure the peace, a compromise transformed Pesach into Easter and gave the Chaldean goddess her subtle place in current cultural practices.

Shrove Tuesday

"Then I confessed my sins to you; . . . and you forgave all my sins" (Ps 32:5 TEV). The word *shrove,* or *shriving,* means "confession." Shrove, or Confession, Tuesday is the day before Ash Wednesday and the beginning of Lent. It was intended to be a time of relaxation in preparation for the long period of self-discipline, self-denial and self-sacrifice. Beginning in the fourth century Shrovetide turned into revelry and rioting; we know it better as Mardi Gras.

Ash Wednesday

"I turned to the Lord God and pleaded with him in prayer and petition, in fasting, and in sackcloth and ashes" (Dan 9:3). Ash Wednesday opens the door to the season of Lent. Ashes symbolize humility and are a visual reminder of the vast difference between creatures and their Creator. They are a sign of sorrow and genuine regret. Historically the ashes used in Ash Wednesday ceremonies symbolize the need for repentance and a change of heart. The focus is on preparing oneself for the celebration of the resurrection. This is a time to repent and to prepare as a forgiven sinner to be received by the Lord.

Here are some ways to celebrate Lent. (1) Begin by attending a worship service on Ash Wednesday. (2) For the next six and one-half weeks prepare for Resurrection Day. The extent to which it is effective in your life will depend on you. Jesus taught in Matthew 6 that we should fast, pray and give. (3) Lent provides a fresh opportunity for personal renewal. Think of ways to honor the Lord with your praise during these days. (4) Traditionally, ashes are made by burning palm branches used in the previous year's Palm Sunday celebration. If you do not participate in a congregation with this observance, consider writing the sins you wish to confess on a piece of paper. Gather and burn the papers with God's words of assurance that he "blots out your transgressions" and "remembers your sins no more" (Is 43:25).

Palm Sunday

"Blessed is He who comes in the name of the Lord; Hosanna in the highest!" (Mt 21:9 NASB). From the time of the giving of the law, sacrifice was ordained by God (Lev 1—7). Sin must be covered in order for us to be in the presence of a holy God.

The entry of Jesus into Jerusalem was the official presentation to Israel of the Messiah as King. The crowd was excited: shouting, waving palm branches and rejoicing. At last, the "Coming One" had arrived to deliver them. No one paid attention to the shepherds leading the sheep from Bethlehem into the city. It was the tenth day of the Hebrew month, Nisan, and they were "each one to take a lamb for themselves . . . an unblemished male" (Ex 12:3, 5 NASB). As the Lamb entered Jerusalem, the "Home of Israel," the paschal lambs were being led into the city in preparation for the Passover. Everyone knew that the way to be redeemed was to sacrifice a lamb, but they had forgotten.

Try this: Prop a little stuffed lamb on a bed of palm fronds in the center of the table where you eat. Read Exodus 12:1-6, John 1:29 and Matthew 21:1-10. Let these objects and texts help you remember the events as you prepare your heart for Good Friday.

Maundy Thursday/Passover

"A new command I give you: Love one another" (Jn 13:34). The name *Maundy* comes from the Latin words "it is commanded." This is in remembrance of the new commandment given by Jesus as he was celebrating his last Passover with the disciples. Here are some ways to celebrate Maundy Thursday: Celebrate the Passover Seder and Last Supper in your home with your family, or share cooking responsibilities with several families, a small group or a house church. For a Christian Seder, recipes and instructions, see *Celebrate the Feasts* (Zimmerman). Then attend a Maundy Thursday service.

Good Friday

"Behold, the Lamb of God who takes away the sin of the world!" (Jn 1:29 NASB). Traditionally, Friday was the day of preparation for the sabbath.* Clearly Jesus' death on the cross on this Friday prepared everything for us to be able to enjoy a permanent sabbath rest. The day is called good because of the great benefit provided as a result of what took place.

Before celebrating Jesus' resurrection, remember his death: (1) On Friday morning perhaps cover the lights with pieces of black cloth. Be reminded that the "Light of the World" went out for three days. (2) Cover your dinner table with a black cloth. Along with the cutlery, set a nail at each place to remind everyone of personal responsibility in the crucifixion. Gather the family for breakfast. Read John 19:17-30 and Psalm 22. Pretend you are there. Share your feelings. (3) Attend a Good Friday service.

Holy Saturday

Leave everything in black. This is a quiet day of waiting. Read Matthew 27:62-66.

Resurrection Day

Mary announced, "I have seen the Lord!" (Jn 20:18 LB). Celebrate in some of the following ways: (1) Wake up early. With the words "Hallelujah, Christ is risen!" wake up each family member. (2) Spread

165

your dinner table with a white cloth. Decorate with fresh flowers and lilies. Light white candles in safe places. All are reminders that Jesus is alive. (3) Find a sunrise service or plan one yourself. Watch the sunrise and be reminded of God's Son; let him come alive in your heart. Read John 20:1-18 and Hebrews 11:25-26. Gather with family and friends, or a small group for breakfast. (4) Go to the church of your choice. Worship the risen Lord with joy!

See also HOLIDAYS—CHRISTMAS; HOLI-

DAYS—THANSKGIVING; SABBATH.

References and Resources

R. Foster, *Celebration of Discipline* (San Francisco: Harper & Row, 1978); R. E. Webber, ed., *The Services of the Christian Year,* vol. 5 of The Complete Library of Christian Worship (Nashville: Star Song, 1994) 373-426; M. Zimmerman, *Celebrate the Feasts* (Minneapolis: Bethany House, 1981); M. Zimmerman, *Celebrating the Christian Year* (Minneapolis: Bethany House, 1993).

Martha Zimmerman

—HOLIDAYS—THANKSGIVING—

The first recorded celebration of Thanksgiving in North America was in Newfoundland in 1578, with an English minister named Wolfall presiding. There are records of another held in Maine in 1607. In December 1619 thirty-eight men landed safely on the banks of the James River near Jamestown in Virginia. The English captain, John Woodleaf, read a directive from his charter declaring that the day of their arrival "shall be yearly and perpetually kept as a day of thanksgiving to God."

But it was the Pilgrims' settlement at Plymouth, Massachusetts, that is most often remembered as the site of the first Thanksgiving. Governor Bradford ordered a three-day celebration in October 1621. In keeping with the biblical instructions in Leviticus 23:39 for the Feast of the Ingathering, its purpose was to give prayerful thanks to God for the blessing of the harvest.

Importance

The desire of an individual to offer thanks to God goes back to the early chapters of Genesis. When Noah left the ark, having been saved by God, he "built an altar to the LORD . . . and offered burnt offerings on the altar. And the Lord smelled the soothing aroma" and promised, "While the earth remains, seedtime and harvest, and cold and heat, and summer and winter, and day and night shall not cease" (Gen 8:20-22 NASB). Noah modeled the importance of saying, "Thank you."

Corporate thanksgiving finds expression in the annual harvest festival when Moses directed the people of Israel to observe a full week of thanksgiving after the gathering of the harvest: "When you have gathered in the crops of the land, you shall celebrate the feast of the LORD for seven days" (Lev 23:39 NASB). David and Solomon continued the tradition, declaring special times of celebration and thanksgiving to God. After years of captivity Nehemiah called the people together to thank God, thereby reinstituting the instructions from Leviticus regarding the harvest festival. It is recorded that there was great rejoicing (Neh 8:17).

There are at least 140 passages of Scripture that deal with the subject of thanksgiving from a personal or corporate point of view. The word *praise* is used many more times. *Praise* means "to appreciate," "prize" and "consider precious and worthy of honor." Thanksgiving is a combination of words joined to express thanks to God. It is gratefulness followed by expressions of that gratitude. By far the most familiar passages of praise are found in the Psalms: "With my mouth I will give thanks abundantly to the LORD" (Ps 109:30 NASB); "Give thanks to the LORD, call on his name; / make known among the nations what he has done" (105:1); "Enter his gate with thanksgiving" (100:4).

In the New Testament we read how Jesus constantly gave thanks to the Father and one year risked his life to celebrate the thanksgiving festival. Paul began nearly every one of his letters with an expression of thanks and urged us to give thanks in everything (1 Thess 5:18). In Romans 1:21 he describes those under the judgment of God as people who "though they knew God, they did not honor Him as God, or give thanks" (NASB). The writer of Hebrews in 13:15 tells us to "continually offer to God a sacrifice of praise—the fruit of lips that confess his name."

Celebrating

The Bible tells us to "rejoice always; pray without ceasing; in everything give thanks; for this is God's will for you in Christ Jesus" (1 Thess 5:16-18 NASB). There are many ways to give thanks.

□ As a Hebrew proverb tells us, "Put something where you can see it so your eye will remind your heart."

□ Hang a cluster of Indian corn tied with an attractive bow on the front door. Remember the thankful spirit of the Pilgrims at Plymouth.

□ Lovingly assemble a harvest display with seasonal produce as your centerpiece.

□ Place a colorful leaf at each person's place at the holiday meal. On each leaf sprinkle several kernels of dried corn. Before the meal is served, take time to remember the hardships of the Pilgrims' first winter in the New World and how with God's help they overcame great difficulties. Take turns expressing your own gratitude for God's mercy.

□ Encourage children to make lists of all the things for which they are thankful.

□ Through a food bank or Christian agency, discover local needs. Decide together how you will help. This is the season to share with others.

The real celebration of Thanksgiving is *thanksliving*. The best way to thank God for the gift of life is to live your life in a spirit of gratitude.

Deuteronomy 8:10 says, "When you have eaten and are satisfied, you shall bless the LORD your God for the good land which He has given you" (NASB). The chapter warns that when everything is going well, there is a tendency for your heart to become proud and thus forget the Lord. Take time to thank God for all of the good gifts that you enjoy. Live out the words of Deuteronomy 8:18, "But you shall remember the LORD your God" (NASB).

See also HOLIDAYS—CHRISTMAS; HOLIDAYS—EASTER.

References and Resources

G. Gaither and S. Dobson, *Let's Make a Memory* (Waco, Tex.: Word, 1983); J. Santino, *All Around the Year: Holidays and Celebrations in American Life* (Urbana: University of Illinois Press, 1994); S. W. Shenk, *Why Not Celebrate!* (Intercourse, Penn.: Good Books, 1987); D. Steindl-Rast, *Gratefulness: The Heart of Prayer* (New York: Paulist, 1984); M. Zimmerman, *Celebrate the Feasts* (Minneapolis: Bethany House, 1981); M. Zimmerman, *Celebrating the Christian Year* (Minneapolis: Bethany House, 1993).

Martha Zimmerman

—HOME—

The word *home* has a broad range of meanings. On a personal level it can refer to our immediate and physical place of residence: a house, an apartment or condominium, a studio, boarding house, trailer park, retirement community, college dormitory or even a street corner. Home can also be descriptive of our "roots"; the place in which we grew up; our town, state or country of origin. Home can also describe the welcome and embrace of close friends or family* members with whom we have a shared history. Or it can be descriptive of something for which we long; either that which we once had and desire to re-create or that which we have never experienced but ardently dream of.

Whatever definitions we use, our experiences of home are deeply formative. For some, home conjures up warm and secure memories of the past or is representative of all that is good and wholesome in the present. For others, to speak of home resurrects past, painful experiences, a reminder of what one never had or does not have. As we face the ever-present realities of family dysfunction and breakdown, economic struggle and the increasing pressures of urban life, we are confronted with the fact that our experiences of homes shape who we are.

The Home in the New Testament

In line with the Old Testament emphasis on the home as a place of protection, for raising a family, for rest, prayer* and hospitality,* and as part of one's legacy to one's children, the home in the New Testament plays a prominent role in the ministry and mission* of Jesus, and in the unfolding story of the early church.

A place of spiritual encounter. Though it is true that Jesus ministered and proclaimed in synagogue and temple, his favored place of ministry was the home. There was nothing that Jesus did in the name of the Father that he was not prepared to do in the home. His choice of home as a primary place of interaction is consistent with his incarnational mission; no longer was the presence of God confined to the temple, mediated by priests, but it was now the immediate and daily experience of all those who respond in faith. God was encountered through healing and deliverance (Mt 8:14-17; Mk 2:1; 5:35-43; Lk 14:1-4), worship and prayer (Mt 2:1; 26:6-13, 30; Lk 1:39-55; Jn 12:1-8; Acts 2:1-4; 12:12), and through hearing and receiving from God (Mt 1:20; 2:13; Lk 2:6-38; Jn 19:19-23; Acts 2:1-4; 9:11). All these happened in the home.

A place of community. In the New Testament the home is vital to the nurture of community. Jesus spent a substantial amount of time in homes building relationships. One of his favorite activities was eating* in the homes of his friends (Mt 8:15; Lk 10:38-42; Jn 12:2). The Passover meal he shared with his disciples in a home prior to his crucifixion (Lk 22:7-38) signified the beginning of a tradition that is still the mark of community in the Christian church.

In the life of the early church it is apparent that the home played host more than any other venue to the development of community (Acts 2:42-47). The early church was almost exclusively a network of house churches (Rom 16:3-5; Col 4:15; Philem 2). Without the house as a meeting place for teaching, fellowship, worship and mission, it is hard to imagine how the early church would have found its feet.

A place of ministry. The home was the place where the open invitation into

God's kingdom was extended to all who would hear. Jesus chose to do much of his teaching and preaching in homes, often while reclining at a meal table (*see* Eating), sharing his time with "tax collectors and 'sinners' " (Lk 5:30; 15:1-2; 19:5-7). He visited and ate with Samaritans and saw many become his followers (Jn 4:39). He confronted the Pharisees in their homes (Lk 11:37-38; 14:1-6), and he welcomed into the home prostitutes, the demon-possessed and the sick (Mt 8:16-17; 26:6-13; Mk 2:1). The home was the place where Jesus took his disciples aside to explain and instruct (Mt 13:36-52; 17:25; 18:35). The home was where Nicodemus came seeking truth (Jn 3:1-21), and it was where the crowds gathered to hear Jesus preach (Mk 2:1; 3:20-21).

A place of expectation. As we examine the role of the home in the New Testament, two realities emerge. Jesus existed very much in the present. He was the presence of God in physical form, to be touched, seen and heard. Wherever he went, he embodied the immediate concern of the kingdom for the here and now. Just as God in flesh was not a mere convenience but a vital theological reality, so Jesus present in the house was not an irrelevant aside but a tangible expression of God in their midst. All the concerns, duties and relationships embodied in the house were gathered up into the concerns of the kingdom. This is obvious from the number of stories of household duties and objects Jesus told to explain the nature of the kingdom of God (Mt 18:1-35; 25:31-46; Mk 10:29; Lk 11:5-10; 14:7-14; 15:8-10).

On the other hand, we have Jesus' promise that he goes to prepare a place for those who believe, a home with many rooms (Jn 14:2). This is part of the kingdom yet to be. It is this sense of the kingdom now and not yet that validates the tensions felt by those endeavoring to live fully in the present and yet fully anticipating. It is somewhere in between these two realities that believers are called to live.

Contemporary Attitudes Toward the Home

Despite people's longing for a home of their own, they tend to view where they live as a temporary resting place. Because of high mobility,* most people pass through many dwelling places during their lifetime. The phenomenon of the mobile home is simply the latest expression of this. In many cases both marriage* partners are now working outside the home. Domestic space is therefore generally empty during the day and often on weekends, though the emergence of telecommuting is having a small effect on this.

Yet the idea of home remains strong. Most people see having a home as essential for their contentment or fulfillment, as a basis for security and stability, and as a fortress of privacy or "haven in a heartless world" (Lasch). They also tend to view their home as a status symbol, as an extension of their personality or as an opportunity to have a taste of nature on their doorstep. For some it is primarily an investment. Our homes, therefore, are significant to us in a variety of ways. That explains why they occupy so much of our attention and mean so much to us.

We are now living in a time when suburbia, the main context for the places people live, is undergoing change and reconsideration. It is not simply a case of fewer people being able to live there, or the urbanizing of many suburban settings, but the way suburbia has strengthened the gap between private and public life.

Architects and sociologists are voicing their common concern that the way

169

we have been planning and building urban neighborhoods has disregarded the balance necessary to a well-functioning society between the home as private space and a place of community. In his book *A Better Place to Live: Reshaping the American Suburb,* Philip Langdon argues that since the end of World War II the front porch as the place of community interaction and the focus of family activity has been overtaken by the secluded backyard, complete with pool and barbecue area. Take a drive through any new housing development and you will find the front façades of the houses dominated by two and three-car garages, with the main entrance to the home hidden off to the side. In many cases sidewalks no longer exist, and public gathering places are a secondary concern. According to Langdon and others, personal convenience and privacy now determine the architecture of our homes. Neighborhood considerations are of lesser concern. The proponents of New Urbanism contend that the way we build our homes must reflect to a greater extent the fact that we are community and public beings.

A Christian Response

As those seeking to integrate our Christian faith with all of life, how do we interpret God's purposes for the home, and how do we nurture our homes as places of God's presence? Apart from our recognition of our thankfulness for God's providential provision of "a roof over our heads," we should consider the following dimensions of our homes.

A sacred place. When one considers the range of significant events to which the home played host—the incarnation, the commissioning of the disciples, the Last Supper, the resurrection appearances, Pentecost, the opening of the church to the Gentiles, the blossoming of the early church—it is hard to deny

the home its role as a place of God's gracious and transforming presence. God's presence through the Holy Spirit can form, nurture, refresh, heal and call us, and it is ours to be experienced in the home. Unfortunately, we do not often appreciate the very immediate, divine presence that surrounds us there. It is our challenge to find ways to recognize and respond to the presence and call of God, and to experience in the solitude and relationship of the home the immediacy of "God with us" (*see* Spiritual Formation).

A place of relationship. The traditional bonds of community are fragile in today's world. As our lives become more fragmented, finding time together as households is increasingly difficult. Shared mealtimes are often sacrificed in the interests of individual agendas. More often than not, the television* is the gathering point in the home, an object that discourages rather than nurtures communication.* If we are serious about the home as a place of interaction, then careful thought should be given to some practical matters of priority. Creating common schedules that prioritize time together is essential. Consideration could be given to the arrangement of furniture in common areas. Too often the television set is the organizing point in our living rooms. Placing it elsewhere and intentionally creating spaces that invite interaction through the simple rearrangement of chairs and lighting can make a substantial difference.

A place of refuge. While in the majority of instances recorded in the New Testament the focus of home ministry and interaction is on the open door, there are also significant instances of the house as a place to close the door on outside demands (Mt 6:6; 8:14; Mk 5:38-43; Lk 1:24, 56). There will be times in the life of every household when it is more appropriate to focus on the healing and well-being of those within than to extend a welcome to outsiders. The various seasons of life each come with their unique challenges and demands. Our homes must serve as places of refuge, withdrawal, healing, comfort and solitude to varying degrees throughout our occupancy. Sensitivity to the changing needs of members must always be seen as a valid expression of our response to God's call. It is interesting to note the occasions in which Jesus directed one of those he healed to "go home" (Mk 5:19; 8:22-26; Lk 5:25). He did not direct them to go and do, go and proclaim, or go into all the world: he simply commanded them to return to their homes.

*A place of mission.** In a society that values independence and privacy, it is perhaps our greatest challenge to stand apart, to model the welcome and embrace of the gospel where we live. The call to mission is a call to friendship. Such a call requires an open door, inviting conversation and redemptive relationship. The church is often rebuked for being more a fortress that guards the faith than an open table to which all are welcomed and where faith is shared. The home is ideally suited to model the latter. An integrated Christian faith is a key issue here too. Our place of worship and fellowship is most often separate from our place of living. In today's urban world the two can be not only in different buildings but in two completely separate parts of the city. Many today are rediscovering the New Testament house-church model, which helped tremendously in reintegrating these separate worlds and in recentering the home as a primary place of mission in the world. Where possible, we can also use our homes as places for exercising hospitality to those traveling or on vacation,* those engaged in itinerant ministry or home from overseas mission, and those

temporarily homeless. While not everyone is able to have a guestroom available to any who may need it, those who can afford to do so can provide one as a tangible sign of their welcoming attitude to others.

A place of recreation. The home is a place where we can relax, be ourselves, rest and enjoy leisure. It provides opportunities for play* with our families and for creativity in the way we decorate and furnish. The home is a context in which many people pursue their hobbies and crafts, extending and enriching themselves in satisfying ways that may also be beneficial to others. The uncertainty or chaos of the world outside is sometimes compensated for by the stability and order of the home. Meanwhile, the space around the house allows people to re-create the earth through planting flowers, shrubs and trees. In some cases the yard of a home become a miniature Garden of Eden that signals to us our longing for the coming heavenly garden city (Rev 22:1-5).

Conclusion

We should consider carefully not just where we should live but where God wants us to live. First of all, this requires understanding our calling, for this will have much to say about where we should reside. In deciding this we need to take into account our location with respect to our work, schools, parks, the needy and public transport.

Second, we should think through what kind of home we need rather than what kind of home we want, which is often not much different from what most others desire. How much should we be governed by the principles of simplicity, of stewardship of God's creation, and, if we are able to build a home, of its compatibility with other dwellings, integrity in terms of style, and quality in terms of craftsmanship?

Third, we should give thought to having and arranging spaces inside the home so that they serve their proper function and are an expression of our values* and priorities. Do we want our home to be a showcase to impress outsiders, or do we want it to be a place that nurtures relationships and provides security for those who live there? Do we want our home to be a perfect example of orderliness and tidiness, or do we want it to be a place of welcome, embrace and peace for the visitor? Do we want it to open up to the creation around it and the street on which it is placed, or seal us from these?

Instead of assuming that the single-family home or individual apartment is the embodiment of our personal desires and needs, we should also consider the benefits of cooperative housing or shared living arrangements, such as friends buying or renting adjoining houses, or living with others in a Christian community. Congregations can also give thought to helping young families put a deposit on their first home, developing a street community where members live near one another and intentionally minister to their neighborhood, or providing low-cost housing for seniors.

In summary, the home is indeed a sacred place in which the presence and purposes of God can be discovered and responded to. As a people who long for the fulfillment of God's promise of an eternal home to which we are welcomed with open arms, we have the opportunity in the present moment to experience and to be "the household of God" (1 Tim 3:15 NRSV). Our homes can be gathered up in that experience.

See also CHORES; HOSPITALITY; MISSION.

References and Resources
C. Alexander, *A Timeless Way of Building* (New York: Oxford University Press, 1979); R. J. Banks, *Paul's Idea of Community* (Peabody, Mass.: Hendrickson, 1994); T. Howard, *Hallowed Be This House* (San Francisco: Ignatius, 1976); T. Kidder, *House* (New York: Houghton Mifflin, 1985); P. Kratz, *The New Urbanism: Toward an Architecture of Community* (New York: McGraw-Hill, 1994); P. Langdon, *A Better Place to Live: Reshaping the American Suburb* (Amherst: University of Massachusetts, 1994); C. Lasch, *Haven in a Heartless World* (New York: Basic Books, 1977); C. C. Marcus and Sarkissian, *Housing As If People Mattered* (Los Angeles: UCLA Press, 1986); W. Rybczynski, *Home: A Short History of an Idea* (New York: Viking, 1986); J. Solomon, *The Signs of Our Time* (Los Angeles: J. P. Tarcher, 1988); J. F. C. Turner, *Housing by People: Towards Autonomy in Building Environments* (New York: Pantheon, 1976); J. A. Walter, *The Human Home: The Myth of the Sacred Environment* (Tring, U.K.: Lion, 1982); W. M. Wright, *Sacred Dwelling: A Spirituality of Family Life* (New York: Crossroad, 1990).

Simon Holt and Robert Banks

—HOME SCHOOLING—

Education begins with our first wobbly steps, with recognition and naming of things, while we are still very small children in our parents' care. The long process about who we are and where we came from, of acquiring skills for life, does not begin when we step over the threshold of our first school and end when we graduate. Language, expressions, morals and values* are all initially learned from parents.

Scriptural Family Education

For most of history, children's early teaching came from within the family and the community. Now most children go to school. However, it is still parents who are primarily responsible for their child's education. Deuteronomy 4 speaks of God's "decrees and laws" saying, "Teach them to your children and to their children after them" (v. 9). Moses reminds the people of the message God gave him: "Hear my words . . . and teach them to [your] children" (v. 10). Deuteronomy 6 lists the Ten Commandments, saying, "These commandments I give you today are to be upon your hearts. Impress them on your children. Talk about them when you sit at home and when you walk along the road, when you lie down and when you get up" (vv. 6-7). This shows education to be interactive and occurring in everyday activities. Biblical priorities are clear: "Train a child in the way he should go, / and when he is old he will not turn from it" (Prov 22:6). Early education is an investment for the future.

Given the weight of these biblical imperatives, Christian parents must think carefully about their children's education. Most would applaud the reasoning that led to the institution of schools,* which in the West was often tied to biblical literacy and to combating social injustice. As the school movement has become a government-regulated institution, however, it is now an integral part of our society and politics. Despite its admirable beginnings and initial Christian slant, many parents find the school system today has strayed far from its roots. Yet, as the institution of schools has become a mainstay of our society, many assume that in order to get anywhere children must go through school from kindergarten to high school graduation. This leaves many parents feeling that they are trapped between their frustrations and doubts about schools and the certainty that their children cannot succeed in life without schooling.

Most technologically advanced societies require that all children be educated, but in the legal system, education is not defined as occurring only in the state school system. In Canada, for example, the wording states that every child is to be educated "at school or elsewhere." School is one educational option; home education is another. In most countries it is not against the law, although it may be bureaucratically convenient to give citizens the impression that schooling is compulsory. When children reach "school age," parents have to make decisions about this "next step" of their children's education. The switch from preschool learning at home to formal education within a school building can be an interruption to the continuity of a child's educational process. Some parents and children find this transition particularly difficult, while others manage it with relative ease. Whatever choice parents make, it should be part of the continual education of their children toward responsible adulthood.

In their search for the best choice for their children, parents find themselves with many questions about the nature of the education offered at any given institution. When our eldest reached this age, we wondered if he needed to go to school. What would school provide that our growing number of family and friends and we could not provide? Was our expertise now too challenged? Could we meet the next requirements of helping our child to learn to read and to do some basic mathematics? What else did he need to learn? We came to the conclusion at this point in our son's development that we could find ways at home and in our community to provide the opportunities that the school was offering. That realization led to our decision to do home education for his first year of formal schooling. This decision was reviewed each year in the light of his growing needs, our resources and the demands of our whole family.

Alternatives to School

Once parents have made the decision not to send children to school, they face the challenge of how to carry out the next stage of their children's education. If "schooling," as a time-tabled regime of sequential learning according to a set curriculum (as opposed to education), is considered valuable by the parents, they could copy the school system. Copies of the official curriculum for each grade are available to the public. For learning about the recommended topics, local libraries are often great resources. Some other options for guidelines are correspondence courses or workbooks available from various educational supply companies.

Each family has the freedom to supplement a basic curriculum for each year taking into account the interests of each child and building on the interests of the family's circle of friends and contacts. Learning about another country, for example, is greatly enhanced by meeting someone from that country and an opportunity to visit. History can be enhanced by visits to local historical sites. Educators recognize the value of "field trips," but in the school system this is difficult to achieve. Outside school such visits can be woven into family vacations* and weekend visits to friends and relatives. Children themselves begin to realize how much they can learn by asking questions of such people as the old lady across the street, a neighbor with a keen interest in ornithology or the telephone engineer working at the roadside.

Concerns

Some questioned our decision to keep our children at home, concerned that they might not receive an adequate social education or have enough interaction with their peers. One of the ways in which we dealt with this issue was by involving our children in after-school and weekend activities. Many children who attend school all day also attend dance classes, swimming classes and many other learning situations. This availability gives children who stay at home during the day opportunity to interact with peers in both a social and an educational context.

Home educating children is virtually impossible for single parents* or if both parents are in full-time work, but this problem could be avoided if, in the case of two-parent families, one parent works and the other stays at home, or if the parents share the education of their children by each working only part-time. If your child needs time away from a school environment that has become destructive to him or her, then short-term home education can restore confidence, and this could be achieved by a good babysitter or tutor who is willing to pay this kind of attention to your child.

While informal education has occurred and has been largely in parental hands throughout history, schooling for all is a recent development. Formal, state-regulated education systems are the product of modern industrialized capitalist societies. Except for fundraising, parents have been pushed out of education, despite their religious responsibility for their children. Home education, whether approached as "schooling" or as "learning for life" is one alternative. While commitment and imagination are needed for this, credentials are not. Children may be disadvantaged in any context, but home education at its best is fulfilling for all and a wonderful preparation for responsible adulthood.

See also CHARACTER; DISCIPLINE;

HOME; PARENTING; READING; SCHOOLS, PUBLIC AND PRIVATE; VALUES.

References and Resources
J. Holt, *Teach Your Own* (Brightlingsea, U.K.: Lighthouse Books, 1981); H. Horne, *Jesus the Teacher: Examining His Expertise in Education*, ed. A. M. Gunn (Grand Rapids: Kregel, 1998); M. Lieberman, *Privatization and Edu-cational Choice* (New York: St. Martin's Press, 1989); J. Mintz, *The Almanac of Educational Choice: Public and Private Learning Alternatives and Home Schooling* (New York: Macmillan, 1995); R. Moore and D. Moore, *The Successful Home-School Family Handbook* (Nashville: Nelson, 1994).

Sue Lyon

—HOMEMAKING—

Homemaking as a vocation has had very bad publicity in recent years. The media delight in caricaturing homemakers. She—such a person is usually, but certainly not always, female—is pictured as having no intellectual awareness; she makes no contribution to the family income; she has no glamour, status or productivity.

For Christians, the story of Mary and Martha (Lk 10:38-41) seems to confirm what the pundits of the media are saying: homemaking, at least the kind practiced by Martha, is second best. Many a good homemaker has had a sneaking sympathy for Martha. After all, somebody had to prepare the food and do the dishes! Yet implicit in Jesus' approval of Mary is a condemnation of Martha's busyness.

It is not surprising that full-time homemakers make up an increasingly small percentage of the population. Is homemaking a profession that is still necessary? Is an intelligent and competent person wasting God-given talents when deciding to stay at home* to care for the family*? To answer these questions, we need to clarify what homemaking is and see what Christians can bring to it, following the examples of the biblical role models we have been given.

What Is Homemaking?
Perhaps the most dreaded question a homemaker faces is "So, what do you do?" The problem is that the answer seems so mundane: "I care for my family; I clean and organize the house; I plan and cook and serve meals; I welcome and provide for our guests." It is hard to express the intangibles: being there for others, creating a warm and sheltering place,

teaching basic values,* modeling the attitudes and ways of God.

Homemaking can be defined as that which develops and nurtures the family at its central core—its traditions, beliefs, values and strengths, and the unique character of the family. Homemakers care for the physical surroundings and physical needs, not as ends in themselves, but as part of the overall fostering of the family's well-being (*see* Clothing; Eating; Sleeping).

In Jesus' ministry we see how physical acts can have both practical application and spiritual significance. He washed his disciples' feet because they were hot and dirty, thus making his companions feel welcome and comfortable (Jn 13:5). Yet it was also an opportunity for him to describe the cleansing of forgiveness.* Creating and caring for a physical environment bring into being an atmosphere in which people are loved, cherished and nurtured in their whole being.

Homemaking is an act of human creativity. The attitude and personality of homemakers, the spirit with which they approach their task, shape and define the homes they make. In creation God brought order out of chaos. Establishing a home exercises a similar kind of creativity. Homemaking is also an expression of providence. It maintains and enhances order within and around the family, much as God maintains and orders the universe. An obvious point of difference, as any homemaker would be quick to acknowledge, is that God's cosmic order has lasted longer than the order created in a home! The finished product—the home—is as unique as are the creatures that God made.

Christian Homemaking

Homes that are fashioned by Christians will share certain characteristics because of their common striving to be obedient to God. It will be marked by the presence of (or the seeking after) the fruit of the Spirit: "love, joy, peace, patience, kindness, goodness, faithfulness, gentleness and self-control" (Gal 5:22-23). The homemaker, because of the nature of her work at the very heart of the home, is able to influence those in her care and affect the atmosphere in the home.

If love* is present in a home, how will it show itself? Christian love, as distinct from the secular version, is defined by God's love for us. In sending Jesus to live his love before us, God proved in the flesh the value of unconditional love. In sending the Spirit to indwell us, God showed us love intimately involved with the everyday life of the believer. This is not love from afar; this is love close up. A homemaker has an unusual opportunity to exemplify incarnational love because so much of her—or his—work must be done in the details of daily life,

and her presence is as important as anything that she does. Love then will not be merely intellectual or emotional but gloriously practical and down-to-earth, that is, truly incarnational.

Similarly, peacefulness is a goal of the Christian homemaker. This does not mean the absence of noise, debate or argument. A home may have occasional or even frequent discord, as well as constant happy noise, and still be a place of peace. Here conflicts are resolved in an atmosphere of love, forgiveness and mutual submission to God's will. Peace is an intangible phenomenon. A home may be superficially peaceful yet, underneath the veneer of calm, full of hatred and disunity. True peace ultimately can only come from God because forgiveness is its most important ingredient. Those who live in peace with God are more able to generate and promote peacefulness in the home. Alongside incarnational character, then, there is a redemptive dimension as well.

The best homemakers manage to create a place where people matter more than material things. This often marks the difference between a housekeeper and a homemaker, as shown in the story of Martha and Mary. Martha was "worried and upset about things" (Lk 10:41). Her concentration was primarily on the pots and pans and food. Mary chose to sit near Jesus and listen to him. In so doing she demonstrated her priority: her friendship with Jesus. Mary may have seen the things that Martha did as one way to express love and hospitality.* But the way Mary chose, the homemaking rather than the housekeeping way, was clearly acceptable to Jesus.

Homemakers' Contribution

The commitment of homemakers to care for the home and family clearly benefits those around them. Less obvious, perhaps, is their enormous contribution to the whole of society. They have much to give the neighborhoods in which they live. They are often at the forefront of the army of volunteers whose hard work adds so much to the general good. They can give the gift of time, and their focus on caring for others makes them natural resources for churches and community organizations. At a time when the disintegration of the traditional family is contributing to serious societal ills, they proclaim that family means more than the status, money* and job satisfaction offered by a career outside the home. In fact, they are actually making a significant contribution to the welfare and renewal of society!

Traditionally, homemaking has included the care and nurture of children. In the confusing debate over what constitutes the best environment for child rearing, some truths are clear: children thrive in an atmosphere that is stable, loving and consistent, where they are respected as unique individuals and given both guidance and freedom appropriate to their age and ability. There are a number of good reasons, besides historical precedence, for the family's homemaker to care for its children. Homemakers have the time flexibility that allows for adaptation to children's changing needs as they grow. Being cared for in their own home enhances their sense of security and emotional stability. The homemaker's commitment to putting people first makes her an ideal caregiver.

What Homemakers Need

If little value is placed on their skills, homemakers are vulnerable to low self-esteem.* They need strong affirmation from family and friends. Low self-esteem can also result from a lack of a sense of identity because identity is closely associated in our society with what job we do.

Like all other Christians, homemakers need to find their primary source of identity in their relationship with God. It is not what we do but who we are—children of God—that gives our lives worth and purpose.

In a profession that offers little in the way of status, homemakers need positive role models. One picture of the ideal homemaker is found in Proverbs 31. Here is a woman who is industrious, loving and honorable; she has status in her community, the love of her husband and the respect of her children. It is a compelling picture and one that has strengthened homemakers for many generations. Another glimpse is provided in Romans 16:3-5. Priscilla was a homemaker and was involved in the family business; she also cohosted with her husband a church in her home and extended hospitality to itinerant Christian workers.

The Example of Jesus

We must not overlook the best biblical role model—Jesus. Looking closely at Jesus' interaction with various people, we see a man with a homemaker's heart. He too worked at physical tasks that were important but also imbued with spiritual significance. He had neither a home nor a nuclear family, yet he was the quintessential homemaker.

Jesus was concerned about the physical well-being of those he met. He healed people because he cared about them, not just to demonstrate his miraculous power or to authenticate his claims. He urged his disciples to feed the hungry crowds. He may have done this to challenge his disciples to stretch their faith; yet it is equally true to say that he wanted to feed the people because they were hungry; he felt compassion for both their spiritual (Mk 6:34) and physical (Mt 15:32) need.

A similar incident occurred on the

shore of the Sea of Tiberias after Jesus' resurrection (Jn 21). When the disciples returned to the shore after a night of fishing, they found Jesus cooking fish for their breakfast. Perhaps he wanted to prove by eating* that his resurrected body was a real one, not a ghostly apparition. Yet he also must have known how hungry they would have been after a night of fishing. By preparing their breakfast he was reminding them of his deep abiding love. He wanted them to experience the warmth of the fire in the chill of the morning. On that shore he made a home for them where the meeting of their physical needs coincided with the meeting of their emotional and spiritual needs. He did it because he loved them. Here is the essence of homemaking.

As Jesus spoke with his disciples about his ascension, he gave an intriguing glimpse into his occupation until they would be reunited with him for eternity. "I go and prepare a place for you," he told them, "that where I am you may be also" (Jn 14:3 RSV). The image is profoundly moving: Jesus, who knows us intimately and loves us boundlessly, is preparing a home for us in which to spend eternity. An occupation so honored by the Lord Jesus is surely one that any of his followers can be proud to pursue.

See also CHORES; EATING; HOME; HOSPITALITY; MEAL PREPARATION; MISSION; PARENTING.

References and Resources
R. Andre, *Homemakers: The Forgotten Workers* (Chicago: University of Chicago Press, 1981); W. Droel, *Homemakers* (Chicago: ACTA, 1990).

Susan Norman

—HOMOSEXUALITY—

Sexual activities with persons of the same sex have been known throughout history and across all cultures. The term *homosexuality* was coined only in 1892, while the activist terms *lesbian* and *gay* are still more recent (1970s and 1950s, respectively). Such changes mean that there is not only a change in the interpretation of same-sex behavior and attitudes but also ambiguity, when referring to earlier references, whether the same concept is being described. Many contemporary writers seek to interpret the biblical references as relating to temple prostitution and culturally endorsed practices rather than the homosexual acts of today. Hence cultural meaning is often advanced as a way of reinterpreting the morality of homosexual activity.

A Long Story
Homosexual acts have been recorded throughout history. Sociologists and anthropologists have identified many different expressions associated with rituals, initiation rites and use of power. These do not assume a lifetime orientation or even a predominant attraction to the same sex. No society in history has endorsed adult homosexual relationships of the kind advocated today. Evidence of exclusive homosexuality has been sketchy, probably due to its rarity. Much of the evidence relates to the enforced isolation of monasticism, denying heterosexual outlet.

Seemingly higher prevalence only received significant attention after the Kinsey reports (1948 and 1953) mistakenly suggested 4 percent of adult men are exclusively homosexual and 10 percent are predominantly homosexual (and fewer women). This apparently scientific work brought confusion both to science and to morality since it made false claims yet appeared to challenge traditional morality. Kinsey's study combined information about sexual attraction with reports of actual sexual behavior. Thus the traditional Jewish and Christian distinctions became blurred. A full, sensitive response requires a distinction between the person with a homoerotic attraction and one who engages in homosexual behavior. This difference has profound implications for our response personally, pastorally, theologically and politically.

While earlier societies have often institutionalized homosexual behavior, either giving it limited sanction or developing strong taboos against it, homosexual behavior has never been incorporated as normal or natural. Claims that homosexual behavior can be observed in animal behavior do not hold up since this is never a sustained pattern but rather an occasional variant where it occurs. The current ideology of the gay movement is to bring homosexuality into the mainstream of sexuality* as one among several preferences of equal legitimacy. This is a radical alternative to traditional thinking and gains strength in the Western world not only from its appeal to civil rights claims but also from maintaining orientation and behavior as inseparable. By contrast, the large number of nonpracticing homosexuals provide evidence that orientation does not necessarily demand a behavioral response.

Many Viewpoints
A fast-growing literature provides different and conflicting interpretations that arise from their varied starting assumptions. Represented in this literature are
□ personal biographies of Christians and others advocating the endorsement of the gay lifestyle as largely predetermined, something to be accepted
□ personal biographies of those (especially Christians) who have experienced a reorientation away from their homosexuality and proclaim release is possible
□ accounts of therapy by clinicians, some arguing change is never real or lasting and others citing a growing body of evidence that real change can and does occur
□ moral and theological discussions regarding homosexual behavior with varying conclusions depending on the adoption of a conservative or liberal interpretation of the Scriptures
□ evidence from the biological sciences suggesting some fundamental difference (genetic or hormonal) that might indicate a built-in predisposition to becoming homosexual (with a clear political agenda of legitimizing the gay movement, this rush of studies has been shown repeatedly to be misleading and inadequate)
□ evidence from the social sciences suggesting links with early relationships, parenting* patterns or significant seduction experiences

These arguments take many forms, and their variety indicates that no one theory is sufficient for all presentations of homosexual inclination. They certainly do not justify parents automatically taking guilt upon themselves when children disclose.

The absence of a single compelling explanation points to the complexity of the phenomenon and suggests that there are many possible precursors to becoming homosexually inclined, as well as various forms of expression. Nature and nurture appear to contribute to differing degrees for any given man or woman, and stereotyping should be avoided.

Biblical Sources
There is wide disagreement about the

meaning of biblical texts regarding homosexuality. Homosexual practices receive mention in the Bible, but such references are few. The conservative interpretation of passages such as Genesis 19:5-9; Leviticus 18:22; 20:13; Judges 19:22-28; Romans 1:26-32; 1 Corinthians 6:9-10; and 1 Timothy 1:8-11 is that there is a clear condemnation of homosexual behavior that goes beyond the commands to Israel and has binding significance for Christians today. This interpretation comes from setting such specific injunctions into the broader context of sexuality generally, especially the creation principle of male and female.

A great deal hinges on the interpretation of the term *natural* as used in Romans 1. Confusion arises when *natural* is used to indicate "according to nature," as a naturally occurring phenomenon, since there are many things, good and bad, that occur naturally. However, Paul's use of the term is undoubtedly in a moral sense—that is, *natural* as something in accordance with God's purposes for creation and over against that which is *unnatural,* or morally wrong. Making such distinctions, we can assert that homosexual behavior is natural in the first sense (it occurs in nature) but unnatural in the second sense as used by Paul. Such a position needs to be balanced by the limited attention given in the Bible to this matter, suggesting that its significance should not be exaggerated. Homosexual behavior appears in the New Testament among catalogs of sins without any indication that it is more heinous than lying or greediness.

Responses for Family and Friends

Rejection and disapproval of the adult succeed only in increasing alienation. It is possible to take a stand against the gay movement as a political force, yet reach out in love* to those who dare to acknowledge their struggle. Even for the homosexually inclined adult who does not see change as an option or desirable, there are still other kinds of healing needed—especially in the area of close relationships. Christian parents easily slip into a judgmental role as their identity as "good parents" comes under challenge.

If healthy change is to occur, this will happen through affirmation of the person without endorsement of the behavior. It can help to reframe the issue not as a primarily sexual one but as a relational one. It is likely to be a journey of pain and misunderstanding, especially from those who have not been in this situation; yet grace can prevail. Help along the way is needed in the same way that families of addicts need support. Some within the church are willing to provide this. Some organizations and therapists are available to help. A useful book for lesbians and their families is *Craving for Love* (Whitehead), and more generally a good source is *Someone I Love Is Gay* (Worthen and Davies).

What About Change?

The core practical question that confronts us is "Is change possible?" and pastoral responses typically vary according to the answer. The gay movement insists change is not possible and should not be attempted, even arguing that attempts at therapy are unethical. The argument derives support from studies seeking to demonstrate biological origins, such as genetics. These studies have been shown to be seriously flawed (Satinover; Whitehead and Whitehead). Yet there is evidence to the contrary. There are wide varieties of expression and experience, suggesting that up to 90 percent of such behavior is learned. While activists publicly clamor for acceptance, others quietly suffer and long to be different. Change, if sought, is achieved successfully by some, but for others the pattern is, humanly speaking, unchangeable. Acceptance of a celibate lifestyle is one legitimate option for those in that situation.

Defining what constitutes change is difficult. In the past a shift toward heterosexual interest and then marriage* were claimed as adequate evidence for successful change, but some now argue that such changes are secondary to a more fundamental change. Some follow the argument advanced by E. Moberly that the underlying problem is not a problem with the opposite sex but with the *same* sex. Developmental theorists argue that a poor relationship with the same-sex parent produces a woundedness that can be healed only through development of strong, positive same-sex relationships. The issue, then, is not primarily one of sexual needs at all but one of unmet developmental needs. Hence successful change arises first in the establishment of good (nonsexual) same-sex bonding, out of which heterosexual relationships may flow.

A good deal of successful therapy has been reported following these assumptions for those, both men and women, who seek change. This developmental learning model stands over against the many efforts to demonstrate a biological basis for homosexuality. Without denying that some biological linkages may one day get beyond conjecture and speculative reports, it is most helpful to understand the biological contribution as only one predisposing factor among many. The individual's later life experiences combine with significant choices to determine the outcome. The gay movement strongly resists the possibility of choice these days. Nonetheless, those who do change claim that choice is possible. And the research data from Kinsey on clearly suggest that many with homosexual tendencies choose not to be active.

Hence we may conclude that change is possible for some, and the Christian gospel offers hope rather than condemnation. It is also clear that in our present state of knowledge, not all who wish to change can do so. A major theme when change does occur is a move away from the sexual focus to growth into personal wholeness and strong relationships. The Christian homosexual who seeks to live according to God's purposes commonly experiences loneliness, frustration, alienation and depression* but can be offered friendship and support without fear when the stereotypes are challenged. Within the churches there is need for clear teaching about sexuality and its expression in all its forms, combined with a strong pastoral response to those who have emotional, interpersonal and spiritual as well as sexual needs.

See also FEMINITY; MASCULINITY; SEXUALITY.

References and Resources

A. C. Kinsey, W. B. Pomeroy and C. E. Martin, *Sexual Behavior in the Human Male* (Philadelphia: Saunders, 1948); A. C. Kinsey et al., *Sexual Behavior in the Human Female* (Philadelphia: Saunders, 1953); E. Moberly, *Homosexuality: A New Christian Ethic* (Cambridge: James Clarke, 1983); J. Satinover, *Homosexuality and the Politics of Truth* (Grand Rapids: Baker, 1996); T. Schmidt, *Straight and Narrow? Compassion and Clarity in the Homosexuality Debate* (Downers Grove, Ill.: InterVarsity Press, 1995); B. Whitehead, *Craving for Love* (Monarch, U.K.: 1993); N. and B. Whitehead, *My Genes Made Me Do It!* (Lafayette, La.: Huntington House, 1999); L. Whitehead and B. Davies, *Someone I Love Is Gay* (Downers Grove, Ill.: Intervarsity Press, 1996).

John Court

—HOSPITALITY—

Hospitality is often confused with entertaining. Although we also speak of entertaining a guest, this word is more descriptive of the act of diverting or of amusing. Entertainment* could represent a superficial hospitality, but it is possible to entertain without being hospitable.

Parenting* is a process of hospitality, giving welcome and a free space for the new addition to a family to develop in his or her own way. Children are able to show hospitality to their parents, especially as they grow older. Often this turns out to be a most challenging ministry. Whole families, whether single parent or extended, can engage in the mission of God by giving hospitality to the stranger, the outsider, the marginalized and the needy (see Mission). It is a way of loving our neighbor as ourselves.

Scripture is the testimonial of God's relentless hospitality toward his creatures. The God who made and sustains us wishes to welcome everyone into his household through Jesus Christ. Therefore, Christian hospitality can be defined as the reality of divine hospitality experienced and expressed in the life of God's children. It is a visible portrayal of the first commandment to love God and neighbor. It is stretching our hearts and resources for the welfare of others and to the glory of God. Consequently, hospitality goes far beyond the act of entertaining to become an all-encompassing approach to Christian life in general and to relationships in particular.

Hospitality in the Old Testament

Ancient Israelite hospitality was more than mere entertainment. In an age when there were no inns or hostels, hospitality was a matter of survival for the traveler, the merchant, the landless Levite, the relative on his way to visit kin, the needy and the foreigner. Hospitality ensures that the guest, whether Israelite or an alien, could expect food, lodging and protection. The well-being of a guest was the host's moral and religious obligation.

Although hospitality in the Old Testament had various expressions, at its core were its religious and social dimensions: to love God was to love* human beings, to be hospitable was a response to Yahweh's own kindness toward Israel. From a religious point of view the manner in which a householder received a guest (such as by providing fresh water for the traveler's dusty feet) and the kind of meal served were interpreted as evidence of the host's character* and commitment to honor Yahweh. Hospitality or the lack of it would, therefore, damage the host's reputation. From a social perspective, through hospitality God created a net and network of human interdependence designed to secure the basic necessities of those who were at some kind of disadvantage, especially the poor and landless.

Despite the lack in Hebrew of a technical word for hospitality, in a number of Old Testament passages it is either clearly implied or directly prescribed, as when God commanded Israel to care for the widow, the orphan and the stranger (Deut 10:17-19; 24:17-22; Prov 14:31; Amos 5:11-12). In some narratives hospitality is indirectly portrayed and serves as the backdrop for a biblical episode or theophany (Gen 24:10-60). In the prophetic books hospitality is related to true justice expressed in terms of respecting the rights of kin, the orphan, the widow, the poor and the stranger (Zech 7:8-14). Boaz in the book of Ruth offers one of the richest examples of this kind of hospitality. Even a religious act such as fasting lost its value when separated from concrete expressions of social righteousness such as hospitality (Is 58:6-7, 10). In the wisdom literature, Wisdom is presented as extending her hospitality to any person lacking understanding (Prov 9:1-6, 13-18). And in the book of Job, Eliphaz interprets Job's misfortune as God's judgment on the latter due to his absence of hospitality (Job 22:6-11).

These passages express the socioreligious importance attributed to the practice of hospitality. God's people were to "remember that you were slaves in Egypt and the LORD your God redeemed you from there. That is why I command you to do this [to care for the needy]" (Deut 24:18). At the root of this lies a deep care by God for his creatures. In an age when there were no civil and human rights committees and no unemployment insurance,* God established a community in which religious devotion and social concern were a part of daily living. In this light, hospitality was nothing less than Israel's response to divine love as well as to human need.

Hospitality in the New Testament
While the basic guidelines presented in the Old Testament carried over into the New Testament, there is a new message, the gospel, as well as a new community, the church, which together reaffirm and dramatically increase the role of hospitality in furthering God's kingdom. As Jesus had reached out to humankind, so the early Christians were to provide material and spiritual assistance to any needy person and to fellow believers in particular (Eph 4:28; 1 Jn 3:16-18). The driving force behind the hospitality of the early Christians was the awareness that because God in Christ had loved them first, they were to love their neighbor (1 Jn

4:10-12, 9-21).

Two of Christ's most powerful teachings on hospitality appear in Luke 14:12-14 and Matthew 25:31-46. The first upholds the unconditional openhandedness with which we are to treat the poor and the outcasts. The second tacitly assumes hospitality in the actions of feeding, giving a drink, providing lodging, providing clothing, caring for the sick and visiting those in prison. These became the common practices of the early church, the visible witnesses of kingdom come. The place of hospitality is also reinforced in Christ's parables that involve food and drink, meals or banquets (Lk 14:15-24; 15:22-31; 16:19-21; 17:7-10). These stories challenge the audience to look at the spiritual implications of commonplace situations: a kind foreigner, a neighbor's midnight request for bread, a beggar at the rich man's door.

The Lord's Supper is the supreme example of God's hospitality. It reassures us of God's relentless care and his unwavering goodwill toward his creatures: his own Son is the host and the sacrifice, the Bread of Life and the Cup of Salvation. God invites us to take refuge under his protective eye, to satiate our souls on divine love, to quench our thirst with life-giving divine truths and to sit and converse with the divine.

The early church also offers an example of Christian hospitality in action as they devoted themselves to alms giving, love feasts, the support of teachers and church leaders, the care of widows, orphans, the sick, the infirm, the poor, the disabled, slaves and prisoners, the burial of the poor, succor to victims of calamities, provision of employment and hospitality to visiting missionaries (Acts 4:32-35; Rom 16:23; Heb 13:1-3; 1 Pet 4:9; 1 Jn 3:16-18; 3 Jn 5-8). This kind of liberality was characteristic of house churches as well as Christian households (see Home). The third letter of John presents the contrast between two church leaders: one named Gaius, who used hospitality to assist the work of missionaries and evangelists, and the other named Diotrephes, who opposed the apostle Paul by precluding hospitality. However, despite external threats from a society antagonistic to Christianity and internal disagreements, the early church carried on with God's tradition of hospitality.

Family Hospitality Today

Today many families do not regularly eat together, let alone spend time listening,* appreciating and encouraging one another. Families need to embrace a countercultural lifestyle that views even meal preparation* as a ministry and a way of including guests. While offering to "take a person out" to a restaurant for a meal or even a cup of coffee is one way of extending hospitality, bringing people into the home for dinner or desert is a more profound way of loving and welcoming. Students who come to their professor's or teacher's home are being invited into their lives and sometimes learn more from this than in the classroom.

As Christ "eagerly desired" to share the Last Supper with his disciples (Lk 22:15), so we must convey the same message to family, friends and friends-to-be. A healthy homemade dinner, candles, flowers in a vase and a fresh tablecloth are ways of sacramentalizing the ordinary. These touches say, "I care. I treasure our time together." Hospitality guards intimacy, which lies not in closed doors but in dismissing the pervasive intermissions and distractions that rob us from togetherness. Hospitality offers a way to reach out to a society suffering the effects of disintegrated families,* loneliness and alienation.

Children learn much about discipleship to Christ through the experience of welcoming people in their homes. They also learn about life from the people whose stories unfold around a dinner table (see Family History). Taking an international student into the home for a short or long stay, giving up their beds to accommodate relatives from a distant place, sharing bread with a poor or unemployed person, are learning-for-life experiences for a growing family. Parents too have an opportunity to show hospitality to the friends of their children, something that is particularly challenging when outsiders bring influences that are antagonistic to the values* cherished by your own family. So there are dangers, and hospitality never happens without risk and sacrifice.

Some families, aware that taking in a stranger or an emotionally unwell relative may pose a hazard to the routine and even the health of their own families, may keep their home as a bastion of privacy, with the parents in total control. This seems the safest way to go, but it neither models neighbor love nor allows children to grow up and become mature. Sometimes such families appear to be "model Christian families" when the children are very young, but their offspring may have a profound need to revolt at a later time and may do so in very dangerous ways. Other families have so many guests, feel so compelled to take in every "stray," including the marginalized acquaintances of their children, that their home resembles a busy mall. They have no boundaries, and their own children may feel neglected and marginalized. Needed in family life are permeable boundaries, patterns of life together that nevertheless may be interrupted and family covenant relationships that will nevertheless admit others into the circle of love, support and nurture. Often it is in the interruptions that God visits, as was certainly the case in the three strangers who visited the home of Abraham and Sarah (Gen 18:1-15). Prayer is critical to this process.

Hospitality and Prayer

Hospitality and prayer go hand in hand. Through prayer God opens our eyes to people's needs that can be met through us. Prayer also prepares our hearts for whatever the encounter with the recipient of our hospitality might bring. While we can control certain aspects of the entertaining process, true Christian hospitality demands that we entrust our guest and ourselves to God. We are completely dependent on God if we wish to give emotional, spiritual and material refreshment. Prayer is as necessary in the church as it is in the home in the context of hospitality. Whether we reach out corporately or individually, prayer will create the ambience for the work of the Trinity. In addition to prayer, the contemporary Christian host can offer time and acceptance.

The Gifts of Time and Acceptance

"I do not have time to have people over!" is one of the common excuses for the lack of hospitality. When we look at Christ, we get a good picture of where and how he invested his time. He spent most of it with people. People were his passion, the reason for him to interrupt eternity and come into human history. At the appointed time people were the reason his life was cut short on the cross. People were the object of his redemptive sacrifice. His time was subject to divine purpose. Often his followers seem to work in the opposite direction: we submit divine purpose to the availability of our personal time. Hospitality helps us counter this tendency because when we receive a guest in the name of Christ, we create a parenthesis in the midst of all our other activities. In it God can meet host and guest. Through acts of hospitali-

ty, we offer our time as a living sacrifice to the God who did not abandon us to random fate and who has called us to invest our days as his Son did.

Acceptance is an expression of our heartfelt hospitality, as it reflects a welcoming attitude. Acceptance is the key to hospitality, as it portrays the welcoming attitude of our God who in so doing never compromised his character. That is why acceptance must not be confused with political correctness. The first has its basis in the experience of God's immutable grace and holiness; the latter is an ever-shifting societal code of expected attitudes. Perhaps there are few other gifts as costly as honest acceptance. But who can measure its impact on someone searching for a solid foundation in life, proof that God still cares or a place of refuge and restoration?

Hospitality as an Act of Worship

As we offer hospitality, we echo the original voice, "Come and sup with me." To welcome, to feed, to comfort or to assist someone in God's name is a way of affirming our devotion and allegiance to the Giver of all good gifts. As hospitality points to God, it becomes a way of honoring God. We have a cloud of witnesses from the Old and New Testaments and beyond that attest to the blessings* that come to those who live hospitable lives. With the nourishment of the Bread of Eternal Life broken for us, we are called to issue the invitation, extend the table, receive the guests, wash their feet, bring out the spread, tell them that God has been good to us. We affirm that hospitality is not merely a nice metaphor of what God has offered us but a spontaneous and genuine act of worship to the God who withheld nothing to bring us back into relationship with himself and with one another.

See also EATING; HOME; LOVE; MEAL

PREPARATION; MISSION.

References and Resources
R. Banks, *Going to Church in the First Century* (Chipping Norton, N.S.W.: Hexagon Press, 1980); R. Banks and J. Banks, *The Home Church* (Sutherland, N.S.W.: Albatross, 1986); R. F. Capon, *The Supper of the Lamb* (Garden City, N.Y.: Doubleday, 1969); R. Duck, "Toward an Understanding of Hospitality in the Old Testament," M. C. S. thesis, Regent College, Vancouver, B.C., 1980; A. Harnack, *The Mission and Expansion of Christianity in the First Three Centuries* (New York: Harper & Row, 1962); A. Heron,

Table and Tradition (Philadelphia: Westminster, 1983); T. Howard, *Splendor in the Ordinary* (Wheaton, Ill.: Tyndale, 1976); R. P. Hromas, *Celebrate the Feast* (Torrance, Calif.: Ark Productions, 1982); J. Koenig, *New Testament Hospitality* (Philadelphia: Fortress, 1980); K. B. Mains, *Open Heart, Open Home* (Elgin, Ill.: David C. Cook, 1976); *New Shorter Oxford English Dictionary* (Oxford: Clarendon, 1993) 1:1266; B. Rowlinson, *Creative Hospitality* (Campbell, Calif.: Green Leaf, 1981); E. Schaeffer, *Hidden Art* (London: Norfolk Press, 1971); J. Vanier, *Community and Growth* (Toronto: Griffin House, 1993).
Patricia Kerr

HOUSE. *See* HOME.

INFORMATION SUPERHIGHWAY. *See* COMPUTER; ENTERTAINMENT; INTERNET.

—INSURANCE—

Insurance is a means by which individuals, families,* businesses and other organizations reduce or eliminate financial uncertainties in areas of life where there are predictable possibilities of financial loss. People exchange a small but predictable amount of money, their premium, for a larger, uncertain loss. Because the insurer can predict average losses over a large population, the risk is evened out and shared. The fortunate many who escape major loss help the unfortunate few who experience it. Kinds of insurance normally purchased by individuals include life, fire, theft or damage to personal property, legal liability, disability, unemployment, health and travel insurance.

The Insuring of Almost Everything and Everyone
Individuals buy some of these types of insurance for personal protection. Groups like businesses or corporations buy insurance for their employees; business partners may buy it to provide the means of buying out a partner's share in business upon his or her death.* In Canada and other countries with a social welfare philosophy, the government or state agencies buy insurance by means of taxes. Insurance provided by the state in

this way is compulsory rather than voluntary.

Insurance, however, protects not only individuals (and by extension their families) but also corporations, nonprofit agencies and governments. They may insure to cover the safe transfer of goods, the reliability of monies deposited in banks, the nonpayment of loans and the loss or destruction of major assets. Though it may not be obvious to the person or organizations purchasing insurance, many significant risks cannot be reduced through insurance: war and insurrection, nuclear holocaust, ecological disaster (acts of humankind widely and over time) and natural disasters of colossal proportion (commonly called "acts of God").

In the Western world many individuals use a significant percentage of their income to pay for various forms of insurance, in excess of 10 percent in many cases if compulsory insurance provided by taxation is also considered. Some people complain of being "insurance poor"—spending so much to cover potential losses in the future that they have not enough to live properly today. Others are underinsured and may face a future without either personal assets or social network to cover major losses or reverses. In most developing countries individual insurance is the privilege of the rich and powerful; the poor and middle class rely on the age-old securities of family and church. Significantly, before there was a major insurance industry, the church pioneered in establishing burial societies during times of plague and mutual aid societies (especially for widows, orphans and the destitute), providing hospitality* and asylum to fugitives, travelers and shipwrecked seamen; and setting up the first hospitals for the sick—a stunning and little-told story (Oliver, 116).

Is insurance merely a modern invention to satisfy an artificially induced need in the consumer society? Is there a biblical foundation for buying and selling insurance? When does protecting against risk become a refusal to trust God?

Thinking About Risk

At first glance the Bible seems to advise us not to think about future risks. The birds and lilies do not worry. "Yet your heavenly Father feeds them" (Mt 6:26). It is the unbelieving Gentiles who run after all these things (food and clothing*). But Jesus is not condemning us for planning for the future so much as warning us not to be anxious about it: "Do not worry about tomorrow, for tomorrow will worry about itself" (Mt 6:34). Indeed, the way we respond to risk is a significant thermometer of our faith and spirituality.

Insurance does not deal with all risks, and perhaps not even the most important risks, such as losing friendships, personal worth, love,* hope or faith. No one through buying insurance can guarantee long life, good health,* satisfying work, personal contentment, a happy marriage,* good neighbors, intimate friendships and children that bring joy to the heart. On a grand scale we cannot insure against the breakdown of a whole society or the ecosystem (though there is much we can do to prevent these). There is no insurance that can be purchased against marriage failure, loss of meaning, personal suffering or, most crucial of all, our eternal salvation.

We cope with risk in several ways: by ignoring it, assuming (or retaining) it, eliminating the possibility of loss, transferring the loss to someone else, or anticipating the loss and planning toward it.

On the first two options, it is folly to ignore risk. We must assume or retain the most important risks and the most crucial potential losses. For the Christian this means trusting in God's providential care, believing that even temporary reverses will be transformed into general good, as exemplified by the victory of the cross of Jesus. By retaining or assuming these noninsurable risks, we are called not only to trust God but to exercise faithful stewardship of our life, marriage, home, driving, possessions and ultimately the environment. God is the ultimate owner of everything; what we render is stewardship. So the proper management of our lives is intended to reduce risk. Keeping an automobile* in good repair, for example, is assuming the risk and managing it by good stewardship.

In most cases the third option, eliminating the possibility of loss, can be done only by refusing to accept the adventure of life. Driving a car, traveling, investing our talents in a community, getting married, having children and even joining a church are risky enterprises. Tragically, some people are like the one-talent man in Jesus' parable (Mt 25:24-25), protecting themselves against any possible loss and so losing what they thought they had. People who refuse to invest themselves in order to eliminate all possible losses end up losing something more precious than what they protected—the joy of life.

Transferring risk to someone else, the fourth option, is not something we can normally do with risks that we must personally undertake. But this is an acceptable way of coping with some potential financial losses that could ruin one's business in a single stroke. For example, a surety bond guaranteeing the completion of a building according to written specifications transfers the risk from the person building the structure to the insurer. Such ways of managing risk are called for in a society that is composed not merely of a collection of individual farmers or tradespeople but of corporations and powerful structures.

The most common way to manage risk is to share it through buying insurance. Most insurance is simply a form of neighbor love* expressed impersonally without knowing who our neighbors are. The insurance company becomes our symbolic neighbor. Through knowledge of past experience, careful prediction of future possibilities and accumulation of funds over a wide population base, insurance companies are able to cover the enormous losses of a few and the minor losses of the many, and have enough left

over to cover their operating costs and make a legitimate profit for the shareholders.

Prayerful Insurance

Here are a few guidelines for Christians to consider when thinking about insurance.

Plan wisely for your family's future. In many cases it is unloving *not* to buy insurance, since it may force your family to embrace involuntary poverty to care for you in a time of extreme need. Wisely insuring is a form of neighbor love and part of our stewardship. But one must be careful that the companies trusted with funds are reliable since there are many cases of bankruptcy. Companies like Standard & Poors and Moody's, and a new index called TRAC rate insurance companies for their strength, liquidity and solvency. Advertised reliability is not a sufficient guide.

Keep insurance in perspective; do not overvalue it. Our eyes can all too easily be diverted from the uninsurable risks that are much more deserving of our stewardship and prayerful attention: marriages, self-esteem* of children, friendships and the joy of our salvation.

Never let buying insurance be an alternative to trusting God. As Jesus said, our heavenly Father knows what we need and cares for us. Significantly, the problem of the fearful investor in the parable of the talents (Mt 25:24) was not his analysis of a potential loss but his conception of his master (representing God) as one who could not be trusted with his mistakes and reverses.

Beware of overinsuring. It is just as foolish to become "insurance poor" as to ignore insurable risks. We are meant to enjoy life and to thrive, not live cramped little lives. Often, insurance can be reduced or not even purchased (as in the case of collision insurance on a car) if one has put aside savings that can be used in the eventuality of a sustainable loss. Very valuable possessions may be too expensive to insure, and wise management, combined with the attitude of "holding things lightly," is more prudent than covering every eventuality. Simpler living is a matter of perspective and not just net worth. A wise philosophy is to self-insure for small problems and use an insurance company's money for large ones. When looking at disability insurance, for example, we should choose a longer waiting period (90 to 120 days) so that in the event of disability we can use our own resources for the short term, thereby reducing the cost. Some people recommend as a rule of thumb purchasing ten times one's income in life insurance.

Help family members sustain their losses. It is lamentable that the basic unit of Western society has become the isolated individual covering all his or her potential losses rather than the family looking after one another. Insuring everything possible may inadvertently assist in the dissolution of the one organic community, besides the church, that can provide care and support during times of crisis and loss. Families can agree together what risks they will undertake mutually, including care of people when they are sick or old. Jesus roundly condemned the Pharisees for neglecting their responsibilities to their parents, a form of "honoring" them (Ex 20:12) by dedicating their assets to the Lord's work, a system called corban (Mt 15:3-6). Paul says that if we do not care for our own families, we are worse than unbelievers (1 Tim 5:8).

Lend aid to others in the body of Christ who need it. The church has an important role to play as the equalizer of risk. In the earliest church in Jerusalem, people sold their surplus goods to provide for anyone in need (Acts 2:44-45; 4:32-37). Later came other forms of sharing, such as famine relief (11:27-30), occupational sharing (Aquila and Priscilla with Paul in making tents) and mutual aid gift-giving* (the great love gift from the Gentile church—1 Cor 16:2; 2 Cor 8—9). It is all too easy to claim it would never work in our urbanized, mobile society where most people move every four or five years. But a commitment to a house church or an intentional community not to move (*see* Mobility), while countercultural, may be a concrete step toward true community. We have something to learn from churches in the developing world on this matter. When someone dies in Kenya, the church gathers to make gifts to the family—not just the grieving spouse—to provide a living and a future for the survivors.

Remember those in society who are uninsured (the disadvantaged and destitute), and act on their behalf. In our modern times risk and loss are systemic problems, not merely matters of personal character and integrity. The Scriptures warning against idleness assume that unemployed people are lazy, whereas today the unemployed are often victimized by systemic problems, sometimes through economies halfway around the world. So in coping with risk today, we must exercise cultural and organizational as well as personal stewardship. We must fight against the abuse of unemployment and health insurance schemes if they are government-funded and abused. We need to lobby for legislative change to care for disadvantaged and marginalized people in our society.

Conclusion

Like most advances in the Western world, the growth of the insurance industry is a mixed blessing. With careful management, reaffirmation of the providence of God and wise stewardship of our lives, buying some insurance is an act of neighbor love and personal responsibility, doing what we can so we will not be a burden on others (1 Thess 4:12; 2 Thess 3:8). In reality, we can never eliminate that possibility fully. And where true family and church community exist, mutual caring is not a burden but part of the unlimited liability of family love. The temptation of too much insurance, or a wrong attitude, can lead to an illusory feeling that we can control our own futures and live autonomously without God. Like many facets of everyday life, this one calls us to a life of prayer, spiritual discernment and loving action.

See also CREDIT CARD; DEBT; FAMILY; MONEY; TITHING.

References and Resources
J. L. Athearn, *Risk and Insurance* (St. Paul: West, 1981); K. Black Jr., "Insurance," in *The Encyclopedia Americana* (Danbury, Conn.: Grolier, 1989) 15:233-39; K. Black Jr. and S. S. Huebner, *Life Insurance* (Englewood Cliffs, N.J.: Prentice-Hall, 1982); E. H. Oliver, *The Social Achievements of the Christian Church* (Toronto: United Church of Canada, 1930); N. A. Williams, *Insurance* (Cincinnati: South-Western Publications, 1984).

R. Paul Stevens

—INTERNET—

Many parents feel a sense of helplessness as they see their children embracing the new communications medium known as the Internet. Others anticipate new opportunities for learning and personal development for the whole family.

The Internet is a network of computers linked together by high-speed telecommunications that facilitate the fast transfer of information from one computer* to another. With the advent of sophisticated computer software and hardware it is possible to view instantly any information on the Internet from anywhere at any time in any place. The Internet will change the way we think, live and relate with others in the global community. It will exercise an increasing influence on life together as a family.* As in any information medium, it contains the full spectrum of ideas and values* that can be found on cable TV, at the video* store or in the magazine rack. As a parent the key to guiding children successfully in a positive online adventure is active participation in the child's Internet experience.

Children, however, are often more adept than their parents at learning the new languages and skills necessary to navigate the world of cyberspace. My nine-year-old daughter is able to retrieve her e-mail, send electronic postcards, look for weather reports and access kids' chatrooms. She has been quicker in learning these new skills than her mother, who is a family doctor!

Parental Responsibility
How should we respond to this new medium and our children's technological freedom? There are dangers linked to the Internet (pornography, hate groups and child exploitation). Some want to stop their children from using the Internet completely. However, it will become in-

creasingly difficult to prevent access. The Internet is everywhere—in the child's classroom, at a friend's house, at the library and the coffee shop.

Parents have a responsibility to raise their children "in the training and instruction of the Lord" (Eph 6:4). Part of this responsibility is to help them to determine right from wrong (1 Kings 3:9). On the Internet, children are two mouse clicks away from much that is right and much that is wrong. The Net is an inanimate tool that can be used for good or for evil. It is not the tool itself that is the challenge, it is the way in which it is used that can be a problem. There are not only moral issues associated with its use but spiritual ones. As Hal Miller says, "All power-based technologies offer an implicit temptation to idolatry. . . . Many people spend too much time on the Net and direct their major energies to exploiting its potential. . . . It is important to keep the Information Superhighway in its place, as a servant" (532).

A thoughtful response is to approach the Net as you would any new learning experience. The curve may be steep at first, but with a little perseverance you can gain enough proficiency to work with your child and help guide their use of this communications tool.

Wise Counsel on Internet Use

The first step is to gather together the facts about the Internet, its benefits and its dangers. Discuss these facts with your children. Go online together and explore the potential for research and learning. Look for information on safe surfing that can be found at the Focus on the Family website <www.family.org> or other sites such as <www.safekids .com> or the Consumer Reports website <www.consumerreports.org>.

Establish the rules of use—no viewing of inappropriate material and never give out identifying information to people you do not personally know. Children should notify parents if they encounter people or information that make them feel uncomfortable. Post these rules by your computer or television—whichever you use to access the Internet—and check that your children are following them.

Monitor where your child has been on the Net by checking the Internet history folder on your hard drive. Put the Internet computer in a family space where everyone has access and can see what the child is viewing. Make sure the child knows that you reserve the right to read what they are viewing or chatting about in a chatroom or on their e-mail. You also may want to set limits on the amount of time your child spends on the Net.

Check out blocking or filtering software that can prevent children from unintentionally finding information you do not want them to see. While these programs are helpful, they should not be used to "baby-sit" your child online. Often the information is outdated and ineffective. These programs are not a substitute for proper adult supervision. There are also Internet service providers (ISPs) that can provide a family-friendly surfing environment. These ISPs will do the filtering for you and keep better track of objectionable material and sites.

Most of all, maintain an open and transparent use of the medium both by yourself, your family members and others who use your Internet access. It is important for your children to see that you are also accountable in the use of the Net.

See also COMPUTER; COMPUTER GAMES.

References and Resources

J. D. Baker, *Christian Cyberspace Companion: A Guide to the Internet and Christian Online Resources* (Grand Rapids: Baker, 1997); Z. Britton, *Safety Net: Guiding & Guarding Your Children on the Internet* (Eugene, Ore.: Harvest House, 1998); M. and W. Dinsmore, *Homeschool Guide to the Internet Information Superhighway* (Elkton, Md.: Holly Hall Publications, 1997); Q. J. Schultze, *Internet for Christians* (Muskegon, Mich.: Gospel Films, 1998); B. Wilson and B.Lang, *A Christian Parent's Guide to Making The Internet Family Friendly* (Nashville: Thomas

Nelson, 1999); H. Miller, "Information Super-highway," in *The Complete Book of Everyday Christianity*, ed. R. Banks and R. P. Stevens (Downers Grove, Ill.: InterVarsity Press, 1997) 528-33.

Mike McLoughlin

LAST WILL. *See* WILL, LAST.

—LEISURE—

Leisure is what we do with our discretionary time—it is doing the things we want to do. Because leisure is discretionary and often enjoyable, it is often taken for granted and not seen as important. However, there is an increasing recognition of the importance that leisure time plays in both individual and family development.

Theological Justification

Often leisure has been associated with idleness and the devil. Coupling these suspicions with a long history of the Christian Protestant work ethic, it is no wonder that so many have confused notions about leisure. It must be remembered that God himself enjoyed rest after finishing creation. God created us and understands our need to rest and rejuvenate ourselves outside our areas of work. Those whose lives are focused only on work soon become narrow and driven. Only focusing on work results in producing weeds of the spirit rather than fruit of the spirit. We have no time for love;* we are joyless, irritable and nonrelational. Workaholism is just as sinful to God as slothfulness, and a driven lifestyle does not yield the fruit of the Spirit.

God desires play,* leisure, delight and joy for his children. Yet so often what is communicated to young and old alike is that such things are questionable; our gospel is so serious that there can be no such time for frivolity. The sad result is that not only do we teach our children that anything fun is outside the kingdom (tragically, this is where many Christian youth go looking for it), but we believe it ourselves. Jesus once pointed to the children around him and said that unless we became like one of them, we would never enter the kingdom. Recreating, kicking back and just plain having fun ensures that our children know that such delightful experiences are not outside of God's plan but fully within it.

Paul Stevens suggests that there are three biblical themes that should guide us in developing a Christian understanding of leisure. First, we need to take seriously the mandate to enjoy God's creation. The Westminster Confession of Faith states that the chief aim of man is to "know God and enjoy Him forever." One of the ways we do this is in our leisure time. Second, we need a sound theology of grace. Notably, the Bible tells us that we are saved by grace, not by works. Grace is central to the Christian experience. All we have is due to the goodness of God, and it is important to take time to enjoy these good gifts. Finally, we need to understand that time is not a commodity to manage as much as it is a gift to be enjoyed. We are to be wise with the time God has given us. Being wise with time includes being productive at both at our vocational work as well as the work God has called us to do (which is done in leisure time), as well as recreating, relaxing and rejuvenating.

Leisure and the Family

Most of us spend a significant amount of leisure time and develop our most intimate ties within the context of our family. The majority of family interactions occur outside of work during leisure time. Leisure meets personal and relational needs through opportunities to bond, providing relational identification, interaction, stress management and social support. Special trips, vacations,* times of play or family gatherings are remembered and woven into the family story that develops. Because leisure time is more pleasurable, it provides families an opportunity to try new roles. It allows members to see each other in a new light, promoting relational bonding. In today's society, where life is lived at a frantic pace, leisure activities can substantially reduce the stress,* tension and conflict that so many families experience. While it has been said that a family that prays together stays together, it can also be said that a family that plays together stays together. Leisure is the vehicle in which parents maintain ties with their children and develop ties with their children's children.

For couples, it is often leisure activities that become one of the major factors in keeping the marriage* healthy and strong. Research has consistently shown that one of the most important indicators of marital satisfaction has to do with whether or not spouses spend leisure time together. Conversely there is a negative effect on the marriage when spouses spend most of their leisure time in separate solitary activity (Orthner, Barnett-Morris and Mancini). After many years of marriage many couples divorce because they realize that they no longer have anything in common with their spouses. Couples facing the empty nest* or retirement often find themselves in marital crisis if they have not worked on developing mutually satisfying leisure activities.

Leisure plays an important role in developing a sense of ourselves, exploring our relationships with each other and learning about the society around us. There is a developmental quality to leisure for both individuals and family. Infants play, which is important for bonding and developmental needs. In preschool, play becomes more physical and imaginative in nature, which encourages cognitive and physical growth. As children age, play becomes more sophisticated, and leisure possibilities broaden to include athletics, music, academic interests and hobbies. Leisure for the teenager is one of the critical ways to meet the challenge of identity formation. In fact, it has been argued that leisure is the primary context for socialization and identity formation with the teen. As they grow older, leisure becomes more sophisticated, and adolescence becomes a time when the children will want to spend less time with their family and more with their friends. A healthy approach to leisure understands that each member of the family shares leisure time both with and as family but also outside the family. Children should play with other children, adolescents should engage in extracurricular activities with their peers, and adults should enjoy the company of other adults.

Guidelines

Despite the profound significance leisure plays in the family, it fails to receive the time and thought it deserves. In order to make the most of the leisure we have, there are a number of guidelines that we should observe. First, we need to ensure that we understand that our leisure is one of God's good gifts to families, and we need to ensure that leisure is one of the ways in which we relate to God.

Second, we need to ensure that the leisure activities we choose reflect a value system congruent with a Christian lifestyle. Leisure is a powerful way in which self-identity is formed. It must then be asked, not only does this leisure help form identity, but what is the nature of that identity? For example, is indulging a young boy's fascination with a WWF wrestler promoting a value system that is biblical? Third, the question must be asked, does our leisure promote selfish living? Jesus clearly stated that there is great danger in pursuing one's own interests as ends unto themselves. To be sure, there is value in hobbies and recreation as an expression of living out of a salvation of grace. However, this can be spiritually unhealthy if leisure is understood as being a right to have one's own time, which no one else is going to get. Teaching children to use their leisure in order to minister to others is one of the most powerful ways there is in helping them live out of a kingdom value system.

Fourth, we need to use wisdom in choosing activities that are truly restorative and creative and that provide the family with quality bonding time. The values of our modern culture of competitiveness and functionality have greatly undermined leisure. A ten year old's Little League game often has the same intensity among children and adults as a World Series playoff game. Spontaneity, sportsmanship and just plain fun have been lost in the objective of winning at any cost. Sound judgment needs to be exercised in not only choosing what we will participate in but also how we will participate in it. This is equally true for collective family activities. While there is nothing wrong with a family video night, research has shown that such a passive activity does not promote as much bonding among family members as playing a board game.* Some evidence suggests that outdoor leisure activities promote the greatest amount of spontaneous interaction. It is important to consider everyone's wishes in picking developmentally appropriate activities. Though it is nearly impossible to pick something that everyone will like, eventually everyone should get a chance to pick what they want to do.

Someone has made the observation that in our modern culture we worship our work, work at our play and play at our worship. To realign all three areas into what we are supposed to do in each would go along way to bringing us closer together as families as well as honoring God.

See also COMPUTER GAMES; ENTERTAINMENT; GAMES; PLAY; SABBATH; SLEEPING; VACATIONS.

References and Resources
J. Balswick and J. Balswick, *The Family* (Grand Rapids: Baker, 1991); R. Banks, *The Tyranny of Time: When 24 Hours Is Not Enough* (Downers Grove, Ill.: InterVarsity Press, 1983); D. Orthner, L. Barnett-Morris and J. Mancini, "Leisure and Family over the Life Cycle," in *Handbook of Developmental Family Psychology and Psychopathology,* ed. L. L'Abate (New York: John Wiley, 1994) 176-201; P. A. Heintzman, *A Christian Perspective on the Philosophy of Leisure* (Ottawa: National Library of Canada, 1985); J. H. Huizinga, *Homo Ludens: A Study of the Play-Element in Culture* (London: Paladin, 1949); R. K. Johnston, *The Christian at Play* (Grand Rapids: Eerdmans, 1983); J. Oswald, *Leisure Crisis: A Biblical Perspective on Guilt-Free Leisure* (Wheaton, Ill.: Victor, 1987); R. Rapoport and R. N. Rapoport, *Leisure and the Family Life Cycle* (London: Routledge and Kegan Paul, 1975); L. Ryken, *Work and Leisure in Christian Perspective* (Portland, Ore.: Multnomah Press, 1987); L. Steinberg, *Adolescence* (New York: McGraw-Hill, 1996); R. P. Stevens, "Leisure," in *The*

Complete Book of Everyday Christianity, ed. Ill.: InterVarsity Press, 1997) 576-82.
R. Banks and R. P. Stevens (Downers Grove,

Mark Davies

LIFE INSURANCE. *See* INSURANCE.

—LISTENING—

If speaking is a spiritual discipline, refraining from speech to listen to the words of others or to God's word is equally crucial to living Christianly. The control factor, however, is more subtle and more demanding in the case of listening. Jesus says, "Consider carefully how you listen" (Lk 8:18), not only because all will be revealed eventually (v. 17), but because if you listen well, you will gain even more to hear. So listening is a key to the inner treasures of the soul.

Listening and Self-Discipline

James says, "Everyone should be quick to listen, slow to speak" (Jas 1:19). The context refers to both listening to others and listening to the Word of God (Jas 1:21), two facets of listening that are inextricably interrelated. Instead of finishing another's sentence we should listen to the soul expressed in the words. Dietrich Bonhoeffer in his classic *Life Together* says, "Thus it must be a decisive rule of every Christian fellowship that each individual is prohibited from saying much that occurs to him" (92). So both speaking and listening involve discernment.

So the self-discipline involved in the ministry of listening is not just *how* we listen but *to what*. While we are inundated by a thousand advertisements and appeals to the flesh every day, we should heed Solomon's advice of "turning your ear to wisdom and applying your heart to understanding" (Prov 2:2; compare 23:12), whether it is a life-giving rebuke (15:31), the law (28:9) or the cry of the poor (21:13). Listening not only *is* selective; it *should be*. We must systematically reduce certain influences in order to attend to those that make us truly wise.

Listening as a Relational Gift

James exhorts all believers to be "quick to listen" (Jas 1:19), which he links in the same verse to "slow to become angry." We are less likely to feel thwarted and therefore get angry if we know what is going on inside another person. Further, if we listen deeply to the soul of another, we will more likely be confronted with our own shortcomings (Jas 1:21), more willing to listen to ourselves and less likely either to provoke to anger or to be so provoked. By listening we renounce control over the one speaking and communicate worth.

Listening is a relational compliment. This is true not only for fellow human beings but of God. By opening our hearts to hear God's word, we worship God and pay the greatest compliment possible. The reverse is also true: that God speaks "with his ears." By patiently attending to our cry (Ps 17:6; 31:2; 34:15; Is 59:1), God communicates his love* as eloquently as in his articulated speech. His silence is both revelatory and evocative. In the same way, our willingness to cultivate the discipline of solitude is a profound statement of the esteem with which we hold God and our availability to his speech.

195

How to Listen

The starting point in all counseling relationships is listening. The same is true for friendships and in deepening a marriage* relationship. By listening we convey our desire to understand, to take seriously the viewpoint of another. When we listen, we refrain from giving advice, preaching or even expressing an opinion until we have first taken the person seriously and gained trust (Collins, 290). Adapting the advice given by the psychiatrist Armand Nicholi, we can summarize the following dimensions of listening: (1) having enough awareness of one's own conflicts to avoid reacting in a way that interferes with the person's free expression of thoughts and feelings; (2) avoiding subtle verbal or nonverbal expressions of negative judgment; (3) waiting through periods of silence or tears until the person summons up the courage to say more; (4) hearing not only what the person says but what he or she is trying to say; (5) using both ears and eyes to detect messages that come from tone of voice, posture and other nonverbal cues; (6) avoiding looking away while a person is speaking; (7) limiting the number of mental excursions into one's own fantasies while another is speaking; (8) practicing the full acceptance of the person no matter what is said (Collins, 26-27).

The last point deserves more comment. To accomplish acceptance through listening without condoning or condemning is spiritually demanding. To do this without condemnation, one must have experienced deep forgiveness* in one's own life, since we condemn or condone what is still unresolved in our own past. And to show acceptance of a fellow sinner without excusing sin cannot be done without compassion, that quality that links us so closely with the heart of God. So listening, like speaking, reveals the person, casts us on God for his grace and invites us to move forward in the life of discipleship.

Listening as a Spiritual Discipline

Just as speech reveals the person, so the quality of listening reveals the soul within. Stopped-up ears come from hearts "as hard as flint" (Zech 7:11-12). Open ears reveal a tender and responsive soul. This is true whether one listens to God or to another person. By learning to attend to the thoughts, feelings and values* of others, we are positioning ourselves to attend to God. Of course, the reverse is equally true. Bonhoeffer puts it negatively: "But he who can no longer listen to his brother will soon be no longer listening to God either; he will be doing nothing but prattle in the presence of God" (98). That prattle leads to the famine prophesied by Amos, not of food or water but "of hearing the words of the LORD" (Amos 8:10-12). Good speakers are good listeners. They have the "instructed tongue" of those who have learned from God in their own lives and therefore are able to sustain the weary with their own words (Is 50:4). God opens the mouth of his servant by wakening the ears of that servant, just as Jesus opened the mouth of the mute person by opening his ears (Mk 7:33), a sign that the day of salvation had truly arrived (Is 35:5-6).

Those unready to obey what they hear from God are called "dull of hearing" (Mt 13:15 KJV). Sometimes this willful stoppage is accomplished by externally plugging the ears (Acts 7:57), but more commonly it is an internal predisposition *not* to hear because they are unwilling to obey, something that the apostles of Jesus called "uncircumcised in heart and ears" (Acts 7:51 NRSV). The ear has not yet heard the full joy and beauty of heavenly sound (1 Cor 2:9). Heaven will be the ultimate listening experience, as the book of Revelation shows (Rev 4—5), and we live with true heavenly mindedness by practicing the disciplines of faithful (that is, faithfull) listening to Scripture, to the hearts of others and to the voice of God speaking to us in our life experiences.

See also COMMUNICATION; CONVERSATION; HOSPITALITY; LOVE.

References and Resources

D. Bonhoeffer, *Life Together*, trans. J. W. Doberstein (New York: Harper & Row, 1954); G. R. Collins, *Christian Counseling: A Comprehensive Guide* (Waco, Tex.: Word, 1980); R. Foster, *Celebration of Discipline* (New York: Harper & Row, 1978); M. McLuhan and Q. Fiere, *The Medium Is the Message* (New York: Bantam, 1967); J. Pedersen, *Israel: Its Life and Culture*, 4 vols. (London: Oxford University Press, 1963); H. W. Wolff, *Anthropology of the Old Testament*, trans. M. Kohl (Philadelphia: Fortress, 1964).

R. Paul Stevens

—LOVE—

Love, the most crucial and central concept in Christian theology and ethics, is also one of the most theologically, ethically, psychologically and culturally ambiguous concepts, with diverse interpretations and contradictory definitions. Love requires not only a theological base and a philosophical framework but also a psychological dynamic and ethical content and context.

Theological Base of Love

Love is considered one of the three primary theological virtues along with faith and hope. Throughout the centuries of theological writing, the analysis of love has centered on love as self-giving *agape*. The nature of *agape* has moved through a progression of emphases. As (1) benevolence, that is, to love the unlovely and the unlovable, *agape* is the generous, altruistic, compassionate love that values the neighbor self-forgetfully, in a self-disinterested concern for his or her welfare. It is in no way dependent on the recipient's merit or worth but only on the lover's generosity. As (2) obedience that acts to love the other because of role, command or moral imperative, *agape* is the faithful, willing obedience to the moral imperative to act for the good of the neighbor in fulfillment of the command of Christ. As (3) self-sacrifice that seeks to love the other at the lover's expense—the other's need comes first—*agape* is self-sacrificial service to the neighbor, which puts the other's needs above one's own, even at great cost to the self. As (4) equal regard that perceives the other as equally worthful, even as one knows the self to be precious and of irreducible worth, *agape* is thus both an act of the will—to exercise compassion toward the other without reservation—and an act of the heart—to value self and other unconditionally. Such love regards the neighbor as loved even when enmity exists, that is, when the other is the enemy.

The first view, benevolence, has been the dominant interpretation of love in Christian history. Most theologians critique it for its paternalistic element. The fourth view, equal regard, is now more frequently pursued since it is capable of embracing the other three, that is, benevolence, obedience and self-sacrifice in a way that takes wholeness, justice and well-being seriously for all humankind, including enemies.

Agape has frequently been defined as "disinterested love," which allows, even

197

supports, an atomistic individualism. When it is seen as a total, unselfish form of love that utterly disregards any response, this unilateral love becomes entirely a matter of what I unilaterally offer to do for someone out there or down there in benevolent generosity. But *agape* cannot be individualized in such a manner; it is a sharing of experience, a recognition of our underlying kinship in the kingdom of God. It is an equal regard grounded in our common existence as creatures from the hand of the Creator, who loves all equally.

We have often been limited by etymological analyses of words, such as the terms for love in the Scripture. Our understanding of Christian love ought not to hinge on the root meanings of classical Greek verbs, nor on particular usages, but on the decisive test of the central understanding of love in the overall meaning of the New Testament witness to love, of the incarnation's demonstration of love, of the full impact of the life, teaching, death, resurrection and presence of the loving Christ. The past, present and future reality of the people of God—the church—as the community of love is the body of Christ.

In the biblical world there were at least five words used to designate forms of love, although only three of these appear in the New Testament: (1) *eros,* the search for an object in aesthetic, passionate or spiritual love; (2) *philia,* the preferential bond of affection, friendship and social solidarity; (3) *storge,* the caregiving love of compassion; (4) *agape,* the nonpreferential, self-giving love of equal respect; and (5) *koinonia,* which is love in the mutuality of community, in the sharing of the common life in covenant and commitment. The fifth love is more than a search for an object (*eros*) or altruistic self-giving (*agape*); it is an expression of mutuality in which giving and receiving are united (*koinonia*).

This is the authentic word for Christian love, the end of the trajectory of the multiple words (*eros, philia, storge, agape, koinonia*). The word *koinonia,* from *koinos* "in common," expresses the fellowship-creating drive toward mutuality, the fellowship-fulfilling goal of equality, the fellowship-celebrating joy of community, the fellowship discipline of impartiality: "May the *grace* of the Lord Jesus Christ, and the *love* of God, and the *fellowship* of the Holy Spirit be with you all" (2 Cor 13:14, emphasis added).

A Philosophical Framework

Agape is a profound concern for the welfare of another, to be understanding and to understand the other without any desire to control, to be thanked by the other or to enjoy the process. *Agape* is a decisive distributing of benefit to self and others. We may view it as a continuum from other-forgetfulness to self-forgetfulness with intermediary steps of preferring self, equal parity and preferring other. Forgetting the other allows the person to choose a course of action with no concern for the other's welfare. *Preferring self* may take into account the other's good but gives more value to one's own need or advantage. *Equal parity* offers equal weight to both self and other in a mathematics of truly equal division of good and bad. *Preferring the other* demands that a person, while taking self-needs seriously, should always give preference to the other. *Self-forgetting* suggests that the person prizes the other so highly that thoughts of the self occur only in relation to the other's needs of fulfillment.

When *agape* is tempered with justice, equal parity becomes a criterion for evaluating what is creative for the other, for the relations and also for the self. The balance point between a just concern for both parties and their needs may vary with the context, the circumstances, the special situations of either. Yet *agape*, accepting the human need as a necessary point of preferring the other, works toward the parity of equality.

The Psychological Dynamic

Love is the moving power of life that seeks the unity of the separated. The individual needs to find unity with other selves but without sacrificing its own or violating the other's identity. This retains the centeredness of each person without absorption or abandonment by the other. These polarities—absorption or abandonment, engulfment or ignoring, union or separation—express the basic fears as well as the essential needs for balanced personhood. More than a balance point, love is an active process of mutuality. Mature love seeks the mutuality that expresses the reciprocity of give and take in a relationship. But the practice of a love that seeks mutuality can be pursued by one person whether the other reciprocates or not. Unconditional positive regard can be given whether the other responds or returns such valuing, as Carl Rogers has taught.

Many psychological theorists assume the principle of psychological hedonism, which holds that all human beings are driven to seek pleasure for themselves and to avoid pain. The contrasting view is that of psychological altruism, which supports the human capacity of self-love as distinct from pleasure for the self, which is selfishness. Love of self and love of other are complementary. A true concern for one's own welfare cannot be divided from concern for the welfare of significant others, and true self-love motivates one to see others with equal respect. Eric Fromm has articulated this perspective and points toward the possibilities of humans' coming to value self and other as a means of reducing the alienation of human society and of increasing the possibilities of persons' val-

uing giving above getting, valuing being above having or doing. This vision of an innate harmony between egoism and altruism has become a basic assumption for human potential, existential and the many varieties of popular psychology, in contrast to the analytic and object relations theorists, who see the two in eternal tension.

Ethical Content

If the concept is to have any meaning, love requires an ethical community. Ethical practice does not occur in human isolation or in individual decision. It arises within community and directly by the commitments of the person. It is in a particular community that the practice of love takes form, receives content, finds direction, achieves fulfillment. The ethic that has emerged from the tradition of Immanuel Kant places central emphasis on reason to the belittlement of feeling. He grounds ethics on a foundation of laws that are universal (in that all rational beings would need to subscribe to them). Thus, he held that the universal principle of respect for all rational beings as ends in themselves and never as mere means constitutes the measure of genuine love. The Aristotelian perspective, in contrast, views love not as a universal law but as a virtue that is central to the formulation and sustaining of human community.

Christian theology is grounded in the passionate, eternal, self-giving, unconditional love of God. The presence of God in the birth, life, teaching and death of Christ presents divine love in human experience and community. The incarnation, crucifixion and resurrection are not as much the infusion of supernatural love as the transformation of the natural human experience, the restoration of created human possibilities, the gift of grace that restores the courage to love, the commitment to care even for the enemy, the participation in the power of the Spirit, which enables us to go beyond the common human capacity to love to an uncommon experience of *agape* in relationships and community.

See also CHARACTER; GIFT-GIVING; HOSPITALITY; MISSION; SELF-ESTEEM.

References and Resources

E. Erikson, *Insight and Responsibility* (New York: Norton, 1964); E. Fromm, *The Art of Loving* (New York: Harper, 1956); C. S. Lewis, *The Four Loves* (New York: Harcourt Brace Jovanovich, 1960); G. Outka, *Agape: An Ethical Analysis* (New Haven, Conn.: Yale University Press, 1972); F. Perls et al., *Gestalt Therapy* (New York: Dell, 1951); C. Rogers, *On Becoming a Person* (Boston: Houghton Mifflin, 1961); P. Tillich, *Love, Power and Justice* (New York: Oxford University Press, 1954).

David Augsburger

—MARRIAGE—

The good news for most married couples is very good indeed. There is a resurgence in faith about marital faithfulness, which researchers are calling *faithful attraction*. Andrew Greeley reports, on the basis of four surveys of couples, that 90 percent of American spouses have been faithful since they were married. Also, more than 60 percent say their marriage is very happy, 75 percent say their spouse is their best friend, and over 80 percent say they would marry the same person again if they had to do it over. *Faith Alive* magazine (July 1994) asked their Canadian readers (mostly church attendees) to rate their marriages, and on average they rated their marriages with a B+. Over 95 percent of women and men had not had an extramarital relationship, though about 12 percent of men reported that they had been tempted. Of those who rated their marriages with an A+, the most common thread was "seeking God's kingdom first."

The marrying couple may well not know what they are doing, but they know what they want. Willard Harley in his book *His Needs, Her Needs* points out what he has discovered as the priorities of the sexes in the order of importance. A man desires sexual fulfillment, recreational companionship, an attractive spouse, domestic support and, finally, admiration from his wife. Harley's research indicates that a woman desires affection, conversation,* honesty and openness, financial support and family commitment. With such different expectations, it is little wonder that the process of becoming one is so fraught with challenges and opportunities.

The Bible speaks often about marriage, but nowhere so eloquently as in the creation story in Genesis 2:18-25. The section begins with this striking announcement by God: "It is not good for the man to be alone. I will make a helper suitable for him" (Gen 2:18). Adam is alone, and that state is "not good"—the only thing in creation that God judges to be not good. As the man began to function as God had intended him (naming the animals), he became profoundly aware that all the beasts had "equal others," but he did not. He became lonely. Being alone is always a negative concept in biblical history, for the full life is found in community with all of God's people (see Eccles 4:9-12; Jer 16:1-9).

The Need for a Helpmate

Christian marriage is particularly unpalatable to some because of the sacrifice or submission implied, so it is thought, in the phrase "suitable helper." God, however, takes this word *helper* upon himself in several passages in Scripture, for example,

Who is like you,
a people saved by the LORD?
He is your shield and helper
and your glorious sword.
(Deut 33:29)

The word *helper* essentially describes one who provides what is lacking in the other. The woman by relative difference but essential equality would be the man's fitting complement. What he lacked, she supplied. And it is equally true that what she lacked, he would supply. The man was thus created in such a way that he needs the help of a partner. Human beings cannot fulfill their destiny without such mutual assistance. What the Bible does not do is spell this out in terms of specific roles. What the man lacks, the woman supplies. So Scripture explains the need for a companion; it also explores the process of becoming married.

Marriage as a Three-Stage Process

Mike Mason, author of *The Mystery of Marriage,* comments that "a marriage is not a joining of two worlds but an abandoning of two worlds in order that one new one might be formed" (91). The concept of offering up your own life for the blessing* of another is both biblical and profoundly psychological. Marriage is a continual three-stage process that involves leaving, being united and becoming one: "For this reason a man will leave his father and mother and be united to his wife, and they will become one flesh. The man and his wife were both naked, and they felt no shame" (Gen 2:24-25). Each of these three dimensions is needed for a complete marriage.

Marital leaving. The process of leaving means disengaging from one's family of origin (the family that you were born into and where you formed your initial preadult values*). It has to do with ending the dependency on the original family and becoming "jointly autonomous" with your mate. It may also mean giving up adolescent* expectations of sexual intimacy so that the marriage can be free to enjoy the pleasures and disciplines of marital love* or relinquishing the fantasies of being forever nurtured and adored. Whatever kind of leaving is required, the leaving will be ongoing. There is a continual leaving of the old to engage the new, even after many years of marriage (*see* Family Systems).

Many couples in marriage counseling find they must work through this issue of leaving. When the first or second child comes around and needs extra care, they begin to parent as they were parented. The problem is that both parents were parented differently and conflicts arise. Both will need to rethink their ideas of what parenting* is about. This is the process of leaving. It is a continual process and is provoked by the inevitable conflicts of living in marital proximity.

Marital union. The idea of being united with one's wife or husband as found in Genesis 2:24 raises the question, How do spouses become intimate? This too is a continual process in which none of us is an expert. To be continually united involves many everyday skills of friendship. This is why good friendships so often lead to secure and satisfying marriages. Being united involves mutual affection and appreciation. There is no one who can live in the intimacy that marriage requires without the affirmation of one's partner. Also, it is impossible to become close friends without the glue of emotions and their effective communication. These emotions may be unpleasant ones (e.g., anger or resentment) or the more pleasant emotions of marital arousal and love. Further, becoming united requires simple acceptance of the other and the skills of conflict resolution* and anger reduction. No one masters all of these skills on the wedding day. Husband and wife are continually becoming more united, more unified, more intimate with each other.

Intimacy is hard work. Many couples, however, think that marital intimacy is a hormonal gift that bubbles them into ecstasy. It is easy for them to fall into despair when they are disillusioned by the necessary work (by the way, it is great to give up illusions that are untrue). But when a couple gets over the disappointment that intimacy is work, they can galvanize their resources to be a missionary to each other's intimacy needs. This is what it means to be united.

Young people grow up looking for the "right one." When our teenagers talk this way, I interrupt them with the terribly parental judgment: "How are you becoming the perfect person for your future mate?" They need to be converted from the idea that their future marital bliss is caught up in finding the perfect one. Rather, marital intimacy is the mutual commitment of being the right one for the other.

Marital sexuality. Sexual intimacy is also hard work—though perhaps it was not for Adam. I can envision Adam running across plains and through rivers, brushing aside giraffes and pelicans in pursuit of his equal other, Eve. Along the way he utters the first hymn of praise in the Bible ("here at last"; Gen 2:23 NRSV) and the first poem ("bone of my bones"; Gen 2:23). Having seen all of creation designed for a partner, he discovered his own and did not need a course in sexual education to know what to do. Adam

and Eve enjoyed a naive integrity, absolutely without the experience or knowledge of sin, as the motif of nakedness suggests. They experienced no shame* and felt no fear of rejection.

This is the hope of all young adults who decide to live together. They are desperately trying to get back to Eden. They want the simplicity and naiveté of the Adam and Eve who knew no sin. But they are cheating and lying to themselves. They have had imperfect parents, who have transmitted generations of fear, unhappiness and twistedness (along with much good) to them. They have developed conflictual personalities that make them suitable to be bachelors and spinsters but never to be husbands and wives. They have developed competing ambitions that place them at loggerheads with each other. They are not naive at all. They know too much. And their experience of sexual union is something less than full communion.

The idea of becoming one flesh expresses the complete personal community of one man and one woman as spiritual-physical-sexual-family unity. How do two become one? It is difficult, say the psychologists. It is impossible, say the realists. It is a miracle, say the religionists. And it is all three. I call it the "mystery of transfiguration." When Jesus was on the mountain with his friends, he was transfigured in their view (Mt 17:2-3). He acted the same, talked the same, but he was now seen in right relationship with all of eternity. A similar transfiguration occurs when a man becomes a husband and a woman becomes a wife. These are not role changes; this is the beginning of the process of becoming the other's *other.* Two are becoming one in view of each other.

The Vows of Mystery
The wedding vows express the process of transfiguration. The wedding vows not

only describe the commitments of marriage, but they obligate one to another. They are not merely descriptive; they carry the weight of the word spoken. Just as God created life out of the spoken word, the vows powerfully implement the process of transfiguration. Carelessly spoken vows carry such carelessness throughout the duration of the marriage. Vows taken as if God sustains the covenant carry the sacredness throughout the couple's journey. The marriage vows from *The Book of Alternative Services of the Anglican Church of Canada* illustrate the mystery well.

"I take you" suggests the activity of a freely disposed individual who entrusts himself or herself to another. It is the most profound ontology: to choose and to be chosen. Marital "taking" has great power. It is the power of acceptance. It is one of the needs of all human beings—to be accepted as we are. In marital taking we accept our spouse without the anticipation of changing. Too many spouses endeavor to create the spouse over into their own image.

"To be" speaks of the transition from one state of being into another. Marriage is not so much a role change as a profound transfiguration into being a husband or wife, not a mere man or woman. The marital transfiguration usually leads to parental transfiguration—the becoming of a father or a mother (*see* Parenting). These transfigurations are a continual process and therefore involve continual change.

"My lawfully wedded wife/husband" speaks of the community aspect of marriage. It is accepted and affirmed as good for society and is the covenantal hope of the community for the future. Marriage always has this beyond-ourselves dimension. In the marriage ceremony the pastor may address to all present, "Will you do all in your power to support and uphold this marriage?" As the community answers in faith, "We will," they echo the covenant of the couple to each other. Sometimes when a couple is remarrying, they quote the passage from Ecclesiastes 4:12: "Though one may be overpowered, two can defend themselves. A cord of three strands is not quickly broken." Their confession is that they were not together on their first try. Their hope is that with God empowering their marriage and with faith making it alive, their covenant will not be ruined. It is with great confidence that a minister marries a couple who depend fully on God.

"To have" speaks of the delight and pleasure of the marital covenant. *To have* is to be thrilled with the discovery that now the spouse has what he or she has waited for. It is a my-beloved-is-mine experience. Having also includes tragedies as well as joys. Problems and challenges are not interruptions in the marriage. Embracing the complexities, disappointments and genuine hurts is as much a part of marital having as relishing the excitements.

"And to hold from this day forward" speaks of the permanence of the having. *Holding* your spouse speaks of sustaining the power of the vows throughout the marriage. How do you hold your spouse? Ask yourself these questions: How do you talk about your mate when he or she is not there to hear? Do you hold him to be valuable to your children or when jesting with friends? Is it your plan every day to discover more of his or her giftedness, to empower and not to limit your spouse? Are you trying to hold him or her back out of fear? Or are you holding to empower the other?

"For better, for worse; for richer for poorer; in sickness and in health" is a reality statement. There will be many highs and lows, and the covenant is sufficient for all of them. If a couple has not significantly suffered, it is probably because they are still young in their marital journey. James tells us to "consider it pure joy . . . whenever you face trials of many kinds" (Jas 1:2). There is an inevitability about these trials—they will come—but they can be appropriated for the good of the marriage and for the blessing of the couple. Some couples do not think that trials produce a good marital crop. When struggles inevitably materialize, they think that they have married the wrong one. Challenges are reminders to become the right one.

"To love" emphasizes the emotion (eros) and the motivation (agape) of the covenant. This kind of love* is both vertical (from ecstasy to sadness) and horizontal (from now to eternity). Much is said in popular marriage books about the various kinds of love. There is friendship love, erotic love, steadfast love and dependency love. At different times of the couple's journey, different loves are required. The love of middle-aged spouses is quite different from the love of aged grandparents* preparing to move into a retirement village, where their grandchildren can come for lunch on Sundays. Newlywed love is unique and quite unrepeatable (thankfully). Marital permanence and satisfaction have to do with reading the stages of your marriage as to the kind of love that is best.

"And to cherish" speaks of the attitude of prizing the chosen other. Cherishing is to put the right value on the marriage and the one loved. Cherishing is the penicillin to the sickness of coveting, coveting another or another's marriage. The remedy for coveting—in relation to both God and one's spouse—is cherishing: receiving and valuing fully what has been given. This is the everyday plea of marital therapy clients the world around: "Cherish me. Value me. Love me."

"Until death do us part" is also a reality statement of marriage. In the midst of the teary happiness of the wedding vows, reality enters in. This covenant will be broken by death.* In the birth of marriage intimacies, the d word is spoken not so much as an interruption but as a reminder of reality. This aspect of the vow reminds the couple of the permanence of the covenant.

"According to God's holy ordinance" speaks of the One who enacts and empowers the covenant. It is God's ordinance because it is God who "holds the paper." While the registrations of our marriages are filed in the appropriate governmental offices, God holds and sustains the covenant that is the marriage itself. It is God who transfigures man to husband and woman to wife. It is God who empowers this union. What vows! But what a God! And what a mystery marriage is!

A Picture of Christian Marriage

Richard Selzer in his book *Mortal Lessons* wonderfully pictures what marriage is.

> I stand by the bed where a young woman lies, her face postoperative, her mouth twisted in palsy, clownish. A tiny twig of the facial nerve, the one to the muscles of her mouth, has been severed. The surgeon had followed with religious fervor the curve of her flesh; I promise you that. Nevertheless, to remove the tumor in her cheek, I had cut the little nerve. Her young husband is in the room. He stands on the opposite side of the bed, and together they seem to dwell in the evening lamplight, isolated from me, private. Who are they, I ask myself, he and this wrymouth I have made, who gaze at and touch each other so generously, greedily? The young woman speaks. "Will my mouth always be like this?" she asks. "Yes," I say, "it will. It is because the

nerve was cut." She nods, and is silent. But the young man smiles. "I like it," he says. "It is kind of cute." All at once I know who he is. I understand, and I lower my gaze. One is not bold in an encounter with a god. Unmindful, he bends to kiss her crooked mouth, and I am so close I can see how he twists his own lips to accommodate to hers, to show her that their kiss still works. (45-46)

See also CONFLICT RESOLUTION; DIVORCE; FAMILY SYSTEMS; FEMININITY; LOVE; MASCULINITY; SEXUALITY.

References and Resources
H. Clinebell and C. Clinebell, *The Intimate Marriage* (New York: Harper & Row, 1970); B. Farrel et al., *Pure Pleasure: Making Your Marriage a Great Affair* (Downers Grove, Ill.: InterVarsity Press, 1994); M. Mason, *The Mystery of Marriage* (Portland, Ore.: Multnomah Press, 1985); J. H. Olthius, *I Pledge You My Troth: A Christian View of Marriage, Family, Friendship* (New York: Harper & Row, 1975); R. Selzer, *Mortal Lessons: Notes on the Art of Surgery* (New York: Simon & Schuster, 1976); R. P. Stevens, *Married for Good* (Downers Grove, Ill.: InterVarsity Press, 1986); R. P. Stevens, *Marriage Spirituality* (Downers Grove, Ill.: InterVarsity Press, 1989); E. Wheat, *Love Life* (Grand Rapids: Zondervan, 1980); N. Wright, *Communication: Key to Your Marriage* (Glendale, Calif.: Gospel Light, 1979).

Paddy Ducklow

—MASCULINITY—

Since the industrial revolution, marital roles have been sharply divided between male and female tasks. Parents have been likewise concerned with the masculine development of their sons and feminine development of daughters. However, there is growing confusion about the meaning of masculinity and how males in family life are to live it out.

Masculinity and femininity are the two categories of gender—differences between females and males that are learned or taken on as a result of socialization. The concept of gender is often combined with gender role to refer to behavior deemed appropriate for persons whose sex is correspondingly female or male. Gender is distinguished from sex,* which is used to refer to purely biological contributions to male or female behavior. Family roles and behavior that are deemed appropriate for males and females can be thought of as gender-appropriate "scripts." Also, while the contributions of biological sex might be assumed to be constant in families across cultures, the family scripts given males or females (gender roles) will vary from culture to culture.

The Concept of Masculinity

As a concept, masculinity is more ambiguous than gender because it is used in social science to refer to maleness based on biological or sociological factors. In its widest and most conventional usage masculinity refers to behavior that is deemed to be most appropriate for a person who is a biological male. While masculinity is in part biologically and in part sociologically based, present knowledge is unable to assess with any precision the relative contribution made by these two factors. In all probability each has both a separate, and a combined, effect upon masculinity and femininity.

In the social sciences there was an initial attempt to conceptualize masculinity as one polar point on a continuum, with femininity as its opposite. The obvious weakness in this approach is that defining qualities of masculinity and femininity were conceived as mutually exclusive.

The accumulating research on masculinity and femininity has contributed much to the ideology of both the contemporary women's and men's movements. This began with an emphasis on assimilation (women were encouraged to compete with men on their own terms), moved to an emphasis on androgyny (women and men were encouraged to blunt gender distinctives and incorporate the best of both male and female characteristics), and resulted in the present emphasis on differentiation (in which women and men are encouraged to recognize and embrace their own unique ways of being female and male respectively). The latest model is supported by evidence that suggest males and females are normatively different in regards to moral decision making (Gilligan 1982), style of conversing and relating (Tanner 1990), and the basis on which each gains self-esteem.* The differentiation model is also consistent with the biblical account of God's creation of humankind—"male and female he created them" (Gen 1:27).

Biblical Models of Masculinity

Those who defend a traditional family form in which male and female roles are clearly divided argue that the current redefinition of gender roles goes against the Bible. However, Scripture sheds little light as to how God desires men and women to be different in the way they behave and relate in the family. Scripture has much more to say about how parents (both fathers and mothers) are to be in family life than it does about how fathers as distinct from mothers are to parent.

Jesus can be used as a biblical model of masculinity. The most dominant emotional characteristic we see in Jesus is his compassion or love.* On numerous occasions Jesus showed both internal feelings (he loved and pitied) and external action (he helped the needy). Jesus' compassion was also expressed in sorrow, as he wept over Jerusalem because of the unbelief of its people, and with Mary and Martha at the death of Lazarus.

At other times Jesus' love moved him to express great joy (Lk 10:21; Jn 15:10-11). Although Jesus was sensitive and nonmanipulative, he was also capable of anger and indignation. In a world under the curse of sin, Jesus responded angrily to human beings' cruelty, hardness of heart, unbelief and hypocrisy. The same Jesus who said, "Let the little children come to me" (Lk 18:16), drove out those who bought and sold animals in the temple and upset the tables of the moneychangers.

Jesus possessed a wide range of emotions and was harmoniously complete in his human individuality. Jesus seems to have embodied the best of the characteristics that by traditional standards are divided and assigned to males on the one hand and females on the other. The scriptural narratives do not support a masculinized or feminized image of Jesus. Instead they suggest the rich depth that characterized Jesus' human life, which can serve as a strong model for how masculinity is to be lived out in family life.

Masculinity and Family Life

Masculinity is now an issue in family life. According to the traditional model of gender roles, women's place was in the home* and men's place was in society. Correspondingly, in the past parents assumed that their sons quite naturally grew up with the strong and rational characteristics suitable for working in the marketplace, while daughters grew up to be sufficiently feminine with the personal nurturing qualities needed within the home.

The emergence of the social sciences called into question how much of this was "natural" and in so doing contributed to the current redefinition of gender roles. The contemporary redefinition of femininity, which has focused on women's involvement in society and family life, began in the late 1960s and has continued to the present. Men in support of the women's movement formed a men's movement in the mid-1970s that called into question the traditional definition of masculinity as the reverse image of femininity. In challenging the traditional model of gender roles, the more modern model deemphasizes any sharp distinction between masculinity and femininity. For women this has meant a greater freedom to obtain a higher education and pursue a career and develop a life outside of their roles within the family. For men, the redefinition of masculinity has freed them from defining themselves solely in role of the breadwinner. In addition to his work, a husband can devote greater energies to his role in the family and come to define himself in terms of his involvement in family life. The core arena within which issues of masculinity are most salient in the family center in the father-son relationship.

The Father-Son Relationship

Absence of strong fathering is a major contributor to the lack of adequate masculine development among boys. Before the Industrial Revolution most boys most likely learned to worked along side of their fathers. Today fathers are more involved in work outside of the home. Mothers took over most of the parenting tasks. Since the Industrial Revolution each successive generation of fathers has experienced less and less fathering from

their own fathers. This means that the present generation is trying to father their own sons while not having been fully fathered themselves. The void created by the father's absence from the home, although detrimental to both sons and daughters, has proved to have the most adverse effect upon sons. In one survey of over seven thousand men, almost none said they had been or were close to their fathers, while another found that fewer than 2 percent of sons described only good relations with their fathers. At the present time 40 percent of American children will sleep in homes without a father living there (Blankenhorn; see Single Parenting). In response to the absence of fathers in so many homes, we might ask why fathers are necessary.

Fathers are necessary because they predominantly orient their sons to the world from a male perspective. What it is to be a man is mirrored back to the son through the father's actions and words. A son acts out what it means to be a man based upon what he has learned from his father or adult male caretaker. As he is embraced for these actions, his masculinity is validated and affirmed. However, it is possible for fathers to be physically present but emotionally absent. Emotionally absent fathers mirror to sons a distant masculinity. Since these fathers do not express emotions or communicate about things of the heart, their sons experience them as emotionally absent.

Men who were not validated and affirmed as males in their growing-up years will often be haunted by a fear that they are not man enough. Men who have heard from their fathers "I love you" are much less driven by the fear of not being man enough. But the sad part is that many fathers today, in being deprived themselves of fathers who mirrored manhood to them, are merely repeating a cycle of nonfathering. As a result they too are driven by fear, and the sight of their own sons mirroring back to them this fear and confusion only serves to reinforce their sense of masculine inadequacy.

The effect of being reared primarily by a mother is profoundly different for sons and daughters. An abundance of mothering, at the near neglect of fathering, makes girls better prepared than boys to become parents. Boys are at a disadvantage because they grow up lacking nurture from their parent of the same gender. This begins a different process of maturation in boys and girls.

While both boys and girls begin their lives with a primary emotional attachment to their mother, boys must learn to identify with their father by denying attachment to their mother. Girls, on the other hand, can continue to identity with and hold their primary attachment to their mother. Yet a girl's relationship to her mother is significantly different from a boy's relationship to his father. While the girl is likely to be involved in a face-to-face relationship with her mother in the home, the fact that the father is absent from the home for long periods means that the boy must learn about masculinity from his mother or the culture at large. He does not have the advantage of an ongoing personal relationship with his father. The close tie girls have with their mothers means that they will likely desire to be nurturing mothers. Since boys are not closely tied to their fathers, and they deny their attachment to their mothers for the sake of their own masculinity, when they in turn become fathers, they will likely be emotionally distant from their children.

Coparenting: Bringing the Father Back In

In traditional families most of the parenting is, in reality, mothering. Yet Scripture does not hold up mothering as more im-portant than fathering. It is difficult for one parent to be all that he or she needs to be to the children. But together, a mother and a father can complement each other by each being strong when the other feels weak and overextended and is in need of support. The important thing is that the parental unit is strong and that both parents be equally involved and bonded in the lives of their children.

There has been an accumulation of recent evidence demonstrating the benefits of coparenting for children and parents alike (Balswick and Balswick, chap. 12). When both the father and mother are jointly involved in parenting, a family has what family therapists refer to as a strong parental subsystem: both father and mother take clear leadership when it comes to nurturing and guiding the children. When the mother and the father are not together in parenting, the parental subsystem is weaker and less effective.

Research has shown that coparented children have a number of advantages when compared to non-coparented children. Coparented children have a more secure sense of basic trust, can more successfully adapt to brief separations from the mother, and have closer relationships to both mother and father. They also develop better social discrimination skills such as discerning who can best meet their needs. Finally, they display greater creativity and moral development, have less animosity toward the other gender and are better able to develop strong friendship bonds with opposite-sex children (Balswick and Balswick, 168-70).

The effect of coparenting upon sons is especially noteworthy. Sons who had a strong bond with both their father and mother were more able to display empathy, affection and nurturing behavior, thought highly of the way they were parented, and were more likely to state that they wanted to be a father when they grew up.

When fathers take a more active part in parenting, mothers also benefit by being relieved from having the major responsibilities of parenting. In the process they too become effective mothers because they do not carry the burden of needing to be the primary caretaker.

The pay-off for greater involvement by fathers with their children can in addition have positive effects upon themselves and their own relationships. Fathers who are highly involved with their children become more able to express their feelings as they develop the relational side of their personality. There is even evidence that highly involved fathers become more relational in their roles outside of the home, such as in their work relationships.

Implications

It is important that men reclaim their full masculinity. Since the family* and the way parents interact with their children is a primary learning ground for how to be a male, it is imperative that family life be lived out in a way that reflects a biblical model of masculinity. The Old Testament image of God as father is of one who has a tender strength, who loves with an unconditional commitment, who offers grace when the children of Israel failed him, and who wants his strength to be theirs. Jesus provides a fuller model of Christian masculinity. Jesus was just as much a man when he wept and showed tenderness as when he drove the moneychangers out of the temple. A Christian model of masculinity includes firmness, strength, determination, rationality and all the characteristics culturally identified with traditional masculinity, as well as tenderness, nurture, caring, emotionality and other characteristics traditionally identified as feminine. One set of characteristics is not our masculine side and the other our feminine. Both are a part of our true, complete manhood. When the image of God as father is combined with the person of Jesus Christ, a model of masculinity emerges that is greatly needed, and can be the basis for how men are to be as they live within the complexities of modern family life.

See also FEMININITY; LOVE; SEXUALITY; SINGLE PARENTING.

References and Resources

G. Bilezikian, *Beyond Sex Roles* (Grand Rapids: Baker, 1985); J. Balswick, *Men At The Crossroads: Beyond Traditional Roles and Modern Options* (Downers Grove, Ill.: InterVarsity Press, 1992); J. and J. Balswick, *The Dual Earner Marriage: The Elaborate Balancing Act* (Grand Rapids: Revell, 1995); J. Blankenhorn, *Fatherless American: Confronting Our Most Urgent Social Problem* (New York: Basic Books. 1995); C. Gilligan, *In a Different Voice: Psychological Theory and Women's Development* (Cambridge, Mass.: Harvard University Press, 1982); J. Nelson, *The Intimate Connection: Male Sexuality, Masculinity, Spirituality* (Philadelphia: Westminster Press, 1988); D. Tanner, *You Just Don't Understand: Women and Men in Conversation* (New York: William Morrow, 1990).

Jack Balswick

—MASTURBATION—

Masturbation is nearly universally practiced (more frequently by men then women) from infancy through old age. The practice is subject to varying interpretations that range from being a gift of God to always being a sin.

God's Original Intention

God created man and woman with sexual desires in order to create and nurture the bond between husband and wife (Gen 2:24; 1 Cor 7:3-5), to provide intimate pleasure (Prov 5:18-19) and to sustain creation through offspring (Mal 2:15). Since God created the male and female bodies for one another, for intimacy and relationship, masturbation by its very nature falls short of the full expression of sexuality* God intended. Yet it is interesting that there are only two forms of sexual expression not prohibited in the Bible: sex within the marriage* relationship and masturbation.

Because we are fallen creatures, our passions can lead us away from God and healthy sexuality. According to the New Testament, to be driven by the passions of fallen human nature is to be enslaved to sin. This affects the whole person, including the mind and the will (Rom 1:26). A person's desires can lead to ungodly acts (Eph 4:22), to gratification apart from good (Gal 5:16), to the breakup of marriage (compare Mt 5:28), to distance from God (Eph 2:3). Even prayer* can be misused (Jas 4:1-3).

The solution to fallen flesh in the New Testament is to receive God's love and Holy Spirit and to follow after the prompting of the Spirit (Rom 8:9-11; Gal 5:16-18). With regard to sexuality, both by the purchase accomplished by Christ on the cross and by the indwelling of the Holy Spirit, one's body belongs to the Lord, not to sexual immorality (1 Cor 6:9-20). Further, self-control is one of the fruits of the Spirit. Self-control is the grace-enacted restraining or moderating of one's desires or having power over oneself rather than being mastered by anything (1 Cor 7:5, 9; 9:25; Gal 5:23). Redeemed sexuality, then, could include the following: accepting sexual desire and sensuality as God's good creation; repenting from the cultural sexual ethic toward God's purposes for sexuality; developing the ability to accept nurturing from others, including God, and to nurture self, that is, to know and express desires, wants and areas of discomfort; developing warm and caring friendships that are not sexual; and seeking a special mutual intimacy in marriage in which each person willingly abandons the self to the other sexually in a temporary surrender of ego and control that grows and matures over time.

Understanding Masturbation

Masturbation is an expression of the passion of fallen human nature. In children masturbatory behaviors can become a negative behavior pattern leading to extreme withdrawal when children do not have enough interaction with people or activities, are severely punished for playing with their genitals or are inappropriately sexually stimulated by others. In adolescence* and beyond, fantasy generally accompanies masturbation. We know from behavioral psychology that pleasure, more than pain, shapes behavior. What gives pleasure is likely to be repeated.

When an individual repeatedly masturbates to an unhealthy fantasy (i.e., one involving power, manipulation, coercion, or one-sided, nonconsenting same-sex or multiple-partner relationships), the pleasure experience imprints the fantasy's sexual misbeliefs ("What feels good is good"; "What feels good must be right"; "I must be gay"; "I am so horny that I can't control myself") and increases the proclivity to act out the fantasy. Counselors repeatedly see unhealthy masturbatory fantasies as part of inappropriate and illegal compulsive sexual behaviors. The personal cost of an unhealthy masturbatory fantasy/behavior is an increase in isolation and loneliness, the creation of unrealistic expectations and imprinting that may lead to destructive behaviors. In marriage an unhealthy masturbatory fantasy/behavior may weaken the marital and emotional bond, increasing the distance between spouses. In these situations the person is mastered by his or her passions and is out of control and in need of God's grace as well as clinical wisdom in order to follow after the Spirit, to regain self-control and to honor the Lord with his or her body.

Second, we look at masturbation as an expression of redeemed sexuality. To experience and accept one's body as a gift from God means that looking, touching and experiencing pleasure is a normal, developmental part of healthy sexuality. Further, a healthy masturbatory fantasy/behavior (i.e., one that anticipates or images a monogamous, mutual, heterosexual marriage relationship) can assist a person in developing sexual awareness and sensitivity, in learning about genital arousal and orgasm, in anticipating or focusing on appropriate future marital relationships rather than being promiscuous, and in easing the transition into shared intimacies in marriage. There are often times in marriage when one's spouse is not available for sexual intimacy; masturbation with a fantasy imaging mutual positive experiences with one's spouse is an acceptable alternative if it increases openness and closeness rather than distance. On the other hand, not all arousal needs to be pursued. Arousal can be allowed to subside with no impediment to the self or the relationship.

Practical Strategies

In making decisions about masturbation and fantasy you may find the following points and questions helpful.

☐ Thank God for your sexual feelings and for the Spirit, who redeems our passions and leads us in self-control (whether present or still to come).

☐ Know that you can control your fantasy and that you are responsible for your behavior. God has created you in Christ for this maturity.

☐ If you feel stuck in a negative pattern, resist despising yourself; resist focusing too much on this one area of your life. Seek competent counsel and remember that God welcomes you and will not cast you off.

☐ When you sense yourself becoming aroused, engage your mind and ask yourself a few questions before you decide to masturbate. By being in touch with your emotional experiences and open before God, you can decide whether to continue or to allow the arousal to dissipate and deal with the feelings and thoughts accompanying the arousal. Ask yourself what has triggered this arousal: positive desire? delight in passions? anger? sadness? frustration? If the emotions are negative, deal with these. Masturbation will be inappropriate. Also ask yourself what consequences you will experience in relationship to God, to significant others and to yourself: appreciation? positive anticipation? coolness? distance? regret? guilt? Make your decision in light of your answers.

See also LOVE; SEXUALITY.

References and Resources

D. G. Benner, *Baker Encyclopedia of Psychology* (Grand Rapids: Baker, 1985); G. R. Collins, *Christian Counseling: A Comprehensive Guide* (Waco, Tex.: Word, 1980); J. R. Johnson, "Toward a Biblical Approach to Masturbation," *Journal of Psychology and Theology* 10, no. 2 (1982) 137-46; C. Penner and J. Penner, *Counseling for Sexual Disorders* (Dallas: Word, 1990); C. Penner and J. Penner, *Sexual Facts for the Family* (Dallas: Word, 1992); J. White, *Eros Defiled* (Downers Grove, Ill.: InterVarsity Press, 1977).

Mike Nichols

—MEAL PREPARATION—

Meal preparation can be a delight; but for most of us, most of the time, it is more like drudgery. This conflict between drudgery and delight lies at the heart of the Mary-Martha story (Lk 10:38-42). Martha's preparations for Jesus' visit were not the real problem—a look at the wording is revealing: "Martha was *distracted* by *all* the preparations that *had* to be made" (emphasis added). It is clear that Martha opened her home to Jesus with the strength of frenetic, hard work—but not with her heart, soul and mind as did her sister, Mary, who listened. Thus her necessary preparations were all drudgery and no delight.

The Meaning of the Mundane

In the busyness of preparing our meals, we need to see the meaning in the mundane, the delight beyond the drudgery. We do not merely prepare feedings (as if for animals). The simplest meal, even when we are alone, can be a communion with God through his creation—which is why we say grace before we eat. To gather foods from garden or orchard is to be reminded of the richness and diversity of creation; God said, "Everything that lives and moves will be food for you" (Gen 9:3). Likewise the peeling, chopping and slicing of vegetables, the testing and tasting of sauces, the kneading and shaping of breads are both labor and a means of loving. Meals can sustain both body and soul, and can with care be celebrations of all that it means to be a human being made in the image of God. This transformation, through loving preparation, of "feeding" into a meal becomes a way to love God with all our heart, soul, mind and strength.

The Ministry of Hospitality

But in North America we increasingly avoid the whole bother of meal preparation by eating out. More and more we rely on restaurants for "special" meals, not only for ourselves but also for a relief from the pressure of home hospitality.* Sometimes this substitute is a necessary means of coping with a busy schedule. But we should look with critical eyes at the busyness in our lives that keeps us from preparing meals for family* and friends. We would do well to remember Jesus' example and the biblical maxim to "practice hospitality" (Rom 12:13). Preparing meals is part of a larger pattern of opening our home* life to others. Giving up meal preparation can be a danger signal of Martha-living versus Mary-listening.

Part of the problem may be that we have so increased our expectations of how the house ought to look and what we ought to serve and how very perfect everything—including ourselves—should be that we have lost sight of the whole point of preparing a meal. A way back is to remember the beautiful phrase from Psalm 23: "You prepare a table before me." God creates a place for us always—no matter what is going on or who is around ("in the presence of my enemies").

Sometimes it is hard to rationalize the time it takes to make meals over and over, day in, day out. At such times we might find it helpful to take a slightly different approach to help us recover the joy of preparing and serving meals in the midst of all the work. Here are a few suggestions:

Make food from scratch. It is usually better that way and has more of your own love in it. But a good meal from basic ingredients need not be a complicated, multicourse extravagance. Soup and warm bread or biscuits can be deeply satisfying and mean only two preparations, a simple place setting and a minimum of up-and-down from the table after serving. Such a meal focuses attention on the daily bread of sustenance and on the enjoyment of the meal together.

Cook from ingredients obtained directly from their source. The plants and animals that produce our food are God's creations, not just raw material. Whether the ingredients be from our own garden or a farmer's market, knowing where our food comes from helps us to appreciate both those other creations and the kind of husbandry that brings them to our table. Our urban culture often traps us as unknowing participants in patterns of agriculture that we would deplore if we knew about them. Checking out the sources of our food and buying from farmers who care about the creatures they grow for us can shift us, and our whole society, toward patterns of life that are more responsible to creation and Creator.

Serve with creativity. Any meal—even toast and tea—gains elegance and a great deal of spiritual and emotional flavor from the way it is served. A tablecloth and folded cloth napkins, wood or pottery serving bowls (or even shells for jam or a sauce), candles—any one of these can transform a simple meal into a statement: "We love you; we care for you; we want this meal to be a special time for you."

Prepare a meal with friends. If the prospect of making a complicated meal seems overwhelming, one wonderful solution is to cook it together with our guests. When we work alongside friends to accomplish a goal—such as making a casserole or a pie—often the getting-to-know-each-other part of the meal is made easy. When our hands and bodies are busy, our souls can relax from the social pressure to say the right bright thing.

Celebrate the Lord's Supper in the context of a real meal. All meals have been hallowed by the meal of bread and wine that Jesus gave to his disciples as a pattern of remembering for all believers. Usually our Communion meal is a pale wafer-and-sip substitute for the richly meaningful complete meal, the Seder supper, that is the ancient Hebrew origin of the Christian Eucharist. Placing Communion in the midst of that meal—or any meal—is a way of restoring community to Christian Communion.

In 2 Kings, a war was averted when the king of Israel, at Elisha's command, prepared a great feast and served it to the raiding bands from Aran. Our meals may not stop wars, but they may be one of the best ways to bring family members, friends and churches together.

See also EATING; HOMEMAKING; HOSPITALITY.

References and Resources

R. F. Capon, *Supper of the Lamb* (New York: Harvest Books/Harcourt Brace Jovanovich, 1969); A. Schmemann, *For the Life of the World* (Crestwood, N.Y.: St. Vladimir's Seminary Press, 1982); J. H. Schlabach, *Extending the Table* (Scottdale, Penn.: Herald Press, 1991); M. Zimmerman, *Celebrate the Feasts* (Minneapolis: Bethany House, 1981).

Mary Ruth Wilkinson

MEALS. *See* EATING; MEAL PREPARATION.

—MENSTRUATION—

The menstrual cycle can be a source of frustration, anxiety and pain. Not only is my cycle highly irregular, but I suffer from a more extreme type of dysmenorrhea. I have accepted some treatments and chosen to reject others. Most women experience only mild symptoms, but I am one of the unfortunate few. Though I often dialogue with God on these matters, my end of the conversation usually consists of fragmented thoughts: *Oh God, please do not let me get my period today—I've got so much to do! Oh, why didn't you make me like my friends who barely notice their cycle? Why does this have to interfere with my life? Oh, make this pain go away . . . please!* But recently I have been engaging in a new stream of reflection. It is an inquiry into the relationship between my spiritual formation and my unique monthly rhythms.

The Spirituality of Every Month Life

If God is forming me spiritually in my everyday life, is he doing the same in my "every month" life? If he is involved in the very dimension of routine that causes me such frustration and anxiety, then surely he is present in every other aspect of my life. If he can work through my menstrual cycle to form me into all he knows me to be, then he can work through every other "nonspiritual" part of my life.

The physiological event and the rhythms of menstruation are not only biological processes. Psychological research has attested to the fact that these are an integral part of women's emotional lives (*see* Femininity). And if this is so, then any discussion of spirituality for women cannot afford to ignore them. The type of gnostic dualism that divorces the spiritual from the body may have done far more harm to Christian women throughout history than to Christian men.

In her reflection on family spirituality, Wendy Wright discusses the importance of setting this dualism aright:

In contradistinction to our Christian heritage that has been shaped by men's perceptions and has drunk deep of philosophical springs that often make a sharp distinction between body and spirit, the experience of woman in family cannot separate the two. Woman's attention is given much of the time, at least subliminally, to the experience of being held and entered, to the cyclical wetness and dryness of fertility and infertility, to the flow and cessation of menstruation, to the profound body-changes of pregnancy, to the fluids of lactation, to the carrying, washing, feeding, and caressing of bodies, to the physical sensations of menopause. To pray a woman's prayer is to celebrate . . . and grieve out of the miracle of the female body. It is to pray the whole person, body and spirit entwined. It is to pray with the rhythms of all created life. (113-14)

For a woman to set out to learn to pray with the rhythms of her created life is to embark on a lifelong journey.

The menstrual cycle itself is a fruitful concept for spiritual reflection. One can consider its link with the miracle of life and reproduction or images of the womb in Scripture (Ps 139). It involves the flow of blood, which is a rich symbol in the Christian faith, related to our salvation. The changes from one stage of the month to another are reminders of all the cycles of life.

Menstruation reminds us of how sin has affected women. Menstrual disorders are linked to childbearing pain, the first result of sin mentioned in Genesis 3:16. Both the groaning and the curse lead me to consider the other result—patriarchy. Though as a woman I live in an unjust world that oftentimes oppresses women, I am sustained by a God who, through incarnation as the Word, displayed once and for all that he is not a patriarchal tyrant. On the contrary, Jesus came to set me free from the law of sin and death, and he inaugurated the kingdom within which the effects of the curse begin to dissipate. I feel especially comforted by his act of healing a bleeding woman, which is found in all three of the Synoptic Gospels (Mt 9:20-22; Mk 5:25-34; Lk 8:43-48). Although through the centuries misreadings of Old Testament regulations for women such as Leviticus 15:19-31 have "canonized the view that something natural to women . . . was especially unsuitable for intimacy with God" (Carmody, 20), Jesus clearly demonstrated a profound distinction under the new covenant by drawing public attention to his willingness to become unclean by touching and healing this woman.

Reflection has also led me to see that the structure of my experience month after tedious month shapes my spiritual life. It does this by providing built-in gifts that I would never be drawn to seek voluntarily but are gifts nevertheless.

Rhythms of Grace
First, my cycle ensures that I am given weeks of peak performance. I tackle my tasks with strong determination, efficiency and abundant energy. I sleep* peacefully, love* courageously and laugh at life. It is not difficult to see the gift of God here, although it must be acknowledged that these weeks would not seem so precious were it not for the others. After ovulation I experience a time in which my emotions are tender, and I am prone

to tears. I have tended to label this as just an emotional shift caused by fluctuating hormones, but I am beginning to see that it is more. Through the shift God often miraculously grants me a deeper awareness of his loving heart, as well as a softening of my heart toward family* and friends.

The part of my cycle that causes me the most consternation is the week or more in which I invariably experience many symptoms of what is commonly called premenstrual syndrome. Symptoms may include water retention (causing tenderness, bloatedness, weight gain, backaches), altered blood sugar levels (causing hostility, headaches, food cravings), and sodium and potassium imbalance (causing fatigue, tension, depression; Wilson, 21-30). The term *PMS* has been mindlessly applied to all women, even though evidence suggests that only a small percentage of women suffer from the syndrome. Most women merely experience normal premenstrual changes.

During this time I feel extremely jittery, experiencing elevated levels of unrest, irritability, anxiety and tension. This change invariably drives me back to God, for it is then that I become aware of my deep need for the power of the Holy Spirit to live a holy life. At other times I rely heavily on my habits of courtesy and deference in my relationships and forget to love with his strength. But during PMS days the illusion of niceness is shattered. I come face to face with the awful humiliation of knowing that without his love I am nothing. Without a continual prayer for his love to overcome my irritability, I am completely capable of treating those closest to me with angry injustice. Without God's intervention the potential for discord and heated conflict lurks in my very cells.

This experience is a matter for both a

theological and an experiential understanding of sanctification. How do I walk the balance between being compassionate with myself during a vexing temptation and simultaneously taking responsibility for my own actions, refusing to slough off any sin committed by blaming it on "that time of the month"? This is the time when I am especially conscious of the war of sin within me.

The most disheartening part of my monthly life is the actual onset of menstruation. This is due to the extreme nature of my dysmenorrhea—debilitating cramping that causes pain to shoot outward from my uterus to my entire body. I feel the pain from the tips of my fingers to the tips of my toes. If I fail to take medication at the first awareness of cramping, I will invariably spend an hour or two huddled on the floor in agony. After this, medication and the administration of heat dull the pain to a tiring ache that puts me out of commission for a day and leaves me in need of extra rest for another.

There are many reasons why this is a discouraging time. Because my cycle is highly irregular, I cannot accurately predict the exact day I should expect my period. My body can spend days sending me false alarms in the form of cramping; this has often led me to refuse to act, certain my period will interfere. Often it does not. So it is with resolve that I have recently begun to change my perspective and be as engaged in life as I can, until the moment the real pain strikes. This shift to active waiting, to participating fully in plans and forming commitments, knowing they may be abruptly canceled, is a metaphor of the life of the church as we await the return of Jesus. While we live and act in anticipation, we are not to "stand here looking into the sky" (Acts 1:11). The unpredictability of such a disrupting event gives me twelve times each year to decide to accept

God's timing or resent it and chafe at it.

Accepting the timing is no easy task, for menstruation often comes in what I judge to be extremely poor timing—in the midst of a crucial assignment or just before a long-anticipated celebration. I do not control my cycle, but I can choose my response. This means twelve opportunities a year to practice submission and acceptance.

The recurring encounter with physical pain is also part of my discipleship. Although the pain is to a certain extent controllable, is always alleviated each month and is from a known cause, I monthly share in the fellowship of suffering with those who suffer chronic pain. I wonder what level of patience I would be able to maintain with others' physical ills in the absence of this always-ready-to-return experience. Through sharpness of pain God sharpens my compassion, as Tilden Edwards also observes: "Though I hate aching, I recognize that tinge of grace in it that brings me closer to the suffering side of everyone, and opens up a little more compassion" (Edwards, 208). My own experience with pain means that I join the many, identifying with and learning from their insights. As Christians we are called neither to masochistically enjoy pain nor to focus much attention on the cause of suffering. Rather we are to take concern for our own reactions to it. The result: God often appears to be concerned with is our spiritual formation (Rom 5:3-5; Heb 12:10-11; Jas 1:2-4; 1 Pet 1:6-7). If this is so, then my own responses to bodily aching each month need redemption so that I may become more like Christ.

So the question becomes, How can I give God my trust, believing that he will bring something of value from the inevitable down days in my life's rhythm? And if this commitment is the decision to rejoice, then I am led to an even more difficult question: How can I rejoice in the midst of what, on the surface, would seem to be an entirely unredeemable part of my everyday life? The answer may lie primarily in an openness to the truth that God is present and wants to bless me with that presence—not only in the structure of my cycle but also in the days of suffering themselves. It is through a new awareness of that presence that I will be able to rejoice at *all* times of the month (Phil 4:4-5).

God is present in my menstrual period, not through any conjuring of my own, but through his grace, a concept I experience yet hardly comprehend. Tim Hansel maintains that our limitations can "become the very invitation to discover fully the dimensions of grace, the improbable path to God's otherwise hidden blessing" (Hansel, 108-9). Through the limitations imposed by my menstrual period, God issues an invitation to experience his gracious presence in ways that are otherwise foreign to my daily life.

Menstrual Sabbath

The most prevalent obstacle to entering this "invitation to life" is my propensity for what Susan Muto and Adrian van Kaam call *functionalism*. Functionalism takes over our lives when we "feel pushed and pulled to perform efficiently and effectively, no matter what suffers . . . [thinking that] to do is vastly more important than to be" (Muto and van Kaam, 146). Christians are not exempt from functionalism, for we come to value service as the meaning and measure of Christian commitment. If we relax, the guilt we exhale shakes the unvoiced conviction that the only meaning of life is to be useful to God. The fruits of functionalism are incompatible with grace. How better to come face to face with grace than through a humdrum time when "my relationship with the world is one of giving in and giving up, surrendering, yielding, and letting go," when I must "renounce temporarily all agent and manipulative purposes" (Cummings, 71)? How better to let grace heal my overrefined conscience, which convinces me that to see a need is to incur an obligation to meet that need? How better to let grace set me free from the "cramping legalism of time" (McConnell, 69)? How better to renounce self-justification and grasp the significance of the gospel I so often betray with my functionalistic lifestyle—that it is through Christ's work alone that I find worth, acceptance and justification?

Precisely because it is a useless and unproductive time, my monthly menstruation is one of the means that God, in his grace, has given me for dealing with the principalities and powers (Eph 6:12) that exploit my weakness in this area. Parker Palmer believes there is a vast conspiracy against such times. So it is vital to pay attention to those unintentional moments that come "whether or not we seek them, are ready for them, or know what to do when they arrive" (Palmer, 26). I have no control over the limitation of painful, exhausting menstruation. But it is possible for me to more consciously pay attention to God's grace in the quiet, contemplative moments that come unbidden during each monthly downtime. A helpful way to do this is to view this time as a type of sabbath.*

There are a striking number of sabbath elements present in my time of menstruation. Marva Dawn describes four elements of sabbath: ceasing, resting, embracing, feasting. With the exception of the last, all are possible within these two days each month. Ceasing is the most naturally embedded in my experience precisely because my body is too exhausted to allow any other response. In my debilitated state I cease not only from work but also from anxiety, from my "incessant need to produce and accomplish" (Dawn, 29) and from my self-sufficient striving to be god of my life. This stems not from a noble heart but from a weary heart that has no choice but to let go. I become acutely aware of my poverty.

There is more intentionality involved in resting. I can choose to go beyond physical repose to spiritual rest. I recall times when I have received spiritual rest in the midst of the aching, the moments when God has had my exclusive attention and we have had meandering conversations. But I am now interested in how I might set aside this recovery time as an intentional sabbath, embracing sabbath values. I can choose to deliberately fulfill the spirit of the command to keep the sabbath by cultivating an attitude of "rejoicing in God's care, trusting dependence . . . renewed dedication to him . . . remembrance of his saving deeds" (Cummings, 73). Is this possible in the midst of physical pain? After the first few hours of sharp pain are gone, it is.

Wasting Time with God

My menstrual period can make space in my life for what Richard Foster calls the *sabbath prayer* or the *prayer of rest*. I am in no shape for long bouts of intercessory or authoritative prayer. But I can choose to renounce both manipulative control over God and my world and "listless passivity" in favor of leaning into cultivation of solitude, silence and recollection. After abstaining from normal patterns of activity and interaction in order to discover that my strength comes from God alone, I need to go further and renounce all the "agitated creaturely activity" of grasping control, which hinders God's work in me (Foster, 101). This is an active choice, for without it my menstrual period can easily

degenerate into an impatient time of frittering away the aching hours with television or novels or demanding my husband's company in my misery. But if I cannot engage in this type of prayer during a day characterized by the grace of limitations, how do I expect to do it on any other day?

Foster encourages me to radically alter my expectation of menstruation, to look forward to the recovery hours as a lovers' tryst with God: "Our Eternal Lover lures us back regularly into his presence with anticipation and delight. . . . We are glad to waste time with God, for we are pleased with the company" (Foster, 77). And as I know from my walk with him, "the hour of discomfort and anxiety is totally forgotten. What we remember forever is the hour of love" (Saunders, as quoted in L'Engle, 33). To engage in sabbath prayer is to encounter God not only in that moment but in all of everyday life. It is also to bow to the truth that God's purposes for my life (unlike my own) do not need to be revised to adjust to limitations embedded in any part of my menstrual cycle. Rather, the rhythms of my life move according to his original plan. My call is to be alert to the realization that these rhythms find true life within the larger rhythms of God's amazing grace.

See also FEMININITY; SABBATH; SEXUALITY.

References and Resources

D. L. Carmody, *Biblical Women* (New York: Crossroad, 1988); C. Cummings, *The Mystery of the Ordinary* (San Francisco: Harper & Row, 1982); M. J. Dawn, *Keeping the Sabbath Wholly* (Grand Rapids: Eerdmans, 1989); T. Edwards, *Living Simply Through the Day* (New York: Paulist, 1977); M. J. Evans, *Woman in the Bible* (Downers Grove, Ill.: InterVarsity Press, 1983); R. Foster, *Prayer* (San Francisco: Harper & Row, 1992); T. Hansel, *You Gotta Keep Dancin'* (Elgin, Ill.: David C.

Cook, 1985); M. L'Engle, *And It Was Good* (Wheaton, Ill.: Harold Shaw, 1983); W. T. McConnell, *The Gift of Time* (Downers Grove, Ill.: InterVarsity Press, 1983); S. Muto and A. van Kaam, *Commitment: Key to Christian Maturity* (New York: Paulist, Press, 1989); P. J. Palmer, *The Active Life* (New York: Harper-Collins, 1990); R. Wilson, *Controlling Pre-Menstrual Syndrome* (Markham, Ont.: Fitzhenry & Whiteside, 1988); W. M. Wright, *Sacred Dwelling* (New York: Crossroad, 1990).

Valerie Pyke Parks

MINISTRY. See CHORES; MISSION; PARENTING; SPIRITUAL FORMATION.

—MISCARRIAGE—

Miscarriage is increasingly being given significance as not only the loss of pregnancy* but the untimely death* of an individual person who has to some extent been part of a family* (*see* Conception). In the eyes of society, miscarriage often occurs unnoticed. The lost child is unseen, unnamed and unacknowledged. There are often no physical remains to bury in rituals that usually afford comfort to the grieving family. It can be a lonely vigil—shock, ambivalence, guilt and anger. Unfortunately, it can be a time of alienation, rejection and shame.* The premature death of these unbeheld children confronts us with our own mortality and provokes us to wrestle with the meaning of human suffering.

Multifaceted Loss

Kowalski notes that "perinatal death encompasses each type of loss—loss of a significant person, loss of some aspect of the self (reproductive health), loss of external objects, loss of a stage of life, loss of a dream inherent in the parents' desire to have a child and loss of creation" (cited in Ney, 1193). There is a growing trend to encourage couples to realize the full extent of their loss especially if later on in pregnancy. By holding, naming, blessing* and saying farewell to their stillborn children and by keeping mementos: footprints, a hair lock, photographs or ultrasound images, the bereavement process is facilitated.

Parents' involvement in a memorial service when there is no body may be helpful even if only "two or three come together" and informally share their feelings (Mt 18:20). The value of rituals cannot be overstated. We use them to navigate the passages of birth, initiation, marriage* and death. Live born children are blessed and welcomed after birth by passing through water (in many Christian traditions). A stillborn child can be transformed by ceremony to a properly deceased person with a soul that has been commended to God, giving the grieving closure.

Although each person responds individually, there are accepted patterns and tasks of grieving. Initially uncertainty progresses to shock and denial. Parents may express anger outwardly as injustice or inwardly as guilt as they accept the reality of the loss. During the stage of searching and yearning they identify and release their distress, sorrow and pain. Disorganization occurs as they adjust to life without the thoughts and plans for the new baby. Painful reminders of the miscarriage occur when having to tell others the news, seeing the nursery, pregnant women or other babies, marking the first menstrual period, sexual intercourse, the baby's due date and the anniversary of the loss. During the stage of reorientation parents successfully withdraw emotional energy from the loss and reinvest it in other activities and plans for the future.

The degree of prenatal bonding and grief may vary considerably. Each woman's experience is uniquely influenced by what the pregnancy meant to her and her family. Some factors that influence the perceived value of the pregnancy include the ease of becoming pregnant, the perceived age of the mother and pressure to conceive, and whether the pregnancy was planned. An experienced mother may have a deeper sense of loss, having endowed the unborn child with specific characteristics and perhaps even a name. Alternatively they may sense some relief if the pregnancy had come sooner than planned. Women who have not successfully carried a child to term may feel more profound doubt of their reproductive health. If an ultrasound examination has been done, the images add to the reality of the fetal existence as do hearing fetal heartbeats and perceiving movements that may have been shared with a spouse and other children. Also, the duration of the anticipatory time during the warning symptoms of bleeding and cramping can influence her attachment and hope.

Adding to the complexity of the recovery, a D & C (surgical dilatation and curettage) may be required to remove remaining placental and decaying fetal tissue that have not passed spontaneously, preventing ongoing bleeding and infection. The operation itself may be perceived as a possible threat to the mother's health and, despite ultrasound confirmation of the fetal death, in periods of uncertainty or denial she may feel that they are taking her baby. In later stages of gestational death, when a D &

C is not possible, induction of labor after a brief but agonizing waiting period is often recommended for the protection of the mother's health. Labor and birth ensue with no reward of a child's cry.

Unfortunately, caregivers may be vulnerable to frustration when "they cannot cure." They may be paternalistic, indifferent, impatient and unfamiliar with grief. Giving permission to express a range of feelings, providing explanations and information, checking back for understanding, giving specific directions about what to expect and do during recovery, adequate pain control and compassionate listening* are all valuable ways to assist a woman through this difficult time. Specific reassurances include the fact that miscarriages are common and represent an inevitable process that cannot be prevented or arrested by maternal or medical efforts. It is nature taking its course.

Specific concerns may arise about the cause of death, requiring many follow-up visits to unravel all the nagging questions and worries. It is particularly valuable to address unnecessary guilt for causing or failing to prevent the loss. Scientific evidence suggests that physical activity, vomiting, sexual intercourse, stress and ambivalent feelings toward the pregnancy do *not* cause miscarriage. Toxins and disease are rarely causes of miscarriage. As science unravels the mystery of conception,* evidence points to a staggering degree of naturally occurring loss from perhaps half of all fertilized ova failing to implant, to many pregnancies that are lost during late menstrual flow before their presence is even surmised. A significant number of examined embryos and fetuses that have spontaneously miscarried have microscopically evident chromosomal abnormalities. It is probable that genetic errors detectable on a molecular level and immunologic rejection will likely account for the balance. Although this may provide reassurance that the pregnancy "wasn't meant to be," many families feel the additional blow of failure and guilt that an abnormality has occurred and ambivalence toward losing something "less than what was intended." Disappointment in God's apparent lack of intervention on behalf of their child can be difficult to express.

Response of the Family

Partners grieve but often express themselves in different ways. The intensity, duration and progression of responses are not usually synchronous. A delicate balance alternating between intense communication and the guarding of each other's solitude is necessary for couples to respect and support one another at this time. Couples who share intimately can enlighten each other's darkness and carry faith for one another at a time when hope seems lost. We must, however, ultimately trust that God will answer us in places of deepest questioning and doubt, strengthening our faith through adversity.

Siblings experience their own grief and need to be comforted. Excluding children by withholding news of what has occurred or failing to share feelings can alienate them. In the absence of age-appropriate explanations, children are prone to fantasy and a correspondingly greater degree of distress. "Magical thinking," whereby children imagine they have caused the death of a sibling, is common and needs to be addressed. At this time especially, children need to be validated. Children born after a pregnancy loss can become "replacement children" and may experience increased parental expectations and confusion of their identity. Ideally, the deceased sibling is neither forgotten nor replaced, and the family can embrace a new child fully and uniquely.

From Despair to Hope

It is little wonder that in many cultures pregnancy is kept secret until it no longer can be concealed. Technology can now provide confirmation at earlier stages of the presence of this new individual. There are Scriptures that affirm our belonging and intrinsic value even in utero (Job 10:8-11; Ps 22:9-10; 139:13-16), and it is clear that pregnancy loss was mourned even in biblical times. A progression can be traced from Old Testament to New Testament that is analogous to the grieving process itself, leading us from despair to hope.

Jeremiah, in profound depression,* cursed himself and the man who told his father of his birth (Jer 20:14-18). Job also cried: "Why then did you bring me out of the womb? / I wish I had died before any eye saw me." (Job 10:18). "Why was I not hidden in the ground like a stillborn child, / like an infant who never saw the light of day?" (Job 3:16). Scripture does not euphemize, gloss over or glorify death.

In David's grief for the loss of his son conceived after adultery and murder, we see premature death as an unalterable state associated with guilt. "Can I bring him back again? I will go to him, but he will not return to me" (2 Sam 12:23). Premature death sometimes counts as death incurred through sin (1 Sam 2:3; Job 22:15; 36:14). However, a careful look at Genesis 2 reveals that there is a distinction made between threatened death that is deserved and death that belongs to the natural state of the creature. Death, when it finally occurs, is explained in reminiscence of man's creation:

You return to the ground,
  since from it you were taken;
for dust you are
  and to dust you will return. (Gen 3:19)

The psalmist tells us that God's hand

reaches into the world of the dead (Ps 139:8). The first heralding of the resurrection occurs in Isaiah 26:19: "Your dead will live, their bodies will rise." The author of Revelation assures us that "God himself will be with them and be their God. He will wipe every tear from their eyes. There will be no more death or mourning or crying or pain" (Rev 21:3-4). God's promise is that this time of anguish will pass making way for the hope of ultimate healing and reconciliation. In contemplating the earthly tragedy of the Piéta—Mary cradling her dead son—we find ourselves full circle from the stable. Relinquished is the hope shared by all parents that we will be the ones cradled in old age by our surviving children. The miscarried or stillborn child is a person whose development is interrupted by natural defects, an extinguished flame that awaits final consummation when they, with us, will be fully restored in the likeness of Christ.

See also CONCEPTION; DEATH; PREGNANCY.

References and Resources
E. C. Hui, *Questions of Right and Wrong* (Vancouver: Regent College, 1994); D. Manca, "Women's Experience of Miscarriage," *Canadian Family Physician* 37 (September 1991) 1871-77; G. G. Márquez, *The Circle of Life: Rituals from the Human Family Album* (San Francisco: Harper, 1991); P. Ney, "The Effects of Pregnancy Loss on Children's Health," *Social Science Medicine* 38, no 9 (1994) 1193-1200; K. B. Nielson, "The Day the Heart Beat Stopped," *Focus on the Family* (March 1993) 10-11; R. Smolan, *The Power to Heal* (New York: Prentice Hall, 1990); R. W. Swanson, "Parents Experiencing Perinatal Loss: The Physician's Role," *Canadian Family Physician* 32 (March 1986) 599-602; D. van Biema, "The Journey of our Lives," *Life* (October 1991); H. W. Wolff, *Anthropology of the Old Testament* (Philadelphia: Fortress, 1974).

Carol Anderson

—MISSION—

Christian family* is first and finally the life of the church. It includes singles and marrieds, those with and without children—all called to exercise unique but complementary missionary advantages. Its purpose is to witness, through its shape and practice, to the kingdom of the God. Christian family is where we live not so much in a "private" haven from the world but in a mission base to the world. But it is also where we learn to "do" mission as rest and play,* where welcoming friends and reading novels and planting gardens and making babies are among our most noble moral endeavors. It is where we do our most strenuous and refreshing work—for what could be more strenuous and more refreshing than rearing children?

Singles and Family Mission
One of the immediate effects of Jesus' creation of a new family is that unmarried people are very much a part of family. It was in the light of the kingdom come that Paul could write, "He who marries his fiancée does well; and he who refrains from marriage will do better" (1 Cor 7:38 NRSV). How could singleness be better than marriage? Paul recognized that the age of the kingdom does not come painlessly. Jesus announced and embodied God's kingdom; the church after him witnesses to this Lord and his kingdom. The rule of the principalities and powers—the undue, overreaching

claims of governments, markets, fashions, cultures, educational and other institutions—is revealed to be illegitimate and ultimately destructive. Because the powers of the old age remain real and often malignant, Christians can survive only with the hope of Jesus' return and the complete manifestation of God's loving, just rule.

In these circumstances, Paul notices that the married person may sink more deeply into the affairs of the passing world than singles (1 Cor 7:33). With spouse and children, the married person takes on additional responsibilities and anxieties. The single person can live and serve in less complicated "devotion to the Lord" (1 Cor 7:35).

For our day, Paul's awareness of the advantages of singleness can serve as a reminder that in the Christian (or first) family, singleness and marriage* are complementary. Christian parenting,* for instance, is a task for the entire church. It is a responsibility (as baptismal ceremonies in many traditions imply) even for those who have never conceived or legally adopted a child. This is not to dispute the primacy of biological or adoptive parents. But in Jesus' and Paul's first family, Christian parents are agents of the church. And they are engaged in a task too big and important for them alone. Single Christians should not be exempt from either the joys or the responsibilities that children bring. Singles are significant role models. In a transient society where many children are separated from biological relatives by thousands of miles, singles can serve invaluably as surrogate grandparents or aunts and uncles (a service most important, of course, to the parent without a spouse—see Single Parenting).

Serving the church's mission, singles also have the advantage of mobility.* On balance, it is simpler for the single, should it seem right, to move to a new sit-uation, to make do with less money or even to confront potentially dangerous circumstances. This is not something for married Christians to exploit: no Christian, married with children or not, is exempt from moving, giving up possessions or facing danger. Yet singles can affirm a unique missionary advantage and take it seriously.

Marriage and Family Mission

If singles have the missionary advantage of mobility, married Christians may possess the missionary advantage of hospitality.* Christians are peculiar people with a long tradition of welcoming strangers. God called the Israelites to love and care for strangers, since they were strangers themselves in the land of Egypt (Lev 19:33-34; Deut 10:17-19). Jesus welcomed strangers or outsiders of many sorts, even to the point of inviting them to table with him. So too the early church put hospitality at the center of its life. As noted (see Family), Christians generously opened their homes to fellow believers. Christians are called to be hospitable within both the first family of the church and the second, or biological, family, and Paul effusively praises families whose homes are the hub of the church in several cities (Rom 16:5, 23; 1 Cor 16:15; Col 4:15; Philem 2).

Among the significant strangers Christian parents must welcome are their own children. Our children are strangers to us in many ways: they come to us as aliens and have to learn to live in our world; they ask awkward questions ("If Christians are supposed to love each other, how can they kill each other in wars?" "Why is God letting my little sister die of cancer?") that remind us how strange we are. Christian parenthood, then, is practice in hospitality. Welcoming the strangers who are our children, we learn a little about being out of control and about the possibility of surprise (and so of hope). Moment by mundane moment—dealing with rebellion, hosting birthday* parties, struggling to understand exactly what a toddler has dreamed and been so frightened by in the night—we pick up skills in patience, empathy, generosity, forgiveness.* And all these are transferable skills that we can and must use to welcome other strangers besides our children. We become better equipped to open ourselves to strangers who are not our children but our brothers and sisters in Christ. Thus the Christian home can be a mission base in many ways.

The Christian Home as Mission Base

The Christian home is a mission base when Christians live in intentional community. But the Christian home is also a mission base when Christians who happen to live in the same neighborhood enjoy meals together, share a lawnmower and tree-trimming tools, or "exchange" kids for an occasional evening.

The Christian home is a mission base when members of a church move into the same apartment complex, sponsor Bible studies and organize supervision of the playground. It is a mission base when it takes in a teenager who has been evicted from home, or a spouse going through marriage difficulties needing time away. It is a mission base when it opens its doors to missionaries on furlough, friends marooned between apartment leases, someone out of work or a family that has lost its home to a fire. It is a mission base providing us resources and encouragement from which to launch into new mission endeavors—whether across town or across the world.

In a world that offers less and less nominal support for Christian practices, in a world increasingly fragmented, hostile and lonely, there is no end to ways the Christian home can serve as a mission base. The limit, quite literally, is our imagination.

See also CHARACTER; FAMILY; HOSPITALITY; MOBILITY; PARENTING; SINGLE PARENTING; SPIRITUAL FORMATION.

References and Resources

R. S. Anderson and D. B. Guernsey, *On Being Family: A Social Theology of the Family* (Grand Rapids: Eerdmans, 1985); B. Berger and P. L. Berger, *The War over the Family* (Garden City, N.Y.: Doubleday, 1983); R. Clapp, *Families at the Crossroads: Beyond Traditional and Modern Options* (Downers Grove, Ill.: InterVarsity Press, 1993); M. Eastman, *Family, The Vital Factor: The Key to Society's Survival* (Melbourne: Collins Dove, 1989); D. E. Garland and D. R. Garland, "The Family: Biblical and Theological Perspectives," in *Incarnational Ministry: The Presence of Christ in Church, Society and Family*, ed. C. D. Kettler and T. H. Speidell (Colorado Springs: Helmers & Howard, 1990) 226-40; S. Hauerwas, *A Community of Character* (Notre Dame, Ind.: University of Notre Dame Press, 1981) 155-95; J. A. Henley, *Accepting Life: The Ethics of Living in Families* (Melborne: The Joint Board of Christian Education, 1994); W. H. Willimon, *The Service of God* (Nashville: Abingdon, 1983), 170-86; N. T. Wright, *The New Testament and the People of God* (Minneapolis: Fortress, 1992).

Rodney Clapp

—MOBILITY—

Mobility is a way of life in modern societies, especially in newer ones like the United States, Canada and Australia. In these countries approximately one person in five moves each year.

People move not only within countries but also between them. In some cases, such as the northward drift to the United States from various parts of Latin America, this is motivated by the dream of a better life. Within a generation Hispanics will number more than 50 percent of the population of cities like Los Angeles. In other cases people are driven from their own country or feel compelled to leave it because of persecution, oppression or even genocide. On a different level altogether, travel and tourism have become big business, resulting in increasing numbers of people moving intensively and extensively around various parts of the world as well as around their own countries.

Though they reside in one location, most people frequently move around cities or regions over long distances on a daily or weekly basis. Some work is mainly mobile. This is true for drivers, salespeople, journalists, deliverers, realtors, seasonal workers, sailors and pilots. In some cases previously fixed workplaces are becoming mobile, especially as cars develop into complete mobile office systems with cellular phone, fax machine, word processor, printer and even perhaps two-way radio. Employees are also moving more frequently from workplace to workplace or from one line of work to another. Virtually gone are the days of the lifetime company employee: the average worker now holds down five or more different types of job during the course of a lifetime.

Why Are We So Mobile?

The roots of mobility in newer Western societies lie primarily in their mobile beginnings. These countries were entered by people who chose or were forced to move to them. Once there, many immigrants did not stay in one place but continued to move across the countryside. It was Frederick Jackson Turner who, toward the end of the last century, first argued that the experience of successive frontiers in the United States significantly shaped individual character and democratic institutions in America. The frontier mentality was characterized by repeated hopes for improvement, by struggles with primitive conditions, by an emphasis on expediency and acquisitiveness, by restless energy and optimism, by individualism and materialism. Though the outcome was somewhat different in Canada and Australia, where the wilderness was not won but itself won against the intruders, the expansion of people into open spaces and their movement between them still had a marked effect.

Somewhere in the midst of this ongoing mobility a subtle but decisive change took place. The immigrants' belief that their hopes would be fulfilled if they could find the right place in which to settle down turned into the belief that the very process of continually moving was itself the way to experience fulfillment. In his influential book Wendell Berry calls this the *unsettling*, rather than the *settling*, of America, for people tended to exploit, rather than care for, the land on which they settled and, when they realized this, left it behind for greener pastures. This exploiting and leaving was the beginning of the disposable society, which eventually transformed itself into the phenomenon of the disposable individual, one who successively leaves a worn-out or failed version of the self behind and by moving on again and again hopes to remake or reinvent his or her selfhood.

What Are the Effects of Mobility?

Mobility can have a number of positive effects. These include freedom from persecution or a restrictive context and the opportunity to begin again, to move to a healthier or simply more pleasant environment, to get closer to family* or leave behind an abusive situation, to increase educational or cultural possibilities, to find a better job and commute fewer hours, to develop a lifestyle more consistent with basic values,* or to fulfill a sense of vocation or mission.*

There can also be negative effects. Among these are the loss of a sense of roots and place, leaving behind extended family and friends, difficulties in readjusting, higher levels of restlessness, a diminished desire and capacity to become committed to people and contexts, and a tendency toward greater relativism in beliefs and values. Though few people are aware of it, the increase in mobility during the last century has also increased the degree of bureaucratic control and regulation of people moving or traveling.

A significant effect of mobility that people do not take sufficiently into account is an increase in levels of stress.* The Social Readjustment Rating Scale helps people determine how much stress they are likely to encounter as they undergo various experiences. As well as a change in residence (20 points), a move generally involves a change in schools (26 points), a different line of work (36 points) or work responsibilities (29 points), a spouse's having to stop or begin work (26 points), and a change in church (19 points) and social activities (18 points). Sometimes a move involves increased marital arguments (35 points), separation from a member of the immediate family (29 points), or a change in living conditions (25 points) or in recreational habits (19 points). When we add the energy expended on adapting to a different climate and to unfamiliar locations, these points often add up to a fair degree of stress: once they reach 300, there is a 90 percent probability of people's experiencing

acute insomnia and developing an illness.

Finally, mobility involves a change in churches, which deprives the congregation left behind of the ongoing presence and contribution of those who are moving. One of the most serious unrecognized factors militating against developing community in local churches today is that roughly 20 percent of their members are turning over each year, among them some of their most committed people. How do you build deep community in such a transient setting?

What Does the Bible Say About Mobility?

The Bible presents us with a complex picture of people moving around and staying put. Significant figures within the nation of Israel and among the early Christians—from Abraham through Jonah to Paul—were highly mobile. This was largely true of Jesus himself. The lives of others, such as Moses and Peter, were a blend of mobility and stability. In contrast, others—like Solomon and James—had a largely settled existence. The nation of Israel itself went through long stretches of stability in Egypt and Canaan, intermixed with wanderings through the desert and a time of exile. In a deeper sense, as the writer to the Hebrews puts it, all these people were "longing for a better country—a heavenly one" (Heb 11:16), but this is not to say that their earthly existence was made up of continual pilgrimage.

Paul is an interesting example with regard to mobility. The apostle worked out the geographical boundaries within which he would move around and beyond which he would not go (Rom 15:19-20). Moreover, Paul did not equate the need or opportunity to do something with the call of God to attend to it—sometimes another factor also had to be present (2 Cor 2:12-13). He viewed his work as completed in a particular area once he had established it in an influential center from which it would spread elsewhere of its own accord (Rom 15:21-23). Except when Paul was forced out, he did not leave a place until he had completed what he had set out to do and had done so in a quality way (1 Cor 3:10-15). Furthermore, the apostle limited how much he attempted within these boundaries to the divine gifts and instructions he had been given, allowing others to look after the rest (Rom 12:3, 6). For all the difficulties and anxieties Paul encountered (2 Cor 11:26-27), overall he learned to be content in whatever circumstances he found himself (Phil 4:11-13).

What Are Our Criteria for Moving?

Building on the criteria found in Scripture and assuming there is no overriding decisive argument for moving, such as health* or lack of work, we ask what concrete guidance can be given to those contemplating a move.

First, make a list of all those affected by the decision. This would normally include family and relatives but should also cover friends, fellow churchgoers, colleagues and neighbors, as well as other people and institutions who have been part of your life and who will lose something by your leaving. This same list will help you assess how much you will lose through being physically separated from these people. Too often a decision to move is based purely on whether it will improve a person's job prospects or provide higher pay or whether relocation will be to a "nicer" area with a better climate. I know of more than one couple who decided that what they and their children were gaining from and giving to their church at the time was more important than a higher salary and status. In all this it is important to count the hidden costs and gains, internal as well as external, that are often overlooked in making a decision.

Second, if you do not have it already, develop a clear sense of your own values and priorities. What is most important to you in your life, and what priority would you give to those items at the top of the list? What would you most miss if all of a sudden you were deprived of it? What stage of life are you in or moving into with respect to family, work, Christian ministry and spiritual growth? If you have a spouse, what does he or she most require over the next few years, and what can you most give to or gain from the one closest to you? All too often decisions about staying or moving are made without springing from or taking into account the basic values around which our lives as Christians should revolve.

Third, work out where the authority lies for making the decision. Does it lie with the person who will be most advantaged by the move, often the male in the household? When a couple or children are involved, does the decision depend on both spouses coming to agreement or on the whole family, at least including children of a reasonable age, reaching a decision? When people belong to a small group, how much involvement should this primary Christian community have through asking questions, contributing wisdom, engaging in prayer and seeking a word of knowledge from God? What roles do nearby friends have in this process, since they will be seriously affected by the outcome? In other words, how is God's will best discerned in such a corporate situation as opposed to a matter that is purely individual or familial? Should a discernment group made of several confidants and key stakeholders be called together to help work through the issue?

Further Considerations

Two clarifications are in order. Sometimes the answer to the question about moving is neither yes nor no but *not yet.* Often a delay enables some factors that are hindering to dissolve or some of the reservations people are experiencing to dissipate. So waiting, which most people find difficult, is a genuine option. Also, deciding to stay rather than move is just as much a choice in its own right. Occasionally such a process unearths stronger grounds for staying than beforehand. Given the rate of mobility today, and its detrimental effects on community generally, the question that God may be asking of many people is not "Who will go for us?" but rather "Who will stay for us?" How else will community be revitalized and deepened in our churches, neighborhoods and cities today?

To whatever extent we are or are not mobile, most of us would benefit from knowing how to handle mobility better. It is helpful here to begin by identifying those aspects of the move that are most threatening or that promise the quickest rewards. Also, work out with family members concrete strategies for minimizing problems and maximizing satisfactions. Consider whatever plans you make as a commitment to those who find the move most difficult and put them into practice as soon as possible. Involve any willing to help in the move so that the burden is shared more widely. Try to find one person in your new location who can answer questions you might have, act as an interpreter of local customs and direct you to any services that may be helpful. Give yourselves a buffer zone of at least one or two weeks to prepare for the move and to settle in and recover from it.

See also AUTOMOBILE; FAMILY; HOME.

References and Resources

W. Berry, *The Unsettling of America: Culture and Agriculture* (New York: Avon, 1972); M. B. Emerson and C. Cameron, *Moving: The Challenge of Change* (Nashville: Abingdon, 1988); J. McInnes, *The New Pilgrims* (Sydney: Sutherland, 1980); J. Naisbitt, *Megatrends* (New York: Warner, 1982); W. Stegner, *The American West as Living Space* (Ann Arbor: University of Michigan Press, 1987); F. J. Turner, *The Frontier in American History* (New York: Henry Holt, 1920); J. A. Walter, *The Human Home: The Myth of the Sacred Environment* (Tring, Herts, U.K.: Lion, 1982).

Robert Banks

—MONEY—

Money matters. It seems that money, like sex,* is at the core of everything that we human beings do. The life-giving power of money in modern society is godlike. It is easy for the moral scold to declaim that it should not be so. But the simple fact is, like it or not, that money has nearly omnipotent control over the human race. Its powers range over life and death* and everything in between. Money matters very much because if we have it, we live, and if we have a lot of it, we flourish, we ascend to Olympian heights of freedom and power, and we live long and prosper. But without money, we perish, or if we have only a precious little of it, we (as much of the earth does) wallow in a squalor of mere subsistence. It does seem that money—mammon—rules the earth.

Money Matters to Families

Money has the authority to bestow food, shelter and facilities that are basic to lives of human dignity. In family life children learn that the presence or absence of money means the difference between good food and mere survival, between a family holiday or a summer spent doing chores* at home. Are we stingy, or overly generous, giving away at the slightest opportunity? Do we spend hours hunting down a bargain or pay full price because our "time is money"? Are we content with what we have or always striving for more, even taking on extra jobs in order to have greater purchasing power? In abundance, money gives us an almost royal freedom to do whatever we please—to travel, to enjoy fine things, to educate our children, to grow old in good health* and security. And an excess of money gives us the power of life and death over others. Even our paltry pocket money placed monthly in the right envelope can literally save people from hunger, disease and worse (see Tithing).

So part of our moral and spiritual education of children is financial education, and this happens, whether we intend it or not, at home* (see Allowances). The way we handle money as parents serves as instruction in the grace of stewardship, but it also reveals how important money is to us and the idolatrous potential of money. Idolatry is simply making something one's ultimate concern rather than the One who is ultimate. "Mammon" is an alternative god. As Jacques Ellul shows, wealth has some of the pretended claims of deity: (1) it is capable of moving other things and claims a certain autonomy; (2) it is invested with spiritual power that can enslave us, replacing single-minded love for God, and replacing neighbor relationships with buying-selling relationships in which even the soul is bought (Rev 18:11-13); (3) it is more or less personal. So money, "wicked mammon," is a form or appearance of another power (Lk 16:9; Eph 1:21; See Ellul, 76-77, 81, 93). According to Jesus, "You cannot serve both God and Money" (Mt 6:24). What can this mean? In what way ought money matter to the Christian? In what way ought it not to matter?

Money Matters in Christian History

In its history, unlike many of the world's faiths, Christianity was never purely spiritual in its vision. That is mainly because Christianity erected its entire worldview upon a strong doctrine of creation. As the first article of the Apostles' Creed implies, to the Christian the material world is something much greater than a mere physical presence or a transitory stage on which more deeply spiritual stories will play out. The material world is God's creation, and it is thus good. The material world is not indifferent, illusory or evil, as it is in many religious visions (consider the great faiths of Hinduism and Buddhism). It is itself something real, essential, good and, we dare say, even sacred.

In the Christian tradition, material wealth is directly associated with God's good creation and thus with God's will and vision for human beings on earth. There is something about material wealth and poverty in almost every section of Scripture. In the Bible it matters that we are rich or poor. The whole story connects money with the story of God and God's people. It is not too strong to say that money (or at least material life) is at the root of all that God is said to have done in history, and it is at the root of all that counts as good or evil among the people of God. No subject was addressed by Christ more often than this one, and there really is no Christian doctrine we can think about very long before we come up against questions about economic life—especially if we are relatively rich in the context of a world that is generally poor. To the Christian, then, money not only matters in a transitory way; it is somehow connected with the redemption and eternal destinies of human beings.

Christians realized from the beginning that the matter of wealth was a matter of great theological and spiritual urgency (Gonzalez, x-xvi). Early Christian thinkers all knew that spiritualism or dualism would not do. From sacred tradition, especially the prophets and Jesus, they knew that how we live as economic persons reveals, even exposes, who we are as spiritual persons. The economic life, they reasoned, is a kind of incarnation of the spiritual life. It is a sequence of actions that speak our hearts more loudly than pious words can do. To the extent that our works cannot be disjoined from faith, the ancients rightly judged that the matter of money (or wealth generally) was a matter that had the mark of eternity about it.

As there are now, there were arguments, debates, disagreements and plain old muddles over the problem. Should we have personal possessions at all? If yes (as most agreed we must), then in what quantity and form? How much was too much or too little? The answers of the early Christians tended toward the ascetic (Gonzalez, 71-214). Most looked upon an excess of wealth as spiritually dangerous and morally evil. Throughout the Middle Ages to the Protestant Reformation, the most brilliant thinkers were disposed to denigrate the pursuit of material prosperity. Their model was mainly Jesus, whom they interpreted to have lived a life of poverty and to have enjoined such a life upon his followers.

There is a tendency in today's consumer society for certain Christians to lionize these historic figures as models of spirituality. But before romanticism sets in, we ought to keep in mind that the moral contest of gaining and having money in their day was very different from that of our own time. Not always but generally in ancient times, it was the rule that one person's gain was another

person's loss. Only a very small and powerful elite had material wealth in excess, while the vast majority lived in conditions that we would find beneath the dignity of any human being. To such a world—the world of Augustine, Aquinas and Calvin—Jesus' words about mammon were unambiguous. It was difficult to go out and acquire great fortune without doing things that amounted morally to theft from weaker brothers and sisters. But even as great men spoke old words to an old time, a new economic world was being born. It would require new words.

Like its thinking about science, philosophy, music, art and much else, Christian thinking about economic life stood well until the modern revolutions struck. Then it seemed that nothing stood very well anymore. In the centuries before, life seemed an unbroken, nearly changeless and endless rule by monarchs and a condition of poverty for the vast majority (who as the poor, it was just presumed, would always be with us). The following centuries brought one destabilizing shock after another to the older order. The social order that had stood for more than a thousand years fell like some great old tree. A new world grew up in its place at such dazzling speed that we have not caught up with it yet. All the systems of civilization were reordered, and this was made possible in large measure by the astonishing success of the new economic system that had emerged.

For the first time in human history a people began seriously to think that poverty (just as tyranny) might be erased from the face of the earth (Lay Commission, 10-17). In a new land, under a new political and intellectual order, a new people began to flourish in a new way. Ordinary men and women became wealthy as only nobility had done in ages past. But they had not attained their good fortunes through the genetic line of heredity, nor had they gained by exploiting weaker folk. They had attained it through the honest labor of their hands, even by providing needed services to others in a cycle of prosperity. Their gain had, in effect, been gain for their fellows. In a remarkably brief span of time this new middle class of people became the majority of the population. The poor became a minority, yet even they had hope of one day being set free from poverty. They knew that we cannot serve both God and mammon, but it seemed that God had served them with it and that he had called them to serve him in prosperity. New words were needed for this new time, and they are needed still.

Money Matters to the Christian Today
Today debates rage among Christians over money and the material goods of this world. What should be done with the great fortune we have amassed? How should we live? What would God have us think and do? How ought we live our economic lives in such a world? When does our respect for money become worship of the god mammon? How much may we freely enjoy? How much ought we in justice to give? For most, the various questions boil down to one: how are we to view the realm of the superfluous, that which exceeds the mere "necessaries of life," as Charles Wesley called them?

Some rail against the superfluous wealth while others in the world hunger and thirst. In their view any countenance of the superfluous is immoral. Our lives and national systems must be rebuilt upon the principle of meeting only our real needs and then the needs of others (Sider). Their appeal is primarily to the biblical prophets and Jesus who, they say, stood against the rich and for the poor.

Others disagree. They argue that the economics of necessity spell global depression of our consumption-driven systems. The outcome would hardly be liberation of the poor from poverty but instead poverty for almost everyone. They also point to many passages of Scripture that give God's blessing on the enjoyment of extravagant and superfluous things (Griffiths). What are we to think and do about money, about the superfluous?

The Two Voices of Scripture on Money
We are forced by the nature of the debate to return to our first principles. We must go to Scripture and seek to hear the Word of God in a new way. But when we turn to the Bible for help, we discover that the text seems to speak with two voices that are in conflict. One voice says that to be rich is to have received a blessing from God. It says that material riches are a means by which God expresses redemptive love for his people and makes them flourish. Material riches bring to pass the very vision of delight that our good God had for us.

The other voice is dark with warnings about money. It says that money is a curse, that the rich are accursed, that riches are the wages of sin and unrighteousness, especially toward the poor, with whom God takes his stand against the rich. Many would say that this second voice is essentially the voice of Jesus and that it does not speak good news to those who have more than enough money. Can we hear the two voices of Scripture as one harmonious word from God? Or are we doomed forever to a dialect of dissonance and paradox? The harmony is difficult to hear, but with care it can be done.

Delight and Compassion Embrace
If we listen to the deepest levels of each voice—the one that blesses and the other that curses the rich—we learn that de-

light and compassion are not alien to each other. Since the one entails the other, in their truest shapes they embrace. Of course, they may become alien to each other—there is a delight that turns hard, into self-indulgent and unjust hedonism, and there is a compassion that turns cold, into righteous, pitiless and joyless moralism. But they need not do so. Indeed, in Scripture we never really have delight in its truest and fullest sense without compassion, nor do we have compassionate justice without delight.

Consider four representative biblical narratives: the creation, the exodus, the exile and the ministry of Christ. In these narratives God has given us the elemental structures of a worldview.

In its lyrical, almost liturgical way, Genesis 1 (and Gen 2—3) pictures God making a material world that is good and even sacred. Here the spiritual and physical worlds are as one. More so, God breathed into the lump of earth that was to become a human being. Human beings are pictured as spiritually endowed physical beings that God designed to inhabit a physical world. And it was "good," as God wished it to be. Even more so, the physical realm is characterized as a pleasure garden that humans are to till and keep as well as enjoy, except that they must not touch the wicked fruit of the knowledge of good and evil. So the most basic vision of human existence as God intended it to be is one of luxurious delight in physicality within a world of moral limits and obligations. This goes to the core of life itself as the ancient Hebrews thought of it (Schneider, 43-64).

The story of the exodus carries on the same double-tinged theme. God rescues the Hebrew people from physical bondage in Egypt and consummates their liberation by giving them a land flowing with milk and honey. It is God who makes them rich and powerful in the land. Because they represent God, they must be especially concerned with those in their midst who have no wealth or power—the widow, the orphan, the sojourner, the poor. In their delight they must seek justice, wherein justice means not allowing that any fellow Israelite be poor. Theirs must be a land shining on a hill to the nations, where delight and compassion embrace in a sacred and plainly political way. The whole of the law thus weds delight with compassion, compassion with delight (Limburg, 25-38).

The same double-edged theme shapes the narrative of the exile. The reason God sends his people back into captivity is that the ruling rich have gorged themselves without grieving for the poor. They are not God's people in the most profound spiritual sense of that concept. The exodus is thus reversed physically, just as it had already been turned back spiritually. The prophets thunder, not against the sacred delight that God blessed but against the dark hedonism that God warned about in the first place. We cannot elaborate how these themes unfold throughout the so-called wisdom literature—Job, Ecclesiastes, Proverbs, even the Song of Songs—but indeed they do (Van Leeuwen, 36-39).

If there is a place in biblical history where we might think delight is sacrificed on the altar of compassion, it would be in the story of Jesus. But delight in the physicality of the world does not die in the heart of Jesus; in him it is reborn and set free again on its way to true shalom for this earth (see Sabbath).

Moral theology has awakened us to the Jesus who stood like a stern prophet against the powers of his time. Without reserve Jesus used his tongue like a whip against those who were rich and blessed the poor, who would inherit the earth (Wolterstorff, 73). Many have drawn from this that Jesus was himself literally poor and that material poverty went with his life of self-denial and suffering (Sider, 61). But this image of Jesus simplifies things too much.

Today's moral theologians neglect the "Christ of delight," who bewildered his religious peers by eating* and drinking, rather than fasting. He was the suffering servant, but since he came eating and drinking, pious ones who knew better labeled him a drunkard and a glutton. They, like Judas, could not fathom the freedom he had for wasteful celebration. When he permitted the woman of ill repute to pour the jar of pure nard over his head that was worth a year's income at a good job and could have been sold and given to the poor, Jesus broke the seal of the vessel that bottled up the forces of darkness that would betray and crucify him.

Christian economic life should flow naturally from a Christian identity that is in perfect harmony with both delight and compassion. We should be in our bodies—our biological families and the church—little Israels, miniature versions of Jesus in our circumstances, those who know the difference between the blessedness of delight and the accursedness of debauchery. Of course, it is not always possible to be so blessed and faithful at the same time. At times we may have to be poorer than we would like to be in order to keep our souls from harm. But there is no ideal to

be found in this, any more than it ought to be our ideal to keep the poor around us from flourishing in true shalom. If possible, let our lives be written epistles of wonder at the blessings that God lavishes upon us so that we, as God's people, might go forth and do likewise among those who hunger and thirst in poverty for the coming kingdom of God.

See also ALLOWANCES; CREDIT CARD; DEBT; INSURANCE; SABBATH; SHOPPING; TITHING.

References and Resources

J. Ellul, *Money and Power* (Downers Grove, Ill.: InterVarsity Press, 1984); J. L. Gonzalez, *Faith and Wealth: A History of the Origin, Significance and Use of Money* (San Francisco: Harper & Row, 1990); B. Griffiths, *The Creation of Wealth: A Christian's Case for Capitalism* (Downers Grove, Ill.: InterVarsity Press, 1984); Lay Commission on Catholic Social Teaching and the U.S. Economy, *Toward the Future: Catholic Thought and the U.S. Economy* (North Tarrytown, N.Y.: Author, 1984); J. Limburg, *The Prophets and the Powerless* (Atlanta: John Knox, 1977); J. Schneider, *Godly Materialism: Rethinking Money and Possessions* (Downers Grove, Ill.: InterVarsity Press, 1994); R. Sider, *Rich Christians in an Age of Hunger,* 3rd ed. (Dallas: Word, 1990); R. Van Leeuwen, "Enjoying Creation—Within Limits," in *The Midas Trap* (Wheaton, Ill.: Scripture Press/Victor Books, 1990); N. Wolterstorff, *Until Justice and Peace Embrace* (Grand Rapids: Eerdmans, 1983).

J. Schneider

MORTGAGE. *See* CREDIT CARD; DEBT; HOME; INSURANCE; MONEY.

—NEIGHBORING—

Throughout the last two centuries, many factors have changed the nature of neighborhoods and thus neighboring. Most people no longer live near where they work, which has fragmented the cohesion that many areas once had. Greater mobility* means that families do not stay as long in a given area, breaking relationships and weakening stability. The breakup of families through divorce* also disrupts some members' connections with people who used to be close by. Inventions such as the telephone* and automobile* have increased the distances people can travel and reduced the time they spend in their localities. Meanwhile radio, and especially television,* keep people inside their homes more. The growing use of computers* and coming of the information superhighway means that people do not even have to leave their homes, let alone talk to their neighbors, to communicate with others. The increasing busyness of many people and the growing individualism in our culture do mean, however, that many people have less time these days for those who live around them. Even the use of high fences and grid rather than cul-de-sac forms of streets has an influence here.

In light of all these changes, it is not surprising that many people lament the loss of neighborhood. Though this also tends to weaken the experience of being neighbors, we should not jump to conclusions about this before checking whether being a neighbor has simply changed its character. For example, it is generally believed that the flight from the inner city to the suburbs resulted in people becoming less neighborly than they were. Studies suggest, however, that this is not usually the case. Also, newer forms of communication such as the telephone, automobile and computer have created additional links between people or strengthened existing ones. This has expanded people's ability to be or remain neighbors. Relationships continued this way are not necessarily any less frequent or intense. This extended sense of neighborhood should not be alien to Christians, who prize highly Jesus' story of the good Samaritan with its challenging definition of neighbor (Lk 10:25-37).

A Biblical Approach to Neighboring

In the Old Testament the word *neighbor* refers almost exclusively to a fellow Israelite. Neighbor relationships assume certain moral obligations based on the command "[You shall] love your neighbor as yourself" (Lev 19:18) and play a significant role in the detail of the Old Testament Law. In the Ten Commandments we are forbidden to "give false testimony about [our] neighbor" or "covet [our] neighbor's house" (Ex 20:16-17). We are to respect our neighbor's property (Ex 22:14) and show mercy to our neighbor (Ex 22:26-27). We are warned against cheating our neighbor or endangering our neighbor's life, but we also are required to confront a neighbor when wronged by one without taking revenge (Lev 19:13-18). We are to show charity (Deut 15:11) and have a concern for one another's welfare (Deut 22:1-4). Elsewhere we are advised not to hurt our neighbor but to strengthen the relation-ship of trust between us and not fend our neighbor off but to share with a neighbor when requested to do so (Prov 3:27-29). Where justice and compassion are absent in a neighborhood, God's judgment is severe. It is directed against anyone who would slander (Ps 101:5), cheat (Jer 22:13) or defile (Hab 2:15) a neighbor, as well as against anyone who would kill (Ex 21:14).

In the New Testament Jesus reiterates the need to love our neighbors as ourselves (Mt 19:19). He redefines the term neighbor to reflect the inclusive nature of the kingdom he had come to establish (Lk 10:29). Much of his earthly ministry was neighborhood centered as he wandered from village to village and ministered in houses and streets (Mt 8:14-17; Lk 7:12). Many of his parables were drawn from aspects of neighborhood life, illustrating the presence of God "in our own backyard" (Lk 11:5-10; 15:1-32). Elsewhere in the New Testament the command to "love your neighbor as yourself" is restated no less than nine times. Paul describes this injunction as a summary of "the entire law" (Rom 13:9; Gal 5:14), and James as the "royal law" (Jas 2:8).

Karl Barth highlighted the importance of being neighborly as a test of how well we are putting our faith into practice. He argues that our responsibility to our neighbor is the concrete form that the Word of God takes in our daily life, especially that word concerning reconciliation. Commitment to being neighborly moves us beyond inherent capacity for individual or family self-interest to our more general responsibilities to accept, love and do right by others. As such, it often confronts us with the need for repentance since we so often fail those who live around us or with whom we are in regular contact. The centrality of the neighbor is a constant reminder to us that issues of morality have a public as well as personal face. Showing neighborliness is also a way of bearing witness to the loving heart and welcoming embrace of God toward others, as incarnated in Christ's coming and living, as well as dying and rising, among us.

Ways of Being Neighborly

Although the meaning of neighborhood is being redefined in the ways outlined above, it is important to nurture our residential neighborhoods. There are bottom-line, self-interested and high-end ethical reasons for this. Unless there is some sense of local identity and pride, neighborhoods tend to lose important services. For instance, unless local parks are used, they often become centers for drug handling or undesirable behavior. It is precisely because so many neighborhoods are empty during the day or at certain times in the year that crime increases. When crises happen in the

home, neighbors are often the only ones close enough to help, and if we do not know them, we are less likely to call upon them.

In more general ways, neighborhoods are also an underappreciated source of community. The importance of the small encounters they make possible should not be underestimated. This includes such apparently minor actions as greeting one another over the back fence or in the street, also assisting each other in small ways when some difficulty arises. It also includes fraternizing and sometimes cooperating when everyone is affected by the same difficult conditions; as well, borrowing or loaning some household or garden item; keeping an eye on each other's property when people are away.

There are various ways in which Christians can encourage and enhance neighborliness. They can

□ sit out in front yards or on porches, where they have them, so that contact with neighbors can be made

□ from time to time invite neighbors for a lemonade or barbecue outside or for a meal inside their homes

□ go for walks regularly around the neighborhood, especially at times when people are more likely to be home, so that they encounter neighbors and begin to develop an acquaintance with them

□ welcome new neighbors and arrange farewells for departing ones

□ consider holding a neighborhood reading group, discussion circle or Bible study

□ hold annual block parties or organize neighborhood caroling at Christmas and draw in some neighbors to plan them

Where appropriate or necessary they can also

□ offer their home as the local polling booth

□ establish neighborhood hobby groups

or exhibitions for those who have common interests

☐ develop voluntary associations for raising local issues or helping needy neighbors

Churches that couples and families belong to could

☐ make a special effort to become part of their immediate neighborhood

☐ decentralize many of their meetings into their neighborhoods rather than concentrating them all on their campus

☐ encourage some members to live near one another so that they can engage in joint ministry to those around them

☐ become involved as a congregation in addressing justice issues and social needs in their neighborhood

☐ put before some members a vision for taking up civic responsibilities

☐ make their buildings available for community meetings and activities as well as their for their own congregational use

☐ set up a small neighborhood park on church property, a drop-in center, counseling service, preschool or Christian bookstore and coffee house

☐ visit their whole neighborhood and ask in what ways they could be of practical service to the people in it

Difficulties with Neighbors

Now and again difficulties with neighbors do arise. This might be as basic as having neighbors who just do not want a connection of any kind, even at the most basic level. They might not even want to indicate they are aware of your presence, let alone make some greeting. There is no easy way to deal with this, but it is worth continuing to make the effort, trusting that in time it will win through or that God will do something to open them up to you. Sometimes tensions can arise between our neighbors and us. This can be over something we have done that they have misunderstood and taken wrongly. It is then up to us to

try and clear the air, indicating in some concrete way our regret that they should have taken offense. A problem can also arise over a matter on which we just happen to have different attitudes. In such a case, there may be reasons on both sides for thinking and acting the way we do. It is always better to talk about significant changes we wish to make in our lifestyle or on our property with our neighbors beforehand, but sometimes it does not occur to us that a particular change will cause any difficulty. In other cases, hopefully there will be an opportunity to talk these through, and, if a stalemate continues, we are faced with the choice of insisting on our preference at the risk of losing a neighbor or giving way for the sake of the relationship. In time our neighbors may change and give us the opportunity of fulfilling our wishes.

At times, however, neighbors can be too intrusive, failing to recognize our time, family or property boundaries, often without realizing what they are doing. In such cases we have to draw loving but firm boundaries and gradually help them understand why these are important. On occasions, we may also find ourselves alongside neighbors who are just inconsiderate, prejudiced or quarrelsome, perhaps even abusive toward one another or toward us. This is the most difficult of situations. Apart from seeking to keep the channels of communication* open, holding our ground when they really step over the line, and continuing in a lot of prayer, there is little we can do. Occasionally others who are affected can support each other in approaching such neighbors. In extreme cases we may even have to bring in the police, though that is always a last resort. The general principle governing our behavior in all this is the Pauline one of "if it is possible, as far as it depends on you, live at peace with everyone" (Rom 12:18).

See also COMMUNICATION; HOME; LOVE.

References and Resources
C. S. Fischer, *To Dwell Among Friends: Personal Networks in Towns and City* (Chicago: University of Chicago, 1982); C. S. Fischer *The Urban Experience* (New York: Harcourt, Brace & Jovanovich, 1984); F. Lappe and P.

Du Bois, *The Quickening of America; Rebuilding our Nation, Remaking our Lives* (San Francisco: Jossey-Bass, 1994); M. Slattery and M. Droel, *Christians in their Neighborhood* (Chicago: Southwest Catholic Cluster, nd); M. J. Weiss, *The Clustering of America* (New York: Harper & Row, 1988).

Robert Banks

NEW AGE RELIGION. *See* ALTERNATIVE RELIGIONS.

—NEW REPRODUCTIVE TECHNOLOGY—

Formerly a mysterious, elusive event that occurred only in the secret and dark places of a woman's body, conception* is now subjected to the blinding light of the laboratory and the scrutiny and manipulation of medical technology. Behind the dazzling miracle of healthy children born to long-suffering infertile couples lies a shadowy moral twilight. The same technology affords contemplation of the possibility of "designer children" through prenatal diagnosis, sex selection, abortion,* and, ultimately, cloning and genetic engineering. The advent of surrogacy and egg and sperm donation is the logical extension of separating the procreative and unitive acts that began with the widespread use of contraception.* Placed outside the temple of a covenantal relationship, modern conception is often complicated by consumerist influences of a marketplace.

Reproductive Miracles
The bitter agony of barrenness is well-recognized biblically, and God's faithfulness to his promises is exemplified in reproductive miracles (Elizabeth in Lk 1:13, Sarah in Gen 18:10 and Hannah in 1 Sam 1:10). It is no less prodigious for those couples whose infertility, be it blocked fallopian tubes or low sperm count, can be overcome by the *in vitro* (literally, "in glass") uniting of their own sperm and ovum. In vitro fertilization (IVF) is accomplished outside the mother's body when sperm and ovum spontaneously meet in a laboratory dish or by microinjection of disabled sperm directly into the ovum. Through hormonal hyperstimulation perhaps a dozen eggs can be harvested from a woman during one

menstrul cycle. A group of successful embryos that have begun dividing are placed in the womb, where one or more may implant and result in pregnancy. The ownership, freezing, storage and use of unplaced embryos are fraught with controversy. Some couples claim them and feel responsible to give each embryo an opportunity for womb placement. Others sell their embryos (along with sperm or harvested eggs) to finance these expensive treatments that have variable success rates.

Successful pregnancies are often complicated by multiple gestations, forcing selective abortion of some implanted embryos to ensure that a smaller number (twins or triplets) will reach viability. There are higher rates of prematurity and complications for which society ultimately bears responsibility in the care of the disabled and vulnerable. Many people feel public funding would be better spent in prevention of infertility (usually a result of sexually transmissible diseases) and in the encouragement and support of women who wish to carry a baby to term with the intent to give an inestimable gift to an adopting couple (see Adoption).

Once conception can occur outside the relational context of human sexuality, reproductive capabilities are imparted to single people, homosexual couples and postmenopausal women. Through research social scientists have demonstrated the success of the biblical procreative model—the marriage-based heterosexual family,* although successful exceptions can always occur with the grace and support of the community. The fewest people object to nonanonymous arrangements occurring between family members (e.g., a woman donating eggs or carrying a child for her sister). But what are the rights of the child? To whom do they belong: to the genetic, gestational (birthing) or social parents? The complex ramifications of parenting nonbiologic children are akin to the established practice of adoption. Questions of responsibility and rights are raised when more then one set of parents have claims on a child, who may ultimately become torn apart in a court lacking Solomon's wisdom.

Another facet of new reproductive technologies (NRTs) is *prenatal diagnosis.* Under the guise of providing reassur ance of normalcy or preparation for defects, there is the thorny issue of whether parents can justly subject both society and an abnormal child to "wrongful birth." Does a child have a right to have intrauterine euthanasia to prevent inevitable "indignities" and suffering as predicted by prenatal tests

should the pregnancy* continue and birth occur? Prenatal diagnosis is the first of many potential steps in altering the type of children that society will admit. At the present time it involves sampling fetal cells from the placenta at an early stage in pregnancy (chorionic villus sampling) or from amniotic fluid accomplished more safely but closer to the time of quickening (amniocentesis). In the case of IVF early cells can be removed from the multicellular embryo prior to being placed in the womb. In research settings these cells have also been successfully duplicated or cloned (artificial twinning). In the future, fetal cells that appear in the maternal circulation may be sampled, providing information without potential harm to the fetus.

As with most genetic diagnoses, a positive result represents a "fate" without hope of a cure at this stage of technology. The alternatives include termination of a pregnancy or, with IVF, a decision not to implant that particular embryo. Gene therapy and intrauterine interventions are experimental but distinct possibilities for the future.

With the advent of DNA manipulation the power to correct critical genetically coded errors becomes a possibility. In the blinding excitement of the genetic revolution, we too easily forget the responsibilities inherent in the biting of this apple core—as we seek knowledge of the "good and evil" inherent in our genes, navigating with fewer ethical absolutes than ever before.

Ethical Considerations
While the full exploration of the ethical ramifications of genetic engineering and NRTs exceeds the scope of this article, the following two concerns are foremost: the commercialization of reproduction and the redefinition of human dignity in narrower terms.

Commercialization of reproduction. Desperate infertile couples are at the mercy of a profit-driven reproductive industry and prone to exploitation in research settings. The selling of human tissue, eggs, sperm and embryos contravenes human dignity. The very fact that couples on lower socioeconomic rungs must sell embryos, eggs and sperm to finance their IVF challenges us to seek higher levels of distributive social justice that exists in countries such as France and Austria. Disadvantaged women may sell their reproductive capacities by entering into surrogacy arrangements where they may carry a genetically related or unrelated child to term and relinquish their rights to the child (if healthy), all for a sum of money that is usually less than what the legal brokers receive. The transfer of funds is never enough to occupy the void and compensate her grief, let alone the dehumanization she suffers. Remunerated surrogacy is ominously reminiscent of slavery. Children begin to be viewed as technological accomplishments, commodities and luxury accessories that enhance social status. Identically cloned embryos may one day be frozen and banked for future use as organ donors or replacement children. Even aborted female fetuses can provide eggs, making it possible to be a genetic parent without having been born.

Is human dignity most threatened by the disease or the cure? What are the motives we bring to the reconstruction of the human race through NRTs? What values will be paramount in shaping the chosen characteristics of future generations? Challenging responsible stewardship, NRTs give human pride and rebellion every possibility for expression. Will we be motivated by vanity, perfectionism and elitism in choosing cosmetically appealing physical or superior intellectual characteristics? By sex selection (accomplished by preferential sperm treatment, selective implantation or abortion), will we produce "ideal" families with offspring of both sexes or offspring representative of the more valued sex (usually male)? Even the seemingly altruistic desire to prevent suffering and promote health is worn thin by the means by which it is achieved—intrauterine euthanasia and embryo experimentation.

The unspoken corollary of the option for prenatal testing is that no one should *knowingly* permit a less than perfect baby to be born. We wrongly sense a moral obligation to dispatch ourselves before we are violated by nature. What is being lost is the essential fact that human beings do not lose their dignity by virtue of an inability to control what cannot be controlled, such as birth defects, disability, illness, aging and death.* "It is the equivalent of saying that to possess human dignity with any degree of certainty one must be forever free of adversity" (Stolberg, 146). We are reminded that Christ on the cross maintained his human dignity in the face of suffering and slander.

Recovering Reproductive Reverence
Ultimately, the hope we have for the future is not eugenics but Jesus. Children represent expressions of our trust in God's intent that "the world should go on," but they are not the means to ultimate sanctification, permanence and perfection. It is unlikely we will ever splice out all the genes that contribute to our brokenness and separation from God. The severing of procreation from sexual activity within the confines of marital fidelity is the harbinger of the disintegration we experience when we threaten our dignity by attempting to separate soul and body. Doubt is the shadow cast by faith. As we plunge into the genetic age may the transcendent presence of God's

justice, beneficence and compassion guide us in the complex decisions that await our ethical scrutiny.

See also CONCEPTION; MISCARRIAGE; PREGNANCY; SEXUALITY.

References and Resources

P. Baird, *Proceed with Care: Final Report of the Royal Commission on New Reproductive Technologies* (Canada: Minister of Government Services, 1993); P. Teilhard de Chardin, *The Appearance of Man* (New York: Harper, 1965); E. C. Hui, *Questions of Right and Wrong* (Vancouver: Regent College, 1994); J. A. Nisker, "Rachel's Ladders or How Societal Situation Determines Reproductive Therapy," *Human Reproduction* 11, no 6 (1996); S. B. Rae, *Brave New Families: Biblical Ethics and Reproductive Technologies* (Grand Rapids: Baker, 1996); S. D. Stolberg, "Human Dignity and Disease, Disability, Suffering," *Humane Medicine* 1, no. 4 (1995) 144-47; S. D. Stolberg, "Talk of the Streets," *Time*, January 23, 1995, 10.

Carol Anderson

—PARENTING—

Parenting is an interactive family process in which adults undertake a primary role in forming children in body (through conception* and care), soul (through personality development and love*), and spirit (through nurturing hunger for God). Ironically, this relationship forms not only children but parents. Children, without knowing it, help their parents "grow up."

Parenting today is a threatened calling from both the outside and the inside. From the outside there is the professionalization of parenting (letting the experts do it for us) and preoccupation with the technology of parenting. On the inside there is erosion of confidence that ordinary people can parent well and that it is worth doing at all. It has not always been this way.

In earlier cultures and some developing countries today children were prized as wealth and parenting was passionately desired even though people inevitably experienced failures. In the identity culture of the West—where people are bent on finding and actualizing themselves—parenting is frequently viewed as an unwelcome and troubling distraction from one's primary vocation outside the home.* This is especially tragic when the parent, like Eli in the Bible (1 Sam 2:12-36), is in religious or public service and refuses to regard parenting with the same vocational importance as preaching, counseling or public leadership. The intention of this article is not to focus on the question of how to parent, important as that is, but to explore the underlying theological and spiritual questions of why we should parent at all and why parenting has such spiritual significance.

Parenting as Vocation
What is lacking in the Western world is a rationale for having and rearing children. In older cultures becoming a parent was assumed of those who married. In modern cultures, however, marriage* and conception are not necessarily linked. Because of advances in birth control, it is now possible to delay having children indefinitely while one pursues buying a house, establishing a career and gaining personal happiness. The urgency of this question—Why have babies?—is raised a

notch further by the new reproductive technologies,* which call into question the church's traditional teaching that it is copulation that produces (and ought to produce) offspring. Never before has it been so urgent to lift parenting above a simple biological urge and elevate it to a holy calling.

A vocation or calling is a life direction and service that is embraced not merely by one's will or through social constraint but as a response to a divine summons and for purposes beyond our own personal fulfillment. Our vocational service is meaningful because we are accountable to God for walking worthy of our vocation (Eph 4:1). Vocation means our life matters to God. So parenting is a vocation because it is divinely constituted (Gen 1:27-28), is accomplished in partnership with God, invites a life of faith and stewardship and is implicitly spiritual—a Godlike thing. Parenting is a path to God, not a diversion from spiritual life. It is not merely a setting in which spiritual disciplines take place—around the family meal, for example—it is a spiritual discipline itself.

Parenting is something we accomplish with God, even if we are unaware of the divine partner in the process. When we procreate, we are creating "before" (pro) God and cooperating with God, without whom the creation of a new person would be impossible (Gen 4:1). Parenting is a divine-human partnership, not an exclusively human achievement.

Parenting invites us Godward. For all, and especially for those who have difficulty conceiving, bearing and rearing a child is a matter of "waiting on the Lord," a waiting that may lead to taking other initiatives to become parents, or even to other expressions of vocation such as serving the children of others. Even after a child is conceived or adopt-

ed,* we must wait on the Lord for the outcome of his or her life—something we can neither predict nor control. Implicit in this is the idea of stewardship. We are entrusted with children; we do not own them.

Parenting as Stewardship

Children are gifts from God to us, gifts we never "own" but of which we are stewards, in a way so deeply understood by Hannah in the Old Testament (1 Sam 1:28). This same idea is communicated by the concept of hospitality.* We create a welcoming space for children where they can be free to be themselves, neither smothered nor "dumped." Both stewardship and hospitality suggest that parents have more responsibilities than rights. Stanley Hauerwas suggests that a child is always, in this sense, adopted, since the child belongs to the parents in a provisional and limited way (Henley, 1990, 21). This is reinforced in the actual experience of parenting when parents discover that they do not have dominion over the child. They cannot determine that their child will replicate them in the world. A child will not, no matter how hard we try, fulfill our unfulfilled ambitions for this life, or give us a status we have not found ourselves in being a child of God.

One practical expression of parental stewardship is the simple truth that no one chooses his or her parents. In like manner we do not choose our children, even should we adopt them. So this vocation of parenthood is distributed among people of various talents, a phenomenon that may lie behind the commandment to "honor" one's parents (Ex 20:12) even if one has little reason to be grateful to them (Henley, 1990, 20). But there is more to this than a divine randomness. Grace can be discovered even through very negative family experiences if these are processed.

Parenting as Ministry

The family as predicament and blessing reflects the gospel in daily life, and pleads it, as poignantly revealed in the parable of the prodigal son (Lk 15:11-32). More than obligation is built into the structure of the human family. There is the possibility of grace, belongingness, belovedness, undeserved kindness. We do not need to bring the Lord "into" our homes by a program of spiritual formation* or even family devotions, good as these are. God is already "where two or three are gathered," whether the family is "good" or "not so good." There are no perfect families, but there is no better family for us to be formed into personal and Christian maturity than the one into which we were born, adopted or entered by the marriage covenant. Thus parenting is truly vocational in its origin, but it is a ministry in its effect on people—both parents and children.

Parents too are under the "nurture and admonition of the Lord" (Eph 6:1-4 KJV; see Blessing). The parenting experience allows us to give and receive ministry from God and others through the issues of everyday life in family, including such things as the need for unconditional acceptance and self-worth, the challenge of "leaving father and mother," the images of God as Father, and issues of who is in control. The Greek word for ministry is the same word as service. So we can consider parenting as a form of family service in which people are touched for God and by God in the normal everyday transactions and relationships of family life. One way of describing this two-way ministry (God to people and people to God) is the biblical concept of priesthood.

Parenting as Priesthood

In a family where some or all the members are Christians, the priesthood of all believers (1 Pet 2:9) means that the father is not *the* priest of the family but rather one of them! So the challenge of parenting is not only to raise godly children but to become godly parents. This comes about through a communal ministry in the home. Each believer is priest to the others. Often the children are priests to the parents—declaring through their innocent wisdom the direct accessibility and trustworthiness of God. In this way children demonstrate the childlikeness that parents themselves are called to emulate. Put differently, every member of the family has the potential to be a spiritual director to the other members, and the family as a whole acts as a corporate priesthood for one another. We do this by praying, by playing, by raising questions, in affirming where and how God is at work in our midst and by directing one another to find our ultimate security and hope in God, not in our family.

Prayer* is an important part of this priestly ministry. The Bible does not specifically require that a family pray out loud together—though it can be a good thing to do—but it strongly advocates prayer *for* one another. The prayers of Paul in Ephesians 1:16-23 and 3:14-19 are great patterns for priestly intercessory prayer for other members of the family. As children approach adulthood, discerning parents will pray more and say less. By the time they become grandparents,* parents learn that prayer is probably their most important continuing ministry to their children and grandchildren.

Some parents, too anxious to have their children declare faith at the earliest possible age, stuff them with Christian information so they arrive at the teens "knowing it all" and immune to discovering something personal, instead of hungering for God and wanting more. Another way of expressing this developmental approach to parenting is through the biblical concept of discipling.

Parenting as Discipling

The connection between the words *discipline* and *discipleship* (both stemming from the Latin *discipulus*, meaning "learner") is a complicated one (Lee, 268-71) and has led some to advocate parental discipline* by punishment and others to reject punishment completely in favor of noncoercive education. In fact, the Bible includes the element of punishment in its idea of discipline but always in the context of something greater: the covenant love that encourages growth and not simply to control.

Discipleship, so perfectly exemplified in the relation of Jesus and his disciples, is a helpful model of parenting for several reasons: (1) the context is not the classroom but life-on-life relationships; (2) learning is continuous and unscheduled; (3) the learning relationship is primarily one of imitation rather than the transmission of information (Lk 6:40); and (4) the primary motivation of discipline is not the need to control but the desire to encourage self-control and other fruits of the Spirit.

Obviously this cannot happen without the parent's being self-reflective. This is especially needed because a family is constantly changing like a mobile with elements moving and influencing all the other elements; congruent with this is the biblical idea of family as covenant.

Parenting as Community Building

The covenant is a binding personal agreement to belong, involving mutuality, love and loyalty. A healthy family is a covenant community in which we are more one because of our diversity, rather than being unified by blurring the differences and merging members into a homogenous unit. The process of building such a community involves constant change for all the members of the family.

The development of a child should start with bonding, attaching to at least one significant adult who is really "crazy" about him or her. Without this bonding a child will grow up looking for the bonding he or she missed and, according to Bowlby's attachment theory, will more likely become a driven person, possibly even addicted.

But this early dependence must progress toward interdependence. The covenant actually starts in a unilateral way by the parents' action in claiming the child as their own, at a stage when the child cannot reciprocate. But the covenant becomes bilateral as the growing child affirms a family identity while becoming differentiated from parents. In one sense parents are continuously preparing their children to leave home from the very first months, and the failure to do this (assuming healthy initial attachment) leads to enmeshed families where the children cannot "leave father and mother" (Gen 2:24) even when they marry, and the parents are unable to "let go." In their covenant ministry parents encourage belonging and differentiation at the same time, giving them both roots and wings. Ultimately, in a mature covenant, when the parents are old and infirm the circle is completed as children care for their parents when their parents can no longer care for themselves (Balswick and Balswick, 1987, 41-42).

Throughout this process of development within the family, parents are powerfully teaching their children the meaning of covenant and therefore suggesting the fundamental basis of our relationship with God—one of belonging rather than performing. In addition, parents are preparing their children to be capable of forming their own family covenant through marriage, if God should so lead. Indeed, even a dysfunctional family experience, if properly processed,

243

can be an asset in preparing for marriage. Understanding intergenerational sin (problems passed on from generation to generation until they are broken) and, more significantly, intergenerational grace (Ex 20:5-6) is crucial to being free to leave home and to form another family.

So an important ministry of parents is the covenant community in which people are encouraged to change and develop uniquely. This view of family ministry profoundly challenges both the Western family (as a collection of individuals) and the Eastern (as a merged unit). It also challenges parents to be constantly adapting to their changing ministry. During the developmental stages of children various parenting styles will commend themselves: more authoritarian (directive) in the earliest months, more authoritative (high control with positive encouragement) during the growing years, and more permissive (nondemanding and warmly accepting) when children reach adulthood (Atkinson and Wilson, 61).

There are several practical implications that arise from a theology and spirituality of parenting. First, recognize parenting as a vocation more important than service outside the home because it is the most tangible expression of God as parent. Second, give up ownership of your child to God; your child is a trusted gift and a precious guest. Third, hear the gospel and live it through living graciously at home, not giving everyone what they deserve. Fourth, pray for your children and encourage them to pray for you. Fifth, put discipline in the context of discipleship. Sixth, build community that balances the need to be *we* with the need to be *me*. Finally, enjoy your children.

Can Christian parents guarantee that their children will become believers? No, not even by "doing it right" in all spheres of parenting. Indeed, some research suggests that inward and authentic faith in young people is found just as much in families where parents were authoritarian as among those who were permissive at the wrong stage (Atkinson and Wilson, 51-62). Good parenting can facilitate a child's growing up to become whole and open to God but cannot guarantee faith. That is the result of a miraculous and mysterious cooperation of human and divine wills. When a child reared in a healthy, affirming home does not embrace faith, at least in the present, it is not a sign of bad parenting. The story is not yet finished, as we learn when the curtain comes down in the story of the two prodigal sons: one at home but in the far country in his heart, the other at home in body and soul.

Parenting does not have guarantees, except the growth of the parents. Parenting is not really *for* anything: not for the certain transmission of faith to another generation, not for the pleasure of having children rise up and call us blessed, not for the satisfaction of producing high achievers. Parenting as a spiritual discipline is for God, who in the end is the only one who can say, "Well done." And God approves of our parenting not because of the merits of our performance but because we did our parenting for God. "God with all his angels and creatures is smiling," said Luther, "not because that father is washing diapers, but because he is doing so in Christian faith." Everyone who has reflected deeply on this ministry and vocation attests that parenting is an act of faith. But faith is not a leap in the dark but a hearty trust in the God who has made himself known in Christ and will one day show us what we really did in parenting our children.

See also ADOPTION; BLESSING; CHARACTER; COMMUNICATION; CONCEPTION; DISCIPLINE; FAMILY; FAMILY PROBLEMS; HOME-

MAKING; PRAYER; SEXUALITY; SPIRITUAL FORMATION; VALUES.

References and Resources
H. T. Atkinson and F. R. Wilson, "The Relationship Between Parenting Style and the Spiritual Well-Being and Religiosity of College Students," *Christian Education Journal* 11 (Winter 1991) 51-62; J. O. Balswick and J. K. Balswick, *The Family: A Christian Perspective on the Contemporary Home* (Grand Rapids: Baker, 1989); J. O. Balswick and J. K. Balswick, "A Theological Basis for Family Relationships," *Journal of Psychology and Christianity* 6, no. 3 (Fall 1987) 37-49; E. Boyer, *Finding God at Home: Family Life as a Spiritual Discipline* (San Francisco: Harper & Row, 1991); R. Clapp, *Families at the Crossroads: Beyond Traditional and Modern Options* (Downers Grove, Ill.: InterVarsity Press, 1993); V. Hearn, ed., *What They Did Right: Reflections on Parents by Their Children* (Wheaton, Ill.: Tyndale House, 1974); J. Henley, "The Vocation of Parenting—with Surrogates," *St. Mark's Review,* Winter 1990, 16-25; J. Henley, *Accepting Life: The Ethics of Living in Families* (Melbourne: Joint Board of Christian Education, 1994); C. Lee, "Parenting as Discipleship: A Contextual Motif for Christian Parent Education," *Journal of Psychology and Theology* 19, no. 3 (1991) 268-77; B. Narramore, *Help! I'm a Parent* (Grand Rapids: Zondervan, 1972); M. Novak, "Family out of Favor," *Harper's,* April 1976; C. M. Sell, *Family Ministry: The Enrichment of Family Life Through the Church* (Grand Rapids: Zondervan, 1981); G. Smalley and J. T. Trent, *The Blessing* (Nashville: Thomas Nelson, 1986); R. P. Stevens, "A Day with the Family," in *Disciplines of the Hungry Heart* (Wheaton, Ill.: Harold Shaw, 1993) 35-64; J. Taylor, *Innocent Wisdom: Children as Spiritual Guides* (Cleveland: Pilgrim Press, 1989).

R. Paul Stevens

—PETS—

It seems that dogs were the first animals to be become pets, probably in Paleolithic times. Evidence from paintings and carvings in ancient tombs of Mesopotamia and Egypt suggests this. These dogs also assisted in the hunting of food. At a later date, c. 2000-1600 B.C., horses and cats became domesticated, the former for riding, the latter to keep the rat population under control. Being domesticated does not necessarily mean that these immediately became pets. Human beings, however, seem to have developed an affection for the animals with whom they worked.

Some animals, such as the seeing-eye dog, continue to have these dual roles today. On farms all over the world the distinction between pet and worker is often blurred, with dogs being used to herd sheep and cattle, sheep to "mow" the grass, and chickens and ducks to produce eggs. All these animals develop personalities that demand relationship. It is only recently that animals have become pets in the sense in which we use that word today, with their purpose being solely for the comfort and companionship of human beings. Though dogs, cats and horses remain favorites as pets, many other species make up the inventory of a modern pet store—rabbits, guinea pigs, hamsters, gerbils, birds, fish, turtles and even reptiles. There is now also the phenomenon of breeding animals to produce more aesthetically pleasing varieties of pets. Some people will pay a high price to own a pet that comes with a piece of paper proving its pedigree.

For centuries humans have celebrated their relationship with animals in art, music and literature. From the earliest times dogs were depicted in caves and on tombs. The crypts in European cathedrals are full of casks topped with effigies in brass or stone of the master or mistress with a whippet at their feet. To see how humans have come to value their pets, you only have to consider the number of advertisements on television* and the varieties on display in supermarkets for pet food, the array of books and manuals about pets available in shops and libraries, the range of pet shows and ornaments in the shape of pets, or the amount of money* that we spend annually on our pets. In some circles the latter is a cause for concern, for it is interpreted as an indication that our pets have become too important in our lives. It is definitely time to pause and think when we learn that in the West most people spend more money on their pets than they give to people less fortunate than themselves, whether to charities in their own country or aid programs overseas!

Indeed we are no longer content to provide our pets with the basics of life. We want to supply them with luxuries. Once upon a time pets were fed scraps supplemented by as little deliberately bought food as possible; now we feed them scientifically balanced formulas for whatever stage of life they are at. Once we treated their sicknesses ourselves; now we not only take them to the vet when they are sick but also give them annual checkups with vaccinations and teeth cleaning. Some animals are on long-term costly treatments for heart disease, arthritis and other complaints. There is even a growing business in funerals and cemeteries for pets, as well as in pet psychology and counseling.

A Proper Perspective on Pets

Though the Bible has plenty to say about the welfare of animals and portrays God's concern for those that live among humans (Jon 4:11) as well as in the wild (Ps 104:10-18), it has nothing to say about pets in our sense of the word. While its general interest in animals—extending to their resting on the sabbath* as humans do (Ex 20:8-11)—encourages us to care for those with whom we develop a special relationship, it also counsels us against giving too much attention to any living being or material object. Have we not crossed the line here and gone from caring for our pets to giving them too big a priority in our lives, making idols of our pets? Some would argue, like Judas in the Gospels, that the money spent on pets would be better given to the poor. However, the poor, as Jesus said, are always with us (Mt 26:11), and we need to balance our commitment to the poor with the enjoyment of God's gifts, including pets.

Pets add much richness to our lives. They bring companionship, affection and a listening* ear. For this reason it is not hard to understand why dogs and cats are by far the most popular choices as pets. They are there to greet us when we arrive home, they offer us unconditional love, asking only a modicum of attention in return, they sense our moods and know when we are in need of comfort and affection, and they are willing to listen to us without interrupting. The warmth of their bodies as we stroke them or their nestling on our knees brings great psychological and physical comfort as well.

Those in the health professions are slowly realizing what wonderful allies they have in pets. As a result, pets are beginning to be provided to people in hospitals and in seniors' homes. Even those involved in caring for emotionally disturbed youngsters are realizing that pets have an important role to play in their rehabilitation. Animal therapy, as it is called, is a growing phenomenon.

Parents have long appreciated how much their children have to learn from having a pet in the home.* Through having to look after a pet, children learn that animals have to be cared for, helping develop responsibility. A pet has to be fed regularly, provided with hygienic conditions to live in and given regular affection. Without these the pet will not thrive, and neither will children nor any other animal deprived of such care. While it is true that animals cannot talk, anyone watching a child with a loved pet knows that communication takes place. As children develop a relationship with a pet, they begin to read the pet's body language. The children start to know when the pet wants something to eat or drink, needs to go outside or just wants attention. They even learn when the animal is pleased or displeased. These are good skills to learn. They have wonderful crossover value in the child's relationships with other humans. Where there is more than one species of pet in a home, such as a dog and a cat, children have the opportunity to learn that animals who are natural enemies can live in peace when they are loved by the same person.

Pets can also be a means of spiritual grace and understanding. Just as animals are referred to throughout the Bible to portray divine things (Is 53:7; Mt 3:16), so too God makes himself known to people through their pets. I have heard people claim that they first understood God's unconditional love through the love their pet extended to them. I have often watched my own cat, seemingly fast asleep but instantly alert at the slightest noise, and reflected on the example of what it means to rest in the Lord.

See also CHORES; FAMILY; PLAY.

Resources and References
J. Sobosan, *Bless the Beasts* (New York: Crossroad, 1991).

Julie Banks

—PLAY—

Christians know they are to work (Gen 1:28; Jn 9:4; Col 3:23-24; 2 Thess 3:10-13). Whether father or mother or even the children, we are increasingly driven to produce and achieve. The typical work week has been lengthening since the early 1980s; women still do a disproportionate amount of work in the home besides holding down a job in the workplace; and children feel the pressure to get good grades in school and are then sent to practice dance, baseball or piano almost every afternoon before beginning their homework.

Given the encouragement of both church and culture, it is not surprising that North Americans are continuing to work longer hours and to *play* less and less. Since World War II there has been an increase in purchasing power, paid vacations,* life expectancy and recreational opportunities. Yet the predicted leisure* revolution has failed to materialize. From a 1974 low of 38 hours of work in a typical workweek, in 1998 it had risen to over 44 hours a week. In the United States since 1980 the percentage of those working more than 50 hours a week has consistently increased, and the number of leisure hours for adults has continued to drop (from 26.2 hours in 1973 to 16.6 hours in 1987). According to one estimate, middle-class parents together work six weeks more a year in 1999 than they did a decade earlier.

The Problem and Promise of Play

The inability (or perhaps unwillingness) of Christian families to find quality time for play is compounded by several factors: (1) the difficulty for those in poverty to have the freedom of spirit to truly play (for the poor, play is often "escape"); (2) the trend of women to work both in the workplace and disproportionately to men in the home (many mothers have no time to play); (3) the effect of consumerism in producing hectic and frenetic lives (we too often "work" at our play); and (4) a twisted understanding of play as escapism, passivity, hedonism or narcissism (cf. children spending hours mindlessly in front of the television*). No wonder Christians struggle with play. Yet when we play authentically, whether as adults or children, we immediately sense its value.

When Is "Play" Play?

As with love* or art, the definition of play is elusive. It is, however, possible to describe some of the central features. Johan Huizinga says play is "a free activity standing quite consciously outside 'ordinary' life as being 'not serious,' but at the same time absorbing the player intensely and utterly. It is an activity connected with no material interest, and no profit can be gained by it. It proceeds within its own proper boundaries of time and space according to fixed rules and in an orderly manner. It promotes the formation of social groupings" (Huizinga, 13). Child psychologist Jean Piaget adds helpfully that play is always done "for the pleasure of the activity" (92-93).

We can best understand the essence of play by looking at four pairs of descriptors.

Playtimes and playgrounds. Play always carries with it a new time and space that function as "parentheses" in the life of the participant. Everyday life comes to a standstill for the duration of the experience (e.g., the ballgame, the concert, the solitaire game), and the boundaries of one's world are forged anew (e.g., one does not ask if the movie *The Lion King* is true or good, or to the degree that one does, he or she is no longer playing).

Individual freedom and loving community. People voluntarily choose to play; it cannot be coerced. Yet players also sense that they have been invited into play by a potential coplayer or play object. While at play one treats other players and "playthings" as personal, creating with them a community (compare the child talking to the baseball as it is thrown against the concrete building or the parents who express their love to each other in a mutual process of give and take). When parents "play" with their children, they must be engaged with them as coplayers. It is not enough for a parent to shoot baskets with a child while thinking about a project at work.

Spontaneity and design. Regardless of prior preparation, which is often quite rigorous (compare the dancer or the concert pianist), there is spontaneity at the heart of play. As we jump, sing or skip our spirits soar. But such abandon is never at the expense of play's orderliness. Every game* of baseball is an occasion for new possibility, but without the rules it is not baseball. Music is the occasion for the spirit to wonder, but only through the strict appropriation of certain rules of tone, harmony and timing. For many families today, play has become overstructured or routinized with little room for spontaneity. Play is a both/and experience. Families need to be sure there are elements of both spontaneity and structure when they participate in play together.

Nonutilitarian yet productive. Play cannot be entered into with continuing outside interest if it is to become play. Although the insurance agent might play golf with a client to get a contract, it is only when business can be suspended that the game of golf ceases to be a form of work. Yet although play can have no ulterior motive or material interest (compare worshiping God as an act of play), it is not without fruitful consequence. In play one is able to do at least four things: (1) create strong bonds with others and the world, (2) emancipate one's spirit, (3) rediscover life in its entirety as the player becomes involved in the wholeness of her or his being, and (4) experience joy and delight that lingers. In these ways the player finds perspective for reengagement in the workaday world. Is there any family that can afford not to play together?

Parents need to take stock as to whether their family is engaged in authentic play. And this is not hard to do. For although play can be corrupted, all of us have experienced its fullness and value. Why is it that I still care about what happens to the USC football team or that I look forward to next year's ballet season? Because I have a longing for play. Parents should trust their instincts. If you doubt whether a family activity is actually play, it probably is not.

Biblical Paradigms and Models
Throughout its pages the Bible recognizes the importance of play though we have often failed to see it. Ecclesiastes advises us to enjoy our food and drink and the person we love (9:7-10). The Song of Songs is devoted exclusively to the playfulness of human sexuality.* The sabbath* has as its most basic definition a time of "nonwork" (Ex 35:1-3). Throughout the Old Testament we encounter the festivals and dances of God's people (see Holidays). The practice of hospitality* was an occasion for work to stop and a wholeness in life to be regained (cf. Gen 18). Similarly, Jesus' own life exhibited a healthy rhythm of work and play. His

times alone and friendship with those like Mary, Martha and Lazarus show us that play was important to him.

Yet we have systematically ignored or misinterpreted these texts. Christians have wondered how Ecclesiastes ever made it into the canon and have misinterpreted the author as writing only about life "under the sun" (i.e., secular existence; Eccles 1:14). For centuries the church has attempted to reinterpret the Song of Songs as an allegory about God's love for them. Many of us grew up in a context that interpreted the sabbath ordinance as applying primarily to our Sunday worship. We have failed to understand that Old Testament practices concerning hospitality have aesthetic as well as ethical dimensions—they were occasions for a party. Were the instances of friendship in the life of Jesus simply another way of proclaiming his messiahship, or were they also expressions of his own humanity? In ways such as these, Christians have failed to let Scripture teach us concerning a God-intended rhythm of work and play, play and work. Like our wider culture we have too often adopted both as individuals and as family units an undialectical commitment to work as our basic ideology.

Central to a biblical understanding of play is recognition that Scripture's concerns include creation as well as redemption. There are multiple theological emphases within the Bible. In Genesis 1 and 2, for example, God is portrayed as working and resting. His rest included enjoyment of creation and fellowship with humankind. Here is the basic paradigm for all of us: created in the image of God, we are to be creatures who both work and play.

This creational perspective is picked up in the sabbath's call for a fundamental rhythm within human existence (e.g., Ex 34:21-22). For the Hebrew the sabbath was not chiefly a time for worship but an occasion for relativizing one's work (compare Ex 16:22-30). It was not by the efforts of those who gathered up manna but only through the gracious provision of God that the Israelites found life and safety. Although the restatement of the Ten Commandments in Deuteronomy 5 justifies the sabbath practice in terms of all of us being God's coworkers, in the prior account in Exodus 20 the rationale for the sabbath is referenced to God alone. Through the sabbath we are invited to "remember" that life is a divine gift, not just a task.

This creational perspective is also expressed in the wisdom literature of the Old Testament as well as in the Song of Songs and many of the Psalms. The Song of Songs opens a window into the beauty and playfulness of human love, instructing us as to our own sexual relationships. Psalm 23 sings a song of trust in the Lord by using two analogies that include work and play—shepherding and hospitality. Psalm 104 celebrates the fact that as God's creatures we are to cultivate the earth not only to provide bread for our needs but wine to make our hearts glad and oil to make our faces shine (Ps 104:14-15). Ecclesiastes mounts a frontal assault on the workaholic who would foolishly try to find meaning in life independent of the God who has created us (Eccles 1—2). Instead, the Preacher finds in Genesis 1—11 sufficient insight to portray our lot in life as enjoying our work and our play (Eccles 9:7-10).

The Christian at Play

The evidence for play in the Bible is extensive, particularly in those discussions that are rooted in creation theology. But even in the books of the Law and the Prophets, as in the New Testament, we find culturally specific examples of Israel at play. A God-intended human lifestyle

of work and play finds its basis in creation and its full possibility in Jesus' recreation (compare Heb 4).

Writers as diverse as C. S. Lewis, Peter Berger and Dietrich Bonhoeffer have portrayed the importance of play within human existence. In *Surprised by Joy* Lewis describes those moments of play—having his mother read to him Beatrix Potter's *Squirrel Nutkin*, smelling a currant bush in his backyard or listening to Wagner—when he felt himself ushered into a reality that was illuminating for all existence. In *A Rumor of Angels* Berger finds "signals of transcendence" when our living toward death* is bracketed and we experience "eternity" in play (52). And in *Letters and Papers from Prison* (193), Bonhoeffer, writing out of his cell as he faced death because of his opposition to Hitler, commented on the general shape of human life:

> I wonder whether it is possible . . . to regain the idea of the Church as providing an understanding of the area of freedom (art, education, friendship, play). . . . Who is there, for instance, in our times, who can devote himself with an easy mind to music, friendship, games, or happiness? Surely not the "ethical" man, but only the Christian. (January 23, 1944)

As Christians we are given the freedom to play. After all, "this is my Father's world!"

See also COMPUTER GAMES; ENTERTAINMENT; GAMES; LEISURE; SABBATH; VACATIONS.

References and Resources
P. Berger, *A Rumor of Angels* (Garden City, N.Y.: Doubleday/Anchor, 1970); D. Bonhoeffer, *Letters and Papers from Prison*, ed. E. Bethge, rev. ed. (New York: Macmillan, 1967); P. Heintzman, G. Van Andel and T. Visker, *Christianity and Leisure* (Sioux City, Iowa: Dordt College Press, 1994); J. Huizinga, *Homo Ludens* (Boston: Beacon, 1955); R. K.

Johnston, *The Christian at Play* (Grand Rapids: Eerdmans, 1983); W. Kerr, *The Decline of Pleasure* (New York: Simon & Schuster, 1962); C. S. Lewis, *Surprised by Joy* (New York: Harcourt, Brace & World/Harvest Books, 1955); W. Oates, *Confessions of a Workaholic* (New York: World, 1971); J. Piaget, *Play, Dreams and Imitation in Childhood*, trans. C. Gattegno and F. M. Hodgson (New York: Norton, 1962); L. Terr, *Beyond Love and Work: Why Adults Need Play* (New York: Scribners, 1999).

Robert K. Johnston

—PRAYER—

Patterns of prayer, modeled by Jesus and Paul, pray God's eternal life into our families. Therefore, they are appropriate anytime, anywhere, at every age and in every circumstance. They teach us how to pray with regard to both order and content. God is acknowledged first: his name, his purposes, his resources, his activity on our behalf; then, within that framework, we present our needs. In this big picture our circumstances become arenas for God to work in and through for the sake of others; our needs become a place for his glory to be seen.

"I pray . . . for those you have given me, for they are yours" (Jn 17:9). As we pray these prayers *for* our children, they should naturally emerge when we pray them *with* our children. Anytime we pray in the presence of our children things we want them to hear or imitate, we are praying with them. Both formal and normal times of prayer are important. *Normal* is talking with God together about everyday things as they happen; *formal* is having set times of prayer—meals, bedtimes, set apart family times—which say prayer is important enough to make time for. If we invite the Creator to join family* brainstorming sessions, he will give insight into ways to put our prayers into action, ways we can be a part of what we have asked him to do.

Children learn to pray the way they learn most foundational things: through imitation and imitative play.* It is a biblical pattern. Jesus said, "The Son . . . can only do what he sees the Father doing . . . whatever the Father does, the Son also does. For the Father loves the Son and shows him all he does" (Jn 5:19-20). "Follow my example, as I follow the example of Christ," Paul urged in 1 Corinthians 11:1. "Be imitators of God . . . as dearly loved children" (Eph 5:1-2). "Whatever you have learned or received or heard from me, or seen in me—put it into practice" (Phil 4:9).

If we as parents can throw ourselves with abandon into a lifelong game* of Follow the Leader with our children, following Paul as he follows Jesus as he follows the Father, we will grow up "in Christ" to look like our "Dad," which is what salvation is all about.

The Lord's Prayer
The Lord's Prayer (adapted here from Mt 6:9-13) invites each family to be God's children together, trusting our Father to be with us, to know what we need, to lead us in safe paths, to deliver us when we get trapped by unwise choices. The words are few and simple. Jesus says, "When you pray, say,

"Our Father in heaven (by whom all things were created, we are your children. You have loved us, chosen us, adopted us and given us your name),

251

hallowed be your name (May we treasure and honor your name and reflect your character in every attitude, word and deed today, especially in our priorities and our motives).

Your kingdom come (Be enthroned in each heart so that your rule of mercy, hospitality,* righteousness and love* will define our family),

your will be done (May we eagerly anticipate opportunities throughout the day to love the people in our life the way you have loved us since this is the work you have given us to do). . . .

Give us today our daily bread (We acknowledge that all we have is from you; therefore we will trust you to provide what is needed in every aspect of our lives).

Forgive us our debts (Forgive us for putting ourselves first instead of you: setting up our own kingdoms, exalting our name instead of yours, legislating our will, trying to secure our own lives with position and material things)

as we have also forgiven our debtors (those who wound, devalue, or violate us; forgiveness,* which is for giving to another who doesn't deserve it, is your gift so that we can both be healed and made whole).

And lead us not into temptation (Protect us, we pray, from the temptation to play God in other's lives: to judge, condemn, demean or control; protect us from the lies of the evil one about ourselves, about God, about each other),

but deliver us from the evil one (the evil of practical atheism, of trying to live life on our own, without you. Only you can bring us into your kingdom, by your power, for your glory).' "

As we order each day, so may we order our lives. The content and order of this outline are vital to eternal life. It is the trunk of the tree from which the foliage and fruit draw life (Ps 1).

The Psalms

For some of us, the Psalms, the hymnbook and prayer book of generations of God's children, show us that "fruit and foliage." Psalms describe our God, our Creator, our Father, our strong tower. Psalms reveal the awe and splendor of God's name; they proclaim delight in his rule and affirm his purposes. There are psalms that relate God's story and our personal story; psalms that cry out for deliverance and justice; psalms that relate temptation in which someone's foot "almost slipped"; psalms that compose variations on themes of forgiveness, provision, protection, security, sorrow, joy and celebration; psalms that assure us of God's lovingkindness and faithfulness. The Lord's Prayer gives us the structure; Psalms flesh it out in realities of daily life.

Your family might look for psalms that tell your story. Or write your own psalms about how God has been involved in your family life. (See Eugene Peterson's *Psalms* [NavPress, 1994] for a fresh, earthy expression.)

Paul's "Mini-Prayers"

The simple sentence prayers from 1 Thessalonians may not seem like much, but they are like keys on a key ring. Their power lies in the doors they open for God to come and work with us in this task we were never meant to do alone.

(1:2) *"We always thank God for all of you."* Habitual thanksgiving for our children and for what God has done for them and is doing in them, brings trust for what he will do.

(3:10) *"Night and day we pray most earnestly that we may see you again and supply what is lacking in your faith."* Family routines and family labels (e.g., dependable, difficult), as well as events of the day, can obscure the "state of the heart." As we consistently breathe this prayer, the Holy Spirit can prompt us to respond in ways that "build up, not tear down" (2 Cor 13:10) when faith is fragile or fractured.

(3:11) *"May our God and Father himself and our Lord Jesus clear the way for us to come to you."* God will clear away the daily debris as well as entrenched defenses of family systems,* to make a way for his love to flow freely through us to our children and through our family to others.

(3:12) *"May the Lord make your love increase for each other and for everyone else."* Paul defines love for beginners in six words: "Love is patient (longsuffering); love is (actively) kind" (1 Cor 13:4). This is what God is like—full of lovingkindness and faithfulness—and this is how we reflect his character. Love can only increase when it is applied in the hard places time after time.

"How do I love, today, Lord?" is the key question. It is not easy to keep loving and loving. And so we pray (3:13) *"May* [the Lord] *strengthen your heart"* to give thanks to God for every person in your life. May he strengthen the eyes of your heart to respond to needs you cannot know. May he strengthen your heart to pursue open, uncluttered relationships with God and people. May he give you strength to love intentionally, generously, spontaneously, relentlessly. Strong, enduring love is from God. You cannot do it in your own strength, so be strong *in the Lord.*

Prayers to Unpack

In these prayers of Paul for his "children" (the believers in the New Testament churches), God's activity comes before their activity. In God's presence Paul gives thanks for who they are and what they have received in Christ. In light of this, and the resources and future that are theirs in Christ, he prays— affirming, encouraging and refocusing their attention on what really matters: faith in Jesus Christ and love for one another. Only then does he address their issues. Digging into the letter itself will help "decode" the prayer and apply it more specifically (e.g., 1 Cor 1:4-9; Eph 1:15-19, 3:16-19; Phil 1:3-5, 9-11; Col 1:3-14; 2 Thess 1:3, 11-12).

Doxology: This Is Our God!

Technology demands doxology. Jesus, encircled by children in the meadow or carrying a lamb, needs to be counterbalanced by Jesus "by whom all things were created: things in heaven and on earth, visible and invisible, whether thrones or powers or rulers or authorities; Jesus, whom God—who lives in unapproachable light, whom no one has seen or can see—has exalted to the highest place; the King eternal, immortal, invisible, the only God; [to him] be honor and glory for ever" (e.g. Rom 11:33-36; 16:27; Phil 2:6-11; Col 1:15-20; 1 Tim 1:17; 6:15).

Benedictions: Sending Out Prayers

There are many wonderful ways to say goodbye (God be with you) with Scripture when family members go off to sleep,* to play, to school* or to work. Even at the end of a meal, as the family scatters to varied activities, a blessing* reminds them that God's presence goes with them. Words of peace, hope, grace from God can nestle in the memory and warm the heart (e.g., Rom 15:13; 2 Cor 13:14; Eph 3:20-21; 1 Thess 3:12, 13; 5:23-24; 2 Thess 2:16-17; 3:5; 3:16-17; Jude 1:24-25). Check various translations of the Bible for other ways of phrasing. Praying a silent benediction whenever the family goes its separate ways (even when you forget and do it later), helps to continue the flow of blessing from your heart to theirs.

Scriptural patterns of prayer place our children and us in God's hands. Every prayer revolves around God's activity in our lives, past, present and future.

Knowing we are chosen and called to participate in God's purposes, loved beyond our limits, and safe now and always, we are free to play as we pray together in God's kingdom. We can explore new paths, build solid foundations and climb higher for a fresh perspective on life.

See also ALTERNATIVE RELIGIONS; CHARACTER; EATING; PARENTING; SPIRITUAL FORMATION; VALUES.

Maudine Fee

—PREGNANCY—

Once conception* has occurred, a human life miraculously unfolds in the nurturing womb, inspiring the scriptural metaphor of pregnancy as "fruitful waiting." The mother's experiences are as diverse as seasonal changes as she marks time in contemplation, preparation, prayer and hope. Intrauterine life is celebrated in Psalm 139 and Ecclesiastes 11:5, confirming God's faithful presence as we are "fearfully and wonderfully made." It is a mysterious journey, marked by growth and development not only for mother and child but for the entire family, as love* expands to embrace a new member.

A Mother's Seasonal Expectations
Invested with an inner garden, a pregnant woman becomes the object of processes beyond her control in a way not unlike the seasonal changes a gardener observes. Scripture reassures us of God's purpose for the future (Ps 104:19; Is 43:1-2; Jer 29:11). The child's presence is signaled by detectable hormonal and physical changes from the very start. In autumn the excitement of the news is heralded by a brilliant arboreal display of colors. As the fog rolls in off the sea, there may be a temporary clouding of volition and certainty held just weeks before. Perhaps even the wisdom of the decision to become pregnant may be doubted as nausea and fatigue obscure joy, calling into question the energy and ability to become a responsible and loving parent. Tearfulness rains in torrential bursts of emotion. Concentration is fragmented by anxiety, and distraction makes everyday tasks more burdensome. Nausea and hypersensitive taste and smell confer vigilance in avoiding exposing the vulnerable embryo to toxins such as alcohol and nicotine. As trees release their leaves, so is relinquishing essential for this season of preparation. The woman yields the constancy of her body shape to metamorphosis and surrenders her independence as she considers how her activities and decisions will affect the child she carries within. If it is a first pregnancy, forever altered is the exclusivity of being "just two." This is a time to plant bulbs of hope deep beyond the reach of frost's fingers (*see* Miscarriage).

The clear winter days afford a heightened scrutiny of people that before had escaped her notice—pregnant and nursing mothers, children in fathers' arms. Anticipating new responsibilities, values* and priorities, and changes in identity demands tremendous effort and time. Burying herself in quiet seclusion, the woman nourishes roots, reconnecting with her concept of family* by reliving childhood memories. She may retreat to reading* and inner places of imagining and prayer (Rom 12:12).

Midway through pregnancy subtlety and secrecy give way to the visibly expanding cradle of the womb. Now undeniable, the pregnancy becomes publicly anticipated. Anchored no longer in her monthly menstrual cycle (see Menstruation), she finds new identity as a mother-to-be. She is the object of others' encouragement and advice, sometimes conflicting and excessive (Mary and Elizabeth share their pregnancies in Lk 1). Like spring's stirring beneath the ground, the baby's movements become distinguishable from internal intestinal sensations. The tangible relationship of a mother and child begins when she notices her baby's pattern of activity and responses to shared sounds of music and voices. Fathers and siblings finally become participants, appreciating the baby's vitality by touch or sharing the visual ultrasound images that delineate the fetus' form and movement.

Summer ripens in a plethora of glow and sweat. With heavy abundance she is a tree laden with fruit and swollen breasts. She chronicles long days and short nights with insomnia arising from mild discomforts. This change is more bearable when considered a conditioning or preparation for the sleep deprivation and altered rhythms that inevitably accompany the birth of baby.

The Fetal Dance
Complete at conception, within the fertilized ovum are the DNA designs whose secrets will be elaborated in this mysterious "becoming" that persists well beyond birth—in fact until death.* Cells divide, migrate, polarize and specialize, becoming organs, cartilage and bone. Only two weeks after the first missed menstrual period, a primitive tubal heart is already beating in an embryo the size of a small bean. Common to fish eggs and the mammalian embryo is a yoke sac, a source of nourishment; in the human embryo it provides blood cells until bone marrow forms and it is no longer needed.

As the fetal brain cells develop, we are reminded of God's prompting to advance life toward greater awareness of self and Maker. "He has set eternity in the hearts of men; yet they cannot fathom what God has done from beginning to end" (Eccles 3:11). By birth, all of the 100 billion brain cells of adult life are present, although the labyrinthine connections are woven throughout early life and are influenced by experience and inhibited by alcohol. This loom's complexity is elaborated by the fact that each cell may ultimately communicate with between one thousand and ten thousand other cells through sixty different chemical messengers (neurotransmitters). The total number of possible interactions exceeds the number of particles in the universe. The human brain is the most highly organized structure known! There is no lack of stimulation in the womb, and the hard wiring begins long before birth.

Consider the growing awareness of the fetus swimming in a warm intrauterine sea. Our blood is the sea continued in our veins. As surf pounds rhythmically against the shore, so the earliest perception of sounds from the fourth month in pregnancy is the primitive drum of our mother's heart. Unlike a swimmer who dives down from the surface, trapping a muffling air cushion in the ear canal, the fetus experiences amplified sounds when transmitted through water to the eardrum. The womb is anything but quiet. Externally we share the sound world, and internally the fetus hears profound bowel gurgling and the rhythmic surging of placental blood to its own quicker-paced heartbeat superimposed on the slower maternal base beat.

Children sing before they speak and sway before they walk, interpreting and synchronizing themselves with the rhythms of human pulsations. Dance

255

has been historically the earliest outlet for emotion, at the dawn of rituals and the arts, giving the inarticulate a voice as a personal form of prayer* ("a time to dance," Eccles 3:4). John the Baptist "leaped for joy" in the womb at Mary's arrival (Lk 1:44). The lively movements of the fetus are visible on ultrasound as early as ten weeks from the last missed period—months before they are perceptible by the mother or an outside hand.

The sensuous world of the fetus consists of the tactile embrace of the womb, the response of the mother's pat to the place of a kick, and positional changes sensed in the inner ear. Tiny stones falling with gravity stimulate hair cells in one of three canals translating "up," "down" and "side to side." There is uniformity in the protective amniotic bath, with constant satiety, warmth and darkness or a reddish glow. It is a safe, sterile and buoyant place to practice the primal skills of sucking, grasping, clinging and dancing. The relaxation response appears essential for health and coping with illnesses, pain or stress. By imagining her child's intrauterine experience, the expectant mother practices relaxation and rhythmic, controlled breathing, so preparing herself for the trials of labor.

Cocreators with Each Other and God

As creation unfolds within the expectant mother at the instigation of the awaiting father, they acknowledge that the child is not formed by their own concepts. They have worked but cannot take credit; they are creating but not possessing. Pregnancy's task is to begin to relinquish our hold on the individual within, whose love, respect and obedience are engendered be-

yond parental control. Our child's destiny, although of utmost concern, is not entirely in our hands.

As the child begins so near to the heart of the mother, it is understandable that in contemplating birth she anticipates a rending that is lifelong, a vulnerability to hurt and be hurt. We are inevitably imperfect parents in the forgiving arms of our heavenly Father. Even in the womb we glimpse our humanity. Amniotic fluid is the brine of sweat and tears, secreted around the developing fetus, welling up from the deepest recesses of joy, sorrow and toil, a salient harbinger of the inherent suffering that our connectedness entails being parent and child. The baptismal tides of confession and forgiveness* can cleanse and preserve the vitality of unconditional love within the family and our identity and hope as children of God, "sowing in tears and reaping with shouts of joy" (see Ps 126:5). We are all pregnantly awaiting ultimate healing and reconciliation in the new heaven and the new earth; each season is weathered in faith and trust that God will be faithful to his promises.

See also BREAST-FEEDING; CONCEPTION; MENSTRUATION.

References and Resources

F. G. Bushe, "When in This State: The Relaxation Response," *Wellness* 2, no. 5 (November/December 1992) 28-33; C. DeMarco, *Take Charge of Your Body* (Winlaw, B.C.: The Well Woman, 1994); L. Nilsson, *A Child Is Born* (New York: Dell, 1993); C. J. Shatze, "The Developing Brain," *Scientific American*, September 19, 1992, 60-67; J. M. Ward, *Motherhood, a Gift of Love* (Hong Kong: Running, 1991).

Carol Anderson

PROBLEMS. *See* FAMILY PROBLEMS; STRESS.

—READING—

Reading is the process by which we arrive at meaning in response to the stimulus of print. But from this definition we may miss the wonder of reading, which is the miracle of mind meeting mind in a conversation* that transcends time. Reading can be a lifelong source of information, instruction and delight.

Reading and Literacy

Because the Christian faith is grounded in and sustained by a body of sacred literature in the form of the Old and New Testaments, literacy has been linked to the proclamation of the good news concerning Jesus. In England literacy was the great gift of the Reformation and the printing press. William Tyndale's wish that the Bible would be available to every plowboy and milkmaid in England became increasingly realized throughout the late sixteenth and early seventeenth centuries, so that by the mid-seventeenth century even a poor man's son like John Bunyan could read the Scriptures and write his response to them for an eager audience of readers from the same social class. This emphasis on education for literacy helped form a word-centered society, which existed for several centuries before being challenged by the visual media.

The many kinds of reading we do may be roughly categorized under three headings. The first, reading to learn, is the approach we take to informative texts. In this kind of reading we usually preview the material, formulating questions that will guide our reading; we then read, review the material in terms of recalling answers to the questions we had shaped and reread where necessary to complete our understanding. The second, reading to function, is the approach we take to utilitarian materials like labels and manuals and do-it-yourself instructions. In this kind of reading we test our understanding by action. The third, reading to satisfy personal inter-

ests, is the approach we take to literary works. Reading to satisfy our hunger to hear God's voice and know God personally is a special aspect of this last category and sustains our spiritual life.

Reading the Bible

The Bible can be read by believers individually with an openness to hearing the Word of God; this is the practice of many in their quiet time or private devotions (Bockmuehl). But the Bible needs also to be read corporately by small groups of Christians in community and as they gather in larger groups for worship, for remembrance of Christ's death* and for the preaching of the Word. It needs also to be read corporately in an ongoing discussion between theologians, scholars, pastors and the laity, as the church searches for an ever fuller understanding of the Bible to guide its beliefs, doctrines and practice.

In modern literary criticism there is an increasing awareness that every reading act comprises an interaction of what the reader brings to the text and what the text brings to the reader. Attention is being paid to the way in which we reconfigure what is configured in the text (to use the terminology of hermeneutist Paul Ricoeur), taking into account the personal and cultural lenses through which we view textual materials.

But there is something more involved in the process of reading than reader interaction. The Holy Spirit is present when believers read the Scripture and will continue to be present in the church until the end of the age. Because of the Spirit's guiding presence within the Christian community, we can have confidence that the Scriptures will continue to instruct and challenge the church in its faith and practice, with new light breaking forth (for historical examples of this process, see Swartley).

Reading Other Works
While the Bible will form the core of the Christian's understanding of God and of life, there is a wide domain of good books beyond the Bible to enjoy and be nurtured by. Christians are sometimes afraid to encounter ideas that do not reinforce their own or are taught to think of time spent reading fiction as frivolous. But we should explore our ideas and others' ideas through reading and thoughtfully weighing them against the Scriptures. One purpose of doing this is to have our own vision of life enlarged or challenged by the visions conveyed by excellent writers of fiction and drama. Guides to good literature might be used to begin such a pilgrimage into literature; the Great Books approach will lead the reader into the basic texts of Western civilization; more simply and flexibly, course descriptions from university or college courses can be used to guide explorations of specific fields or areas of interest.

Literature can be approached in a number of ways: by time period (you might want to read medieval poetry and prose or novels of the eighteenth century), by author or by theme. As an example of theme, one might consider death and dying from the point of view of the yearnings expressed in ancient literature (*The Epic of Gilgamesh;* the biblical books of Job and Ecclesiastes); in descriptions in classic and contemporary literature (Chaucer's *Book of the Duchess;* Bunyan's conclusions in both parts of *The Pilgrim's Progress;* William Faulkner's *As I Lay Dying;* Rudy Wiebe's *My Lovely Enemy*); in discussions in

contemporary psychotherapy (Ernest Becker's *The Denial of Death* and Elisabeth Kübler-Ross's *On Death and Dying*); in readings from Christian experience (David Watson's *Fear No Evil*); in resources for Christian pastoral care (David K. Switzer's *The Dynamics of Grief*); and finally in the riches of Christian theology (Jürgen Moltmann's *The Crucified God;* John R. W. Stott's *The Cross of Christ*). Accompanied by meditation on such biblical passages as Psalm 23, Psalm 90, the passion and resurrection narratives in the Gospels, their expositions in Acts and Pauline passages like 1 Corinthians 15 and Philippians 1, such an exploration through reading would open up a wide perspective and equip one to think clearly and Christianly about the "unthinkable"— that is, death.*

Encouraging Young Readers
With the visual media taking over many hours of children's lives, Christian parents should be serious and intentional about helping their children form the habit of reading. Reading encourages a use of the mind and imagination that is not required in television* viewing. Reading also extends the period of "charm, malleability, innocence and curiosity of children" which the visual media transform into "pseudo-adulthood," according to Neil Postman (xiii). Habits of lifelong reading are most likely to be developed in a home in which the adults read for enjoyment, information and personal growth themselves. If books are present in the home and read and discussed in the view and hearing of the children, reading will be seen as a natural part of everyday life. Good reading habits begin with an association between books, reading and loving care; the child enjoying the total experience of love* and story, pictures and voice is a child on the way to becoming a reader (*see* Fairy Tales).

Parents are often highly anxious about their children's learning to read and try to promote it by means of phonics workbooks and other aids. Most reading experts agree that putting pressure on children in this way is more likely to turn off developing readers than to help them (on this, see Elkind). Since reading requires an array of skills and experiences, the home* that provides rich visual and tactile learning experiences and creates opportunities for storytelling and conversation lays the foundation on which more formal instruction can be based (see Home Schooling).

Some form of regular Bible reading with children, kept short and made an integral part of mealtime or bedtime rituals, provides the best basis for a lifetime love for and knowledge of the Scriptures. Families could begin with simplified, sequential Bible stories and move on to participatory shared readings at levels appropriate to children's abilities. Or, very simply, families could include a brief reading of a few verses of Scripture as part of the blessing at the beginning or conclusion of a meal. Still, the best pattern of instruction is the one laid out in Deuteronomy: "Fix these words of mine in your hearts and minds. . . . Teach them to your children, talking about them when you sit at home and when you walk along the road, when you lie down and when you get up" (Deut 11:18-19). The Scriptures wholly integrated into life and thought will be passed on lovingly from one generation to another.

Conclusion

Reading is of great importance throughout the Bible. Christians, like Jews, are people of the Book. The writing of the New Testament documents presupposes that many among those who were first called Christians were literate and that others would listen to the oral readings of the stories of Jesus' life, death and resurrection. Although Jesus himself left no written records, his many citations from the Old Testament show his deep biblical literacy. He opened his earthly ministry with a reading of the Hebrew Bible within the congregation at Nazareth. In this scene all the elements of reading sacred text are delineated: a congregation or body of people who hold the text to be sacred and the public reading and discussion of that text, in which the current readers take their place in succession with previous generations who have read and commented on the text. It is in the context of these elements that Jesus offers a radical rereading of the text, declaring, "Today this scripture is fulfilled in your hearing" (Lk 4:21).

One of the early conversion narratives, the story of the Ethiopian official, is the story of an evangelist's offering a rereading of an Old Testament text so that the reader can see Jesus in it (Acts 8:26-40). And the book of Revelation not only sees future events as written on a sealed scroll (chap. 5) but is itself self-consciously a book that is to be read by the church until the return of Christ (1:3; 22:7-21). We would do well to cultivate ourselves as readers as we whisper or cry, with the readers of all ages, "Come, Lord Jesus."

See also ENTERTAINMENT; FAIRY TALES; GOALS; LEISURE; PARENTING; SPIRITUAL FORMATION.

References and Resources

M. J. Adler and C. Van Doren, *How to Read a Book: The Classic Guide to Intelligent Reading* (New York: Simon & Schuster, 1972); K. Bockmuehl, *Listening to the God Who Speaks* (Colorado Springs: Helmers & Howard, 1990); D. Elkind, *The Hurried Child* (Reading, Mass.: Addison-Wesley, 1981); N. Frye, *The Great Code: The Bible and Literature* (New York: Harcourt Brace Jovanovich, 1982); H. J. Graff, *The Legacies of Literacy* (Bloomington:

Indiana University Press, 1987); J. Lindskoog and K. Lindskoog, *How to Grow a Young Reader* (Wheaton, Ill.: Harold Shaw, 1989); N. Postman, *The Disappearance of Childhood* (New York: Dell, 1982); J. W. Sire, *How to Read Slowly: Reading for Comprehension* (Wheaton, Ill.: Harold Shaw, 1989); W. Swartley, *Slavery, Sabbath, War and Women: Case Studies in Biblical Interpretation* (Scottdale, Penn.: Herald, 1983).

Maxine Hancock

REST. *See* DEATH; LEISURE; SABBATH; SLEEPING.

RISK. *See* DEBT; INSURANCE; MONEY.

—SABBATH—

Sabbath is what our leisure-hungry and work-addicted culture desperately needs. But the word brings to most minds negation, absence and all the restrictions well-meaning Christians have placed on Sunday over the years. This article will explore the biblical meaning of rest, the theological meaning of sabbath and sabbath as a life-giving discipline. In the end we will see that we do not keep sabbath so much as sabbath keeps us!

The Ultimate Rest

The negative view of sabbath has some foundation. The Hebrew word *shabath* means "to stop," "to desist," "to cease from doing." The first formalized reference to sabbath in the Ten Commandments requires desisting from labor one day a week, though it does not legislate six days of labor: "Remember the Sabbath day by keeping it holy. Six days you shall labor and do all your work, but the seventh day is a Sabbath to the LORD your God. On it you shall not do any work" (Ex 20:8-10). As Witold Rybczynski notes, viewing the weekend as a day or two in which one is not required to work and viewing it as a period in which one is required *not* to work are not the same thing (60). A weekly experience of rest is fundamental to our regaining perspective and entering the rest that is essential to personal, social and creational survival.

But sabbath rest is more than keeping one day a week. Rest is not merely cessation but appropriation. Israel was commanded to enjoy the day—to enjoy rest! Rest is a state of body, mind and soul that is essential for health,* both physical and spiritual. It involves restoring balance, rejuvenating energies, regaining perspective, allowing our emotional energies to recover, being in harmony with our own bodies and, especially, enjoying God. Rest is a multi-faceted blessing that includes sleep,* dreaming, recreation, vacations,* play* and leisure.* But sabbath is rest in its purest and most complete form, probably because it involves gaining the threefold harmony of God, humankind and creation.

Harmony with God means that we have peace with God, enter God's own rest and enjoy God. Harmony with humankind means that our own persons are rejuvenated and given perspective. Unlike leisure, which is concerned primarily with cultivating oneself, sabbath ministers to the self indirectly by recovering our focus on God, renewal being a byproduct. Harmony with creation suggests that God's desire is not only that people have rest but even animals and the land, every seven years as well as one day a week (Ex 20:10; Deut 15:1-12). This threefold harmony can also be expressed in the terms of prayer* (God-humankind harmony), play (harmony with oneself) and peacemaking (humankind-creation/social harmony): enjoying God, enjoying ourselves and celebrating creation.

To show how fundamental sabbath is to the life of faith, Scripture describes the creation of Adam and Eve on the sixth day as the penultimate creation, the climax coming the next day, the sabbath. Nothing is closer to God's mind and heart than the creation of sabbath. Adam woke up from his unconscious sleep not to start his work of caring for God's world but to experience rest. Adam and Eve's first vocational experience was to waste time for good and for God. Only if we do the same can we understand why we are to take care of God's world, build community and pray.

No Trivial Pursuit
There is a theology of leisure in the Bible, but it is secondary to the great and extensive material on sabbath. What we find from Genesis to Revelation is not the cultivation of a perfect balance of work and leisure but of work and sabbath. There are deep theological reasons for this.

Sabbath reveals the heart of God. God rested on the seventh day (Gen 2:2), but this was not mere cessation; it was refreshment (Ex 31:17). God literally put aside the work of creation both to enjoy rest ("It was very good"; Gen 1:31) and to put creation in its place (it is good but not God). So the people that were first called to bear God's image on earth—Israel—were given two archetypal images of salvation to proclaim good news to others and to be refreshed in

their own faith: the exodus (symbolized in the festival of Passover) and the sabbath (their weekly reminder that God is in charge; Moltmann, 287). Both exodus (a dramatic rescue accomplished by the mighty hand of God) and sabbath (a period that implies trusting in God's provision enough to set aside one's work) are tangible signs of having faith in a God of grace. The kind of God we actually worship is revealed by whether or not we keep sabbath.

Sabbath was not to be an experience of multiple restrictions; Israel was to "call the Sabbath a delight" (Is 58:13). This delight was not eliminated by the coming of Christ but rather was intensified as we wait for full manifestation of Christ and the kingdom, when full rest will be attained. Jesus claimed to be Lord of the sabbath (Mk 2:27-28) and declared that he fulfilled rather than annulled it. Being sabbath's lord did not mean Jesus could break it at will; rather, it means that the Lord fulfilled sabbath's meaning and intent. Therefore Jesus healed and gleaned in the fields (as a poor man) on Saturday, the Jewish sabbath. More importantly he embodied sabbath by restoring people to God through forgiveness* of sins, healing the sick and bringing unmitigated joy, the first stage of the threefold harmony of God, creation and humankind that will receive its final fulfillment when Christ comes again. In the New Jerusalem (Rev 21—22) the Lamb is everywhere (we enjoy God in uninterrupted communion), creation is renewed (not only the new heavens but even a new material earth!), and people are released for permanent creativity and exquisite joy.

Sabbath reveals God's intentions for the world. It is the celebration of creation. Jürgen Moltmann speaks of this as the "feast of creation." Put differently, sabbath involves the redemption of both space and time, the reharmonizing of

God, humankind and creation in both spatial (and material) as well as temporal terms.

The first mention of holiness in the Bible refers to time: "And God blessed the seventh day and made it holy" (Gen 2:3). In contrast, humankind seems preoccupied with making holy places. In his brilliant exposition of sabbath, Abraham Heschel observes that all pantheistic religions are religions of space and sacred places, in contrast to the faith of Israel, which is concerned with the redemption of time (4-6). The prophets maintained that the day of the Lord was more important than the house of the Lord. The great cathedrals, he maintains, are cathedrals in time. And sabbath is the holy architecture of time. The meaning sabbath is precisely this:

> Six days a week we live under the tyranny of things in space; on the Sabbath we try to become attuned to *holiness in time.* It is a day on which we are called upon to share what is eternal in time, to turn from the results of creation to the mystery of creation; from the world of creation to the creation of the world. (Heschel, 10)

Surprisingly, God's work in creating the world is presented in Scripture as play. Wisdom describes herself as "the craftsman at [God's] side . . . filled with delight day after day, / rejoicing always in his presence, / rejoicing in the whole world and delighting in mankind" (Prov 8:30-31). Sabbath and play have much in common.

Sabbath reveals the playfulness of God. Sabbath for humankind is playing heaven. The best way to learn to work is to play at it! Children do this naturally before the process of growing up drives a wedge between work and play. When we "play" heaven—by cocreating with God, by delighting in creation, by making things fit a heavenly model and by worshiping—we are anticipating the joys of being fully "grown-up" men and women in Christ in heaven (where we truly become children again!). Once again Heschel is eloquent on this subject: "Sabbath is an example of the world to come" (73) and heavenly minded people are, as C. S. Lewis once said, those who are also of most earthly use (51).

Having the Time of Our Lives

We have been exploring sabbath as a lifestyle, something that informs and transforms all the facets of everyday life: work, leisure, family life, vacations and even sleep. We have good scriptural warrant for universalizing sabbath in a way that makes it an everyday reality rather than a one-day-a-week affair. The apostle Paul said, "One man considers one day more sacred than another; another considers every day alike. Each one should be fully convinced in his own mind" (Rom 14:5). Sabbath is *optional,* which opens up the possibility of every day being regarded as such: "He who regards one day as special, does so to the Lord. . . . For none of us lives to himself alone" (Rom 14:6-7).

Sabbath lifestyle. In Jesus' day many had reduced sabbath observance to a task, a work to be performed. The religious people of his day were hedging the day with a myriad of prohibitions either to make it happen or to protect it from impiety. So the day came to be served both for its own sake and for the merit people obtained in doing it just right. In contrast, Jesus viewed sabbath as something given by God for people's benefit, not bondage: "The Sabbath was made for man, not man for the Sabbath" (Mk 2:27). Jesus regarded himself as Lord even of the sabbath. He enjoyed the day by doing what his Father loves to do on the sabbath: creating and recreating, resting and bringing rest to others.

It is difficult to resist the conclusion, given the number of miracles Jesus worked on the sabbath, that Jesus deliberately chose to do most of his healings on Saturday! He had a point to make: sabbath is not the absence of work but experiencing the joy of God and entering into God's work. The author of the letter to the Hebrews had this same thought when he called us to "make every effort to enter that rest" (Heb 4:11), "for anyone who enters God's rest also rests from his own work, just as God did from his" (Heb 4:10). This author hints that entering sabbath is, ironically, hard work for us because we are so driven to make sabbath a personal performance, a thing we make happen, rather than a delicious relaxation in God. So sabbath becomes the model of salvation.

Mini-sabbaths. Most Christians find that whether or not they have kept a special day, they need a time dedicated to God every day. It is important to explore the reason for a daily quiet time. Spiritual disciplines are not ways of finding God or of attaining sanctification but of chasing away obstacles that keep us from being continuously found by God. It is a mighty work on our part to make ourselves truly available to God. The farmer cannot make the seeds grow, but he must work hard in cultivating the soil. That is what daily sabbath involves.

There is a further reason. Our society continuously inundates us with messages to buy, consume and experience. It is impossible to be unaffected by the ubiquitous appeal of the advertising world to the flesh. That is reason enough to spend time each day in a mini-sabbath. But the purpose is not merely to bank good thoughts before we are besieged by the world. The purpose is to shape how we are to live. It seems imperative that persons committed to making every day sabbath must learn how to reduce the stimulation they receive from society. They will see fewer movies, watch less television* and moni-

tor more carefully what they read. According to the gastronomic world we are what we eat, and in the realm of the soul, we are what we see and hear. We want to live each hour for God, experiencing God's presence and pleasure.

Adopting a sabbath lifestyle will result in less need for leisure activities and diversions. The world offers work and leisure (without sabbath). The Bible offers work and sabbath (with leisure). Leisure and sabbath are not necessarily the same thing. Sabbath involves the threefold harmony of God, creation and ourselves. Prayer and Bible reading are part of this but so may be digging a garden, making a model boat, trying a new recipe, visiting the lonely and liberating the oppressed (Is 58:6). For a full experience of sabbath we will contemplate creation, redemption and our complete consummation in heaven. Sabbath is contemplative; it directs us toward God and informs us of the meaning of life. But it also leads to an active lifestyle in line with the Old Testament Jubilee year: the sabbath of sabbaths (Lev 25; Lk 4:18-19). Leisure, which is so much less than this, can become a diversion from sabbath and an unsatisfying one at that.

Part of sabbath living is to see that we get a good night's sleep every night, as far as it is possible. God literally refreshes his beloved daily in sleep (Ps 4:8; 127:1-2). Refreshed in sleep and renewed by our exposure to the life-giving power of Scripture and prayer, we can face the demands of work.

Sunday sabbath. Having considered the universalization of sabbath in a lifestyle, we must now address the question of sabbath as one day a week. The emergence of the Jewish sabbath in the context of societies that did not have a seven-day week is a fascinating study in itself. The further emergence of the Christian Sunday in relation to the Jewish sabbath is a complicated matter. Obviously early Jewish Christians celebrated both the sabbath (sundown Friday to sundown Saturday) and the Lord's Supper on Resurrection Day (Sunday) before returning to work on Sunday. In time, sabbath observance diminished, normally without having the Christian Sunday take on all the characteristics of Jewish sabbath (Rybczynski, 66). But the Christianization of the Roman Empire had its effect on Sunday. Formal law relating to Sunday observance was first enacted in 321 by Emperor Constantine, who forbade people to work on "the venerable day of the Sun." But it was not until the twelfth century that the term *Christian sabbath* was used, marking as it does the grafting of the sabbath tradition, especially in its negative restrictions, on to the Lord's Day (Rybczynski, 70-71).

Some form of weekly or regular sabbath is not an optional extra for the New Testament Christian. It is fundamental to spiritual health and even to emotional health, as some medical studies have shown. But keeping one day as a special day of reflection on the meaning of the other six is increasingly difficult in a secularized society that now exploits Sunday as the ultimate day for shopping* and leisure activities. For pastors Sunday is a workday, and I recommend that they perhaps keep a Jewish sabbath: Friday sundown to Saturday sundown. Each person will find a pattern that fits, at least for a while. Different occupational experiences and changes in family responsibilities will cause us to adjust our pattern from time to time.

Often these special-day sabbaths are splendid opportunities to follow one of the many spiritual disciplines that have enriched the spirituality of the church over the centuries: Bible meditation, confession, waiting prayer, intercession for others. An excellent guide for this is *Celebration of Discipline* by Richard Foster. A whole book of the Bible can be read at one sitting, or a single verse can become the subject of meditation for several hours. Time can be spent reflecting on parables or waiting for new ones to come through God's creation. Sabbath is also an ideal time for the journey inward. Active people need to stop long enough to let their soul catch up to their body. *Religion,* in the true meaning of the word, is that which binds together, so making us whole. When we create space and time to be real with God, important questions often surface, questions that can lead to more connectedness.

I have, until now, been exploring an individual use of sabbath as a special day. I have done so deliberately because I am convinced that one can only afford to be in Christian community if one has learned how to be alone with God. Otherwise we tend to feed parasitically on the corporate life of the church. But now I must offer a word about sabbath in regard to the church. I have come to believe that worship in the context of fellowship is the most important thing we do in the gathered life of the church. If sabbath is being liberated from the tyranny of performance to rediscover our identities through love,* then worship is an obvious way to keep the sabbath. We do not worship for what we get out of it. That would bring our utilitarian work ethic into worship. Ironically, praise "works" precisely because it lifts us above our compulsion to make everything useful. It is mere enjoyment of God, nothing more, nothing less. All our worship on earth is like a grand rehearsal, worth doing for its own sake, but intended to prepare for a grander occasion. Sabbath days help us to "play heaven." May we not also view sabbath as a way of "playing" with God, celebrating the mutual delight God and we, his covenant partners, have in each other and the work we do together?

In the deepest sense we do not keep sabbath; the sabbath keeps us. On our own we are not capable of sustaining our orientation toward God and our heavenly direction. That leaves us with a biblical paradox: we must labor to enter that rest (Heb 4:11). Sabbath keeps us focused on the heart of God, the intentions of God for the world, the playfulness of God. Sabbath keeps us heaven-bound.

Ultimate sabbath. In reality, Sunday for the Christian is not simply the Jewish sabbath moved a day later. As Moltmann points out, Sunday is the messianic extension of Israel's sabbath and a witness to the new creation brought by Christ. It seems pointless to debate whether sabbath should be kept on Saturday or Sunday when the New Testament points to a greater experience than simply "keeping the sabbath." Sabbath cannot be contained in the practice of "keeping one day." Therefore, a curious phrase appears in the second century in the *Epistle of Barnabas:* "the eighth day." In this primitive Christian document, Barnabas looks forward to an ultimate fulfillment of sabbath when the Son of Man comes. Speaking for God, Barnabas says,

> The present sabbaths are not acceptable to me, but that which I have made, in which I will give rest to all things and make the beginning of an eighth day, that is the beginning of another world. Wherefore we also celebrate with gladness (on Sunday and the rest of the week) the eighth day in which Jesus also rose from the dead and was made manifest and ascended into Heaven. (*Barn.* 15:8-9)

So it is with good reason that the Russian theologian Nikolai Berdyaev spoke of the event of Easter as the eighth day of creation. What was created at the beginning, all that we are and have and all the days of the week, enter at Easter into the beginning of the glorification of everything, a glorification in which the gulf between toil and rest is closed.

Because the eighth day has begun, we live simultaneously both *in* this world and *for* the coming world. The transfiguration of everything has begun. So the purpose of keeping one day a week, keeping one hour a day and living every day sabbatically is to make ourselves available for God to redeem all the time and space of our lives. All seven days are holy because the eighth day is dawning.

See also HEALTH; LEISURE; PLAY; SPIRITUAL FORMATION; VACATIONS.

References and Resources

S. Bocchiochi, *From Sabbath to Sunday: A Historical Investigation of the Rise of Sunday Observance in Earliest Christianity* (Rome: Gregorian University Press, 1977); M. J. Dawn, *Keeping the Sabbath Wholly* (Grand Rapids: Eerdmans, 1989); T. Edwards, *Sabbath Time* (New York: Seabury, 1982); Richard Foster, *Celebration of Discipline* (San Francisco: Harper & Row, 1982); A. D. Goldberg, "The Sabbath as Dialectic: Implications for Mental Health," *Journal of Religion and Health* 25, no. 3 (Fall 1986) 237-44; A. Heschel, *The Earth Is the Lord's and the Sabbath* (New York: Harper & Row, 1950); C. S. Lewis, *Christian Behaviour* (London: Geoffrey Bles, 1943); J. Moltmann, *God in Creation,* trans. M. Kohl (London: SCM, 1985); E. O'Connor, *Eighth Day of Creation: Gifts and Creativity* (Waco, Tex.: Word, 1971); E. Peterson, "The Pastor's Sabbath" *Leadership* 6, no. 2 (Spring 1985) 52-58; H. Rahner, *Man at Play* (New York: Herder & Herder, 1972); W. Rybczynski, *Waiting for the Weekend* (New York: Viking Penguin, 1991); W. Rordorf, *Sunday: The History of the Day of Rest and Worship in the Earliest Centuries of the Christian Church* (London: SCM Press, 1968); R. P. Stevens, *Disciplines of the Hungry Heart* (Wheaton, Ill.: Harold Shaw, 1993).

R. Paul Stevens

SATANISM. *See* ALTERNATIVE RELIGIONS.

—SCHOOLS, PUBLIC AND PRIVATE—

John Dewey's progressive education was as popular across North America following World War II as it had been in the 1930s. It was ideally suited to America's melting pot philosophy—the idea of a common political loyalty, a common set of values and a clarity about the heritage that should be transmitted to succeeding generations. Then came Sputnik in the fall of 1957. Lawrence Cremin, an expert on the history of progressive education, dates the death of that movement from the days immediately following the successful launch of the Soviet satellite. Sputnik was indeed an educational watershed.

Changes followed fast after Sputnik: first came a drive to raise academic standards, then followed intensive research on what determined success in schools. One outcome of the latter was the discovery that parents exercise critical influence on performance in schools and hence their views and involvement needed to be given new priority. Alongside these changes came the societal revolution that accompanied the widespread usage of television* and computers.* No longer was the melting pot philosophy meaningful. Both the content and process of learning came under scrutiny. Traditional values were frequently rejected, leading to a growing concern by parents, a concern that still dominates their thinking.

Values* are at the heart of educational practice. While every parent wants a good education in terms of content, preparation for college and career prospects, there is a larger concern: the question of which values will undergird classroom practice. Are they consistent with those held by the parents? At one end, is there a danger of indoctrination leading to confrontation with the home? At the other, might there be a moral vacuum, a maze of relativistic ethics, destroying all sense of right and wrong? Values are evident whenever educational plans are made. Everything that happens in a school is value laden. The notion of value-free education is a myth: every choice of teaching materials, every mode of instruction and every action by the teacher carries a set of values.

Public Schools

Harmony with parents is difficult in the public school system. Teachers and school administrators are expected to represent the interests of the people they serve, namely, the values of the multicultural society of North America. Since no institution can operate without some ground rules, the likely pattern of values acceptable to all segments of the community will be the lowest common denominator: respect for the rights of others, honesty and work ethic. These will be advocated since, in theory, they have universal acceptance. However, naturalism or secular humanism will often be a dominant value. In such, humanity is seen as an accident of evolution, so the human being is the measure of all things and can create his or her own truth and morality. The outcomes are predictable—permissiveness, moral relativism and situational ethics. Values are neutral.

Awareness of God, acceptance of the

Judeo-Christian ethic and knowledge of the Bible's content are generally avoided on the fallacious assumption that they violate the separation of church and state. In many schools they would be treated as harmful, unsuitable for a child's intellectual growth, even regarded as the private interests of narrow-minded parents. This does not mean that Christian parents cannot influence or be happy with sending their children to public schools. Competent teachers and principals know that the student's home background profoundly influences performance in school, and they will often want a harmonious partnership with parents.

The increasing recognition of parental values is now apparent among political leaders. Over the past few years the importance of education has been stressed, focusing sharply on the role of parents. Many leaders now urge educators to give top priority to parental values. Clearly the older style where teachers decided which values would govern must give way to a system in which parents and teachers adhere to a common set of values.

The voucher system is one of the best ways of meeting parents' wishes. It allows them to choose any school, public or private, in which they have confidence and where fees match the voucher. The voucher is based on the per capita cost of education in the public system of the community concerned. In Milwaukee, parents who were very unhappy with the performance of their public schools accepted vouchers for half the regular per capita cost of schooling, which was all they could secure from the municipal authorities. With this money they sent their children to Catholic schools. The result: attendance and standards of achievement rose dramatically.

One Gallup Poll showed that the majority of parents throughout the United States would opt for a voucher system if given the opportunity. The vested interests of teachers' unions and educational structures are often the main hindrances. Even public school teachers frequently favor the voucher system for their own children. A poll taken in the late 1980s revealed that a quarter of all urban schoolteachers sent their children to private schools, while the population as a whole was less than a sixth.

Many Christian families are glad to have their children attend public schools. Some believe that the home influence will be strong enough to counter any negative values. Others arrange compacts with particular schools so that they are assured of support for their values. In New England in the 1980s, school districts and groups of parents who shared common values forged partnerships. Parents could then select the school that met their values and coincided with their curricular interests. Similar arrangements are being made in British Columbia, Canada. School districts are establishing alternative traditional schools in which parental wishes are given top priority. Traditional values are emphasized and a variety of new practices are sometimes introduced: school uniforms, strict discipline,* increased homework, and extensive consultation between parents and teachers on all aspects of school life.

Private Schools

The dominant role of the parent is at the heart of private education. The choice of the school and the paying of fees ensure a position of control. The attributes that parents consider vital and worth paying for will govern school practice. As a general rule, classes are smaller, a major asset for the teacher who wants to give attention to the whole person of the student. On the negative side, costs may be prohibitive. This is becoming less and less of a problem as private schools multiply and a wide range of fees can be found in a given community.

For those who want a private Christian school, there are two kinds of institutions: at one end are parents who want only the teachers to be Christian. The teaching materials and procedures may be the same as are found in the public system. At the other end are those that insist on having Christian teachers and all teaching materials supportive of Christian values. Books that teach evolutionary theory, for instance, are either banned or linked with biblical descriptions of the origins of life. For parents who choose the second type, the school is seen as modeling Christian society; children are aggressively persuaded to choose Christian belief and demonstrate the application of their faith in everyday living.

The Christian school movement dates from the 1960s, when the issue of values first surfaced. Since that time Christian schools have grown rapidly in numbers, and today they represent the fastest growing movement of any aspect of education. From a doctrinal point of view evangelicals dominate, but their desirable characteristics make them popular with a much broader clientele. They are safe and orderly, with an emphasis on basic academic subjects and with teaching staffs dedicated to their work. Self-discipline along with moral and spiritual values are emphasized.

Choosing a School

Until there is general recognition of the rights of parents to choose appropriate schools for their children, choices must be made among the best available. There is no such thing as a perfect school. Here is a four-point approach to finding the school that best fits your child's needs, whether it be a public or a private institution:

1. Study the full range of alternatives available. Use references like Jerry Mintz's book, which is listed below. Do not overlook the smaller private schools. They are often the best.

2. Focus on the curricula and philosophy of those that have some appeal. Keep in mind both your own preferences and the personality of your child.

3. After narrowing your list, visit the schools that interest you and spend some time with one or more of the teachers. Most schools welcome this. Inquire into curriculum content, how the role of the teacher is viewed, the handling of disciplinary problems, and how much time is given to athletics, art and music—subjects that are often neglected.

4. Once you have made a tentative choice, visit the school along with your child before making a final decision. Make sure that adequate time is allowed for your child to feel comfortable with the school.

Summary

The choice for parents who want to have home and school values identical is no longer a matter of selecting a private instead of a public school. There are many alternatives between these two polar positions and many locations across the country where particular choices are appropriate. There is no panacean solution for every family or every community, but there is a key to a successful outcome: it lies in the quality of relationships between parent and teacher and between teacher and child. Morality and values are most effectively taught or sustained when there is a trusting, caring relationship between teacher and child, and where parents trust the teacher.

See also CHARACTER; DISCIPLINE; HOME SCHOOLING; PARENTING; SPIRITUAL FORMATION; VALUES.

References and Resources

G. Austin et al, *Research on Exemplary Schools* (London: Academic Press, 1985); A. Burron et al., *Christ in the Classroom: the Christian Teacher and the Public School* (Denver: Accent Books, 1987); F. Gaebelein, *The Pattern of God's Truth: The Integration of Faith and Learning* (Colorado Springs: Association of Christian Schools International, 1955); H. Horne, *Jesus the Teacher: Examining His Expertise in Education*, ed. A. M. Gunn (Grand Rapids: Kregel, 1998); M. Lieberman, *Privatization and Educational Choice* (New York: St. Martin's Press, 1989); J. Mintz, *The Almanac of Educational Choice: Public and Private Learning Alternatives and Home Schooling* (New York: Macmillan, 1995); K. Sidey, ed. *The Blackboard Fumble* (Wheaton: Victor, 1989); G. H. Wood, *Schools That Work: America's Most Innovative Public Education Programs* (New York: Penguin, 1993).

Angus M. Gunn

—SELF-ESTEEM—

The term *self-esteem* is often confused with other "self" terms such as self-worth, self-love, self-image, self-acceptance and self-concept. Self-esteem has a particular meaning: how a person feels about who he or she is. The feelings may be positive or negative; the basis of assessment varied. Self-esteem differs, for example, from self-concept. Self-concept refers to "what a person thinks he or she ought to be or could be." While self-concept affects self-esteem, the two terms refer to different processes. In Western culture positive self-esteem is considered essential to happiness. The self-esteem motto goes something like: unless you value yourself and feel good about yourself, you will not be happy.

The Effects of Low and High Self-Esteem

Low or high self-esteem is *not* a cause or an effect of behavior. Low self-esteem does not make someone perform poorly. High self-esteem does not make someone more successful. Low self-esteem can in fact be a prod to higher accomplishment. Low or high self-esteem cannot be tagged as the primary cause or effect of behavior.

While self-esteem is not a cause or an effect of behavior, it is associated with a variety of personal and interpersonal characteristics. For example, individuals who show anxiety, neurosis, social inadequacy and report illnesses attributed to psychosomatic causes also tend to assess negatively their self-worth. Those who negatively assess their self-worth are more likely to be approval oriented and sensitive to criticism, fear arguments, report that they are unable to overcome their disabilities, engage in dependent relationships and feel unlovable.

Individuals who are nonconformists, intellectually curious, goal-oriented, aspire to leadership and generally find life more satisfying tend to positively assess their self-worth. Those who positively assess their self-worth also exhibit less defensiveness in relationships and more trust in relationships, are less likely to be depressed and report a more positive relationship with God.

The Development of Self-Esteem

Basic self-esteem is learned early in life in parent-child interactions. Because there is limited influence on a young child outside of parents, the parents' impact on the child's self-esteem is sizable and stems more from the emotional realm than verbal involvement. There are two primary building blocks: acceptance and achievement. As two *I-statements,* these would be *I am loved* and *I am able.* Feelings of worth accompany the experiences of being loved and accomplishing tasks.

Parents express acceptance through gentleness, touch, time together, play,* meeting appropriate needs and through encouraging and affirming positive behaviors with appropriate praise and affection. Parents validate achievements by noticing the child is growing in ability to do more things for himself or herself (e.g., from feeding and tying shoes to making decisions, creating things, forming relationships, and living through failure and disappointment), communicating that recognition verbally or nonverbally and giving the child increased opportunity to exercise age-appropriate skills.

Though they are not skilled interpreters of what they observe, children learn basic self-esteem from parents because they are excellent observers of their environment and their parents' responses. Children may learn low self-esteem from their parents' poor responses or from their "childish" interpretation of their parents' responses. If one parent validates the child's abilities while the other contradicts the validation, the child's sense of self-worth will manifest itself inconsistently. If a parent overly rewards or punishes a child, the child will reflect a more rigid *I am good* and *I am bad* sense of worth. If a parent repeatedly labels a child's actions as stupid, the child will believe he or she is stupid. If a parent pushes a child to compensate for the parent's low self-esteem, then the child will struggle with reaching high standards.

The same holds true for positive ex-amples. If a parent gives and receives affection well, the child will learn the same. If a parent is appropriately proud of an accomplishment and can celebrate failures or setbacks with dignity, then the child learns how to live with a sense of worth in the world. As children enter the teen years and adulthood, they carry with them their basic self-esteem: their positive and negative experiences of love* and achievement, their feelings and interpretations associated with these experiences, and internalized values* from parents, teachers, peers and culture.

The Ups and Downs of Self-Esteem

Self-esteem is never static, but growing or decreasing. The ups and downs of self-esteem stem from a comparison between one's ideal self and one's experience of reality. When the gap between ideals and experience is small, self-esteem increases. When the gap between ideals and experience widens, then self-esteem decreases. A person's ideal self is formed primarily from internalized values of parents and others (e.g., hard work before play; it's better to be nice than tell the truth) as well as from the culture through the media (e.g., the rich and beautiful achiever is the ideal to strive after). A person's experience of reality is formed from self-observation and through feedback from others (i.e., the person's perceived self). The use of comparison between ideal and real as a basis for self-esteem means that one is constantly vulnerable to emotional ups and downs while assessing worth. Adopting cultural values as the basis of ideals means that those who seek to compensate for low self-esteem will do so though seeking power, privilege, wealth or rights, which is not the biblical way to seek or find self-worth.

The Christian and Self-Esteem

Taking one's self-worth from values in the

culture, feedback from others, and comparison to others or to ideals are substantially different from basing one's worth upon what God thinks of us and acts toward us. Starting with God rather than culture yields a different basis for self-esteem. The *pursuit* of self-esteem could be seen as idolatrous for two reasons. First, we are called to seek God above all else (Deut 5:7-8; Mt 6:33). Second, self-esteem, like happiness, is nearly impossible to achieve by pursuing it directly. Self-esteem, much like blessedness, comes as a byproduct of seeking something else and someone other than self (Mt 5:6).

Positive self-esteem is based on the fact that God created us with the utmost care (Ps 139), in the divine image, nearly as angels (Ps 8), and has called his creation good (Gen 1:31). Further, God has chosen and redeemed his people not on the basis of their being better than others but simply as an expression of love toward them (Deut 7:7-9; 1 Jn 4:7-21). As those who are created, redeemed and justified (1 Cor 6:11) and await heaven, God now calls us to love one another humbly in community (Jn 13) through servanthood. This frees us from a life of comparison (Gal 6:4, Col 3:1-7). Community in Christ is to be a place where we live out acceptance, confess sin, and receive forgiveness* and encouragement (Mt 18:21-35; 1 Thess 5:11; Jas 5:16). One of the primary building blocks of self-esteem—acceptance—is woven throughout God's actions toward us and intentions for the church.

The other building block of self-esteem—achievement—is based biblically on the fact that part of God's image in us is creativity and part of God's call is to be vice regents over creation. We are also called by God to make his name known and build the local church. Equipped by the Holy Spirit we are called not only to the achievements of human growth but to creative and spiritual achievements—all for the glory of God. For the Christian, positive self-worth is the byproduct of life in Christ.

Developing Healthy Self-Esteem

Three primary steps to healing can be taken with adults who display low self-esteem. First, seek understanding of the factors, such as early childhood experiences, that may have contributed to low self-esteem. Once these are understood, it is time to move on. It is important to move beyond blame and anger over the past, for there is no healing in blame and anger. Further, simply understanding the past does not in itself produce change and healing. We can prayerfully apply biblical truths to the understanding gained. Then, it is time to get on with the primary task of taking responsibility for one's self-esteem in the present.

Second, address the cognitive distortions or the negative self-talk learned by the person from the internalized values, ideals and childish interpretations of experiences—from all the factors that have contributed to low self-esteem—and replace this negative self-talk with positive self-talk.

Third, develop relationships in which the person can give and receive acceptance and love. With those in a pattern of abusive relationships, this third step may only be possible at first with a counselor who is outside the circle of abuse* and can assist with the development of new behaviors of giving and receiving.

As an example of the work involved in these steps, I offer an exercise in replacing negative self-talk with positive self-talk. This exercise is based on Deuteronomy 7:7-9, which begins with these words: "The LORD did not set his affection on you and choose you because you were more numerous than other peoples."

1. Read aloud the following statements that reflect the identity, the self-talk, of God's chosen people. Add your own statements that you feel fit with the spirit of Deuteronomy 7:7-9.

It is not because I am beautiful that God chose me and called me by name. It is not because I am spiritually strong or sensitive that God chose me and called me by name. It is not because I am great in comparison to others that God chose me and called me by name. It is not because of my accomplishments that God chose me and called me by name. Your statements:

_____

_____

_____

_____

_____

_____

2. Now read aloud these positive statements that reflect the self-talk of God's chosen people:

God chose me because he desired to set his love upon me. God chose me because he is faithful to his promises. God chose me because he desired me to be part of his people who are set apart to serve him. God chose me because he desires to reveal his mighty power to me in delivering me from sin's bondage through Christ. God chose me because he wants me to know that he is God, who will bless my love for him for a thousand generations. Your statements:

_____

_____

_____

_____

3. As you finish reading these statements, pay attention to the feelings that accompany this positive self-talk. List them. These positive statements repre-sent the identity of a person chosen by God who knows to whom he or she belongs, from whence he or she has been brought by God and who he or she is as a chosen person and part of a chosen people. This identity can not be bought or created—it can only be accepted (by one who is steeped in the truth of what it means to be chosen by God) *and lived out.*

If you have accepted this identity, what was important in doing so? If you have not yet accepted this identity, what makes accepting it difficult?

The quest for improved self-esteem has intensified due to the study of self put forward by humanistic psychology. The challenge for Christians is to base our self-worth on how God has created us, values us, acts for us and calls us to be increasingly like Christ. For the Christian, healthy self-esteem will always be a byproduct of redemption and redeemed relationships that await completion in God (Rom 8:18-21).

See also ADOLESCENCE; DEPRESSION; LOVE; PARENTING.

References and Resources

W. Backus and M. Chapman, *Telling Yourself the Truth* (Minneapolis: Bethany House, 1980); D. G. Benner, *Baker Encyclopedia of Psychology* (Grand Rapids: Baker, 1985); D. K. Clark, "Philosophical Reflections on Self-Worth and Self-Love" *Journal of Psychology and Theology* 13, no. 1 (1985) 3-11; W. Fitts, *Tennessee Self-Concept Scale: Manual* (Nashville: Counselor Recordings and Tests, 1965); E. Piers, *Manual for the Piers-Harris Children's Self-Concept Scale* (Nashville: Counselor Recordings and Tests, 1969); V. Satir, *Conjoint Family Therapy* (Palo Alto, Calif.: Science and Behavior Books, 1983); P. C. Vitz, "Leaving Psychology Behind," in *No God But God,* ed. O. Guinness and J. Seel (Chicago: Moody Press, 1992) 94-110.

Michael Nichols

SEXUAL ABUSE. *See* ABUSE.

—SEXUALITY—

Contrary to the popular idea, sexual intercourse within the covenant is "very good" (Gen 1:31). It is good biologically—reducing tensions and creating new life (see Conception). It is good socially—strengthening the capacity for love.* It is good ethically—balancing fulfillment with responsibility. It is good spiritually—becoming a powerful experiential parable of Christ's will to bless the church. But crucial to the discussion of a theology and spirituality of sex is that God says sex is good, not god! In what follows, we explore what the Bible has to say about sex, its God-given purpose, how sex relates to prayer, how parents undertake sex education in the home, and finally sex and singleness.

The Bible and Sex

The Bible contains references to almost every conceivable sexual experience, both healthy and sinful. Only a few references will be given here.

Divine intent. God's purpose in creating male and female is to create a community that reflects a God of love (Gen 1:27; Eph 5:22, 25), to end loneliness, to communicate love within marriage (Gen 2:18) and to continue the human race (Gen 1:28). Married love is dignified, holy and a joy to God (Gen 2:24; Song 1—8; Mt 19:5-6). Single people, nevertheless, may celebrate their appetite for covenant even while not experiencing its full expression in marriage. Many do this within a covenant community. Far from stigmatizing the single person, the New Testament offers singleness as a calling and a gift (Mt 19:12; 1 Cor 7:17). Sexual restraint is, however, needed whether married or single (1 Thess 4:3-8; Heb 13:4) since promiscuous sex is harmful and alienates us from our Creator. Indeed, sexual sins, more than most other sins, have a profound effect on our personality (1 Cor 6:18-20) and our spirituality (Rom 1:27). A life given over to sexual pleasure is profoundly empty as people seek ever more exotic thrills to titillate their satiated desires (Jude 7-13).

The emphasis of Scripture is not only on acts but on attitudes (Mt 5:28; 2 Pet 2:14). Sins of fantasy are as serious in God's sight as sins in body, largely because the body is not the shell of the soul but part of the real person, as is the mind or emotions. Some references bear on the question of pornography (Phil 4:8; 2 Tim 2:22; 2 Pet 2:14). But in God's sight, sexual sins are not worse or less forgivable than other sins, and there is hope of full forgiveness* and substantial healing to those who have hurt themselves or others in this way (Jn 8:1-11; 1 Jn 1:9).

Covenant sex. Sexual intercourse and its normal preparation (foreplay; Gen 26:8) are reserved for the full covenant experience of marriage* (Deut 22:13-29). Family planning, while not named directly in Scripture, must be considered in the light of Genesis 1:28, Psalm 127:3-5 and Hebrews 13:4. The reference in Genesis 38:9 is to failing to perform a marital duty; it is not a condemnation of contraception.* Premarital sex, understood biblically, is really misnamed. There is no such thing as premarital sexual intercourse. The act means marriage and is highly symbolic: the interpenetration of two lives in complete self-giving.

Sexual sin. The general word in the New Testament for unlawful and sinful sexual relationships (*porneia*) includes prostitution, unchastity and fornication (Gal 5:19; 1 Thess 4:3)—in each case the person is not treated with respect, indeed is treated rather as a sexual object. The desire is an evil desire (*epithymia;* Col 3:5) or a lustful passion (*pathos*), connoting a preoccupation with sexual pleasure and personal gratification (1 Thess 4:5). Several English words, including lewdness and lasciviousness, translate the word *aselgeia,* which means "sheer, shameless, animal lust to gratify physical desires" (Mk 7:22; 2 Pet 2:2). Most of this sin concerns sexual activity outside the marriage covenant, but it includes the possibility of married lust.

Prostitution treats sex as a commodity outside the covenant (Lev 19:29; Deut 22:21; Prov 6:23-35; 1 Cor 6:15-20), often leading to venereal disease, which is possibly mentioned in Leviticus 15:1 and Numbers 25:1-9. Adultery breaks the marriage covenant and inflicts wounds on both persons (Ex 20:14; Lev 20:10-14; Prov 5:15-23; Mt 5:27-30), though some of these words also apply to distorted sexual expressions within marriage. The Bible also provides a theological context for the profound respect of women and the relational nature of sexual acts: in Christ a woman's body is not the exclusive possession of the husband (1 Cor 7:3-5), and the sex act is profoundly personal (1 Cor 6:18). Homosexual acts are an offense against the relational image of God (Gen 1:27; 19:5; Lev 18:22; Rom 1:24-27)—in all these cases Scripture deals with homosexual activity rather than the tendency to homosexuality.* Since the Bible reveals the communal purpose of sexuality (showing love and building communion) and the danger of an unhealthy fantasy life (Mt 5:28), solo sex (*see* Masturbation) must always be something less than God intended.

Sexual temptation. The Bible gives clear direction on handling sexual temptation (Gen 39:5-10; Job 31:1; 1 Cor 6:18; Eph 5:1-3) through fleeing, walking in the Spirit (Gal 5:16) and setting our hearts on things above (Col 3:1-14). But the power of the indwelling Christ does not anesthetize our sexual appetite. Just the reverse, new birth makes us fully alive in every conceivable way. But the cleansing love of God (2 Cor 5:14-21) drives out unworthy thoughts and attitudes, and empowers us to love (Jn 15:13; 1 Jn 4:7-21). Christians should be the sexiest people on earth precisely because their natures are being conformed to the image of God (Rom 12:1-2), because their sexual experience within marriage is physical (union), social (intimacy) and spiritual (communion), and because they are lining themselves up with God's intended sexual design for us as human beings. Indeed there is growing empirical evidence that Christians are able to enjoy sex more than others and, within marriage, make better lovers!

Sexual spirituality. Sexuality is also the point of our greatest vulnerability. Ultimately the solution for sexual sin is not psychological. As Jesus noted in the case of the woman with multiple relationships, healing is found in worshiping God in Spirit (or spirit) and in truth (Jn 4:23-24). Tragically, the church adopted the philosophy of Neo-Platonic dualism, teaching that spirit is holy and the body is either evil or inconsequential. In contrast, Paul says the body is for the Lord and the Lord is for the body (1 Cor 6:13), thus inviting theological reflection on our sexuality.

The Purpose of Sex

Answering the question "Why is there sex?" the Bible tells us six things that are enough to start a social revolution, enough to leave us ashamed that we were ever ashamed of our sexuality.

Because we crave relationship. God has designed us to move beyond ourselves. In Genesis 2:18 God says, "It is not good for the man to be alone." Adam discovered that he needed another like himself—but different. So the male by himself cannot be fully in the image of God, nor can the female. The biblical phrase *the image of God* presupposes the idea of relationship. God is a Trinity, humankind a duality, of relationships. So part of our spiritual pilgrimage is to relate healthily to the opposite sex.

To consummate covenant. In the Old Testament covenants were sealed and renewed by significant rituals and signs. This signing of the covenant emphasizes that it is not an idle promise but a solemn act with serious consequences. In the New Testament the Lord's Supper becomes the ritual of the covenant for those who belong to Jesus Christ. These rituals are like any sacraments: God communicates a spiritual grace through a material reality. Sexual intercourse is the consummation and the ritual of the marriage covenant. Just as the bread and wine offer us spiritual nourishment, so in marriage "sexual intercourse is the primary (though certainly not the only) ritual. It is an extension and fulfillment of the partners' ministry to each other begun during the public statement of vows" (Leckey, 17). Intercourse is to the covenant what the Lord's Supper is to salvation. It expresses and renews the heart covenant. If the symbol is not backed by a full covenant, it is merely a powerless, graceless act.

To keep us distinct in unity. At the candle-lighting portion of a wedding ceremony the bride and groom take the two lighted candles representing themselves and, with great solemnity, light a single central candle representing their marriage. But then they stoop down and blow out the two candles. Do they really mean to blow themselves out? Tragically, some do. Sexuality is the urge to be part of a community of two, symbolized by the act of intercourse. The differences and the uniqueness of both people are celebrated at the very moment of oneness and unity. God is the ultimate mystery of covenant unity. Reverently we may speak of the mystery of one God in three persons; we know they are not merged. Nor do we merge in the human covenant. Partners should find, not lose, their identity.

Because male and female are complements. In a covenant marriage each calls forth the sexuality of the other. Eve called forth the sexuality of Adam. Until she is created, the man is just "the human" (*ha-adam*). Only after the woman is created is he "the man" (male person, *ha-ish*). His special identity emerges in the context of needing a suitable helper. Adam saw Eve as one called forth. His cry "At last!" (Gen 2:23 RSV) is an expression of relational joy. Now he has found a partner as his opposite, by his side, equal but different, his other half. C. S. Lewis compared our sexual unity to that of a violin bow and string. Both are needed, and neither can be fulfilled without the other.

It is important to note here that the Bible does not give us two parallel lists of qualities, one male and one female. That should be reason enough not to generalize on male and female stereotypes. The sexual act suggests that men and women are different in their sexuality. In intercourse woman receives the man, making herself extremely vulnerable. The man, on the other hand, is directed outward. While the woman receives something, the man relieves himself of something. It means something different to the man. A woman needs to be psychologically prepared for this self-abandonment, not only by the public commitment of her husband to lifelong troth but also by her husband's ongoing nurture of the love relationship. This difference in sexual identity may also be the reason behind the common male complaint that their wives do not understand their need for sexual release and expression. It is a gross but instructive overstatement to say that men must have sex to reach fullness of love while women must have love to reach fullness of sex.

To create children. Thomas Aquinas believed adultery was wrong because people having sex outside marriage do not want to conceive a child (Aquinas 11.154.11.3). Most people today do not find this a convincing argument. But sex gives the procreative process its own way (which adulterers are always determined to interrupt) and is a powerful statement of why we have this appetite. It would be wrong to say that every act of intercourse must have procreation as its end. In the Genesis narrative the man and woman were in the image of God and enjoyed profound companionship before there were children. But to cut the tie between sex and children is to reduce sexuality. A childless marriage can be a godly community on earth. But a marriage that refuses procreation for reasons of self-centeredness is something less than the God-imaging community that was called to "be fruitful and increase in number" (Gen 1:28). Our society treats babies as an inconvenience, an interruption to a blissful married life or a challenging career. But the Bible says that babies are an awesome wonder. Even if the birth was unexpected and unplanned for—or perhaps even, humanly speaking, unwanted—it is the work of God, a lovely mystery. Healthy sexuality makes marriage the beginning of family.*

Because it incarnates the covenant. God wants us to have an earthly spirituality. These are carefully chosen words. Faith has to be fleshed out to be real. The Christian message is that God became a man. God didn't become just another spirit. The Word became flesh and dwelt among us (Jn 1:14). Spirit became body. In marriage, too, spirit must become body. Love must become incarnate. If in the church there are Word and sacrament, in a marriage there needs to be words and touch. Our society secularizes sex. It treats it as pure body, pure flesh—nothing more. There are no sins and no sexual perversions. The converse, just as wrong although sometimes thought to be Christian, is the problem of hyperspirituality. These Christians talk about God but either live uneasily with the physical or live a double life. Flesh (in the sense of the physical) and spirit have never been reconciled. Sex is looked down upon, almost as a necessary evil. In contrast to the sacralizing and the secularizing of sex, the Bible sacramentalizes sex. It does this by putting it in its rightful place: in the covenant. That does not mean that single people cannot be whole without sexual intercourse. As Smedes puts it, "Although virgins do not experience the climax of sexual existence, they can experience personal wholeness by giving themselves to other persons without physical sex. Through a life of self-giving—which is the heart of sexual union—they become whole persons. They capture the essence without the usual form" (1976, 34).

Sex and Prayer

Sexual spirituality and *spiritual sexuality* appear to be oxymorons, but not to those who have been converted to a full biblical perspective on sexuality. There is a reason for this. The desire for sexual union and for God are intimately related. God is a God of love. God dwells in the covenant community of Father, Son and

Holy Spirit, interpenetrating, mutually indwelling, living for and in one another, finding life in self-giving to the other—all ways of describing what the Orthodox fathers of the church in the fifth century described as *perichoresis*: the intercommunion of the Godhead in a nonhierarchical community of loving, mutual abiding. Made in the image of God (Gen 1:26), humankind was built male and female for communion, created to long for mutual abiding, destined to find fulfillment in self-giving. Commenting on how the sexual appetite is so closely related to worship and prayer, Alan Ecclestone notes:

> The primitive impulse to deify sexual love was not wholly misguided; it has all the features of great mystical experience, abandon, ecstasy, polarity, dying, rebirth and perfect union. . . . It prompts between human beings those features characteristic of prayer; a noticing, a paying attention, a form of address, a yearning to communicate at ever deeper levels of being, an attempt to reach certain communion with the other. (Wild, 23)

But there is an important corrective in Scripture: our sexuality arises from our godlikeness; our godlikeness does not arise from our sexuality. So this profound clue to our true dignity as God-imaging creatures, a clue written into our genetic code, our psychological structure and our spiritual nature, is an invitation to seek and worship God in spirit (truly in Spirit) and truth (Jn 4:23).

Sex and Singleness

Three biblical goals for our personal sexuality are (1) sexual freedom, (2) sexual purity and (3) sexual contentment. Sexual freedom does not mean freedom from constraint but freedom to express our sexuality fully and exclusively within the marriage covenant. When one is not yet married or is called to the single life, sex-ual freedom allows us to appreciate the other sex and to welcome our sexual appetites but to refrain from full physical expression outside of the marriage covenant. What is seldom noted about self-control is that it is a byproduct of a prayerful life, the result of walking in the Spirit, and not something gained by steeling one's will or trying.

Sexual purity is certainly not dull (read the Song of Songs). To live freely and with sexual purity, we must reduce the amount of stimulation we allow ourselves to receive from magazines, movies, videos* and mass media. Job could say that he had made a covenant with his eyes not to look at a woman lustfully (Job 31:1), not an easy thing to do in a sexually saturated culture. Positively, we must increase our attention to God.

Sexual contentment, rather than sexual fulfillment, is a worthy Christian goal. The secret of contentment for Paul and ourselves is the practice of thanksgiving and continuing dependence on God (Phil 4:6, 13). Thanksgiving is essential for single people who will be tempted to seek fulfillment mainly in themselves (see Masturbation) or in dating* relationships that are impure. Single people will find their sexual repose by directing their love with all of its passion to the loving community of Father, Son and Holy Spirit, through which literally we experience God as our spouse (Is 54:5).

Sex and Parenting

Rearing children in a sexually saturated society is especially challenging. Monitoring television,* videos and other media is an absolute necessity. Being prepared to discuss what is being taught at school about birth control, sexual behavior and love is an important informal sex education. If parents feel awkward in discussing this subject, or ashamed of their own sexuality, they will communicate this

277

negativity to their children whether they intend to or not. Parents tend to two extremes: talking about sex too much, and so awakening an unhealthy fascination with the topic, or refraining from speaking openly about this aspect of human experience, and so communicating by silence that this is something dirty and sinful. Answering children's questions—all of them—in an age-appropriate way, is an important part of parenting.* As young people begin to date or spend time socially with the other sex, it is important to have established open communication on the place of sexuality, its purpose (as above) and why it is a beautiful thing to reserve full sexual expression for marriage. In some societies where the extended family lives under one roof, children are inevitably exposed to the adult experience of sexual intercourse, but normally privacy is desirable, if not essential both for the couple to enjoy freedom in lovemaking and for children not to be tempted to a kind of voyeurism. As in all other aspects of parenting this one challenges parents in terms of their own maturity and invites their own growth.

In conclusion, sex is contemplative. This most down-to-earth daily stirring within us invites us heavenward. We were built for love and built for the God who is love. It causes us daily to wonder at the mystery of complementarity, inviting us into a social experience in which there is more unity because of the diversity of male and female, just as God is more one because God is three. It demands of us more than raw, unaided human nature can deliver, a life of self-sacrifice and abiding contentment, qualities that can come only by practicing the presence of God. Finally, it invites us to live for God and his kingdom. As C. S. Lewis once said, if we find that nothing in this world and life fully satisfies us, it is a powerful indication that we were made for another life and another world. In some way beyond our imagination, human marriage will be transcended (Mt 22:30) and fulfilled. Indeed, we will not give or receive in marriage because we will all be married in the completely humanized new heaven and new earth, where God's people daily delight in being the bride of God (Rev 19:7; 21:2).

See also ABUSE; CONTRACEPTION; FAMILY; FEMININITY; HOMOSEXUALITY; LOVE; MARRIAGE; MASCULINITY; MASTURBATION.

References and Resources

J. Balswick and J. Balswick, *Authentic Human Sexuality: An Integrated Christian Approach* (Downers Grove, Ill.: InterVarsity Press, 1999); S. Jones and B. Jones, *How and When to Tell Your Kids About Sex: A Lifelong Approach to Shaping Your Child's Sexual Character* (Colorado Springs: NavPress, 1993), and *Facing the Facts: The Truth About Sex and You* (Colorado Springs: NavPress, 1995); D. Leckey, *A Family Spirituality* (New York: Crossroad, 1982); M. Mason, *The Mystery of Marriage* (Portland, Ore.: Multnomah Press, 1985); R. Rohr, "An Appetite for Wholeness," *Sojourners*, November 1982, 30-32; L. Smedes, *Mere Morality* (Grand Rapids: Eerdmans, 1983); L. Smedes, *Sex for Christians* (Grand Rapids: Eerdmans, 1976); R. P. Stevens, *Married for Good: The Lost Art of Remaining Happily Married* (Downers Grove, Ill.: InterVarsity Press, 1986, portions quoted with permission); H. Thielicke, "Mystery of Sexuality," in *Are You Nobody?* (Richmond, Va.: John Knox Press, 1965); Thomas Aquinas, *Summa Theologia*, trans. Fathers of the English Dominican Province, vol. 4 (New York: Benzigle Brothers, 1948); E. Wheat, *Intended for Pleasure* (Old Tappan, N.J.: Fleming H. Revell, 1977); R. Wild, *Frontiers of the Spirit: A Christian View of Spirituality* (Toronto: Anglican Book Centre, 1981).

R. Paul Stevens

—SHAME—

Shame is a condemnation of self based on a negative judgment of one's self by the individual, others or God. It is a wound (Lynd) and a threat to one's identity as a person of worth to oneself, others and God. In contrast with guilt, which is related to an act, shame is the condemnation of one's whole personhood. For a comprehensive understanding of shame, both internal and external aspects of shame need to be explored. In the same way, the healing of shamefulness must be considered both internally and externally.

Shame affects one's whole person. Psychologically, experiences of shame change one's self-concept (see Self-Esteem) as well as one's mood. Spiritually, shame can either alienate one from or take one closer to God. Shame also has physical effects. It often causes blushing and psychosomatic symptoms. Shame affects interpersonal relationships leading to conflicts. Even vocational life is influenced. A shame-bound person cannot be productive in work because of feeling inhibited and because of the drain on psychological and physical energy.

The intensity of shame one feels depends on the degree of one's interpersonal sensitivity, desire to connect with others, moral conscience, humility, sense of dignity, integrity, discernment of the situation, self-insight and willingness to confront one's inner self. Just as water can be turned into electricity or become a flood, shame has both a positive and a negative side for an individual and the community.

Negative Aspects of Shame

Shame has a constraining and paralyzing power. The self-conscious and ruminative nature of shame freezes one "in the inertness of immobility" (Schneider, 30). Each encounter of shame affects one's self-image, making one feel inadequate, diminished, helpless and unqualified for life. Further, it induces one to waste energy and resources by denying and concealing one's shame. Preoccupied with covering up one's true self, a person can neglect dealing with guilt. Because shamed people are afraid to disclose their real selves, they create superficial relationships within a community.

So shame robs one of the capacity to develop a proper self-understanding and authentic interpersonal relationships. Unhealed shame can make a lasting negative impact and can also be passed down through generations (Fossum & Mason). But shame also has some redeeming qualities.

Positive Aspects of Shame

Shame sharpens one's value system and moral consciousness, whereas shamelessness leads to moral corruption. Feeling shame means that one has a certain standard for one's own behavior as well as for how one should be perceived and treated by others. Behind such a standard lies a yearning for truth and honor.

After going through a painful self-confrontation some people develop new perspectives and consequently a new self-identity and self-understanding. Shame helps in character* formation. Through shame one realizes that he or she is not as good or competent as previously thought before the moment of shame.

The restraining power of shame prevents one from contemplating unethical and selfish decisions that would endanger community building. Shame also contributes to community building by motivating one to seek forgiveness* and establish reconciliation. It has a strong bonding power to unite people who share the same type of shame, for example, in the case of discrimination shame.

Types of Shame
There are three categories of shame.

Self-related shame arises from one's behavior, characteristics, background or situation. Examples include guilt shame; incompetence or inadequacy shame; inferiority shame; blunder shame; problem shame (e.g., mental illness, divorce*); help-seeking shame; character shame (i.e., shame caused by character slandering); birth shame (e.g., an illegitimate child); body shame (caused by physical appearance or defect); sexual shame (e.g., homosexuality,* rape, infidelity); poverty shame; education shame; religion shame; ideology shame; truth or justice seeking shame; vocation shame; ethnicity shame; nationality shame.

Association-related shame involves one's connections with other individuals or groups, such as family* shame; friendship shame (caused by wrongdoings of friends); ancestor shame; conflict shame (caused by interpersonal conflicts); abuse* shame (victimization shame); affiliation shame (caused by affiliation with certain groups); exclusion shame (felt when one is excluded from a group); discrimination shame (caused by being discriminated against).

Environmental shame originates in one's geographical identity. Examples include culture shame (i.e., unfamiliarity with a new culture), home-town shame and social norm shame (e.g., ignorance of social customs).

A Theological Perspective
It is noteworthy that in the creation account in Genesis the pre-Fall and post-Fall state of human beings are contrasted in terms of shame. In their pre-Fall state "the man and his wife were both naked, and were not ashamed" (Gen 2:25). Here we find the first emotional term and the first relationship term in the Bible. Genesis 2:25 shows that God intended human beings to be unashamed. But with the Fall (Gen 3:7-13) Adam and Eve felt shame over their "nakedness" before God and each other. As a consequence, they developed a shame-based identity. Their awareness (Gen 3:7), cowork (3:7), posture toward God (3:8), language and emotion (3:10) were all organized by and centered around their shame. The loincloths Adam and Eve made symbolized the toiling of human beings to cover up their shame completely, an impossible goal. Neither their loincloths nor "the trees of the garden" could hide them from the all-seeing God.

Not only does Genesis illuminate a shame-based identity, but it also demonstrates the role of shame in the experience of community. Genesis 2:25 and 3:7 show us what God intended when he created the first marital unit, the first human community and the first church. The theme of shame, not the theme of love or happiness, is introduced at this point, showing that freedom from shame is fundamental in forming the marriage,* church and human community that God originally intended for human beings. Nevertheless, the first human community was established on the foundation of shame. But the experience of shame also has a redemptive dimension.

After the Fall God related to Adam through his shame, namely, by asking Adam about his nakedness and by providing him with skin garments. Adam also related to God through his confession of his nakedness. So shame became a meeting ground between man and God, the beginning of God's redemptive work enabling them—and us—to start a new life.

Grace-Based Identity
In the light of the gospel, human beings

have only two choices, namely, to live under the dominion of sin or grace (Rom 6:15-18; Col 1:13). The former way of life often leads to a shame-based identity, while the latter leads to a grace-based identity. Grace redefines self not around who one is but around one's relationship with God.

Basing our identity on self-perception or how others view us cannot solve the problem of shame. The potency of shame comes from a sense of worthlessness and one can never feel free from a sense of want, inadequacy and worthlessness. Guilt is related to an act, while shame is the condemnation of one's whole personhood. Whereas guilt can be expiated, shame has a dimension that cannot be fundamentally dealt with except through "transformation of self" (Lynd, 50). But human beings are limited in how much they can transform themselves.

Only the gospel of grace that transforms a person through the experience of the infinite self-giving love of God can give assurance of one's true worth and ultimately resolve our problem of shame. For example, having recounted his shameful act of persecuting the church of Christ and his experience of God's grace of forgiveness and calling, Paul says, "By the grace of God I am what I am" (1 Cor 15:10). He is referring to the new identity he has received through God's grace.

The Bible uses the metaphor of clothing* for this change of identity: taking off our old sinful self and putting on the new identity granted by God's grace. In the creation story Adam and Eve tried to clothe themselves to resolve their shame, but their loincloths made of tree leaves were not adequate. So God provided them with garments of skin gained at the cost of life. This is the prototypical picture of the mighty and loving God leading them from their shame-based

identity to a grace-based identity. Only by God's grace can we acquire a new Christ-like or God-like identity (cf. Rom 8:29; 2 Cor 3:18; Eph 4:24; Col 3:10). This grace-based identity enables us to maintain an appropriate sense of shame that functions constructively, while freeing us from both excessive shame and shamelessness that function destructively.

Grace-Based Community

Where people have experienced forgiveness and reconciliation, members of a church or family recognize one another as those forgiven and recreated by God. This leads them to accept one another as forgiven sinners and people on the way to the consummation of salvation. They can tolerate one another's shortcomings without shaming each other excessively. In fact, they are exhorted to value one another as brothers and sisters "for whom Christ died" (1 Cor 8:11). They are to accept and even protect especially the weak members of their community from suffering shame (1 Cor 8:7-13; 11:17-34; 12:22-26).

A grace-based community functions in two ways. On the one hand, it provides healing for those suffering from a variety of shame feelings that originate from the worldly perception of their weaknesses. On the other hand, it constantly warns "strong" members not to boast of their strength, which would inevitably "shame" the weak members. Rather they are to boast only of the Lord (1 Cor 1:29-31; Jas 1:9-10; 2:1-7). Thus healthy interpersonal relationships are developed while an appropriate sense of shame is maintained. Integrating the positive sides of shame while avoiding the negative aspects is a great challenge both in the church and in parenting.

Implications for Parenting

Starting from the first family on earth, issues relating to shame have been passed on throughout generations. These problems are deeply embedded in families for important reasons.

God has created human beings with various emotional needs such as acceptance, affection, appreciation, approval, attention, comfort, encouragement, respect, security and support. He wants us to love* our children by meeting these needs in them (Ferguson). When these needs are not met during the critical developmental years, children develop a shame-based identity, a view of self that is laden with negative self-evaluation and shameful feelings (West). There are several possible factors that contribute to the formation of a shame-based identity in children.

First, the parents may have a shame-based identity, due to their own neediness and sense of worthlessness. Thus they can neither become role models nor have the strength to validate their children consistently. Second, spouses with a shame-based identity often have marital conflicts because of their unrealistic expectations that their spouses will meet their enormous emotional needs. When they become aware that their spouses cannot meet their expectations, they turn to their children and form an enmeshed relationship with them. Since the children know their survival depends on their parents' well-being, the children try to satisfy their parents' needs. In the process the children develop a deep sense of shame for two reasons: they realize that no matter how hard they work, they cannot succeed, and since much of their energy is spent for meeting their parents' needs, not much is left for their own development. Their sense of failure and deprivation leads them to a shame-based identity.

Third, unhealthy communication* patterns can create shame. In healthy families children learn that they can ask questions and get straight answers. In dysfunctional families they experience double messages and are punished or ridiculed when they try to clarify their confusion through straightforward communication. They conclude that there must be something wrong with them and feel ashamed of themselves. They sometimes disguise their deep sense of self-invalidation with shameless behaviors.

Fourth, family rules can play a part. Each family has its own rules concerning its children's behavior. When a family has too strict and too many rules, especially when it fails to meet the children's emotional needs, the latter are likely to develop a shame-based identity (see Discipline). These children feel that since they can never be successful in keeping all of the family rules, they must be bad or inadequate. Some children react to such a low self-esteem by going to the other extreme, namely, by becoming shameless adults.

Fifth, there is the matter of roles. In dysfunctional families children are expected to play certain roles such as a caretaker of siblings or parents, a fulfiller of parental dreams or a family entertainer. Children develop a shame-based identity in the course of playing these roles because they feel accepted and approved only when they play their roles well and feel ashamed of themselves when they fail. Even when children successfully play their roles, some of them still feel invalidated and unaccepted because it is not who they are but the roles they play that is affirmed by their parents. This is why some high-achievement people still suffer from a shame-based identity.

Sixth, disapproval of children's developmental stage is a factor. Because they want their emotional needs met through their children, some parents desire to keep their children younger or older than their actual age. These parents disapprove of their children going through the God-intended human developmental process. Children raised by such parents receive a nonverbal message from them: "I am not pleased with who you are now." When children hear this type of message consistently from their parents, they develop a shame-based identity.

Finally, shame and aloneness often coexist. God created human beings with relational needs. Therefore a person who is alone is perceived by God—so it is thought by others and even by oneself—as an inadequate being. For children, being alone often means abandonment and not deserving genuine care. Therefore, repeated childhood experiences of being alone, especially when one needs guidance, comfort or companionship, lead to the development of a shame-based identity.

The Church's Role

Many families yearn to see their children equipped with a strong Christian identity and are desperately searching for specific guidelines for building healthy families. The high divorce rate of Christians indicates that churches have failed to teach and demonstrate to people how to keep the great commandment of love among family members.

Often the members of a Christian fellowship tend to provoke and reinforce shame instead of positively dealing with it. Insensitive comments, gossiping, unwise advice, insensitive public prayer requests, boasting of one's status or achievements make others feel ashamed. The same thing happens in families. In order to make the church and the home a healing rather than harming community, it is essential that the gospel of God's grace in Christ in its wholeness be shared, taught and lived. In this way a grace-based identity and a grace-based community can be formed.

It is time for churches to support families actively by initiating family ministry that includes programs for premarital preparation, marriage enrichment, caring for distressed couples, parental empowerment, three-generation bonding, divorce care and single life. It can be implemented through seminars, small group Bible studies, Sunday school classes, preaching, worship services and family retreats. For a successful family ministry, a paradigm shift in church leadership is imperative.

See also DISCIPLINE; FAMILY PROBLEMS; FORGIVENESS; LOVE; SELF-ESTEEM.

References and Resources

D. Augsburger, *Pastoral Counseling Across Cultures* (Philadelphia: Westminster Press, 1986); D. Ferguson, *The Great Commandment Principle* (Wheaton, Ill.: Tyndale, 1998); M. A. Fossum and M. J. Mason, *Facing Shame: Families in Recovery* (New York: W. W. Norton, 1986); H. M. Lund, *On Shame and the Search for Identity* (New York: Harcourt, Brace, 1958); C. D. Schneider, *Shame, Exposure and Privacy* (New York: W. W. Norton, 1992); M. West, *Shame Based Family Systems: The Assault on Self Esteem* (Minneapolis: CompCare, 1992).

Yea Sun E. Kim

—SHOPPING—

Shopping has become the main activity for most people when they are away from home,* work or school.* This is true for not only individuals—especially for young people—but for families as a whole. Even most Christian families spend more time in the shopping mall than they do in church activities. However, apart from a few books written by those advocating a simpler lifestyle, as yet there is little thoughtful guidance on the subject.

The Rise of the Consumer Culture

It was partly the emergence of the mass media and advertising that enabled the fruits of the Industrial Revolution to become so widely marketable and desirable. But it was also partly due to the development among the populace of an increasing number of people who defined themselves in terms of their unsatisfied needs and wishes. Previously, especially in Protestant countries, life revolved around personal self-denial in favor of a commitment to work and family,* work and civic obligations. It was only when the external enticements of advertising connected with inner longings for physical and material well-being that the shift to a more leisure-oriented, consumer culture took place. Christians, especially middle-class ones, gradually became as affected by this as non-Christians. At the heart of this whole development was the growth of the shopping mentality.

One sign of this was the commercial appropriating of the main annual holidays*—Easter, Christmas, Thanksgiving and even Mother's Day. Since some of these holidays were essentially family and religious affairs, commercial attitudes began to invade the home as well as the church. Another sign was the growth of increasingly large retail centers, from the department store to the shopping mall, which increasingly became the focus of family outings. A further sign was the proliferation of road signs and billboards, catalogs and junk mail that have increasingly blanketed the country and filled the mailboxes of virtually every home. The latest sign is the appearance of home shopping, TV* channels and shopping by computer,* right in the heart of the family living area and bedroom. The church has also increasingly turned itself into a market-ing agency, advertising a shopping mall of religious services and meetings. Even God is often treated as a giant vending machine for religious consumption.

On average, Americans now spend about six hours a week in shopping-related activities, or around 6 percent of their waking hours. This is about 20 percent higher than twenty years ago. During the intervening time, Sunday shopping has almost doubled, and expenditure on consumer items has increased almost 50 percent in real dollar terms. While women devote more time to shopping than men, the difference amounts to only two hours a week. About half of people's shopping time goes toward buying groceries, clothing* and other basic articles.

The Shopping Mentality

The spread of the consumer society has resulted in several noticeable changes in attitudes toward shopping. Many people today rely on what they buy for telling them who they are or defining what they want to be. They look to shopping not just to get necessities or to feel pleasure, but to give them identity and meaning. When feeling down about themselves or deciding to try to become someone different, they become prey to believing that buying new clothes, getting a new hairstyle or purchasing a new car will somehow miraculously bring this about. The attraction of the new is central here. Underlying this is often the desire to forge a whole new identity for themselves. Window-shopping provides models to look at. Do-it-yourself home improvement programs stimulate wants or envy determined by others' achievements. By all these means, the way others are outfitted or housed supplies other models, as does the lifestyle of media, sports and fashion celebrities.

Shopping also appeals to certain quasi-religious longings. The experience of shopping can give a brief, if limited, sense of transcendence by helping people to get out of themselves and enter a different, almost magical world. The quest for bargains also promises people of all ages the experience of a kind of material grace. What could be more exciting than discovering something you really want that hardly costs anything? For some this is a reflection or substitute, however pale, for experiencing God's free offer of the gospel. Unfortunately, it is one that never fully satisfies, for we cannot buy an identity or a purpose, intimacy or happiness.

In these ways we have moved from being disciples and citizens to being primarily consumers. This contains the risk that Christians, who have been "bought with a price" and set free from the idolatries of this world, become commodities to be bought by advertising and sometimes even sold off through the sale of mailing lists. In other cases people become compulsive or pathological spenders. For some, shopping becomes a mood-elevating drug that feeds a poor self-image, makes them feel good and beautiful or restores a sense of excitement to their lives. This is a form of addiction as powerful as dependence on alcohol or a chemical substance. Young people who suffer from low self-esteem are also very vulnerable to this temptation.

A Christian Perspective on Purchasing

How can we go shopping Christianly? How can we put material things in their proper place, as did early Anabaptists, Quakers and Puritans? These people thought carefully about what, how much and when to buy, possess and consume, and were inculcated into a responsible

approach through their family upbringing as well as church instruction.

The Bible also provides us with some basic perspectives. As mentioned, we need to remind ourselves that already, through Christ, we have been "bought at a price" (1 Cor 6:20), and therefore we do not have to buy our way to fullness of life. The model we should seek to imitate is nothing less than Christ. As the Spirit transforms us into his image, we become a "new creation," have a new identity and find a new direction. We should basically be content with whatever we have, knowing that God will, at times, lavish good things on us, and at other times we may experience want (Phil 4:11). We ought to remember that since the form of this world is passing away, we should "buy something as if it were not [ours] to keep" (1 Cor 7:30). Indeed, freely giving away a generous proportion of what we earn is a responsibility (2 Cor 9:7-9; see Tithing). It is also important that we look to the Spirit to develop within us self-control, one of the prime fruits of the Spirit. If we "lack wisdom" in this or any other area, we are invited to ask God sincerely for it (Jas 1:5).

What follows are some general principles for resisting the consumer culture. These are designed to help us travel in this world more lightly as resident aliens, whose prime loyalty belongs to a "better country" (Heb 11:13-16) and to a heavenly family whose head is God.

First, as a family* or with other single friends or with your small group in the church, begin to discuss the relationship between shopping and discipleship. Through newspapers, magazines and books investigate the facts about over-consumption and poverty in your country and locality.

Second, where you can do so reasonably and in a nonpressured way, make and grow things yourself or as a family activity rather than always being dependent on buying them.

Third, collate your individual shopping trips into one a week and, when possible, buy cooperatively with other church members or other members of your wider family rather than just for your personal or household needs.

Fourth, look for places where prices are lower and packaging less wasteful. List specifically and budget carefully what you will buy and resist the temptation to engage in impulse buying.

In addition to these general principles, others have found the following specific questions helpful in their shopping. For example, if items are more than a certain price, ask the following questions:

☐ Why do you want the item, and are your reasons for doing so adequate?

☐ Do you have the budget to cover the cost, or will you have to put too much on credit?

☐ Can you do without it, and what would you do with the money* if you didn't spend it this way?

☐ Would you be able to make the item, or would it be enough to get it second-hand?

☐ Do you need it now, or can it wait until you will use it more often?

☐ Have you, or those for whom you are buying it, made use of similar items already owned, or are you simply piling up items which will be little used?

☐ Can you borrow it or buy it with others so that several share a little-used, expensive product?

☐ If it is replacing something, do you have to replace it yet, or can you wait until it is worn-out or broken?

☐ Is it fixable if it breaks, and is there an accessible, trustworthy repair center with reasonable prices?

☐ How much will it damage God's world, either by consuming scarce resources or by becoming nondisposable waste?

For those who are prey to impulse buying and overspending, here are further suggestions about how to go shopping:

☐ Do not go shopping unless you have something specific in mind to buy.

☐ Go to the mall only with a definite purchase or fixed amount of money in mind.

☐ Wear a watch or place a time limit on how long you can "afford" to stay or shop.

☐ Take someone else with you but not a person similarly vulnerable to the mall's enticements.

☐ Evade sale traps and query whether you really need the bargains on offer.

☐ Plan gifts* for major holidays ahead so you do not run around in a last-minute panic.

☐ Delay big expenditures until you have had the opportunity to reconsider their necessity and check out others' prices.

☐ If in doubt about buying something, do not buy it. And every so often go without something significant.

☐ Develop an appreciation for the social aspects of the mall or, if this is insufficient, do not meet others there.

☐ If married, promise yourself that you will tell your spouse everything you buy.

☐ Above all, remember that God loves us just as much whether we have much or less, whether everything matches or not and whether we are in or out of fashion.

All these suggestions can be taught within the family. They are designed to help us shop "as to the Lord" rather than simply according to our own, others' or society's desires. In all this it is important to take just one step at a time rather than trying to change established patterns overnight. Keep in mind that the goal is not modesty or simplicity for its own sake but for what it reflects of the values* of the kingdom. This occasionally leaves us open to buying freely and generously when this is appropriate in terms of God's purposes. Inexpensiveness or cheapness is not necessarily good in itself. Often it is more economical to buy for quality and durability. Also, emphasize the joyfulness and fun of a less consumer-oriented approach to life rather than laying heavy guilt trips on oneself or others.

See also ALLOWANCES; CREDIT CARD; DEBT; GIFTS; MONEY; TITHING.

References and Resources
R. W. Fox and T. J. Lears, *The Culture of Consumption: Critical Essays in American History, 1880-1980* (New York: Pantheon, 1983);

M. Giordan, *The Great Consumer Con: How to Beat It* (London: Temple Smith, 1978); J. Kavanaugh, *Still Following Christ in a Consumer Culture* (New York: Orbis, 1991); L. Shames, *The Hunger for More: Searching for Values in an Age of Greed* (New York: Times Books, 1989); R. Shields, ed., *Lifestyle Shopping: The Subject of Consumption* (New York: Routledge, 1992); R. J. Sider, ed., *Living More Simply: Biblical Principles and Practical Models* (Downers Grove, Ill.: InterVarsity Press, 1980); M. Starkey, *Born to Shop* (London: Monarch, 1989).

Robert Banks

—SINGLE PARENTING—

Today single-parent families are so common that it is virtually impossible to find anyone who does not know a single parent or whose life is not personally affected by the single-parent phenomena. Parenting alone is one of the hardest jobs in the world, one that faces over twelve million parents and over sixteen million children in the United States alone (U.S. Census Data, 1995). But in the past, extended families* opened their arms to envelope the single parent. Several generations lived, if not in the same house, within a short distance of one another. Children with only one parent usually had a variety of family members to care for and love them.

What is different today is that it is not war or disease or famine that has afflicted families. Instead, today we have a culture of low commitment, easy divorce and detached familial relationships. It is estimated that in the United States alone one million marriages end in divorce* each year, affecting over one million children (Dan Rather, *CBS News,* December 3, 1998). As troubling as that is, there are even more families that are parented by one person because there never was a marriage* to begin with. Struggling against the issues of an overwhelming amount of work, financial stress and the stigmatization of being a single-parent family, it quickly becomes clear that this effort needs widespread collaboration.

Understanding the Challenges
Almost everyone is aware of the financial challenges that face single parents. But few people understand how serious the issue is. Eighty-seven percent of the families on welfare are headed by single mothers (Bennett). Although most single parents work outside of the home, their work is often a low-paying position that keeps them struggling between pitiful wages and their return to public assistance. Childcare is expensive and can easily consume more than one-half of the income. When children become sick, day-care centers may prohibit them from attending. Half-days at school, inclement-weather days or in-service days all tend to expropriate funds from a single parent's paycheck.

Nonpayment of child support is an

enormous burden. Less than half of those who are awarded child support receive the money. Approximately 25 percent never receive the first payment (Palmer and Tangel-Rodriguez, 9). Not surprisingly, 57 percent of single-parent mothers live below the poverty level. Researchers estimate that 73 percent of children from single-parent homes will spend some time in poverty before they are eighteen (Armstrong, 3). Many of those families will live in poverty for seven years or more.

Single-parent families move frequently. Even when mothers are awarded the family home* (which is no longer the norm since the advent of no-fault divorce), they may not be able to handle all of the costs associated with retaining it. The vast majority of single-parent families experience a revolving door of changing family households. This disruption destabilizes the social and educational world of the children. A residential move typically means the loss of friends and pets*—elements that normally help ease the pain of a family crisis. It may also mean a change in school districts, which is a highly stress producing factor for all children. Due to custody arrangements, children of divorce shuttle back and forth between their parents' homes on weekends, holidays and summer vacations.* Research indicates that, in their mobility,* children of single parents experience profound feelings of isolation, loneliness, sadness and despair (McLanahan and Sandefur, 25).

Their financial situation often prohibits them from participating in athletics, extracurricular activities, camps and other educational experiences that children from two-parent families can afford. If they have been fortunate enough to receive child support from the absent parent, the support stops being available at the time they most need additional financial assistance to attend college and make the shift from teen to young adulthood. Although many family attorneys urge parents to make provisions for their children's college education, insufficient income or lack of long-term planning often jettisons the best of parental intentions.

Additionally, today's children lack the benefit of adequate role models—usually their fathers, but also grandparents, aunts, uncles or even long-time neighbors—that earlier generations of children of single parents enjoyed.

Until the 1960s community relationships outside of the family were often formed in church. During the last fifty years the culture that has produced skyrocketing illegitimacy, easy divorce and far-flung families has also produced low church attendance. For the single parent, churches are commonly imaged as a place specifically for families that are made up of a mommy, daddy and kids. Not all single parents see the church as a source of safe support.

Sociologists confirm that stigmatization of single parents and their children by the general public has negatively affected academic performance of children, job performance of single parents and socialization of both (Bryan, Coleman, Ganong and Bryan, 169-74). The term *single parent* typically connotes a profoundly negative image—irresponsible, selfish, inadequate and dysfunctional. In church, "single-parent" has added layers of meaning. The single parent is often viewed as guilty of sin!

God's Concern for Single-Parent Families

Early in Genesis the story of Abraham, Sarah and Isaac is juxtaposed against the story of Hagar, the Bible's first single parent and her son, Ishmael. It was sin that created the situation for Hagar, even though she was obedient to her masters.

Her son, Ishmael, was the result of a sinful plot on the part of Sarah (to gain a child) and Abraham's complicity. Hagar was caught in the middle of a series of bad choices made by other people. But God offered his grace to Hagar and a promise to Ishmael (Gen 16:10).

Both the Old and New Testaments affirm that God cares for the widow and orphan. Time and time again, God admonishes his people to be mindful of their special needs:

Do not take advantage of a widow or an orphan. If you do and they cry out to me, I will certainly hear their cry. My anger will be aroused, and I will kill you with the sword; your wives will become widows and your children fatherless. (Ex 22:22-24)

Religion that God our Father accepts as pure and faultless is this: to look after orphans and widows in their distress and to keep oneself from being polluted by the world. (Jas 1:27)

Taking care of the widow and orphan appears to be nothing less than a litmus test of how much the people of God love God. It is "pure" religion, James says, implying that having a religion that ignores the widow and orphan is fundamentally contaminated. We must care for both two-parent families and single parent families not only because we are admonished to do so but also because single-parent families represent one of the largest outreach opportunities for the entire church.

The Church and Single Parents

There are four specific areas where effective ministry can change the lives of these disenfranchised families.

Spiritual. Pray without judgment for a specific single parent and his or her children. It is encouraging to watch a single-parent family that has been spiritually adopted by a couple or another

family move from crisis to health.*

As a single parent it is critical to find a faith community. If you find yourself in a church that does not embrace you, it is important for you to find one that does. Studies show that single-parent families that have their faith as a common bond process through the adjustment stage more quickly and exhibit more wholeness and healthfulness than families that do not have a spiritual foundation (Stinnett and DeFrain, 100-121). God is neither surprised nor embarrassed that you are a single parent. God does not use divorce or illegitimacy to punish us. In God's economy our own choices exact their consequences.

On one hand, God hates divorce and his plan is for children to be conceived within a marriage. On the other hand, many times these very situations provide an opportunity for God to reach individuals that may not have been willing to open their hearts for him until they were at their very lowest. God wants each of us to come to him, and he will waste nothing, including divorce and illegitimacy, to bring people into a saving relationship with him.

Emotional. Single parents and their children need relationship with two-parent families, with other single-parent families, and with people who are older and have already raised their children. The best relationship is that of simply being a friend. Unfortunately, many single parents continue to make bad choices because they lack good role models (for themselves and for their children), wise counsel, and the supportive hands and ears of friends in godly community. Single-parent families who have been surrounded by loving friends who include them in their social activities, encourage and edify them, and lovingly hold them accountable for their decisions are families that are happy, healthy, functional and successful.

If you are a single parent, recognize that it is your responsibility to be a friend in return. Friendship is never a one-way street. If you cannot afford to reciprocate in the way you would like, understand that your friends do not expect that of you. They want to see good stewardship* from you. But what they most want to see is that you genuinely care for them as well.

Furthermore, as a parent, your most important role is that of a model for your own children. How you behave at this time with your friends, and in every other area in your life, will influence their behavior in their life. Learning to be a friend, even when the circumstances are not optimal, will provide generous rewards for them later in life.

Financial. As mentioned earlier, most single parent families struggle with inadequate finances. Perhaps it is possible to help by buying groceries on occasion, by fixing a problem automobile or simply changing the oil, by helping out with household maintenance, etc. These are the kinds of practical needs that single parents have that a church body can handle with the help of many people. Most single parents, particularly single mothers, will require some amount of supplemental income until they get on their feet. It is a good idea for a church to have a benevolent fund specifically for single-parent family needs. It is also an excellent idea for some people in the church with financial skills to be available to help single parents with their budgets and to give them sound financial advice.

As a single parent you may need financial assistance for a period of time. Many government welfare programs are dead-ended. Once on, it is very difficult to get off. Furthermore, the accountability that you need, the encouragement and the hope that you require will not be there. Look instead to the local church for the added measure that you need to give you a hand up. Many churches have benevolent funds, food cupboards and clothes resources. Ask to be put in touch with someone who can help you with your financial questions.

Life Skills. Most single parents can use some programs to help them build their skill levels. Divorce recovery programs may be a good start, but they rarely meet the needs of single parents by themselves. Parenting* and discipline* skills are especially needed. Communication* skills and financial skills are often lacking. Many single parents need job retraining or help finding a job.

A church that provides for these skills to be taught through biblical principles to single parents will be expressing the essence of the gospel—love* in action (Mt 25:42-43, 45). But it is critical for the church leadership to remember that the children of single parents need an opportunity for healing and building new life skills as well. New studies indicate that children who have a venue to process their grief and learn new ways of coping within the first two years in their adjustment will do significantly better than children who do not. Children who do not have an opportunity to process systematically decline in their academic achievement and show greater signs of hostility and violence in later years (Rotenburg, Kim and Herman-Stahl, 43). This is where a group in the church, such as a house church made up of adults and children together, two-parent families and single-parent families, has much to commend it. Indeed, such will often fulfill most of the services mentioned above.

As a single parent, do not fall victim to the myth that your children will automatically bounce back. Children may not manifest their troubles until many years after their crisis—usually at a time when they are finally able to exert some control over their lives and when other developmental issues bring the old pain to the surface. Be ever mindful of what is happening and help them understand and resolve the needs that they have.

See also COMMUNICATION; DIVORCE; FAMILY; FAMILY PROBLEMS; GODPARENTING; LOVE; MOBILITY; MONEY; PARENTING; SHAME; VALUES.

References and Resources
B. Armstrong, *Single Parent Training Manual* (Christian Financial Concepts, 1998); D. Blankenhorn, *Fatherless America* (New York: BasicBooks, 1995); L. R. Bryan, M. Coleman, L. H. Ganong and S. H. Bryan, "Person Perception: Family Structure as a Clue for Stereotyping," *Journal of Marriage and the Family* 48 (1986) 169-74; D. Elkind, *The Hurried Child* (Reading, Mass.: Adison-Wesley, 1989); C. Etaugh and K. Nekolny, "Effects of Employment Status and Marital Status on Perceptions of Mothers," *Sex Roles* 23 (1990) 273-80; J. Guttmann, N. Geva and S. Grefen, "Teachers' and Children's Stereotypic Perception of the Child of Divorce," *American Educational Research Journal* 25 (1988) 555-71; T. McKenna, *The Hidden Mission Field: Caring for Single Parent Families in the 21st Century* (Mukilteo, Wash.: WinePress Publishing, 1999); S. McLanaham and G. Sandefur, *Growing Up with a Single Parent: What Hurts, What Helps* (Cambridge, Mass.: Harvard University Press, 1994); N. Palmer and Ana Tangel-Rodriguez, *When Your Ex Won't Pay* (Colorado Springs: Pinion Press); K. J. Rotenburg, L. S. Kim and M. Herman-Stahl, "The Role of Primary and Secondary Appraisals in the Negative Emotions and Psychological Maladjustment of Children of Divorce," *Journal of Divorce and Remarriage* 29 (1998); N. Stinnett and J. DeFrain, *Secrets of Strong Families* (New York: Basic Books, 1986).

Theresa McKenna

—SLEEPING—

We spend about a third of our lives sleeping but usually focus on sleep only when deprived of it. Since more and more people are suffering from sleep deprivation, at present it is the subject of much attention.

Why People Have Trouble Sleeping
There are various reasons for people sleeping less than they should. When a baby comes into the house, one or both parents lose sleep for a time to tend to its feeding requirements. Parents need to work out how best to share the burden so that each is getting the amount of sleep needed to function effectively. Within the family, or when living away from home in college dormitories, young people also sometimes burn the candle at both ends in their desire to experience all that life has to offer. While their youth makes it easier for them, if such behavior becomes habitual, it begins to have an effect. They begin to tire more quickly, feel listless and have little energy for their studies and other commitments.

Another group in society sometimes goes without sleep because of impoverished conditions. Job provides a vivid description of his world and ours by referencing the poor, who

lie all night naked, without clothing,
    and have no covering in the cold.
    (Job 24:7 RSV)

In our world at least one-sixth of the world's population lives in absolute poverty, for whom even sleep can be problematic. More generally, however, sleep deprivation occurs because some people are attempting to do too much and cut back on sleep to increase the time at their disposal. Others are too uptight at the end of the day to rest properly and therefore lose quality or quantity of sleep. Many carry their worries, plans and desires to bed with them and cannot relax enough to sleep well. Some live and work to an irregular rhythm and find their sleeping pattern sometimes disturbed.

One consequence of sleep deprivation is that insomnia has now become the major medical problem in newer Western societies. This lies at the root of the huge pharmacological industry in sleeping tablets and drugs for reducing stress. When people do not get their proper sleep, they suffer more than a loss of physical energy. They have less psychological stamina, make poorer decisions and find it difficult to concentrate and think effectively. They also lose out on the equilibrium and, at times, insight that come from regular dreaming.

Regular Sleep as an Act of Faith

Giving oneself over to sleep can be a basic expression of confidence, as, for instance, in Psalm 3:5-6:

I lie down and sleep;
I wake again, for the LORD sustains me.
I am not afraid of ten thousands of people
who have set themselves against me round about. (RSV)

Because "he who keeps Israel will neither slumber nor sleep" (Ps 121:4 RSV), we can sleep. Psalm 127 reflects on this confidence, focusing on both God's protection and his gracious provision:

Unless the LORD builds the house,
those who build it labor in vain.
Unless the LORD watches over the city,
the watchman stays awake in vain.
It is in vain that you rise up early and go late to rest,
eating the bread of anxious toil;

for he gives to his beloved sleep. (vv. 1-2 RSV)

Jesus' sleep in the boat during the storm is an example of this confidence (Mt 8:24), a confidence that both natural processes and kingdom growth are accomplished by God even while we sleep. This possibility of sleep is shown in one of Jesus' parables: "The kingdom of God is as if a man should scatter seed upon the ground, and should sleep and rise night and day, and the seed should sprout and grow, he knows not how. The earth produces of itself" (Mk 4:26-29 RSV). Because God provides, we can sleep. Sleep witnesses to a fundamental truth in the same way that keeping the sabbath* or the Lord's Day does: by God's grace we do not need to burn the candle at both ends to achieve prosperity or security. This witness has long found expression in vespers services and family prayers at night.

Sleeping In as an Expression of Foolishness

While sleep may be a gut-level expression of confidence, excessive sleep is simply an expression of folly: "How long will you lie there, O sluggard? When will you arise from your sleep? A little sleep, a little slumber, a little folding of the hands to rest, and poverty will come upon you like a vagabond, and want like an armed man" (Prov 6:9-11 RSV). There are many similar sayings throughout the Old and New Testaments. Both Jesus' sleep in the boat and Jonah's sleep in the boat (Jon 1:5-6) reveal character,* but not the same character: one the sleep of faith, the other the sleep of a slothful escape from duty.

Forgoing Sleep as a Mark of Obedience

While trustful sleep may be the appropriate response in most situations, in some the appropriate response is to deprive oneself of sleep to pray* or work. God's watchfulness allows us to sleep securely, but we are also invited to participate in this watchfulness, forgoing sleep. The Bible suggests that sleep was regularly broken for nighttime prayers, as witnessed in the Psalms: "When I think of thee upon my bed, and meditate on thee in the watches of the night" (Ps 63:6 RSV).

In more acute situations we find references to both prayer (2 Sam 12:16; Joel 1:13; Mt 26:36-46) and work through the night (2 Cor 11:27): "I will not give sleep to my eyes or slumber to my eyelids, until I find a place for the LORD, a dwelling place for the Mighty One of Jacob" (Ps 132:4-5 RSV).

We also find Paul permitting husband and wife to refrain at times from having sex and presumably sleeping more with one another at night. While he insists that neither should unilaterally deprive the other of sex (or presumably sleep), he does allow this from time to time when, with the agreement of the other, one party wishes to devote special time to prayer (1 Cor 7:5). This permission between a couple or within the family can also cover periods of extended prayer in crisis situations. For example, when he speaks of the urgency of the end times, Jesus views sleeplessness as a metaphor for readiness: "Blessed are those servants whom the master finds awake when he comes" (Lk 12:37 RSV). Because sleep needs to be broken off to participate in God's watchfulness, we need to find and follow an appropriate rhythm that expresses both our confidence in God's protection and our participation in God's watchfulness. In this we should take care that the patterns and needs of other members of the family are not disregarded. One way of doing this would be to have occasional periods of prayer together as a whole family.

Permitting Sleep as a Form of Justice

Sleeping becomes an ethical issue largely when our conduct affects others' sleep. Thus a proverb warns:

> He who blesses his neighbor with a
> loud voice,
> rising early in the morning,
> will be counted as cursing. (Prov
> 27:14 RSV)

More substantively, the Israelites were instructed not to take advantage of their neighbors' indebtedness to rob them of sleep:

> If ever you take your neighbor's garment in pledge, you shall restore it to him before the sun goes down; for that is his only covering, it is his mantle for his body; in what else shall he sleep? And if he cries to me, I will hear, for I am compassionate. (Ex 22:26-27 RSV)

This theme reappears in Job's declaration of innocence (Job 31:32). Justice is good news for the sleepless poor. It is striking that these texts do not start with sleep but offer a broad vision of justice in terms of loan guarantees or innocence. In that context the neighbor's sleep comes into the conversation. Our challenge is to let our vision for justice be shaped by that vision so that our actions become good news for the poor in practical matters like sleep.

God's Sleep

What does God's watchfulness mean for those who are in need? Does God never slumber or sleep? The psalms—reflecting a liturgical tradition evidenced elsewhere in the ancient Near East—use sleep to express God's absence:

> Rouse thyself! Why sleepest thou, O
> Lord?
> Awake! Do not cast us off for ever!
> Why dost thou hide thy face?
> Why dost thou forget our affliction
> and oppression? (Ps 44:23-24
> RSV)

To have God asleep and especially the poor sleepless is an intolerable situation. Following the lead of the biblical witness we should learn from people like Job what our justice should look like and also cry out with the psalmist, with the poor and with the church until God does "wake up" and his kingdom come.

So faith not only gives us personal confidence to sleep but also compels us to cry out to God until we all can sleep securely. It is no surprise that secure sleep appears among the Old Testament's end-times promises in Ezekiel 34:22-25 and in Hosea 2:18, where he promises:

> And I will make for you a covenant on that day with the beasts of the field, the birds of the air, and the creeping things of the ground; and I will abolish the bow, the sword, and war from the land; and I will make you lie down in safety. (RSV)

Aids to Sleep

Sleeping properly should be a regular part of our lives. It is honoring to God, beneficial to ourselves and members of our family, and advantageous for others. Apart from reliance on chemical aids to sleep, some nonmedical ways of dealing with insomnia follow.

☐ Respect each other's need for sleep when we arrive home and come in late.

☐ Keep noise levels down so that we do not disturb other members of the family.

☐ Wind down—do not go jogging just before sleep or watch television* until late in the evening.

☐ Avoid caffeine and heavy meals just before going to bed, resorting if needed to warm milk or a light sandwich.

☐ As much as possible, take only short naps during the day, so that you will sleep well at night.

☐ Save the bedroom for sleeping and sex,* not for other things like intense conversation,* working, squabbling and family discipline.*

☐ Develop consistent sleep patterns, rather than ones that vary between cheating on sleep and desperately trying to make up.

☐ Cast any burden you may have on God and ask him to relax you and grant you the gift of sleep.

Sleeping pills may occasionally have their place in a time of great pressure or crisis when you are severely agitated, or when going on a long plane flight into a different time zone and it is important to be refreshed on arrival. Even then, however, adjusting your sleeping patterns two or three days ahead so that you begin to move into the time of the place to which you are going is a very effective nonmedicinal way of obtaining the sleep you need.

See also HEALTH; SABBATH.

References and Resources

J. A. Hobson, *Sleep* (New York: Scientific American Library, 1995); T. Jacobsen, *The Treasures of Darkness* (New Haven, Conn.: Yale University Press, 1976); P. Laxie, *The Enchanted World of Sleep* (New Haven, Conn.: Yale University Press, 1996); T. McAlpine, *Sleep, Divine and Human, in the Old Testament,* JSOTS 38 (Sheffield, U.K.: JSOT, 1987).

Thomas H. McAlpine

SPIRITUAL DISCIPLINES. *See* CHORES; PARENTING; PRAYER; SPIRITUAL FORMATION.

—SPIRITUAL FORMATION—

The Second Vatican Council used the phrase "domestic church" to recapture the ancient idea that the family* is a form of church and a place for evoking and applying faith. The companion article on character* explores the development of good habits, moral and spiritual education, and virtues. The section on discipline* proposes parenting is essentially a matter of discipleship. The entry on prayer* explores communion with God both for and with family. In this article we look specifically at family spiritual formation. How is it to be understood and practiced?

"Spiritual formation" is an old term dating back to monastic practices and refers to "the process whereby men and women who love and trust Jesus seek to take on the character of Christ guided by various spiritual practices" (Peace, 939). Disciplines and practices include spiritual direction, sacred reading, spiritual reading, meditative prayer, retreats, spiritual journal keeping and spiritual autobiographies. These may be summarized in terms of three journeys: upward (in communion with God), inward (in gaining knowledge of self) and outward (in service, compassion and justice; Stevens, 932-38). But do they fit family life?

The disciplines of monastic life and family life seem on the surface to be incompatible. How can you have regular times of prayer, solitude, intentional spiritual direction when there are dishes to be done, beds to be made, meals to be prepared, diapers to be changed and chores* to be completed? Obviously there is value in some intentional spiritual formation in the context of family life—practicing family prayers, family Bible reading and engaging in family mission*—though there is always a danger when these form a routine. It is especially counterproductive to push children to pray out loud and read at the table when this is forced and unnatural. But more important than adding spiritual disciplines to family life is the recognition that family life itself is a spiritual discipline.

Family as Spiritual Discipline

We do not need to bring the Lord into our homes* by a program of Christian education for the family, or even by family devotions, good as these are. God is already there, even if our family has problems.* The reasons are important.

Family has covenant at its core. Covenant allows us to see something of the covenant love life of God; at the same time, God's covenant with Israel and the church inspires our covenant life in marriage and family. Further, family life has a trinitarian foundation. Cohumanity and covenant love are expressions of God's very being—existing eternally as Trinity—three unique persons in relation. Every family in heaven and on earth has been named—derives it being and nature—from God (Eph 3:14). God-imaging creatures therefore exist not as individuals but persons in communion.

The Cappadocian fathers (Basil, Gregory of Nyssa and Gregory of Nazianzus) taught that the essence of God is relational, that God exists in a plurality of distinct persons united in communion. They avoided the twin dangers of collectivism and individualism by speaking of perichoresis (reciprocity, interchange, giving and receiving without blurring). Perichoresis involves a relatedness that is both static and dynamic. The heart of the matter is the sociality of the triune God, an elegant truth sometimes expressed through the metaphor of family: three persons, one family. The net effect

295

of this recovery of perichoretic reflection is doxological reflection on the triune God under the category of community rather than individuality. This has a profound application to spiritual formation. To be like God is to be persons in community, with intercommunion, interpenetration, unity through diversity and not through merger. As God the Father, Son and Spirit are one through diversity, more one because they are three, so God-imaging creatures are one through celebrating the diversity of male and female, parents and children, distinct personalities, while being each for the other and all for the one. So when God made a creature like himself, God made a family. Family life is implicitly spiritual, innately full of invitations godward.

Finding God at Home

One obvious implication of the theology of family life is that the structure of family life and our struggles with this structure are opportunities to find God at home. As we work through issues of codependence (merging) and independence (collectivism), we are invited to discover interdependence (communion without union). The unity of a family is not a homogenous unity with merged lives; nor is it to be a mere bouquet of individuals sharing an occasional common meal. Family is meant to be perichoretic—a real communion without merging (see Problems; Communication).

Not only does the fundamental structure of family life invite us to find God, but the many day-to-day issues set us up to find God freshly and grow in discipleship. The warp and woof of family relational life both suggest godlikeness and invite us to seek God's help in living with relational integrity: forgiving* one another, welcoming one another, offering hospitality.* Parenting,* for example, involves sustaining, guiding and

relinquishing—all dimensions in which we learn from God as our ultimate parent. Childhood involves trusting, acknowledging and honoring—all fundamental to faith formation. Brothers and sisters learn to play* together and cooperate—both fundamental for living by grace through faith rather than by the performance of works. Grandparenting* involves enjoying (rather than using) and comforting; being grandchildren involves appreciating and, usually at some time, grieving—again, all dimensions of the life of faith (Henley, 33-105). What better school for Christian living could be contrived?

Take the question of unconditional acceptance. As the older brother in the parable of the two prodigals discovered, one cannot experience the welcome of God while rejecting one's brother (Lk 15:11-32). Family life sets us up to experience the gospel—unconditional acceptance on the basis of relationship rather than performance. The elder brother in the parable prides himself on his impeccable behavior and hard work (15:29-30) but is really damned because grace and gratitude have not broken his hard heart. It is family life that invites him to live by faith and grace.

Family is the first environment in which we gain images of God as Father and the human paradigm for the feminine references to God in the Bible. Sometimes these images must be unlearned. Even in the best family we do not learn the fatherhood of God from our own parents; rather, we learn our fatherhood and motherhood from God. Nonetheless, our experience of parenting and being parented is evocative—a call to be converted to the fatherhood of God rather than to be convinced from our human parents. Child rearing turns out to be a moral and spiritual education for the parents. Children help parents grow up. We cannot give children affection, correction and a future with promise if we have not received these from God ourselves (*see* Blessing).

The Jacob story in Genesis 25—35 demonstrates that God was determined to bless Jacob in the context of his family life, through his relations with parents, brother, wives and father-in-law, even though that family was riddled with favoritism, deceit, family secrets and multigenerational sin. In the end, when Jacob was reconciled to Esau, Jacob confessed that seeing his brother's face was "like seeing the face of God" (Gen 33:10).

A "perfect Christian family" is not required for faith development; indeed there is no perfect Christian family. The best place to meet God is right where we **are**. Even seriously troubled families can become arenas of spiritual formation if the liabilities and difficulties are processed (sometimes the help of someone outside is needed for this). To run away from our families is to run away from one place God wants to meet us. So we are invited to find God at the center of family life, in all of its relational dynamics and covenantal structure, rather than at the periphery through religious exercises.

See also CHARACTER; DISCIPLINE; FAMILY; GOALS; GODPARENTING; MISSION; PRAYER; PARENTING; READING; VALUES.

References and Resources

R. S. Anderson and D. B. Guernsey, *On Being Family: A Social Theology of the Family.* (Grand Rapids: Eerdmans, 1985); J. O. Balswick and J. K. Balswick, *The Family: A Christian Perspective on the Contemporary Home* (Grand Rapids: Baker, 1989); E. Boyer, *Finding God at Home* (New York: Harper & Row, 1988); J. A. Henley, *Accepting Life: The Ethics of Living in Families* (Melbourne: Joint Board of Christian Education, 1994); T. Howard, *Hallowed Be This House* (Wheaton, Ill.: Harold Shaw, 1978); D. R. Leckey, *The Ordinary Way: A Family Spirituality* (New York: Crossroad, 1982); R. V. Peace, "Spiritual Formation," in *The Complete Book of Everyday Christianity,* ed. R. Banks and R. P. Stevens (Downers Grove, Ill.: InterVarsity Press, 1997), pp. 938-43; R. P. Stevens, "Spiritual Disciplines," in Banks and Stevens, eds., *op. cit.,* pp. 932-38; W. M. Wright, *Sacred Dwelling: A Spirituality for Family Life* (New York: Crossroad, 1989).

R. Paul Stevens

SPORTS. *See* ENTERTAINMENT; GAMES; LEISURE; PLAY.

STEWARDSHIP. *See* CHORES; CREDIT CARD; DEBT; INSURANCE; MONEY; TITHING.

—STRESS—

We experience stress when we experience a physical or psychological threat to our well-being. Crisis occurs whenever the stress we are experiencing overwhelms our perceived ability to cope with it. Families find themselves in crisis whenever they cannot meet the challenges of life or when an important goal is blocked.

Stress and Contemporary Life

Most individuals and families are well equipped to handle a single major stressor that comes from one direction. However, we struggle when facing several minor stressors that come at us from many directions. Yet this is exactly what most families experience in modern life.

It is little wonder that most families to-day report that they experience significant amounts of stress on an ongoing basis. With families experiencing more and more stress, it is not surprising that more and more families are in crisis. Research has shown that most families tend to ignore minor stressors, allowing them to compound. Conversely, if stressors are perceived as overwhelming, then typically they are denied until they become an imminent crisis. Usually families only mobilize to overcome their stressors when the stress is causing significant discomfort and they believe they have the resources to overcome the problem.

Any stress that is unresolved in one part of our lives will compound the stress we feel in another part of our lives. Likewise, whenever one member of the family experiences stress, it affects the stress loads of other family members, as well as the overall stress load of the family itself. An analogy is to picture the family as a large, empty bowl. Surrounding the bowl are individual empty glasses, representing each family member. Stress is like water that is poured into these containers. Whenever an individual experiences stress (e.g., problems in the workplace), not only does the individual glass receive water but so do the other glasses, as well as the large container in the middle. Though each container will receive differing amounts of water (stress) the overall effect is to raise stress levels both in individual family members and in the family as a whole. In the same way, stress that the family experiences as a whole (e.g., chronic conflict at home) is like water being poured directly into the large container in the center—however, the other individual levels rise as well. On each of these containers there is an imaginary red line that marks the crisis point, whereby the stress is now greater than the ability to cope.

As stress is introduced to the individual or to the system as a whole, if it is not dealt with or "poured out," the levels increase until they cross over this line and crisis occurs. But just because a single individual in the family is over the red line does not automatically mean that everyone else is over theirs. Thus, it is possible to have one or more family members in crisis, without the entire family being in crisis. When this is the case, healthy families rally around the member and become a source of support. However, as individual stressors accumulate, so does the family's. Crisis occurs when the family feels overwhelmed by the cumulative effect of the stress of individual members or by experiencing a stressor that confronts and effects the family system as a whole. When the entire family is in crisis, support will have to come from outside the system.

Types of Family Crises
There are four basic types of family crises. The first is the unforeseen crises that happen and dramatically upset the family's equilibrium. Unexpected job loss is an example of this. The second type occurs when long-term stress is left unresolved and begins to compound. A marriage relationship that deteriorates over time and results in separation is an example of crisis born out of long-term unresolved stress. A third type of family crisis is developmental. These crises are a normal and even predictable part of family development. Adolescence* is a natural part of the family lifecycle, yet is often experienced as a time of crisis. The fourth type of family crisis is a hybrid between a developmental crisis and an unforeseen crisis. The birth (developmental crisis) of a deformed child (unforeseen crisis) is an example of a hybrid crisis.

Factors in Causing Stress
Research has found that family stress is

the result of three interacting factors (Hill).

The nature of the stressful event itself. Most people believe that stress comes from the environment and is due to external circumstances. The Social Readjustment Rating Scale (SRRS, Holmes and Rahe) employs this belief. The scale lists numerous possible stressors that one may have been exposed to in the previous year, assigning each event a number of points indicating the magnitude of the stressor. For example, the death* of a spouse is assigned 100 points, divorce* is assigned 75, etc. One simply goes down the scale, checks off any incident that they have experienced and adds the points. The total represents the amount of stress the individual has experienced in the previous year. In this model, stress is understood as objective and external with the individual being a passive recipient.

Believing that stress is inherent in the event itself leads to one of the most frequent strategies employed by families in crisis management, which is to deal with the stressor so that it is removed. Families who deal well with crisis are those who can employ problem-solving skills in order to arrive at practical, workable solutions that resolve the problems.* This approach is an excellent strategy if it is possible to work upon the external stress to bring about change. However, it is important to realize that not all stressors can be changed directly. For example, the stress that many families experience during adolescence cannot be resolved by making adolescence go away.

The family's perception of the event. What we believe about what we are experiencing plays an even more significant role in stress formation than the actual event. This is something many families in crisis fail to understand. Families can be so focused on trying to solve the problem, which they understand as external to themselves, that they fail to understand that it is their reaction to the problem that is the real problem. Crisis usually occurs when a family employs a solution to a problem, and the solution does not work. Most families in crisis do not abandon their original solution but instead repeat it with greater effort and when failure ensues, the magnitude of the crisis increases. At this point, thinking becomes constricted, strategies to cope become unfocused, and desperation clouds rational thinking. A family in crisis often needs outside intervention to help them change the way they are responding. Thus, a second and highly effective strategy in crisis management is helping families to change both their understanding of and reaction to their stressors.

Simply redefining the problem in such a way that it becomes manageable is an excellent way for families to mobilize their resources to meet the challenge. For example, many families see the desire of their adolescent children for more freedom as rejection or rebellion and thus respond in ways that inflame stress within the family. Simply helping parents interpret their child's behavior as a normal developmental desire for independence rather than rebellion can initiate a different set of responses that often relieve stress within the home.

The resources or strengths of the family at the time of the stressor. For crisis to occur there are two primary stages we must go through. First, we must perceive the event as stressful, and second, we assess whether or not we have the resources to cope with it. If families do not have the resources they need to cope with the stressors they face, then they will find themselves in crisis. Thus, family health* plays a significant role in dealing with stress and crisis. Families that are too rigid or chaotic do not do as well in coping with stress as families who maintain a balance between flexibility and structure. Families who cope well with stress learn to adjust and adapt. Being able to accept and manage change is a critical skill in crisis management.

Another important factor is how connected family members are to one another. Healthy families feel connected and work like a team in overcoming their problems. Conversely, families who do not do well in crisis are those where members experience little connectedness or are so connected that they are codependent. Having a strong marital bond as well as healthy parent-child relationships provide a strong foundation in dealing with the stressors inherent in family life (Balswick and Balswick). Communication* and conflict resolution* skills are critical in times of family crisis. Families who work together to solve problems, delegate responsibility, and respect and share values* do well in times of high stress. Families who blame each other, do not help each other out, do not share troubles or resist compromising do poorly.

Another important factor in family crisis is how much external support they have. Families supported by their extended family, friends and church who have monetary resources to access professional help when needed do far better in crisis than isolated families with no support.

Stress and crises are a normal part of the family life cycle. Birth, death* and catastrophe are normal family experiences. Families who are able successfully to negotiate crisis events in their lives typically grow from such experiences and become more adept and confident in overcoming future crisis (Steele and Raider). Normal crises precipitate a process of grief and mourning. In some families this grief process is blocked, and they end up remaining stuck in perpetual anger and denial and always seem to be in crisis. Crisis-oriented families tend to act out the things that have never been resolved, and their ability to cope diminishes over time. These families tend to have few connections with relatives, friends, neighbors and no religious affiliation. Sadly, children who grow up in these families know no other way of life and repeat this cycle in their adult years (Kagan and Schlossberg).

Christian Resources
Christians have a number of advantages in dealing with stress. Foremost is God. The Bible teaches, "The Lord is my helper; I will not be afraid" (Heb 13:6; see also Ps 118:6-7). This is not to suggest that Christian families do not face stress or cannot be thrown into crises. Like Job, many Christian families have experienced catastrophes that threaten to overwhelm them. Foundational to our faith is that we will suffer, but in our suffering we will not be alone. By faith we know that even when the world seems out of control, it is not: God cares for us deeply and is in control. He hears our cries, and when we feel like we have exhausted all our human resources, God still actively cares for us. We also have the enlightening and wisdom of the Holy Spirit, who can lead us in ways of truth. Sometimes this will mean a very painful recognition of our own sin in dealing with stress or our own sinfulness in causing stress.

Much stress is caused because of the way we conceptualize the problem. If we believe from the outset that nothing can separate us from the love, care and providence of God, then much of our fear can be replaced with confidence. This is why crises are often a significant time of spiritual growth—we are forced to rely on God rather than ourselves, and we learn that God is there for us. Many Christians experience far more stress in their lives because they have never really learned to develop a life based on faith. Research has shown that those who have a high degree of meaning and purpose in their lives are better able to withstand stress. As chaotic as crises can feel, those who seek to understand what God is saying to them in their crises will fare far better than those who fail to look for meaning in their times of struggle.

Finally, Christians have the care and support of the body of Christ. The more vulnerable, honest and real Christians can be in sharing their struggles with one another, the more we will be able to support one another in meaningful ways. Grief groups, family retreats, care ministries, prayer ministries, seminars and teaching are all ways in which communities of believers can support one another. It must also be remembered that as Christians we are called to be salt and light to the world around us. Most experts agree that a significant number of families are experiencing crisis. Many of them have none of the resources we do as Christians. To offer them the resources of care, support, education and ultimately the hope of Christ is a profound way that many churches are being salt and light in their communities.

See also COMMUNICATION; CONFLICT RESOLUTION; DIVORCE; FAMILY PROBLEMS; FORGIVENESS.

References and Resources
J. Balswick and J. Balswick, *The Family* (Grand Rapids: Baker, 1991); R. Hill, *Families Under Stress* (New York: Harper & Row, 1949); R. Kagan and S. Schlossberg, *Families in Perpetual Crisis* (New York: W. W. Norton, 1989); T. Holmes and R. Rahe, "The Social Readjustment Scale," *Journal of Psychosomatic Research* 11 (1967) 213-18.

—Mark Davies

—TELEPHONE—

Once the telephone was basically about extending communication; now it runs the danger of adding to the factors that are breaking down community, even in the home.

The Ubiquitous Telephone
The telephone has played a pervasive role and significantly altered personal and business communication* patterns. Telephones are the nerve ends of the modern world: like the body's central nervous system, they connect disparate members, even within the family, and channel messages from one to the other. Though occasionally we wish we could be as far away from it as possible and curse its intrusion on our lives, most of us use the telephone constantly and greatly appreciate what it does for us.

In most Western countries more than 90 percent of the population have one or more phones in their residences. We are also in the midst of significant changes in the world of telecommunications. With the coming of cellular models, the telephone is becoming ubiquitous: instead of relying on scattered public phone booths to stay in touch, we can become mobile. With the invention of modems, the attachment of phones to a computer* opens up the possibility of working from

301

home rather than at the office.

The telephone has become an indispensable part of everyday life. It has played a major role in maintaining cohesion as settlement spread and connected rural and urban areas in vital ways. It has changed the context and meaning of neighborhood. But what are its main advantages and disadvantages in the family? How much has it enhanced or diminished close relationships at home and further afield? To what extent is it a primary cause of our pressured lifestyle, intruding into and fragmenting family life?

Until the last couple of decades there was little discussion of these issues, largely because Christians took the telephone for granted and used it like everyone else. From a spiritual or theological point of view scarcely a thought has been given to it, unless to see it as a way of directly advertising the gospel to people in their homes or providing them with valuable crisis counseling services. In the earlier part of the century only groups such as the Amish debated whether it would be beneficial or not. Leaders of that community warned of its dangers, arguing that it would subvert face-to-face community and allow the secular world to subvert the life of discipleship. There was a church split among the Amish over this, and Old Order Mennonites avoided this only by forbidding church leaders to own a telephone or members to enter hotels to use one. At stake was a vital issue: the extent to which we should allow modern inventions to influence and shape shared life in the home* as well as in the wider Christian community.

The Nature of Telephone Conversations

Telephone conversation* takes place for a variety of reasons. The most common distinction is between intrinsic and in-strumental purposes. The first has a social purpose, giving people opportunity to talk about their interests, concerns, experiences and relationships. The second has a task orientation, enabling people to further their work or make some arrangement.

The first kind of conversation is used to build on and extend existing networks of relationships. Women in particular use the telephone to hold together the fabric of both family* and friends and to carry out important voluntary caregiving activities to people who are lonely, ill or in need. The telephone is especially important to those at home who do not have much face-to-face contact with others—such as the elderly, handicapped and infirm—and to those for whom social contact is extremely important, such as single mothers, teenagers and troubled people. People moving into retirement homes use their telephones to keep in touch with friends and family, and sometimes for shopping.* Immigrants, especially women, use it primarily to build a female support neighborhood* and also to bring language instruction within their reach.

Advantages and Disadvantages of the Telephone

On the positive side, people particularly appreciate the telephone for: its convenience; the way it saves time; the way it allows ongoing contact with family and friends; its opportunities for gossip; the way it overcomes feelings of isolation and loneliness, and reduces the tyranny of distance; the way it allows one to say things he or she could not say in person; how it accesses information without emotional consequences; the way it helps to avoid small talk; how it allows the expression of feelings; the sense of security it provides. On the negative side, what people most dislike, in order of importance, are its expense, interruptions at any time, intrusions on privacy, calls from strangers, frustrations in getting through to people, uncertainty about what to say, the telephone's overconvenience, its impersonal nature and its having brought bad news.

In addition, most people feel guilty if they do not answer the telephone when it rings. For this reason, especially if there are many calls, the telephone can make life too busy, intruding on family meals and time that husband and wife need together, as well as on leisure* times and periods of prayer and meditation. Salespeople can enter the home unannounced through the telephone and take up time and energy. Children can get access to types of calls that are unfit for them or rack up large telephone bills by dialing out-of-state friends.

Putting the Telephone in Its Place

Perhaps in the spiritual realm the closest analogue to the telephone is prayer,* for it too is a wide-reaching, multipurpose, communal phenomenon. One of the unexpected findings of surveys is the important psychological functions that telephone calls play: making people feel wanted, needed, included and involved, and in general providing the opportunity to be social and keep in touch. In other words, telephones seem to contribute to people's self-esteem* and experience of community.

On the other hand, sometimes people feel that the telephone uses them, as when they sense they must answer it, are manipulated, encounter insensitivity, waste time on it or become addicted to using it. In these ways it turns people themselves into machines and leads them to feel insignificant. Where several people in a family compete for use of the same telephone, it can cause friction and a competitive spirit. This is exacerbated by the way telephones are sometimes increasingly tied up as family members use the Internet.* While one answer to this is to connect more telephones to the house, this heightens the possibility of individual family members developing separate lives in their own rooms instead of spending enough time together.

Few families would want to do without a telephone, valuing the way it enables them to keep in touch—through the day as well as at a distance—and also to get on with their individual responsibilities, both in the home and outside it. But too few think about how to maximize its advantages and minimize its disadvantages, how to allow the telephone its proper place without exceeding its limits and affecting the quality of family life adversely. Here are practical suggestions that can help.

☐ Have only one phone for the family and learn sharing, self-discipline and sensitivity to others' needs, only adding and devoting other lines for computer uses.

☐ Use the phone only when necessary. Visit rather than phone those working for or with you if they are in the next room.

☐ Tell people not to call you between certain hours. This helps both them and you establish boundaries for phone use.

☐ Do not answer the phone at mealtimes, even if you eat alone. When eating* it is important to have time with others or to yourself.

☐ Preserve leisure* time from intrusion by work-related calls. This means keeping cellular phones in their place.

☐ Interrupt politely and hang up immediately on all junk calls. This is your right, for they are invading your privacy. Give priority to people with you over incoming calls from others. Answering machines can be a real help here.

☐ When necessary use answering machines to screen incoming calls or try providing family and friends with a recognizable signal.

☐ Fast from the phone occasionally for a

day, weekend or holiday. This prevents addiction and keeps it in proper perspective. Such guidelines will help you make the phone a servant rather than a master within the family setting.

See also COMMUNICATION; CONVERSATION; INTERNET; NEIGHBORING.

References and Resources

S. Aronson, "The Sociology of the Telephone," *International Journal of Comparative Sociology* 12 (1971) 153-67; D. Bell, "Toward a Sociology of Telephones and Telephoners," in *Sociology and Everyday Life*, ed. M. Truzzi (Englewood Cliffs, N.J.: Prentice-Hall, 1968); G. Gumpert and R. Cathcart, eds., *Inter/Media: Interpersonal Communication in a Media World* (New York: Oxford University Press, 1979); J. Meyrowitz, *No Sense of Place: The Impact of Electronic Media on Social Behavior* (New York: Oxford University Press, 1985); I. de Sola Pool, *The Social Impact of the Telephone* (Cambridge, Mass.: MIT Press, 1977).

Robert Banks

—TELEVISION—

Television is surely the most pervasive and influential mass medium of the late twentieth century. At the same time television is one of the most poorly understood media, eliciting both praise and superficial criticism. Moreover, the uses of television defy simple classification since the medium pervades every aspect of life. The merging of film, video* and the computer* with television is making it even more difficult to define and evaluate the medium.

The Appeal of Television
Television's appeal to humankind is apparently universal. From early childhood to the end of their lives, human beings will normally watch television if it is available and if they have the time. Indeed, there is considerable evidence that television viewing is steadily eclipsing all other types of entertainment* and all other forms of leisure.* In North America, for instance, television viewing time is greater than that of all other forms of entertainment combined.

Probably the two most appealing aspects of television are its drama and persona. The most popular uses of the medium present messages as dramatic stories. This is true, for instance, not just of situation comedies, soap operas and police dramas, but even of many commercials, nearly all news stories, documentaries, sporting events (the drama of the game), movies, animated children's shows and music videos.

Television's appealing use of persona similarly pervades the medium. In fictional programming, television *represents* all types of people, who are played by celebrities or stars. At the same time, television *presents* people who are more or less acting as themselves (e.g., talk-show hosts and guests, news reporters and anchors, variety-show emcees, sports players and commentators, and televangelists).

This combination of drama and persona creates a pseudorelationship between viewers and television personalities. Viewers feel as if they know various celebrities. In some cases this kind of pseudorelationship creates an uncritical, largely irrational trust (e.g., trusting a TV preacher or a news reporter), an inability to distinguish between fact and fiction (e.g., soap-opera viewers' emotional involvement in fictional weddings) and even a greater viewer commitment to televised characters than to real-life relationships.

Balancing Television with Real Life

Viewers should maintain a healthy balance between the medium's pseudorelationships and the viewers' real interpersonal relationships. Parents in North America on average spend over four hours daily watching television, a mere four minutes conversing with spouses and an unbelievable thirty seconds daily conversing with their children.

For most families, a daily limit of one or two hours of television viewing would adequately control the tendency to overindulge, especially if the viewing is familial and not individual. In addition, regulating the number of personal television sets in the home can help enormously; too many parents try to solve the problem of deciding what to view by giving each family member his or her own set. Finally, the placement of the television set in the home is also important; if the living or family-room furniture is organized around the set, for instance, television viewing, not conversing,* will dominate in-home leisure time.

Viewing Versus Watching

It is important that Christians learn how to view television instead of only watching it. Viewing is an active, discerning response to televisual messages, whereas watching is passive and largely uncritical. Viewing requires the audience to look for the values* and beliefs that animate television messages.

Neil Postman suggests that television tends inherently to eclipse critical thought by emphasizing image over word. Although there is undoubtedly some truth to this generalization, it

wrongly assumes that viewers cannot be taught to think about the meaning of images, especially moving-image narratives. By equipping people to evaluate and reflect on programs, this type of visual literacy combats the tendency of the medium to trivialize subjects.

From a Christian perspective, viewing fosters spiritual discernment of secular doctrine (Eph 4:14) communicated through popular culture. Viewing places all television programs in the context of God's Word, enabling viewers to identify and evaluate the worldviews behind this popular entertainment.

Viewing can be fostered especially by parents, pastors and schoolteachers. Parents should view and discuss programs with their children. This is most effective as a regular, informal activity. Pastors have considerable potential to foster discernment by using popular TV characters and programs as illustrations in sermons and other Bible teachings. Schoolteachers have many opportunities to encourage discernment by integrating video segments into lectures and discussions across the curriculum. Students thereby learn to think about what they see, as well as to relate popular images to schoolwork.

Children and Television

Children often watch enormous amounts of television to relieve boredom. Many parents encourage this by using the medium as a baby sitter, particularly before and after school, on Saturday mornings and during meal preparation.* Significant research suggests that this type of unsupervised use of television by children is not wise.

Until they reach about eight years of age, children are not capable of interpreting programs on their own with much critical ability. Younger children have difficulty separating television's fictional content from real life. Moreover,

305

they cannot easily make sense of the meaning of televisual stories; their understanding of television is limited largely to describing dramatic action or events. Often children's understanding of a show is significantly different than the commonplace understandings of adults. Therefore, it is essential that parents carefully monitor and supervise their children's use of the medium. This should include (1) wise selection of appropriate programs for young viewers, particularly shows that are slow-paced and provide their own explanations of the stories; (2) parental viewing with children; and (3) parental discussion of programs with children, especially discussion of how each child is responding emotionally to programs.

Parents also need to balance television time with other important activities. Reading* skills are often undeveloped in children because of excessive television viewing. Social skills are sometimes similarly retarded when a child does not spend adequate time interacting with other children. Children's normal patterns of sleep* are even interrupted in homes where parents do not adequately regulate viewing time.

Finally, television viewing can exacerbate a variety of childhood disorders, although the reasons are not precisely known. For example, television apparently worsens hyperactivity among some children. The medium also contributes to attention deficit problems in susceptible children. Because these links between television and childhood behavior are often idiosyncratic to specific children, it is essential that parents monitor the viewing of their offspring.

The Future of Television

Television is a rapidly evolving medium that will likely play a growing role in all areas of society, especially family life and education. As computers merge with television, the medium will expand and specialize its content. This will further challenge Christians to use television wisely.

Television is shifting from a *broadcasting* system to various forms of *narrowcasting*. The growth of cable television, with its specialized drama, sports and information, is only one step on the road to channel-free programming. Viewers will increasingly be able to select specific programs at any time from a broad menu of available options. Channel surfing (rapidly switching from one channel to the next with a remote-control device) will be transformed into menu surfing. This technological revolution will change the television landscape into a cornucopia of specialized fare.

Televisual abundance of this kind offers positive opportunities as well as serious challenges to Christians. There will be many more worthwhile programs, including all kinds of instructional educational material and quality drama. But the new televisual landscape will also challenge the limits of Christian morality by providing specialized fare for people who practice unacceptable lifestyles or who believe in non-Christian religions.

It is imperative that Christians avoid a mindless adoption of the new television technologies. Parents need to establish standards for familial use of new technologies. In addition, local congregations and Christian schools need to help individuals and families to live faithfully by cultivating critical viewing skills and sharing suggestions about worthwhile programs.

See also ENTERTAINMENT; LEISURE; VIDEOS.

References and Resources

J. P. Ferré, ed., *Channels of Belief: Religion*

and American Commercial Television (Ames: Iowa State University Press, 1990); T. Inbody, ed., *Changing Channels: The Church and the Television Revolution* (Dayton: Whaleprints, 1990); N. Postman, *Amusing Ourselves to Death: Public Discourse in the Age of Show Business* (New York: Viking, 1985); Q. J. Schultze, *Redeeming Television: How TV Changes Christians—How Christians Can Change TV* (Downers Grove, Ill.: InterVarsity Press, 1992); Q. J. Schultze, *Winning Your Kids Back from the Media* (Downers Grove, Ill.: InterVarsity Press, 1994); also available as a five-part video series with Gospel Films.

Quentin J. Schultze

THANKSGIVING. *See* HOLIDAYS—THANKSGIVING.

—TITHING—

Tithing is commonly understood as the obligation to pay one-tenth of one's income to the church or religious causes. It is a spiritual ministry that is good for us, the church and the world. But, as we shall see, stewardship—a much larger concept—more than encompasses merely giving a percentage. It is total, though the true meaning of tithing in the Bible points to this larger ministry of Christians and the family.

Biblical Tithing

In the Old Testament tithes were like taxes paid to the temple; they were not discretionary gifts (for an exception, see Gen 14:20). This practice accomplished four things. It (1) celebrated the goodness of God (Deut 14:26), (2) acknowledged God's ownership of everything, (3) maintained places of worship (Num 18:21; Deut 14:27) and (4) cared for the poor (Deut 14:28-29). Even in the Old Testament tithing was only part of Israel's stewardship. The New Testament only once mentions tithing (Mt 23:23)—in the context of Jesus' calling the Pharisees to something more important. The New Testament principle is not one-tenth but "cheerful giving" (2 Cor 9:7). Since everything belongs to God, we should generously disperse what we can to help others. But the use of "should" destroys the very idea of Christian giving; it comes not from law, principle or obligation but from the spontaneous overflow of gratitude for Christ's blessing on our lives (2 Cor 8:9).

It is tragic that Christian stewardship has been so often reduced to tithing as a calculated obligation—giving to the Lord's work one-tenth of one's income ("Is that gross or net after taxes?"). While *stewardship* is commonly used as a camouflaged appeal for funds for church and religious purposes, the term denotes a more comprehensive view of the Christian life affecting time, work, leisure,* talents, money,* the state of one's soul and care for the environment. The Greek word for *steward* means "one who manages a household." Years ago persons called "stewards," rather than huge financial institutions, were employed to manage the financial affairs and households of wealthy people. Their management included not only money but everything that makes a household thrive, not unlike the vocation of homemaking* but on a large scale. A biblical example is Joseph's work as steward of Potiphar's house; his master did not "concern himself with anything in the house" (Gen 39:8).

Stewardship is a term theologically related to service or ministry. If *service*

307

denotes the motivation for ministry—undertaking God's interests for the pleasure of God—*stewardship* suggests the purpose of ministry: to manage God's world in harmony with the owner's mind. These two words, *service* and *stewardship,* taken together constitute the ministry of the laity and therefore are the ministry of Christians in families. They are roughly equivalent to the much popularized term *servant leadership.*

Managing God's Household

God is the ultimate owner of everything (Ps 24:1; 50:10) and has entrusted creation to humankind. We are entrusted with the care of the world and are accountable to God, who owns it and has declared his intended purpose. This trusteeship stems from the so-called creation mandate in Genesis 1:26-29. The stewards are to take care of the earth (Gen 2:15) and develop it in response to the summons of God.

This far-reaching stewardship embraces (1) care of creation, so managing the resources of earth and sea; (2) expressing creativity in all of its forms, so developing God's aesthetic creation and bringing further beauty into the world; (3) maintaining the fabric of God's creation, so making God's world work (*see* Chores); (4) enculturating the world and developing varieties of human expressions of values,* structures and lifestyles, so bringing distinctive meanings to the peoples of the world; (5) harnessing the earth's potential by inventing tools and systems for making things, so bringing benefit to humankind; (6) expressing dominion over time by ordering human life around patterns of time and by keeping one day a week for rest and reflection (*see* Sabbath); (7) developing human society, organizations and peoples/nations, filling the earth with peoples living in distinctive but harmonious communities

and states, so creating structures as contexts for human life. Considered together, these are the ways we take care of God's household. This all-encompassing stewardship is the stewardship of every human being; every living thing and the whole material creation are not exempted from this stewardship in favor of something more "spiritual." This is part of their spiritual ministry.

Israel as Exemplary Steward

Under the old covenant God's gift of trusteeship was especially directed to the nation Israel (Deut 10:14-15). There are three parts to the promise God gave to Israel: the presence (God will be with them), a people (he will be their God; they, his people) and a place (the land will be theirs, i.e., entrusted to the people, not individuals).

The families* (more like clans or extended families today) were the basic social, kinship, legal and religious structure under the old covenant. They were family-plus-land units, as illustrated by the redemption of Naomi's land-plus-family in Bethlehem (Ruth 4:9-12). Thus in the Jubilee year (every fifty years) both God's ultimate ownership and the family's trusteeship were expressed by the return of the land to the original family, even if the land had been mortgaged or sold in the meantime to pay debts (Lev 25:4-18). The reason given is this: "The land is mine and you are but aliens and my tenants" (Lev 25:23). This has implications for the question of providing an inheritance for one's family (*see* Will, Last).

New Testament "Household" Responsibilities

All the promises of God concerning God's presence, people and place find their yes in Christ (2 Cor 1:20). The Gentiles along with Jews in Christ become joint heirs (Eph 3:6) in a joint body so that "in

Christ" answers to all that "in the land" meant to Israel—and even more! Fellowship in Christ for the Gentiles as well as the Jews fulfills the analogous function for the Christian as the possession of the land did for the Israelite. But that does not eliminate the socioeconomic dimension of stewardship. Christian fellowship *(koinonia)* is not merely "spiritual" communion. It is total sharing of life, not regarding possessions as absolutely one's own, bringing economic and social justice and peacemaking. The biological family and the church (the Christian's "first" family) both are arenas for total stewardship *(see* Family): total sharing of life.

Christians share stewardship of the world with the rest of humankind, but they have three additional concerns: (1) the investment and proper use of our personal time, abilities and finances for the benefit of others, something for which we are held responsible by God (Mt 25:14-30; *see* Money); (2) the treasuring and distribution of the grace of God as proclaimed in the gospel (1 Pet 4:10), not only by apostles and church leaders (1 Cor 4:1; Tit 1:7) but by all believers' being stewards and witnesses of the gospel; and (3) the full-fledged sharing of life (including material possessions) as a sign of being "in Christ." In the early church this meant sharing available assets over and above the normal (Acts 2:44-45; 4:32-35), engaging in relief missions to poor believers (Acts 11:27-30) and crosscultural giving to symbolize the mutual interdependence to Jew and Gentile, equality and unity in Christ (1 Cor 16:1; 2 Cor 8:13).

Time, Abilities and Finances

It is unbiblical to relegate personal stewardship to merely the religious portion of our lives: to tithing, using our talents for the church or giving a percentage of our income to the Lord's work. All of us belong to God, and stewardship concerns the whole of everyday life.

The time of our lives. We exercise stewardship of time in our daily occupations, fulfilling God's creational and providential calling to make the world work. We also invest time when we play* with our families or enjoy conversation* with friends. This everyday redemption of time springs from the sabbath,* which is one of the crucial signs that we take the stewardship of time seriously. We cannot lay aside our compulsion to work unless we believe that God is running the world and can be trusted with it while we rest.

Abilities for church and world. It is a sin not to use talents and gifts that God has given. They are to be used for the upbuilding of family, church, neighborhood and society. In the end we are accountable for our use or disuse of them. Not all of this has to be organized through the local church; indeed, most of it will not be.

Finances, where your heart is. Contrary to the secular viewpoint—"If you do not own it, you won't take care of it"—being a steward should increase our care and diligence in the use of property and wealth. It is not ours; it will be taken back by God one day; God will hold us responsible for what we do with it. Our everyday stewardship links us with God, who maintains the world. God wants not just an intact creation but a "return" on his investment.

The Grace of Giving

Many people give donations. The Bible calls us to stewardship. Donations imply that we are the owners and out of the generosity of our hearts we are giving some to others. Stewardship implies that it all belongs to God and is used for God's purposes. Donation spirituality is self-affirming and calculated for effect;

309

stewardship spirituality is other-directed and wholehearted. Donation spirituality looks for a thank-you from the recipient; stewardship spirituality aims at "Well done" when the Lord returns.

Some questions to ponder are these: How much do we give that does not come from a sense of obligation or social expectation? Do we act as if the part we retain is actually ours? Do we regard whatever wealth we have as a stewardship on behalf of the poor? Does the disbursement of monies represented by our checkbook or credit card* invoice reflect God's priorities for everyday life?

How does the grace of giving work out in practice? We should give to support Christian workers and causes as instructed in Scripture. But, in accordance with the Old Testament outlook, we should also see that we are stewards of money and assets in ways that benefit our families. To neglect family through sacrificing for the church is wrong. This is clearly something both Jesus (Mk 7:11) and Paul affirmed. Indeed not taking care of our families makes us worse than unbelievers (1 Tim 5:8). We should also heed Jesus' injunction to "use worldly wealth to gain friends for yourselves, so that when it is gone, you will be welcomed into eternal dwellings" (Lk 16:9). This means investing in people, giving money (anonymously, if possible) to the poor and showing hospitality.*

Family Stewardship
Returning to the larger view of stewardship, we can be stewards as families by (1) embracing the care of creation by recycling, reducing waste and treasuring the earth; (2) encouraging and expressing creativity in each member of the family and the family as a whole, so bringing beauty into the home* and the world; (3) celebrating and releasing the talents and spiritual gifts of members of the family; (4) maintaining the fabric of

God's creation through shared chores; (5) enculturating the family and the world by developing shared values and so bringing meaning to family life; (6) harnessing the earth's potential through work, showing how work itself is cocreation with God; (7) expressing dominion over time by celebrating sabbath and keeping patterns of rest and reflection, and giving our time to serve others and the people of God; (8) engaging in mission* together through hospitality,* witness and community service; (9) sharing resources with the poor, if possible, directly; (10) giving money cheerfully to further the kingdom of God in helping people, supporting Christian workers, relieving the poor, bringing justice and advancing the liberating kingdom of God.

On this last point—financial stewardship—tithing is a useful guide but not an absolute requirement. Allowances* are a good way of encouraging financial stewardship among the younger members of the family. Further, open and candid financial conversations* as a family can both teach stewardship and develop a corporate expression of it, including deciding together how family monies should be spent. Unfortunately, financial openness is one of the last privacies of the person in the Western world today. Family discussions and accountability through small groups in the local church are good ways of developing a Christian approach to time, talents and treasure.

Stewardship gives meaning to our lives and helps us make sense out of everyday life. It captures all our energies, assets and creativity for God's grand plan of humanizing the earth and developing it as a glorified creation. It saves us from the twin dangers of despair (What will come of the earth?) and false messianism (If we do not save the planet, who will?) because we are cooperating with a God who is determined to bring the creation to a worthy end through its complete renewal (Rev 21:5). Stewardship is a thermometer of our spirituality and discipleship. Where our treasure is, there will be our hearts (Lk 12:34). Our response to a brother in need is a measure of our love for God (Jas 2:15-16; 1 Jn 3:17). But stewardship also provides an incentive to grow in Christ. If we give sparingly, we will live cramped, emaciated lives; if we give generously, we live expansively and deeply (Lk 6:38).

In the end what God wants back is not an untouched creation or an intact (but unused) human ability; God wants a "return" on his investment. Stewardship is the way God gets such a return. It is not simply giving things away or keeping them safely in trust, but wisely investing them in contexts in which they will do some good and multiply. On the judgment day God will be asking individuals, families, churches and nations what we did with what we had. How well will we have managed God's household in the time between Christ's first and second coming?

See also ALLOWANCES; GIFT-GIVING; MISSION; MONEY; WILL, LAST.

References and Resources

J. Chrysostom, *On Wealth and Poverty*, trans. C. P. Roth (Crestwood, N.Y.: St. Vladimir's Seminary Press, 1984); O. E. Feucht, *Everyone a Minister* (St. Louis: Concordia, 1974); R. Foster, *Freedom of Simplicity* (New York: Harper & Row, 1989); D. J. Hall, *Stewardship of Life in the Kingdom of Death* (Grand Rapids: Eerdmans, 1988); L. T. Johnson, *Sharing Possessions: Mandate and Symbol of Faith* (London: SCM Press, 1981); M. MacGregor, *Your Money Matters* (Minneapolis: Bethany House, 1988); R. J. Sider, *Cry Justice: The Bible on Hunger and Poverty* (New York: Paulist, 1980); R. J. Sider, *Living More Simply: Biblical Principles and Practical Models* (Downers Grove, Ill.: InterVarsity Press, 1980); R. J. Sider, *Rich Christians in a Hungry World* (Dallas: Word, 1990); C. J. H. Wright, *God's People in God's Land: Family, Land and Property in the Old Testament* (Grand Rapids: Eerdmans, 1990).

R. Paul Stevens

—VACATIONS—

The original meaning of *holiday**—holy day—contains a powerful suggestion: holiday making can become an experience of holiness in time. But for many people, family or personal vacations are times of spiritual dryness or exhaustion. Often people say they must return to work for rest! Even with our huge vacation industry, people are either bored or stressed out on vacations. So far as its original meaning is concerned, the word *vacation* simply means "a vacancy," that is, "doing nothing." But a vacation should have a more positive meaning than that. Getting out of our daily routines and working roles allows people to experience their individuality more fully and to be less programmed by what others expect.

A host of questions surrounds the practice of vacationing: Why do some people never take vacations or feel guilty if they do? In what ways do vacationing and sabbath* observance overlap? Is an expensive vacation in a luxurious setting ever justified? Does the process of trying to justify a vacation destroy the very idea of taking one?

The Difficulty of Doing Nothing

Understandably, vacations are stressful for workaholics who do not want to be, or feel they cannot be, freed from the compulsions of work. Often Christians feel they must justify the expenditure of money* or time on nonproductive and nonreligious inactivity. Justification by faith—that watchword of the Protestant Reformation—has not been sufficiently translated from Sunday faith to Monday faith, from weekend to workday, nor has it been translated into sheer enjoyment of time, place, people and experiences for their own sake. According to Bertrand Russell the modern person thinks that everything ought to be done for the sake of something else, not for its own sake (Oates, 40). This instrumental or functional attitude is deeply ingrained in the thinking of church people and must be challenged for a person to be converted to vacationing, a conversion that is part and parcel of our conversion to Christ.

The idea of a paid annual leave from work is a modern phenomenon, and it is not universal. It is unheard of in some Two-Thirds World countries and by millions who work in the service sector of society. Many professionals and self-employed people take vacations at their own expense, with significant loss of revenue. Increasingly, vacations in North America are becoming shorter, two or three brief times a year, so work is not seriously interrupted (the European trend is different). Not surprisingly, many choose not to take them at all or combine a short vacation with a professional conference in an exotic location. A whole industry has developed around *incentive trips*, which are designed to satisfy wanderlust and the work ethic at the same time, all at the company's expense. It is argued that since they are offered to salespeople and managers whose performance has excelled, mornings in a conference and afternoons enjoying the amenities of a plush resort actually pay for themselves.

On such trips business executives take their cellular phones, fax machines and computers,* even to the beach. The idea of vacationing loses its meaning if one takes along the infrastructure of normal stressful responsibilities. Many Christian academics and pastors have "working vacations" (an oxymoron) or "ministry trips." There is reason to think that in spite of the huge leisure* industry, the industrialized or postindustrialized information societies may have less restorative vacation experiences than older and less-developed societies. So-called backward countries may be more advanced in some of the life patterns that really matter, such as visiting, conversing* and resting. All too often in the so-called developed countries vacations have been reduced to a commodity to be consumed with the compulsiveness with which one must work in order to be "excellent." It has not always been this way.

Is Vacationing a Modern Invention?

Festivals and holy days have been part of the annual rhythm of societies from time immemorial. They provided opportunities to engage in celebration, community events, religious ceremonies, feasting and revelry. Some of these were associated with the rhythms of the year in agricultural life (harvest or sheepshearing) or seasonal changes (solstice) and with annual migrations (for hunting or fishing). Christianity often adopted and transformed these festivals into holy days, Christmas* and Thanksgiving* being conspicuous examples. The Jewish tradition is rich in holidays, such as Passover (Feast of Unleavened Bread; Deut 16:1-8), Feast of Tabernacles (Deut 16:13-17) and Ingathering (or Feast of Weeks; Deut 16:9-12; see also Ex 23:14-19). Three times a year the Israelites were required to set aside the normal rhythm of work and sabbath to undertake a pilgrimage to Jerusalem, often in a holiday mood (Lk 2:41-52). These were far from being dull religious events, for Deuteronomy prescribes buying food, wine "and whatever you like" (Deut 14:26) with one's tithe* to experience the joy of the occasion.

While it is true that until modern times only the rich could afford to travel extensively and stay in luxurious hotels and spas—with opportunities now opened to the middle class through inexpensive air fares—almost all people in all ages have found or exploited something like vacations. Prior to the global trend toward urbanization most people possessed discretionary time in winter during what is still called in farm areas "fence-mending time."

In *Waiting for the Weekend* Witold Rybczynski traces the origin of the practice since the Industrial Revolution of staying home on Mondays, a practice that evolved into the institution of the weekend. The need for breaks in the routine of work is universal and is practiced even today, without calling them vacations, in the market days of Two-Thirds World countries. The sabbath, which gets fuller treatment elsewhere (*see* Sabbath), was intended to be a weekly vacation to remember our roots, to celebrate creation and to gain perspective for the coming week—all facets of personal and communal restoration. The lack of sabbath in contemporary Christian life is a tragic indication of the need for recovering a theology and spirituality of vacationing.

Thinking Christianly

The mandate to enjoy God's creation is an undertaking of grace that liberates us from judging our relationship to God and leisure in use-value terms and is an approach to the theology of time that delivers us from viewing time as a resource to be managed rather than a gift to be received (*see* Leisure). Great vacations, in one sense, can neither be planned nor managed. One further theme warrants consideration in an article on vacationing: a theology of place.

A theology of place is foundational to Christian vacationing. God created the world to be inhabited and filled (Gen 1:28). Adam and Eve's priesthood in the garden involved turning raw space into place: a garden with borders, animals appropriately named, plants nurtured, musical instruments invented and gold mined. The so-called nesting instinct is not exclusively a maternal drive. Even on camping trips men quickly turn raw space into a fire pit with a view, a "table and shelves," where pots can be hung up, and a drying area, where clothes can be set out to dry.

Travelers, whether backpacking or riding the Concorde, long for resting places, an image Jesus used for his provision of a place (or places!) to experience in heaven (Jn 14:2). Movement is another theme taken up in Scripture. If some do not take vacations because they are taking themselves too seriously, others may not take them because they are taking their home* too seriously—the house, garden and cat that cannot be left (for the opposite danger of not taking them seriously enough, *see* Mobility).

Taking a Vacation

In the light of the preceding theological reflection here are some suggestions on how to take a vacation. First, plan to waste time rather than to fill up every hour with prearranged activity. Give God a chance to reach you! Second, find out what truly refreshes you (and your family) and do it: being beside a lake or sea, visiting another culture or sleeping* a lot. Third, enjoy this leisure opportunity to pray, read Scripture and explore some of the spiritual disciplines you normally practice in a hurried way. Fourth, keep a journal and reflect on what you have seen and heard, turning these observations into prayers.

Fifth, avoid mixing work and vacationing, even working too hard at devotional things. Sixth, do things you normally do not have time for, such as reading* books (if you are not reading for a living), refusing to read (if you read for a living), watching the clouds, visiting old friends or walking so slowly you actually see what is around you. Seventh, do not overdo vacations. People not accustomed to taking vacations should not start with a three-month trip with their family! In the same vein it is not wise to wait too long to have a vacation—until you are too exhausted to work and therefore, paradoxically, too exhausted to rest. Eighth, do not expect that some exotic place shown on a travel brochure will make you happy. You are responsible for your own happiness; it has little to do with how much money* you have to spend. Ninth, take off your watch and live by the tides or the slant of the sun in the sky. Walk barefoot or fly a kite. Get in touch with God's creation. Finally, enjoy God.

See also LEISURE; SABBATH.

References and Resources

R. Banks, *The Tyranny of Time: When 24 Hours Is Not Enough* (Downers Grove, Ill.: InterVarsity Press, 1983); R. Capon, *An Offering of Uncles: The Priesthood of Adam and the Shape of the World* (New York: Crossroad, 1982); T. Hansel, *When I Relax I Feel Guilty* (Elgin, Ill.: David C. Cook, 1979); W. E. Oates, *Confessions of a Workaholic: The Facts about Work Addiction* (London: Wolfe Publishing, 1971); "Off the Beach: Eight Awesome Alternatives to Sun, Sand and Surf," *The Other Side* 22, no 2 (1980) 33-39; W. Rybczynski, *Waiting for the Weekend* (New York: Viking Penguin, 1991).

R. Paul Stevens

—VALUES—

In the Western world there is a confusion of values that simultaneously promotes family values such as togetherness, affirmation and forgiveness,* and antifamily values such as personal self-realization, psychic mobility (keeping all your options open), relational rentalism (only short-term commitments to others) and the right to unlimited sexual expression. Nevertheless, even in this day of fractured families it is widely acknowledged that the family is the primary arena for forming spiritual understanding and moral values.

Largely through the work of humanistic psychologists such as Rollo May, Abraham Maslow, Fritz Perls, Erik Erikson, Carl Rogers and others, values are back in the picture, even in the school system, where it is increasingly recognized that value-free education is really impossible. Values are cherished behaviors, principles and attitudes. And the family* is the first location, and undoubtedly the ultimate environment, for values formation. In a family context why are values important? What family values are biblically commended? How can family values be cultivated? (*See* Character; Communication; Family; Goals.)

The Value of Values

Every family has a set of values, often unexpressed, that determines how decisions are made in the face of competing alternatives. Sometimes these are expressed in family mottoes, such as "Birthday parties always come before personal plans," "Dad is the head of this house," or "No secrets allowed in this family." More often values are subterranean. These values express fundamental beliefs about what and who is important; how relationships should be fostered; what is the place of money,* sex* and power; who is entitled to make decisions and where God is in it all. Values determine behavior, give expression to beliefs and give meaning to everyday life. Values shape the culture of the family, the culture of the church as a family of families, and ultimately the culture of the nation.

Every social organization can be pictured in three concentric circles. On the outside are the artifacts of the culture, enshrined in visible symbols (the welcome sign over the door, father sitting at the head of the table), rituals (starting Christmas Day by singing carols) and codes (the last will* and testament). These symbols and artifacts express the reality that can be represented by a second, smaller concentric circle: family values, what the family cherishes. These values, in turn, express the family's beliefs (the smallest concentric circle—whether men and women are created equal, whether sex is a good gift of God, whether God has anything to do with everyday life). Together this family culture forms an all-embracing influence in child development. It is felt by anyone entering a family gathering, especially when one marries into a family and therefore really marries a family! One of the most significant areas of tension when two people get married is the marrying of two different sets of values (see Dating; Family Systems). Some people do not realize how deeply these values were formed within their family of origin until they are confronted in the transforming crucible of marriage.

It is not surprising that Christians frequently find themselves caught between the claims of the kingdom and the sometimes-idolatrous claims of their families (see Family). That is what is behind the somewhat ambiguous words of Jesus about hating father and mother in order to follow him (Lk 14:26) and letting the dead bury the dead (Lk 9:60). Even when Christians live together in a family, there will be some clash of values—a crisis that itself can become an arena for spiritual growth. Indeed, rather than seeing the family as an arena for spiritual disciplines (such as daily Bible reading), we should see the family itself as a spiritual discipline (see Spiritual Formation).

Commendable Values

Values are based on beliefs. Commendable values are based on the following beliefs: (1) the divine origin of family life as a covenant community and an expression of God's own family life in the Holy Trinity (Eph 3:15); (2) grace rather than perfection or excellence as the dominant motif of the Christian life; (3) the vocation of all God's people to be God's holy people and to do God's work in the world; (4) the family as a domestic church, the smallest unit of church life (see R. P. Stevens, 35-42); (5) the family as the primary unit of spiritual, relational and emotional formation, so that even parents grow up by having children; (6) the depoliticizing of the family by the grace of Christ so that Christians in families become a community of companionship, unity and mutual priesthood (Eph 5:21; 6:1-4); (7) the fact that Christ's work of redemption does not make people into angels or religious people but into full human beings to fulfill God's purposes in the world.

Based on these fundamental beliefs, almost all Christian values could be commended for persons living in families. Here we will examine biblically commended values in four categories that belong exclusively to family life (such as honoring parents), are especially suitable as family values (such as inheritance) or most likely to be cultivated in everyday family life (such as contentment). Spiritual education does not begin with Sunday school but with birth, indeed with conception.* In each of the following categories we start with values that could properly be considered part of the human vocation and end with values that are specific to persons of faith.

Relational values include (1) honoring parents, that is, respecting parents for one's whole life, though not subordinating oneself to them after leaving home and cleaving to husband or wife (Gen 2:24; Ex 20:12; 21:15; Lev 19:3; Deut 5:16; 21:18-21; Prov 19:26; 20:20; 28:24; Mt 10:36; 15:1-9; Eph 6:1-4; Col 3:20; see Grandparenting; Marriage; Parenting); (2) blessing or affirmation of one another (see Blessing), showing affectionate loyalty and building each other up with words and deeds (Gen 27; 48—49; Prov 31:28-31; Eph 4:29; Phil 4:8); and (3) forgiveness, letting the past be in the past and creating the possibility of a new future for another and even oneself (Ps 32:5; Prov 10:12; 19:11; Mk 11:25; Jn 8:11; Eph 4:32; Col 3:13; 1 Jn 1:9; 4:20; see Forgiveness; Love). In exalting these relational values a family is showing that people are more important than things.

Social values include (1) procreation, bearing seed to create another generation in one's own image (Gen 5:3), for we are to experience salvation in the context of doing what we have been created for (Gen 1:28; 19:30-38; Ex 6:13-25; Deut 25:5-10; Judg 21; Ruth 4:18-22; Ps 127; 1 Tim 2:15; see Conception; Parenting); (2) togetherness without enmeshment, involving building a common life through interdependence, rather than independence or codependence, crafting a unity that is deeper and stronger because of the diversity of personalities and their gifts (Rom 12:15; Phil 2:4; see Family Systems), including prizing and respecting the other sex as complementary and necessary to fully image God (Gen 1:27); and (3) play, since the family that plays together is likely to stay together (Prov 8:30, see Leisure; Play; Sabbath; Vacations). In exalting these values, members of a family are called to live beyond themselves and to show love to their nearest and dearest neighbors.

Vocational values include (1) service in the world through all the ways that humankind makes God's world work (Gen 2:15), ranging from public service through politics to giving food to the hungry (Mic 6:8; Mk 10:43; see Preece, 1123-29); (2) hospitality through which strangers and visitors are given a space where they are free to be themselves (Gen 18:1-15; Lev 19:33; 1 Tim 3:2; 5:10; Tit 1:8; Heb 13:2; 1 Pet 4:9; 3 Jn 8; see Hospitality) and through which those closest to us are allowed to develop in their own way in an environment of acceptance; and (3) mutual priesthood through which children bring God's message, presence and grace to parents (just as parents do to children; Eph 6:1-4) and through which husband and wives function not in a pre-Christian hierarchical way but in genuine partnership involving mutual submission and ministry (Eph 5:21-33; 1 Pet 2:5, 9). It is often noted that children growing up learn about God from their parents, even when their parents claim to have no faith or do not practice it. Just as infants see themselves mirrored in the eyes and facial expressions of their parents, they gain images of God, some of which require abandoning or transforming later in life. Children also learn whether becoming a pastor or a missionary is the ultimate vocation or whether all of God's people are called to the ministry (Eph 4:1).

Stewardship values include (1) treasuring a multigenerational inheritance involving the conservation of the land and the planet; (2) treasuring family assets for future generations—a matter that undergirded much of the Old Testament legislation, especially the returning of the land to families in the year of Jubilee (see Wright, 119-28)—and saving up to provide for others, especially one's children (Ex 22:10-11; Lev 25:13, 23; Deut 20:19; 21:15-17; 1 Kings 21:3; Job 42:15; Prov 17:6; 19:4; 22:28; 2 Cor 12:14) and parents (Mk 7:11, see Will, Last); (3) sharing, which involves lending, borrowing and almost unlimited liability within a family (Ex 22:25; Deut 15:1-11; 23:19; see Credit Card; Debt; Money), as well as generous more-than-a-tithe giving (2 Cor 9:7) to believers in need and to the Lord's work (Gen 14:20; Ex 34:26; Deut 14:22-24; 26:1-15; 1 Chron 29:2, 9; Prov 3:9; 11:24-25; see Tithing), willingness to work toward equality (2 Cor 8:13-15) between rich and poor Christians through gifts that empower rather than create dependence (Acts 2:44-47; 4:32-37; Rom 15:25-27; 1 Jn 3:17) and compassionate gifts and empowering help to the truly needy whether they have faith or not (Lev 19:9-10; Deut 23:24-25; 24:19-22; Prov 19:17; 22:9, 16, 22; 28:27; 31:8-9; Lk 4:18; Jas 1:27); and (4) contentment, which is living in continuous thanksgiving for what God has provided, whether much or little (Phil 4:12), and deciding not to yield to the siren advertisements that say happiness is achieved by having yet another possession or experience (Deut 5:21; Josh 8:22-27; Prov 1:19; 15:16, 27; 16:8; Eccles 5:12; Mt 6:19-21; Lk 12:15; Eph 5:20; Phil 4:6).

Conspicuously missing from the above list are the traditional Christian values of church attendance, family devotions and religious activities. The reason is significant: these are not values but rites and roles that support values (or discourage their formation). This raises the vital question of just how values are formed. Psychology has reminded us of the scriptural insight (Deut 5:9) that values—good and bad—get passed down generation to generation, even in dysfunctional families. But how can we foster the values mentioned above, and do so in such a way that does not relegate God to the religious periphery of family life fifteen minutes after the supper meal and a brief prayer before sleep?

Reinforcing Values

Thus far I have refrained from defining family, partly because the nuclear family cannot bear the full load. Divorce* and single parenting* have taken their toll. They have also forced us to rethink family in the light of Scripture. Family in the Bible includes the idea of household, those joined by covenant, blood or adoption* in a mutuality that includes not only the primal unit of mother, father and child but uncles and aunts, grandparents and cousins, friends and business partners and even "the alien within your gates" (Ex 20:10)—there not by right but by grace. Many a young person, struggling with her parents through adolescence,* has found profound acceptance and healing through a grandparent who really believed in and prayed for her. So values are formed not merely by parental transmission but through family life in toto: who gets invited to dinner, how the stranger at the door is treated, when we speak of Uncle Frank, the black sheep of the family, what we do when we have overspent our income, who makes the decisions about where a family vacation will be spent, whether

Mom and Dad "still have sex" and view it prudishly or sacramentally (see Sexuality), how the church service is discussed over Sunday dinner, what is done when the daughter comes home with a boyfriend twenty years her senior.

Values clarification. Life is full of learning, most of it unconscious. So our first task in reinforcing values is to clarify the values we already hold. This can be done effectively through values-clarifying exercises outlined for families and church groups (Larson and Larson) or relating to work and vacation (Jones and Jones). Values can also be clarified through journaling, through family discussions and through taking each family crisis as a God-given opportunity to ask, "What are we presently cherishing that lead to this conflict or challenge?" It took Jacob twenty years to get hold of this truth and to admit to himself and God (Gen 32:27) that his name was Cheat/Jacob, though God had thrown up mirror after mirror in his life to bring him to himself—a prerequisite to his being blessed by God (see R. P. Stevens, 43-53).

Values teaching. Parents do not often think of themselves as teachers; still less do children. But family life is a life-on-life environment for learning. The Bible advocates conversational teaching (see Conversation): "Impress them on your children. Talk about them when you sit at home and when you walk along the road, when you lie down and when you get up" (Deut 6:7). We teach all the time—over the supper table (see Eating), when we drive together, when we are making purchases in a store, as we say goodnight and pray by the bedside. Much of family life is sheer imitation of the same pattern as discipleship. The disciple (and the child) when he "is fully trained will be like his teacher" (or his parents; Lk 6:40). We are teaching even when we are not speaking. (One power-

ful memory during my teens is sneaking past my parents' open bedroom door late at night after a school dance or a date* and seeing my father or mother kneeling beside their bed undoubtedly including me in their prayers.)

Teaching is continuous, but there are teachable moments, such as when your daughter asks, "Dad, what's so wrong about premarital sex?" These moments are to be prized, waited for, prayed over and seized as treasures hidden in the field. One of the most precious gifts children can give parents is their questions. Some questions arise spontaneously; others are evoked by patterns and habits (see Character) of family life that at some point or other invite the question by a son or daughter (compare Josh 4:6: "What do these stones mean?").

Values embedded in traditions and rituals. It is important for families to celebrate Christmas, Easter and Thanksgiving (see Holidays); to read Scripture and good books as a daily ritual (see Reading); to tell stories, especially the stories of one's own family; to keep the family genealogy, a family scrapbook or photo album as a treasury of values incarnated in experiences, relationships and events (see Family History); to pray* for one another and with one another; to worship regularly with the people of God. Other rituals—not often considered—that communicate important values are unplugging the telephone* during the family supper, watching television* together (and so discussing the values implicit in mass media; see Television), taking an annual vacation,* keeping sabbath* and other customs unique to the family (such as going swimming in the ocean on New Year's Eve or taking a walk every Sunday afternoon).

One fundamental value to be treasured is the family itself, especially in this day when the family is out of favor.

Michael Novak suggests there are two kinds of people in the world today: individual people and family people. He reflects on how education and the media help children to become sophisticated in everything but the things most needful: "love, fidelity, childbearing, mutual help, care for parents and the elderly" (Novak, 44). Insightfully Novak notes that having children is no longer a welcome responsibility because "to have children is plainly, to cease being a child oneself" (39). Children help parents to grow up, a maturation many resist in favor of perpetual adolescence without the burden of having a family. With equal insight Neil Postman in *The Disappearance of Childhood* laments the loss of childhood. He does not think we will forget that we need children. What he fears is that we are forgetting that children need childhood. Childhood is crucial to learning the discipline of delayed gratification, modesty in sexuality* and self-restraint in manners and speech.

Not only are most of the values mentioned above countercultural, but valuing the carrier of these values, the family, is itself an act of resistance against the prevailing culture. To treasure family, to decide to live near one's extended family (*see* Mobility), to invest

in family life as a holy ministry, to treat each family meal as the table of the Lord, is exactly the revolution so desperately needed today.

See also CHARACTER; FAMILY; GOALS; FAMILY SYSTEMS; PARENTING; SPIRITUAL FORMATION.

References and Resources

G. Jones and R. Jones, *Naturally Gifted: A Self-Discovery Workbook* (Downers Grove, Ill.: InterVarsity Press, 1993); R. S. Larson and D. E. Larson, *Values and Faith: Value-Clarifying Exercises for Family and Church Groups* (Minneapolis: Winston, 1976); M. Novak, "Family out of Favor," *Harper's* 252 (April 1976) 37-46; N. Postman, *The Disappearance of Childhood* (New York: Vintage Books, 1994); E. H. Schein, *Organizational Culture and Leadership: A Dynamic View* (San Francisco: Jossey-Bass, 1991); G. Preece, "Work," in *The Complete Book of Everyday Christianity*, ed. R. Banks and R. P. Stevens (Downers Grove, Ill.: InterVarsity Press, 1997); B. Stevens, "Patterns of Eternity: Toward a Spirituality of Family," *Saint Mark's Review* 143 (Winter 1990) 13-17; R. P. Stevens, *Disciplines of the Hungry Heart: Christian Living Seven Days a Week* (Wheaton, Ill.: Harold Shaw, 1993); C. Wright, *God's People in God's Land: Family, Land and Property in the Old Testament* (Grand Rapids: Eerdmans, 1990).

—R. Paul Stevens

VIDEO GAMES. *See* GAMES, VIDEOS.

—VIDEOS—

Perhaps no new medium has been adopted more rapidly around the world than video. Portable video cameras and especially the videocassette recorder (VCR) have affected everything from news coverage to international politics and family life.

The Home Video Theater
The most significant uses of video occur in the home.* Indeed, video transformed many homes into private movie

theaters, where family members could view at their own discretion commercially produced videotapes of tens of thousands of feature films, educational products, pornographic materials, political propaganda made by special-interest groups, exercise programs and their own family-made productions. Initially teenagers were the principal consumers of videocassettes, and viewing adult-oriented movies with friends became a rite of passage, especially for North American adolescents. By the middle of the 1990s, however, home viewing of movie videos was a massive industry that surpassed movie box-office revenues and encompassed practically all sectors of society.

In one sense, home video is merely an expansion of television.* Many movies available on videotape are also available on broadcast or cable television. Also, VCRs are sometimes used to record cable or broadcast programming for repeated viewing or for viewing at a different time.

Technological improvements in home-video imaging and audio helped to make home video a medium distinct from television. Larger and less expensive television sets encourage families to establish video viewing areas or even entire video rooms in their homes. Moreover, hi-fi sound systems enable viewers at home to emulate the aural impact of the movie-theater screening room. As a result, home viewing of movies is more formal, collective and planned than regular television watching, although not necessarily any more reflective or discerning.

Most people prefer to rent or purchase newly released video movies. Even classic movies are now widely rented at video shops. In Two-Thirds World countries there is an enormous market in illegal copies of recent films, especially action-oriented Hollywood films staring high-profile actors. The video industry caters to this appetite for new films, a strategy that does not always serve well the more discerning video user who seeks older, high-quality movies.

Video Gaming

Video games are part of a large, high-tech industry designed primarily to fulfill one primary human want: the desire to overcome personal boredom in the home. A few games purport to be educational or to enhance small-motor skills, but the vast majority is almost purely for personal entertainment.* Not surprisingly, children with the greatest leisure* time are the prime market for these games. These children have the most time to spend and the least inhibitions about computer* technologies (see Computer Games; Internet).

For all of their high-tech wizardry, video games are a poor substitute for board games* and yard games. Most video games depend upon a market of lone players, whereas other games have depended on small groups searching for relational activities. Even when groups play video games, the play is directed at the monitor, not at players. While most other gaming fosters interpersonal communication among players, video gaming usually eclipses it.

Video games also have addictive qualities for players. Foremost is the rush of adrenaline that players feel during the peak moments of "action." Nearly as important is the competitive determination to beat the game, if not the other players. Rewards are immediate, even if the game has to be restarted for the player to try to advance to the next level. Finally, home-video games temporarily satisfy compulsive personalities that need to be doing something as quickly and as frequently as possible.

Video games are not all bad, but they are clearly inferior and addictive substitutes for relational forms of recreation. The best video games are not time-bound, superenergy visual extravaganzas, but multiplayer inducements to communicate about the subject matter of the game. Unfortunately, males do not feel the need for intimacy as strongly as women, so the video industry matches its male-oriented product development and marketing to these nonrelational players. Video games are largely the province of bored males who satisfy some of their cravings for power by blasting away the enemies.

Home Video as Family History and Parable

Low-cost equipment is a boon to amateur video production, especially in the home. A growing number of families are using video photography to preserve memorable events. This kind of family video history alters both the way family life is conducted and how families relate to their pasts. In the best uses, video can help families enjoy and learn from their own personal stories of life.

Video, even more than film and still photography, leads families to emphasize the preservation of events rather than actual events themselves. In other words, family life is increasingly staged for the camera, and thereby for the memorable record the video provides. Sometimes the change is not exceedingly important (e.g., where the wedding party must stand during the service, or when graduates march during commencement). In other cases, however, the sheer availability of the video camera redirects the action (e.g., the videographer instructs children at the beach to build a sand castle, or a toddler on Christmas morning to frolic in the pile of discarded wrapping paper—all for the drama of "the camera.")

One positive aspect of this video mindedness is the way it can instill a familial sense of the value of special occasions. Video encourages families to find more value in their time together, to see such family times as out of the ordinary (Ecc 3:1). The medium can even foster greater preparation for family events in the hope of maximizing their video potential.

However, video can easily rob family life of its spontaneous joy and irreproducible memories. When the video camera is present, families tend to swap their unplanned antics for staged behavior. Suddenly the normal spontaneity of life disappears, even the spontaneity left in ritualized ceremonies such as baptisms* and graduations. In addition, video focuses a family's collective memory only on the events that can be recorded. Unless a family consciously tries to keep alive the oral stories of nonrecorded events, the video memories will eclipse the recollection of them (see Family History).

The Future of Video

Video technology complements the computer* and has a bright future. Although videotape will eventually be replaced by CD-ROM or other forms of digital storage, video movies and games will likely take up even more leisure time. Three important trends will shape the future of video and will influence the users of this technology.

First, video will become an increasingly interactive medium. A new genre of movies will become something like video games, with the "player" choosing plot directions. Meanwhile, the interactivity of video games will be enhanced by faster action and a greater array of play choices. In its own way, home-video production will share this increased interactivity in the form of greater user control over the production process, including the home use of graphics, editors, sound enhancements and special effects. Interactivity will increase the creative options of users.

Second, video will emerge as an "essential" technology. Like radio and television before it, video will shift from a luxury item to a foundational home medium. In fact, video will subsume television, if not the computer, in many homes. Along the way video will take on all kinds of new uses based on the CD-ROM and other storage devices. These may include such things as home reference work, educational programs, video telephones* and home shopping.*

Third, video will shape domestic life, just as television has for decades. Families will continue to dedicate more of their leisure time to video, seduced by the medium's specialized fare for all ages, lifestyles and ideologies. Domestic architecture and furniture will be influenced by the desires of video viewers, perhaps even more than by the need for strong family life and interpersonal relations generally.

See also COMPUTER; COMPUTER GAMES; ENTERTAINMENT; GAMES; LEISURE; PLAY.

Quentin J. Schultze

VIRTUES. *See* CHARACTER; VALUES.

WEANING. *See* BREAST-FEEDING.

—WILL, LAST—

One of the most sensitive things we do in life is to write a last will and testament. Doing this confronts us with our own inevitable death*—an important and deeply spiritual ministry to ourselves. We are also forced to define who and what is valuable to us, and how we wish our possessions to influence people after we die. A will can be a family blessing,* a form of gift-giving,* and a means of bringing peace and justice to our families. It can bless charitable organizations and encourage causes we embraced in this life. It can also be a hand extending from the grave to control, manipulate, divide and bring retribution for wounds not healed before we died. So the will reveals not only the state of our financial assets but also the state of our souls.

Some people do not bother to make a will, not so much for spiritual reasons, or even because their assets are comparatively small, but because they do not think it important. They do not survive, of course, to see people fighting over their possessions or the hurts caused because the people assumed to be the proper heirs did not actually receive the promised inheritance. Without a will your family assets might be frozen for months; your nearest surviving kin may not have funds to continue normal life; provincial or state laws will determine the distribution of your assets without consideration to your wishes, sometimes ignoring the members of your family who should be the rightful heirs; more of your estate will be spent in administrative costs, and the process may be delayed for months, sometimes for years.

It is not the purpose of this article to advise how a will should be written. Normally this should be done by a lawyer, though simple forms can be obtained in banks that, if properly witnessed by two adults who are not beneficiaries, correctly signed and dated, can be legal. Properly conceived wills name the executor or executrix (the person named to administer the will) and the beneficiaries (those who receive specific portions of the estate). They also need to be updated every five years or when there has been a change of residence, marital status or family circumstances. My purpose here is to explore the meaning of writing a will.

Before There Was a Will There Was a Way

In ancient times the equivalent of the last will was the father's oral blessing of the family before he died (see Blessing). Isaac's blessing Esau, his favorite younger son, in contradiction to God's revealed plan of maintaining the family leadership through Jacob, is a classic story of a "last will" gone awry. In giving his word even in the context of a ruse, Isaac could not recall his promise, though he appointed the one he thought was the wrong person as leader of the family. God providentially arranged for Jacob to be the bearer of the promise. In Israel such final blessings included a double portion of the estate to the oldest male (Deut 21:15-17) since this person would be the responsible leader of the family. Job was conspicuously different from many of his contemporaries in giving his daughters an inheritance along with his sons (Job 42:15).

In the ancient world, and in the Two-Thirds World today, land is not only the most important possession (since it is the means of producing food) but also very often the only possession. While once the passing of such lands to the surviving male heirs took place with the help of village elders, without a written will, today this has become a vexed matter as such estates are now hotly contested in Two-Thirds World courts by second and third wives, by wives who were never legally married but cohabited, and by legitimate and illegitimate children. So not only in the developed world, where the assets are primarily monetary and land recorded with proper title deeds, but even in the

developing world it is crucial today to attend to this important ministry of family love and neighbor love. It is not always, however, a loving ministry.

The Will to Curse

Some people use their wills to control people they were unable to control in this life. A son or daughter may be out of favor, or has brought shame* on the family. Further wounds are inflicted posthumously, by disinheriting that child, though the laws sometimes preclude totally excluding a near relative simply because they were not named in the will. Some states require that a spouse must receive a mandated minimum share of the deceased spouse's estate, even though the deceased person intended to exclude the spouse totally. The Old Testament tried to regulate against such injustice based on personal favoritism rather than equality and fairness. If a man marries a second wife whom he loves more than the first, he may not give the rights of the first-born (the double portion) to the son of the second marriage (Deut 21:15-18).

No one dies with all the problems* fully resolved. Someone is loved less; someone is struggling with addiction and would squander an inheritance; someone is idle and lazy; someone has wounded and shamed the family. Not surprisingly, some people use the will as their last chance to "get even," without remaining to assist in picking up the pieces. Rightly understood, making a will is an act of stewardship—undertaking to manage one's household and transferring appropriately ownership and responsibility. Where a child is incompetent, a lawyer can assist in specifying a trust fund. Last wills cannot do much to solve family problems, but, when poorly conceived, they can exacerbate the ones that already exist.

323

Will to Bless

Normally a will should express justice and fairness in a family. This is not easy when there are great differences in economic strength among surviving members. It may be tempting to write a will based on perceived "need" rather than fairness. "James doesn't need my money since he has a professional income, but poor Martha has never had a chance." What the person cannot foresee is the reverses of life: James struggling with an incurable disease and unable to work; Martha divorced and remarried into a wealthy family. Further, it is impossible to regulate people's feelings. As elder son in the parable of the prodigal complained, "You never gave me . . ." when the father had given him everything (Lk 15:29, 31)! But what we can do is to refuse to play favorites, to express mercy to those who have disappointed us, to provide as best we can for all kin who survive us, and to trust that God will help them deal with such ongoing temptations of life as envy, greed and covetousness.

As a form of gift giving, a last will can do a lot of good. First, a surviving spouse will be able to continue a reasonably normal life. It is a practical way of loving our spouse. Second, we can continue our priorities in parenting* by naming suitable guardians (with their permission) for our minor-aged children and providing for their maintenance. Third, we can bring delight by specifying the transfer of possessions that will bring joy to a particular relative or friend. Fourth, we can empower the next generation to do things they would not otherwise be able to do, such as buying their own home.* Fifth, we can see that all the outstanding debts* in this life, relational and financial, are forgiven. Sixth, we can bless charities and churches with a significant gift. Seventh, we can show impartial love like God's love to every member of the family, regardless of merit and performance, just as God makes the sun to rise and the just and unjust (Mt 5:43-47).

The Contemplative Will

Making a will helps us prepare for our death and begin the process of relinquishment, which is a spiritual work or discipline. This is both a ministry to ourselves and a ministry to our survivors at the same time. But this spiritual work may encompass not only what happens when we die but also what happens as we die.

Many people today write a living will in addition to the one to be executed upon their death. A living will outlines how a person wants to be medically treated in the event of a terminal illness or a condition that requires life-sustaining procedures. It is normally a gracious thing to do this, as close members of the family, without such direction, may feel obliged to prolong life as long as possible, fearing accusations of disloyalty or lack of love. This too can be drawn up by a lawyer. While some people think this is a means of causing death, it really is a way of regulating the unnecessary delay of death through heroic medical interventions. Christians especially should be prepared to die.

Making a last will and testament recognizes several theological perspectives founded in Scripture. What God entrusts to us in this life is a multigenerational inheritance, not to be squandered in one lifetime. The earth, the traditions of culture and family, the material treasures of one's family—these are not for ourselves alone but our children and children's children (Prov 13:22; cf Ps 17:14). Further, we do not know how soon Christ will come and bring the whole human story to its consummate end. Wise stewards, like the wise virgins in the parable of Jesus (Mt 25:1-13) are ready for a long wait (25:4). Rather than living for the moment, which is a perversion of *parousia* or second coming readiness, Christians are called to be ready today but prepared for another thousand years.

Finally, providing for the next generation is an act of responsible Christian stewardship. But we must do this in a way that involves stewardship of life today. The gospel invites us to flourish in life now, not just to plan for the next life. Some people are so concerned to provide for their children that they refuse to enjoy life now; others, so anxious to squeeze everything they can out of today, leave nothing. Scripture properly understood provides the eschatological balance: living today because of tomorrow in the light of what God has done in the past.

We cannot take our money and possessions with us. But what we can take is faith, hope and love. We can take relationships we have made in Christ through the use of our money* (Lk 16:9). And we can take the knowledge that our last determination on earth was that mercy and peace shall survive us as our true inheritance.

See also BLESSING; DEATH; GIFT-GIVING; MONEY; TITHING.

References and Resources

D. Clifford, *Plan Your Estate* (Berkeley: Nolo Books, 1990); E. J. Daly, *Thy Will Be Done* (New York: Prometheus, 1994).

R. Paul Stevens

WORK. *See* CHORES; MOBILITY.

WORSHIP. *See* PRAYER; SABBATH; SPIRITUAL FORMATION.

INDEX OF ARTICLES

Thoughtful parenting : a
manual of wisdom for home &
family